Sydney's Century

A HISTORY

To Benedict and Donald

PETER SPEARRITT

Sydney's Century

A HISTORY

UNSW PRESS

A UNSW Press book

Published by
University of New South Wales Press Ltd
University of New South Wales
Sydney 2052, Australia
www.unswpress.com.au

National Library of Australia
Cataloguing-in-Publication entry:
Spearritt, Peter, 1949
Sydney's century: a history

Bibliography.
Includes index.
ISBN 0 86840 521 3 (hardback)
ISBN 0 86840 513 2 (paperback)
994.41

Copyright acknowledgements
Unless otherwise stated, original illustrations are in the possession of the author. Every effort has been made to contact and acknowledge copyright holders.

Cover Grace Cossington Smith 1892–1984 Australia. Detail from **The bridge in-curve**, c. 1930, tempera on cardboard, 83.6 x 111.8cm. Gift of the National Gallery Society of Victoria, 1967. National Gallery of Victoria, Melbourne

Page i **Top** Map of Sydney by Cyril Samuels, c. 1941 **Below** *Home magazine* cover, 1932 *Title page* Sydney Opera House in the final stages of construction, 1972 *Title page inset* The author (with camera) and maintenance workers on the eastern chord of the Sydney Harbour Bridge, photograph by John Storey *Above* Bondi Pavillion, photograph by John Storey 1982 *Page vi* Unusual birds eye view, Smith & Julius studios

A note on measures

Money
12 pennies (d) = one shilling (s)
20 shillings = one pound (£1)
After decimal currency was introduced (1966):
two dollars ($2) = one pound (£1)

Length
1 inch = 25 mm
1 foot = 30 cm
1 yard = 0.9 m
1 mile = 1.6 km

Area
1 acre = 0.4 hectare
1 square mile = 2.6 km^2

Printer Southwood Press, Sydney
Page design Adrian Young, Canberra

Contents

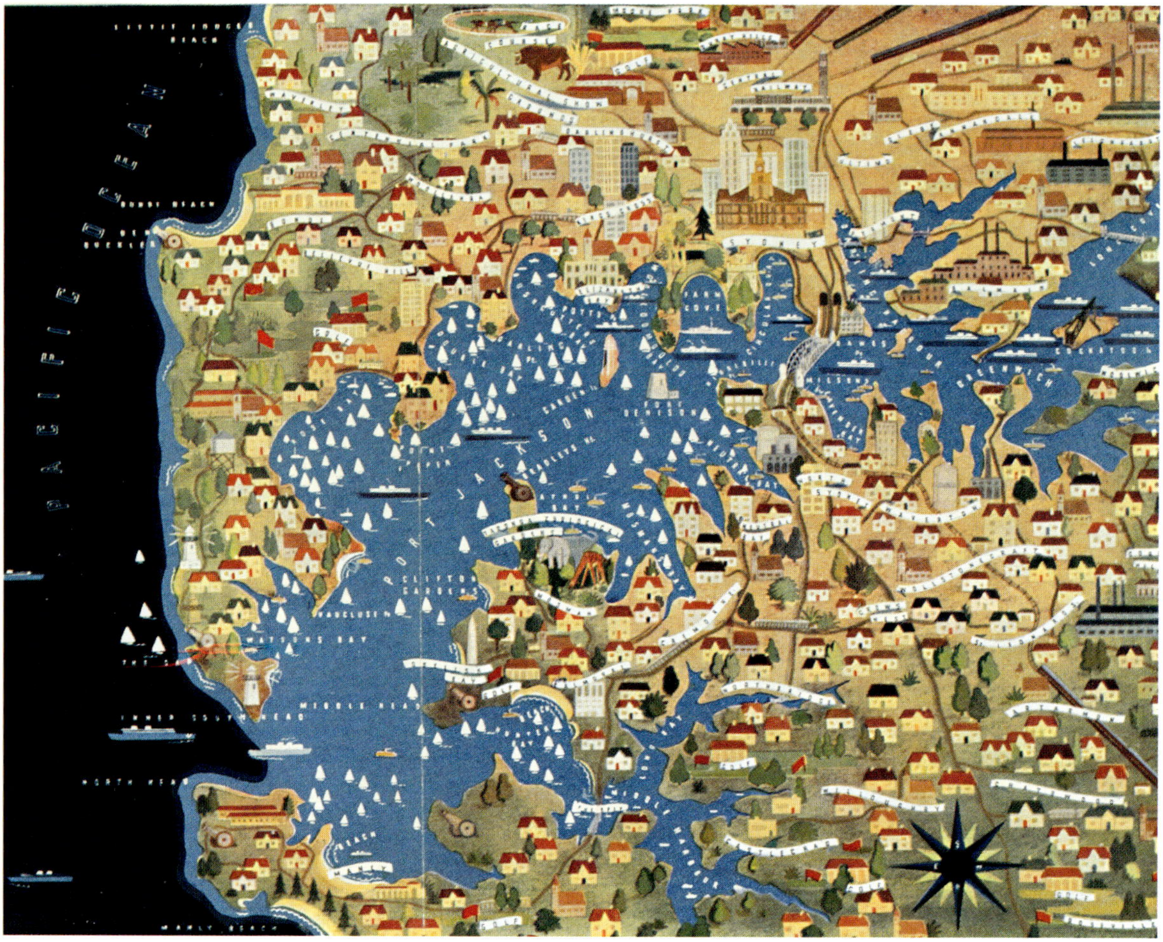

List of abbreviations

ABS	Australian Bureau of Statistics
ACER	Australian Council for Educational Research
ADB	*Australian Dictionary of Biography*, 14 vols to date, MUP, Melbourne, 1967–
AEHR	*Australian Economic History Review*
AFR	*Australian Financial Review*
AGPS	Australian Government Publishing Service
AIF	Australian Imperial Force
AJPH	*Australian Journal of Politics and History*
ALP	Australian Labor Party
ANU	Australian National University
ANUP	Australian National University Press
A & R	Angus and Robertson
ASSLH	Australian Society for the Study of Labor History
A & U	Allen and Unwin
CCC	Cumberland County Council
CPD	*Commonwealth Parliamentary Debates*
CUP	Cambridge University Press
DMR	Department of Main Roads (NSW)
DT	*Daily Telegraph*
H & I	Hale and Iremonger
LD	*Labor Daily*
ML	Mitchell Library
MUP	Melbourne University Press
MWSDB	Metropolitan Water, Sewerage and Drainage Board
NLA	National Library of Australia
NRMA	National Roads and Motorists Association
NSWHC	New South Wales Housing Commission
NSWIG	*New South Wales Industrial Gazette*
NSWPD	*New South Wales Parliamentary Debates*
NSWPP	*New South Wales Parliamentary Papers*
NSWSR	*New South Wales Statistical Register*
NSWYB	*New South Wales Year Book*
OUP	Oxford University Press
REIJ	*Real Estate Institute Journal*
RSL	Returned Services League
SMH	*Sydney Morning Herald*
SSTT	*Sydney Since the Twenties*
UNSWP	University of New South Wales Press
UQP	University of Queensland Press

List of maps and tables

P & O Poster by Rhys Williams

Writing about Sydney

Sydney has long been acknowledged as one of the world's great cities. Its spectacular harbour setting had always occasioned comment, especially from visitors and migrants, who arrived by sea from the 1790s to the 1960s. While arrival by air may be less romantic, it is equally spectacular. The deep blue of the harbour, the bays and the rivers feeding them contrasts with the red roofs of suburban houses and the green of surviving bushland. Once you've glimpsed the city centre and two of the world's great twentieth-century structures—the Harbour Bridge and the Opera House—you know where you are. It is unmistakably Sydney.

When my book *Sydney Since the Twenties* appeared in 1978, it came at a time of growing interest in the past and the future of our cities. Suddenly the handful of universities and the score of scholars who had taken cities as real subjects for discussion found an audience among architects, local government officials, town planners and concerned citizens who were working to make our cities better places to live in. A number of major books about Sydney have appeared since then, making it possible for this rewriting, *Sydney's Century*, to expand the scope of its coverage. There are major new studies to draw on. Many of these books owe their origins to the Sydney History Group, formed in 1978. Max Kelly, Jill Roe and other members encouraged a new generation of scholars to take Sydney as their subject. Local councils, most notably the City of Sydney Council, commissioned scholarly histories, drawn on here and cited in the further reading list.

This book draws on a wide variety of writing about Sydney, from the utilitarian to the imaginary world of the novelist. Millions of words are written about Sydney every year. Metropolitan and local newspapers and magazines contemplate the present state and future options for the city centre and the suburbs. Almost every one of the city's two million vehicles carries a street directory. The humble street directory is vital for anyone wanting to understand the process of suburban expansion—from the creation and naming of streets to those telltale dotted lines indicating 'freeway planned here'. Airport, ferry and bus terminals abound with brochures about how to get the best out of Sydney. And in the 1990s web sites, often elegantly designed but with remarkably messy content, crowd cyberspace.

Sydney also had, at the turn of the century, architects and municipal reformers, including J.D. Fitzgerald and John Sulman, who could write about their passions. A later generation of town planners produced the magnificent County of Cumberland Plan, but since the 1980s most planning documents are badly written public relations exercises. Sydney's famous postwar architects happily record their own structures but have had little to say about making Sydney a better city to live in.

Every local council in Sydney contains important records about its own area, from ratebooks to plans for expanded parklands. A general history such as this relies heavily on the work of local and metropolitan historians; the last 20 years has seen a flowering of work by professional historians, including Shirley Fitzgerald's history of the Sydney Municipal Council and dozens of histories of particular suburbs. Some of these stand out as both literary and historical works, especially Gavin Souter's superbly readable account of Mosman. Historians and geographers continue to write about housing, transport, retailing and the social composition of the city. The reader will find their works in the further reading list.

Revealing their colonial origins, Sydneysiders are always thrilled when a major international writer recognises them. Jan Morris's *Sydney*, published in 1992, received an uncritical reception. It boasts fewer insights about Sydney than earlier writings by some of our best journalists and authors, including J.D. Pringle, Souter and the Melbourne architect Robin Boyd. When international publishers tackle Sydney they are still inclined to approach famous

Closed in the early 1980s, Reschs Waverley Brewery, Tooth's warehouse and the AGM glass plant were demolished to make way for high rise apartment buildings in the 1990s.
Photograph by Peter Spearritt 1985

expatriates, so Time Life asked the Brisbane-born poet Peter Porter to write on Sydney in its great cities of the world series.

Sydney's institutions, from the stock exchange and the universities to schools, department stores and churches, have often found biographers, as have some of the city's famous and infamous citizens. There are histories of the city's grand houses, its workingmen's cottages, its parks, gardens and bushland. This book draws on a number of them but readers looking for a particular individual or business or organisation can do no better than start their inquiry at the Mitchell Library.

In the world of fiction, local writers have long recognised the range of settings that the city provides. In his first novel, *Jonah* (1911), Louis Stone provided a graphic portrait of the lives and landscapes of working-class Waterloo. In *Seven Poor Men of Sydney* (1934), Christina Stead made the harbour a centrepiece of her novel, Watson's Bay a site of adventure, romance and lust on warm summer nights. Eleanor Dark based her novel *Waterway* around the tragic sinking of a passenger ferry. Leonard Mann, in *A Murder in Sydney* (1937), introduced readers to the intricate environments of the city and the streets and lanes of Kirribilli and Neutral Bay. The poet Kenneth Slessor set many of his poems around the harbour or in the eastern suburbs, from his grand epics such as 'Five Bells' to his satirical book *Darlinghurst Nights*.

With the exception of Ruth Park and Jon Cleary and the pulp paperback writers of the 1950s and 1960s, Sydney—bursting its suburban seams—became less popular as a setting for novelists. It came to fictional prominence again in the 1980s with Peter Corris's detective, Cliff Hardy, prowling the inner and outer suburbs in his battered Falcon. Unique among Australian detectives, Hardy even consults reference works at the Mitchell Library. David Williamson, who moved from Melbourne to Sydney, captures the preoccupation with real estate in a number of his plays, including *Emerald City*.

Between the wars the children's writer May Gibbs created a world peopled by gumnut babies from Nutcote, her modest harbourside home in Neutral Bay. Half a century later writers for children again took up Sydney as a setting with gusto; the novels of Libby Gleeson and Nadia Wheatley are among the best-known results.

In the 1970s historians and novelists began to question the rights of Australians to occupy sites that were appropriated by British colonists. While this dispossession was recognised by some previous writers, and marked by Aboriginal protests, most commentators treated the alienation of the continent as a fait accompli. Keith Willey's *When the Sky Fell Down: The Destruction of the Tribes of the Sydney Region 1788–1850s*, published in 1979, was one attempt to understand the fate of Aboriginal people. In the 1990s the land rights movement and the *Mabo* and *Wik* judgments have raised a series of questions about the nature and extent of prior occupation and the regime of European property rights that spread across the landscape. While the great majority of Sydney's land is held in Torrens and strata titles, the Crown still owns vast swathes of bushland, national parks, rivers, harbours and other waterways. Claims for collective ownership of such sites are now emerging,

Jørn Utzon, the Danish architect who won the competition to design the Sydney Opera House in 1957, resigned in 1966. He was not present at the opening of the Opera House as George Molnar, an architect himself, made plain in his 20 October 1973 cartoon (detail reproduced here) for the *Sydney Morning Herald*.

as is a new literature—from archaeological studies to autobiographies—about Aboriginal life in Sydney.

The richness of non-fiction and fictional accounts of Sydney is paralleled by the appeal of the city for professional and amateur photographers and the attraction of the harbour and the beaches for many of our painters. Anyone who writes about Sydney draws on and owes much to the photographs of Harold Cazneaux, Max Dupain and David Moore. The Mitchell Library holds major collections of all this work, and the work of hundreds of other photographers, including unnamed government photographers who captured key moments in the city's history and key elements of the evolution of its built landscape.

Just as photographers have been fascinated by the construction and evolution of Sydney's great structures—the finger wharves, the Harbour Bridge, the Opera House—so have generations of artists depicted the growth and atmosphere of the city. In the interwar years Grace Cossington Smith, Roland Wakelin, Margaret Preston and Dorrit Black produced magnificent oil paintings, watercolours and lithographs of the city. In the 1950s and 1960s Lloyd Rees and Brett Whiteley reflected on the colours and the subtropical climate of the city. Their art influenced a later generation of painters and commercial artists who created mass-produced images of the city of great imagination, with bold colours and compositions of landscape, buildings and people. Ken Done is pre-eminent in this domain, with his images—as paintings, posters, on T-shirts, coffee mugs and placemats—to be found in travellers' households around the world. Telling images of Sydney icons, from the Opera House to the Haymarket, have been represented by a number of artists, including Martin Sharp.

The most socially acute commentary on Sydney has not come from novelists, poets, painters or photographers, but from cartoonists: Bill Pidgeon's portrayal of Bondi and Macleay Street in the 1930s, Emile Mercier's inner city backyards of the 1950s, George Molnar's reflections on city boosting in the 1960s and Bruce Petty's ability to show how a city of high rise apartments, Victorian terraces and suburban cottages somehow hangs together. Some of the best phrases ever written about Sydney have also come from the pens of these cartoonists. Molnar's cartoon at the opening of the Sydney Opera House showing its architect, Jørn Utzon, walking away from his sails was tellingly captioned: 'When I was walking up the stairs I met a man who wasn't there.'

Sydney's Century draws on a rich literature about the city, its people and its cultures. Having lived in Sydney for 30 years and been a frequent visitor since, I have also drawn on personal recollections of family and friends, including my time at the now demolished North Sydney Technical High School (home, these days, to C & W Optus, taverns and a shopping plaza) and the chastening experience of becoming stranded in a rowboat in Homebush Bay while undertaking a heritage study of the Parramatta River.

Some postmodern analysts describe the city as a series of overlapping subcultures, of territories where one individual's experience or one group's experience may be very different to another's. But the chief points of difference in the way people encounter a city do have collective underpinnings. Age, gender, ethnic background, your place of residence and your place of work (if you have work) all have enormous implications for how you use and experience the city. Young children have to be prevented from crossing city roads, women have to be careful where and when they walk and even how they use public transport. Wealth and suburb of residence can protect some Sydneysiders from the more unpleasant aspects of big-city living. Gated estates, alarm systems and security devices offer partial protection from the fear of robbery or harrassment. But one of the good things about big cities, as distinct from gated communities, is that if you want to participate in metropolitan life, you have to go out. Out into the street, out into the traffic, out into the suburbs or into the city centre. These things can be written about collectively, as can the evolving landscape of the city.

Sydney's Century traces the physical growth of the city in the twentieth century, the process of suburbanisation, and the way in which changing employment and transport patterns have shaped the city. While it draws on the rich literature of local history, it is an account of metropolitan growth and change. Readers interested in particular suburbs, individuals, businesses or the history of particular peoples should consult the further reading list before tackling the Mitchell Library. Crime and corruption in Sydney is occasionally revealed in royal commissions and in exposés by hardy journalists, but much of it goes unreported. Businesses, families, political parties, institutions and ethnic groups are now reconstructing their own histories using private records, photographs and interviews. A great deal of work has already been done on migrant history, business history, working-class employment and 'subcultures' including gay history. The Sydney haute-bourgeoisie have long been documented in the *Sydney Morning Herald*, the *Bulletin* and in the pages of

Australia Day parade, 26 January 1985. The Aussie Signs float celebrated Sydney's Bridge and high rise structures.
Photograph by Peter Spearritt

Oil storage tanks at Gore Bay, Greenwich, depicted in the Shell house journal *Together* in July 1930, showed their proximity to housing and industry. A spectacular oil spill from a tanker in the main harbour in August 1999 reminded Sydneysiders of the environmental hazards of their working port.
Together, July 1930

Who's Who. Their lifestyle, their homes, their children, are recorded in many a public and private archive. Understanding the lives of many other Sydneysiders requires a much more time consuming search for records, especially for those who until recently have hardly figured in accounts of the city. We await a detailed history of indigenous Australians in twentieth-century Sydney.

I should briefly mention the standpoint from which I write. All cities are the products of economic, social and technological forces that result in unique landscapes and structures, and shape the daily lives of their citizens. Underlying *Sydney's Century* is the belief that collective action in a democratic society should attempt to create a just city. The pursuit of individual wealth or autonomy at the expense of the public good should be resisted by public debate and legislative action. Home ownership, for example, is beneficial to individual households, giving people a sense of financial and emotional security denied to many tenants. But a society that sits back when decent housing is beyond the means of most of its citizens—which has happened from time to time in the history of Sydney—is courting gross inequality. Similarly, a city that embraces ever-increasing rates of car usage without improving its public transport system will inevitably see private affluence compromised by public squalor. Sydney is one of the world's great cities, but it can be made a better and fairer city. Among its other tasks, this book examines some of the attempts to do just that.

Sydney's Century owes much to the advice of friends, colleagues and students. My parents moved house and offspring from Melbourne to Sydney in 1960. At school I saw, at close hand, the redevelopment of the city centre and North Sydney. With fellow schoolmate and photographer John Storey I developed a fascination with how the city is depicted. At the University of Sydney Heather Radi and John Power encouraged my interest in Sydney's planning. At the Urban Research Unit at ANU Peter Harrison (1918–90), Max Neutze, Leonie Sandercock and Pat Troy provided a mix of encouragement and critique of which Australian universities should be rightly proud. Over 300 students at Macquarie University in the late 1970s and 1980s put up with bus and ferry explorations of the suburbs, as Monash students have done in the 1990s. As the Gregory's is no match for Melbourne's Melways, these field trips included dead ends in toxic sites near Homebush Bay, getting lost on the urban rural fringe, encountering crematoria and identifying school uniforms from some of the city's more suspect private schools. Ben Boer, Don Godden, Trish Holt and Andrew Spearritt have introduced me to finger wharves, abandoned power stations, enclosed convents and the beauties of the national parks. Friends and colleagues will find their advice, their newscuttings, even their own suburbs, workplaces and dwellings drawn on in these pages: Tim Bowden, Jim Davidson, Graeme Davison, Louise Douglas, Stephen Foster, Glenda Gartrell, Jim Gillespie, Murray Goot, Martin Indyk, John Iremonger, Denis Jeans, Max Kelly (1936–96), Paula Lake, Louise Martin, Jack Mundey, John Patterson, Tony Prescott, John Rickard, Gavin Souter, Ruth Thompson, and George Wilkenfeld.

Peter Browne suggested a major reworking of the earlier book and maintained my enthusiasm for the project. At the National Centre for Australian Studies at Monash John Arnold, Jan Field and John Young made the new book possible. Richard McGregor provided much needed editorial advice, from a Melbraic perspective.

Much of my thinking about Sydney draws on explorations of other cities, usually in the company of a friendly guide: London (Hugo Hinsley), Oxford (Gordon Clark), Hong Kong (Christopher Callinan), Berlin (Germanus Pause), Boston (Bob Mack), Los Angeles (Leonie Sandercock), New York (where the late Walter Tevis showed us the great hotel foyers), Melbourne (Nigel Lewis), Adelaide (Anne Edwards and John Mottram) and Perth (Tom Stannage).

1901
LONG LIFE
AND HAPPINESS TO LORD AND LADY
HOPETOUN

CHAPTER 1

The new century

When the residents of Sydney celebrated the federation of the Australian colonies on 1 January 1901, a sweltering Tuesday, they marked the start of a new nation, a more exciting notion than the start of a new century. The half a million people who poured into the New South Wales metropolis had to stop thinking of themselves as residents of the colony, as it was now a state; the land they called Australia was their nation.

FACING PAGE
Sydney welcomed Lord and Lady Hopetoun with an elaborate archway in Martin Place.
NSW Government Printer 1901

Of the state's 1,354,000 residents, 80 per cent had been born in Australia, 17 per cent in the British Isles or elsewhere in the empire, while only 35,000 were of 'foreign' birth, including 18,600 from continental Europe and 11,300 from China. Well over half of the 'foreign born' were resident in Sydney, which numbered almost 500,000 people, depending on how many of the outlying areas one included. At the 1901 census the NSW statistician reported 7734 'full blood' and 'half caste' Aborigines in the state, of whom 509 were 'nomads'. Probably no more than a hundred or so Aborigines remained in Sydney, many less than the 3000 that Governor Phillip estimated lived between Broken Bay and Botany Bay in the 1790s.[1]

Sydney derived its name from Sydney Cove, where Phillip had established the first settlement in 1788. He named it in honour of Thomas Townshend, a wealthy politician who was created Baron Sydney of Chislehurst in 1783. The following year Townshend became home secretary in the British cabinet and in that role arranged for Phillip to command the fleet that would bring convicts to establish a penal colony in Australia. Later made Viscount Sydney, Townshend never visited Australia other than in correspondence.

The imprint of Britain in the new colony went beyond government, education, the legal system and buildings. Visiting British explorers, convicts and free settlers took it upon themselves to name everything in sight, from natural features to the roads they created in a country that seemingly had neither roads nor tracks. Sydney's imperial origins can be seen in its roads named after kings, governors, politicians and assorted aristocrats. As villages and suburbs developed, they also took on names from settlements in the mother country: Ryde, Putney, Darlington, Epping, Richmond, Windsor, Penrith.

Some areas were named after the new arrivals, including the convict surgeon William Redfern, who was pardoned two years after his arrival in the colony in 1801. A handful of outlying regions and settlements were named after Aboriginal tribes, including Ku-ring-gai, Warringah and Parramatta, meaning head of the river, a place where eels lie down and sleep. Kurnell, Cook's first landing place in Australia, is probably named after an Aboriginal word for wild carrot.

Successive NSW statisticians were fond of proclaiming that both the state and its capital city were over 97 per cent British stock. Sydney's convict and imperial origins were much in evidence at the turn of the century. The state Parliament building in Macquarie Street still looked like the Rum Hospital to which it owed its origins. Convict-built and convict-era buildings lined Macquarie Street, Circular Quay and much of the Rocks. Sandstone warehouses showed the telltale signs of convict stonemasonry. Admiralty House, a sandstone mansion on the foreshore at Kirribilli, opposite Circular Quay, housed the admiral commanding the British squadron in Australia, 11 of whose warships were a reminder, during the Commonwealth pageant of 1901, of Britain's commitment to protect Australia as an integral part of its empire. A British-born and British-appointed governor ruled local society from Government House, a Gothic edifice above the Fort Bennelong tram depot. As chair of the Executive Council of New South Wales, his signature made acts of parliament into laws.

The *Bulletin*, with its republican and bushman sentiments, described the Commonwealth pageant as tawdry, unworthy, magnificent and irresistible. It complained that most of the triumphal arches 'looked hasty and feeble', though it did praise the flags and draperies in the long avenue of Oxford Street and Newcastle's arch of coal. According to the *Bulletin* the pageant belonged to 'the mass and cordoned people' rather than to the soldiers, 'gowned dignitaries', politicians, 'ciphers' and 'sycophants' who formed the parade and were invited to the Governor-General's swearing-in at the Centennial Park pavilion. Governor-General Hopetoun, 'the legacy of persistent British rule', came at the tail of the procession, 'looking so puny, so wan—as if in his own person he figured the wan and puny basis of the idea of monarchy which he represented'.

The *Sydney Morning Herald* gave a very different account of the day, describing the swearing in of Hopetoun at Centennial Park as the 'climax'. Seven thousand invited guests, 11,000 choristers and 60,000 spectators cheered Hopetoun as, leaning on his malacca cane, he walked from his coach to the seven-sided white pavilion, surmounted by the royal coat of arms. The Anglican Primate of Australia, with 41 per cent of the population professing his faith, offered a prayer. Cardinal Moran, the leader of the Catholic Church in Australia, claiming 22 per cent of the people, was not invited to say a prayer at the swearing-in ceremony, which his church boycotted.[2]

'So thoroughly tired out', the Governor-General, who caught typhoid on the voyage from London via India, did not attend the state banquet in the Town Hall, the city's most impressive structure. Electrical illuminations covered the city and the harbour, while 7000 needy families were supplied with grocery vouchers so that 'every poor person in the city and suburbs will be furnished with sufficient food for his or her immediate wants on the day that ushers in the new year, the new century and the Australian Commonwealth'.[3]

The *Bulletin* and the *Sydney Morning Herald* were in agreement on one matter, the importance of the farmer to the future of the states, their capital cities and the nation. As the *Bulletin* put it a few days after the Commonwealth pageant:

And far from the city, out and away beyond in the bush and in the desert, the men and women who really make Australia are fighting drought, fighting fire, digging the ground or reckoning their pitiful losses of cattle and sheep, stubbornly winning gold and silver and coal, stubbornly fighting for subsistence, for the wherewithal to maintain Sydney city and the city pageant. And the pageant passed; but these endure.[4]

Table 1.1: Population of Sydney at ten-year intervals, 1871–1991

Year	Population	Percentage of NSW population in Sydney
1871	137 586	27.4
1881	224 939	30.0
1891	383 333	34.0
1901	481 830	35.6
1911	629 503	38.2
1921	899 059	42.8
1931	1 200 830	46.8
1941	1 337 050	47.5
1951	1 795 010	54.8
1961	2 193 231	55.7
1971	2 725 064	59.3
1981	3 204 696	62.5
1991	3 672 855	62.3

Source: *NSWSR* and Commonwealth censuses. The figures are based on the boundaries used for statistical purposes at the time.

Country and city

Sydney's rapidly increasing proportion of the state's population drew much unfavourable comment from rural residents and their political representatives. In 1905 the *Queanbeyan Observer* attacked the 'evil' of Sydney in terms similar to those used to attack Canberra 'centralism' in more recent years, alleging that:

> governments poured the revenue they derive from the country into the pockets of city dwellers. On the city they will lavish our funds in the erection of magnificent buildings, in the construction of relief works, the placing of high salaried officials, the city instead of being the paid servant transacting the business that is sent to it by the producers, has become through press and politics despotically dominant.[5]

Although Sydney's primacy over New South Wales was already well established by 1861, in the following decades its proportion of the colony's population continued to increase. Many reasons were adduced. In 1910 a British visitor, J.F. Fraser, wrote:

> As political influence is always strongest where the population is greatest—strongest at Sydney, at Melbourne, at Adelaide, at Brisbane and at Perth—the Governments of the day, to win support, have converged the [railway] lines in the States upon these various places—to their benefit, truly, but to the disadvantage of other places ... At certain periods of the year a great rush of business comes in conveying wool, live sheep and mutton. Instead of having various exits for export, the aim seems to be to force all the goods out of one door in each State.

Writing in 1916, the English-born Sydney architect John Sulman had a more general explanation: 'the whole tendency of modern life is to concentrate population in urban areas'.[6]

At no time did any other town in New South Wales look like outstripping Sydney's population. The next four largest centres at the 1911 census were Newcastle (55,380), Broken Hill (30,972), Parramatta (12,465) and Goulburn (10,023). By 1921 Parramatta was regarded as part of Sydney and Wollongong (32,381) had replaced Broken Hill as the third-largest city.

In the interwar years conservative rural representatives in the Legislative Assembly frequently opposed the expenditure of money on Sydney—the north shore bridge project was a favourite target. The legislation authorising its construction was passed in 1922 as a result of an unusual consensus between the parties of urban labour and capital. But the consensus did not

Drift to the Cities.
Front cover *Current Affairs Bulletin*, January 1945

last, and the Nationalist minister for Public Works, R.T. Ball (representative of the rural electorate of Murray and the man who laid the foundation stone for the Sydney Harbour Bridge), felt obliged to claim that under his regime 'country and city expenditure had been in the ratio of six to one'.[7]

'The Centralisation Curse at a Glance'.
New State Magazine, June 1923

Complaints about Sydney's growth were not confined to the non-Labor parties. In 1928 the Labor member for the rural electorate of Namoi, W.J. Scully, deplored the alarming drift of the population from the country to Sydney and the larger towns: 'Governments are afraid of powerful city interests and of papers like the *Evening News* which agitate for the construction of the Eastern Suburbs Railway,' he said.[8] Between 1911 and 1947, 343,000 people moved from elsewhere in New South Wales to Sydney, almost as many as the 374,000 born in the metropolis. Only 76,000 people came from other states, while arrivals from overseas totalled only 60,000.[9] Scully's Labor colleague in the Sydney electorate of Leichhardt, Bernard Olde, had an explanation for the city's growth: 'Everyone knows that the drift to the city is an economic and industrial fact. Industry is now in the hands of big capitalists who find it easier to bring men to the machines which they have in operation than to take the machines to pieces and spread them over the country.'[10]

John Sulman had made the same point in 1916—without the ideological overtones—attributing Sydney's expansion to 'its progressively increasing use of machinery in production'.

Recognising the inexorable growth of Sydney, rural parliamentarians suggested drastic solutions, but to no avail. In 1931 the Country Party member for the federal electorate of Cowper, Earle Page, advocated the creation of a new state in northern NSW: 'Amputation', he wrote, 'is the only way to save the clean and wholesome north from the gangrene of extravagance, Communism and repudiation that is eating into the Metropolis.'[11]

Earle Page's *bête noire* of the time, Labor Premier Jack Lang, later wrote with equal venom of the Country Party's attitude:

The Country Party only had one real plank in its platform. That was the very

> simple formula of grabbing everything for the country and giving nothing to the city ... they obtained spur development lines to all kinds of outlandish places. They were losing propositions from the start and still have to be subsidized by the Government ... One of the things [the Country Party] wanted most was the portfolio of Railways. Not necessarily to build railways. Rather to stop certain railways being built for the city dwellers.[12]

So developed the uneasy relationship between the harbour city and its hinterland. But there was no escape, the two were interdependent. The hinterland depended on Sydney's port, financial and governmental facilities to export its produce to other states and overseas, and on the city's merchants and manufacturers to provide the imported or locally manufactured goods necessary for comfort and production. The city, for its part, depended on the rural hinterland for many of the raw materials needed to feed and clothe its residents and on rural exports to keep the port busy and warehouses full.

Despite the unease, city and country did meet at least once a year, at the Royal Easter Show, first held in Sydney in 1889. The show was an annual symbol and reminder of the symbiotic relationship.[13] In 1926 a Sydney solicitor, George Forbes, wrote that 'the utility of the annual show, both to the citizens of Sydney and the men on the land, has long been beyond doubt, and its popularity may be gauged by the attendance ... in 1926, which numbered 675,940 persons'.[14] In that year Sydney's population passed one million, and the rest of the state numbered 1.3 million. Even allowing for multiple visits, probably one-quarter of the state's population attended the show.

Koala Film's comedy showed The Way Backs on their farm and in the big city.
Lone Hand, June 1918

There were, of course, other points of contact, particularly through relatives. Many country people travelled regularly to Sydney to shop and, if they could afford it, to stay in large hotels such as the Metropole. Seaside and harbourside resorts such as Manly were also popular with country residents. The Rev. Stanley Drummond's Far West Children's Hostel at Manly, founded in 1930 for the children of outback parents who could not afford a holiday by the sea, became an example of what the harbour city could offer the hinterland.[15] The harbour, wrote Sulman in 1916, 'acts as a great lung to the city, which can never be closed'. Children were told that 'the fine open-air life must surely appeal to thousands of young men and young women' and were asked in one popular school textbook:

> Which would you rather do—spend your life on a high stool in an office with a green shade over your eyes, or taste something like this:
> *'Twas merry mid the blackwoods, when we spied the station roofs,*
> *To wheel the wild scrub cattle at the yard,*
> *With a running fire of stockwhips and a fiery run of hoofs;*
> *Oh! the hardest day was never then too hard!'*[16]

It is difficult to discover how often Sydneysiders visited the fabled 'sunburnt country' of the hinterland. Many went for holidays, honeymoons and trips beyond Sydney. Some resorts, including the Blue Mountains (with its 'Guest House Capital', Katoomba) and the Jenolan Caves, were available by the 1920s in one-day rail and motor tours.

Sydney's growth as a centre of commerce, industry, transport and government led to the development of other characteristics associated with what planning historian Peter Hall calls 'world cities'.[17] The city became the centre of communication, education, entertainment and high and low culture. Sydney had the state's highest-circulation newspapers, the largest publishers, the biggest libraries, art galleries and museums, and the only university (founded in 1852). Sydney's dominance of the press began with the establishment of the *Sydney Morning Herald* in 1831 and was assured by such later additions as the *Evening News*, the *Telegraph*, the *Bulletin*, the *Sun* and the *Australian Women's Weekly*.

Until the coming of the 'talkies' and radio in the 1920s, Sydney also had a virtual monopoly of large-scale mass entertainment. According to one observer, the new Tivoli at Central Station, seating 2000, was 'not frequented by people seeking entertainment on a higher level than diversions by tumblers, magicians and leg shows'. Built originally as a Grand Opera House, it was to see only one season of opera. Other major live theatres included the Royal, Her Majesty's, and the Minerva at Kings Cross, opened in 1938 as a theatre and later used as a cinema. Of Sydney's little theatres, only the Independent and the New Theatre had seating capacities of more than 300.[18]

The boom in cinema and radio in the interwar years undermined the city's monopoly of mass entertainment. Certainly Sydney had the state's most lavish cinemas—venues such as the State in Market Street—while some of its live theatres, like the St James, were converted to cinemas in the 1930s. The new electronic media were cheaper to transport or transmit than were large companies of performing artists, so most country towns soon had cinemas (or at least movies in a local hall) and most households had a radio. Nonetheless, the film distributors remained headquartered in Sydney, and the Macquarie network purchased a number of country radio stations, which centralised programming in Sydney, as would occur with television in the 1950s and 1960s.

Just as Sydney had a greater diversity of entertainment, so too did it provide more varied job opportunities than anywhere else in the state. This was particularly true for women. In 1919, 94 per cent of the NSW female factory workforce worked in Sydney.[19] The *New State Magazine* explained in October 1921 that north coast women flocked to Sydney because whatever their profession—teaching, music, art, commercial work, domestic work or nursing—the 'only opportunity for training lies in the metropolis, which has the monopoly of high educative facilities'. Only Armidale, the political capital of New England, acquired a university college before the Second World War. Neither Newcastle nor Wollongong, with much larger populations, had a fully fledged university until the 1960s.

A large city provides not only diversified employment but also greater opportunity to move from one job to another. Such a move is much more difficult for a farmer who must dispose of equipment and land or a miner or farm labourer who may have no other job alternative unless he moves to another area. Few city workers faced these limitations. Sydney's extensive public transport system meant that it was possible to change job and job location without necessarily moving house. And if this proved unavoidable, it was easier in a large city with a large housing stock, a large rental market and frequent turnover. For entertainment, outdoor recreation, education, housing, health services and employment, Sydney could be self-contained; much of the hinterland could not.

Capital of the continent

School textbooks and official utterances of the time portrayed Sydney as Australia's 'first settlement', 'a triumph of British exploration and perseverance'. In 1898 Timothy Coghlan, the NSW statistician, wrote in *The Seven Colonies of Australasia*:

> The first settlement in New South Wales, the oldest of the seven colonies of Australasia, was effected by an expedition under the command of Captain Arthur Phillip, who landed at Botany Bay on the 19 January 1788, and formally took possession of the whole continent. Botany Bay being found unsuitable, the fleet was brought round to Port Jackson, and the city of Sydney founded on the 26th January of the same year.[20]

On the cusp of the new century, retrospective studies of the nineteenth century proved much more popular than attempts to imagine the twentieth. In the late 1890s the British publishing company Chambers got together with the North American company Linscott to create the Nineteenth Century Series. They approached Coghlan as author and he in turn secured Thomas Ewing, the member for the Legislative Assembly seat of Lismore, as his co-author for the volume on Australasia. Both men had been born in the colony, Coghlan of Irish Catholic parents in Sydney in 1855, and Ewing in nearby Pitt Town in 1856, his father an Anglican clergyman. Their book is a combination of Coghlan's statistical zeal and Ewing's debater's wit. They were both convinced of the superiority of the British race. Coghlan coveted the post of high commissioner for Australia in London but had to be content with his appointment as NSW agent-general in 1905.[21]

Front cover of *Sydney Old and New: A Pictorial Contrast* (1913) showing 'natives opposing the landing of Captain Cook'. Prior Aboriginal occupation of Australia was much more likely to be acknowledged pictorially than in text.

Readers of *The Progress of Australasia in the Nineteenth Century* were told that for a nation that had started out as 'the dumping ground of the prisons of England', and then attracted 'adventurers and gamblers' bent on finding gold, Australia had developed remarkably high ideals, 'as the constitution just framed after years of calm discussion proves'. Coghlan and Ewing went on to observe that Australia has:

> an advantage over any other nation on the globe. Her population is homogeneous—British and Irish throughout—and is free from the difficulties Canada finds in the French question and the United States in her negro population. The native races are now so weak that they cause the Government no trouble. British ideas, British institutions, can be developed in their purity in Australia; and it is not at all likely that any large bodies of European emigrants will risk the long voyage to the South to make for themselves homes in the Island-Continent.[22]

Writing for an international audience, Coghlan and Ewing spent a considerable time explaining why 'no characteristic of Australasian development has been more marked than the concentration of population in the cities', with 'considerably more than one-third of the population massed in the metropolitan areas'. A similar observation had been made by Adna Weber, the 28-year-old deputy commissioner of labor statistics in New York state, whose book *The Growth of Cities in the Nineteenth Century* appeared in 1899: 'The most remarkable concentration, or rather centralization, of population occurs in that newest product of civilization, Australia, where nearly one-third of the entire population is settled in and about capital cities.'

Apart from New York, with 50 per cent of the inhabitants of its state, and Boston, with 40 per cent of the inhabitants of Massachusetts, Sydney, with 34 per cent of the NSW population, and Melbourne with 46 per cent of Victoria's population, proved how extraordinary the Australian situation was, with its inhabitants 'so massed in a few centres'. Most of the population growth in Australia's cities had come, as in the American cities, not just from people moving from the country to the city, but from new immigrants choosing to stay in the cities. Based on 1899 statistics, Coghlan and Ewing stated in authoritative tone that Melbourne is 'the largest Australian city', with 470,000 people, while

Table 1.2: Populations of Sydney and Melbourne metropolitan areas calculated on a minimum density basis 1901–33

Year	Sydney	Melbourne
1901	481,117 Area 88,289 acres. Least dense area was Lane Cove with 77 people per hundred acres.	480,279 Area 85,275 acres. Least dense areas were Preston and Oakleigh with 40 and 70 people per hundred acres respectively.
1911	629,503 Area 118,299 acres, including Ku-ring-gai and Eastwood. Least dense area was Eastwood with 33 people per hundred acres	582,275 Area not stated, but approximately 100,000 acres. Least dense area was Heidelberg with 33 people per hundred acres.
1921	899,059 Area 118,299 acres, as for 1911. Least dense area was Eastwood with 73 people per hundred acres.	766,465 Area 105,385 acres. Least dense areas small part of Mulgrave (399 people) and Moorabbin with 58 people per hundred acres.
1933	1,235,267 Area 156,149 acres. All areas had a minimum density of over 100 people per hundred acres.	983,173 Area 116,489 acres. All areas had a minimum density of 100 people per hundred acres

Note: The reported census figures have been adjusted where necessary to provide comparable population densities, and hence total metropolitan populations, for each particular year. It has not been possible to use a uniform population density for whole of period 1901–33. Sources: NSWSR, 1891 and 1901; *Victorian Year Book*, 1892 and 1902; Commonwealth censuses 1911, vol. 3; 1921, vol. 2; and 1933, vol. 3. See also the discussion in JW McCarty, 'Australian Capital Cities in the 19th Century' on city size and city growth, in JW McCarty and CB Schedvin (eds), *Australian Capital Cities*, Sydney University Press, Sydney, 1978, pp 9–25.

Sydney, the oldest city, had 427,000 inhabitants. But as Weber remarked, estimates of city populations depended on how much of the surrounding 'suburban districts' one included in the definition. He noted that Sydney, with its 35 suburbs in 96,000 acres, was bigger than any American city except Chicago, with 103,000 acres. Melbourne, at 164,000 acres, claimed a metropolitan area more than twice that of London's 75,000 acres.[23]

Federal Parliament House, Melbourne
Postcard, 1905

At the 1901 census, the first to be held on similar principles for all the new states, it became clear that the populations of Sydney and Melbourne were neck and neck. If one defined Sydney's urban area as the contiguous suburbs with more than 70 people per 100 acres, the metropolis comprised 88,289 acres and housed 481,117 people. Applying a similar definition to Melbourne, 480,279 people lived in 85,275 acres (see Table 1.2). There was no general agreement among statisticians at the time about how to define the metropolitan area, the Victorian statistician preferring the ten-mile-radius definition of 163,480 acres that Adna Weber refers to, but that included 78,000 acres with a mere 15,800 people, mostly in small farming settlements. Once the 1901 census results became available, Coghlan had to revise his figures for Sydney. It became clear that the 40,000 people that Melbourne had lost between 1891 and 1895 would not be promptly made up. In subsequent annual estimates for both cities, Sydney inexorably drew ahead.

City and state pride bedevilled the question of where the new nation's capital would be. One of the concessions made to the people of New South Wales to get their support for federation was the insertion of section 125 in the Constitution, which states that the nation's capital would be within the state of New South Wales but not less than 100 miles from Sydney. A further provision, that 'Parliament shall sit at Melbourne until it meet at the seat of Government', served as a consolation prize to Victoria, which hosted the federal Parliament in its grand Parliament House until 1927.[24] While Victoria's Parliament House is still without its planned dome, it is a much more impressive edifice than its NSW counterpart, the converted rum hospital—hardly the appropriate setting for the parliament of a new nation.

The New South Wales Parliament House
NSW Government Printer, 1954

A number of prospective sites were considered by the NSW and federal governments. As part of the effort to enhance Sydney's position, in 1904 journalist E.J. Brady edited a substantial booklet entitled *Sydney, Commercial Capital of the Commonwealth: Being a consideration and recognition of her national pre-eminence as the civic mother and chief industrial centre of the Australian States*. That Sydney would not house the federal capital Brady portrayed as 'the price paid by the patriotic people of New South Wales for Federation'. The foreword to the booklet made no mention of Melbourne but explained that Sydney's claims to be the 'political capital' 'were waived in order to propitiate our Southern neighbours'. Brady argued Sydney's case as the 'Commercial Capital' of Australasia: 'Although it is not possible in terms of our Federal bargain to have the Central Political Government located in the finest city in the southern hemisphere, we can at least, as patriotic citizens, put forward our claims to the commercial consideration of the world.'[25]

The federal *Seat of Government Act (1908)* settled on the district of

Yass–Canberra as the site for the national capital, with an Australian Capital Territory to be purchased from private land holders and the NSW government. The 1911 census, the first held by the new federal government's statistician, confirmed not only that Sydney was bigger than Melbourne but also that it was growing much faster than its southern rival. Subdivisions were advertised in developing suburbs within seven miles of the GPO, such as Bellevue Hill, Randwick, St Leonards and Annandale, as far afield as Bankstown, Carlingford and Granville and well beyond the metropolitan area, at the outlying villages of Como and Hornsby.[26]

In June 1911 the Melbourne *Argus* informed its readers that Sydney's population of 637,794 represented almost a 30 per cent increase on its 1901 population of 492,907. The following year the *Argus* reported that Sydney's population was increasing by 20,000 people per year while Melbourne was adding 12,000 people per year.[27] Melbourne also experienced a subdivision and building boom, but the mood in Melbourne was less buoyant than in

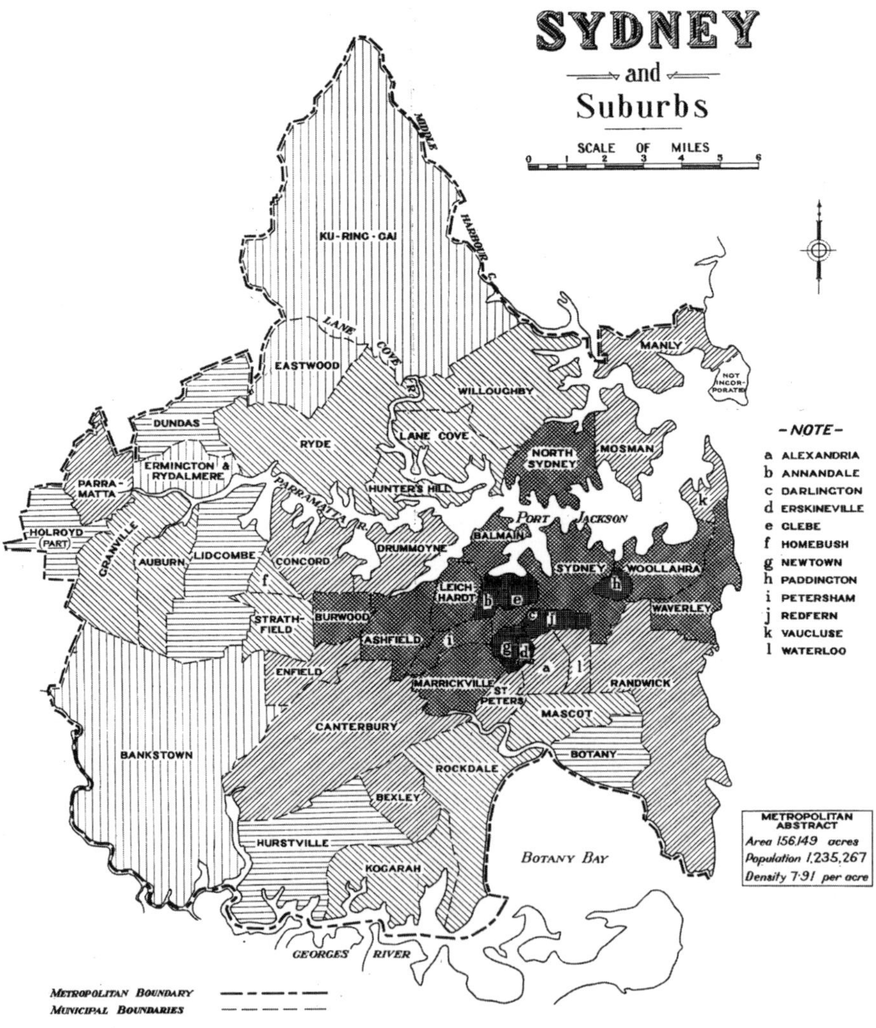

Map 1.1: Metropolitan Sydney 1911.
At the 1911 census the average population density across the metropolis was a little over 5 people per acre varying from the inner industrial suburbs with over 100 per acre, to the outer suburbs with less than one person per acre.
Commonwealth census 1911

Sydney, as it still smarted from the collapse of the late 1880s and early 1890s.

The *Sydney Morning Herald* welcomed the 'outstanding fact' of the 1911 census as the 'enormous expansion of suburban Sydney' and reported that Victoria would lose one seat in the Commonwealth Parliament. In June 1911 the *Herald*, revelling in Sydney's primacy as a port, happily proclaimed 'Sydney cannot escape being the chief port of the Commonwealth and the great distribution centre for the Pacific.'[28] The following year a group of businessmen got together and formed the Millions Club, established in the belief that accelerated migration from Britain would make Sydney the first Australian city to reach a population of one million. By the time of the next census, in June 1921, Sydney's population, at 899,059, was well in excess of Melbourne's at 766,465. Within the next year or so Sydney's population, if one included the outlying suburbs, reached the one million mark, adding weight to the city's claim to be 'the second white city of empire'. A German postcard manufacturer announced Sydney as 'Capital of the continent', developing into a 'metropolis with sky-scrapers'.

'Over one million inhabitants. Capital of the continent, and developing into metropolis with sky-scrapers. Port Jackson is a good natural harbour with several basins, among them the largest is the Circular Quay, shown in picture with grain elevators.' This translation appeared on the back of the postcard, which had text in both German and English.
Trinks & Co, Leipzig, c. 1922.

Sydney began the new century with a population almost the same as Melbourne's. Despite the claims of local boosters, Sydney's future growth, let alone a position of national pre-eminence, was far from certain. Awareness that birthrates in the city were lower than those in the country prompted resentment on the part of rural dwellers, concerned about their state capital in a country whose physical size was not matched by its population and whose interior needed settlers. Many parts of Sydney were unsanitary and unpleasant. Horse manure, poorly maintained roads and inadequate sewage and stormwater disposal gave some areas of Sydney a Dickensian appearance. More than one-third of the population lived in row terrace houses or other dwellings of three or more households. This was in marked contrast to country towns, where terrace housing was rare. In 1901 central Melbourne's population density was 11 people per acre, while in central Sydney the figure was 39 people per acre. In parts of Sydney it was well over 80 people per acre. While this did not approach the high-density living of some British and United States cities, Sydney's inadequate sanitation made it much more squalid than London or New York. At the outbreak of plague in 1901 the newspapers expressed dismay but not disbelief.[29]

The cartoonist Hop portrays the plague—emblazoned on a rodent—as 'a burning question' requiring immediate attention.
Bulletin, 12 May, 1900

Rats were the most visible evidence of the threat of the plague, but it took authorities some time to co-ordinate their extermination.
Max Kelly, *Plague Sydney*, 1982

CHAPTER 2

Plague, planning and the house famine

On 19 January 1900 Arthur Paine, a carter working at Sydney's central wharf, died of bubonic plague. As there were no other victims in the next ten days, the *Sydney Morning Herald*, noting no alarm from the medical profession, concluded that 'there is nothing to show that Sydney is experiencing an unusual season of sickness'. But by 12 March a dozen people had succumbed to plague, carried by rats from ships in port; panic, which 'stemmed in large measure form the centuries old fear of plague', gripped the city.[1] Both the *Bulletin* and the *Herald* reminded readers that plague victims were compulsorily incarcerated at the Quarantine Station on North Head where, if they died, they were buried in a fifty-foot deep grave.

At a time when people thought disease could literally be spread by an 'ill wind', the press reported an 'exodus' to the western suburbs, 'a mad rush to the Blue Mountains' and an increase in the number of Sydneysiders visiting Melbourne, which remained free of plague until May. People planning on visiting Sydney postponed their trip. The other colonies declared Sydney an infected port, its shipping subject to quarantine regulations. The Victorian Railways cancelled a monthly excursion train between Sydney and Melbourne, fearing that its cheap fares would attract the plague-prone working class. One Sydney journalist described this as 'unneighbourly', while the *Bulletin* pointed out that the plague 'isn't a patch on the daily, hourly typhoid as a means of slaughtering the public'.[2] By the end of the year 103 people had died of plague in Sydney; exactly the same number died of typhoid. In the medical terminology of the time enteritis, phthisis, cancer and pneumonia accounted for many more of the 5502 deaths in Sydney in 1900.[3]

Nonetheless, the plague was a dreadful and rightly feared disease, entering the city via the filthy wharves and putrid slums of Darling Harbour. Other major outbreaks followed in Brisbane, Rockhampton and Townsville. Melbourne, Adelaide and Fremantle had no more than 10 cases each.[4] Two-thirds of the 165 plague deaths in Australia in 1900 were in Sydney. This did little for self-esteem in the city that was to host the inauguration of the Commonwealth of Australia on 1 January 1901.

Areas of the city were quarantined and houses and businesses inspected. The epidemic demonstrated, as Curson and McCracken explain in their book *Plague in Sydney*, that the city 'through years of apathy, neglect and inadequate regulation [had] fallen into a dirty, insanitary condition'. Inspections in Kent and Sussex streets, abutting Darling Harbour, found extreme overcrowding and houses unconnected to the sewer, whose cesspits were emptied into the waters of the harbour. Some blamed the 'heathen Chinee' and 'Syrians', but

Children and slums. Little Dowling St, Paddington, 1913
Mitchell Library

the *Daily Telegraph* concluded that 'white people are the worst offenders'. Many houses had walls only one brick thick, saturated with damp, their floors resting on the earth. Toilets were often to be found in kitchens.[5] All the residents of these houses were tenants, but the ramshackle structures were owned by business and professional men.[6] The wooden wharves were not much better. Poorly constructed, they provided excellent haunts and foraging grounds for rats.

The early bouts of cleansing, all in areas regarded as 'slums', involved the removal of garbage, the application of disinfectants and whitewash and the demolition of some houses. But the epidemic continued, so the government finally took the advice of its chief public health officer and targeted the carriers of the disease, the rats. Volunteer rat catchers were offered a bounty for their catch. The lord mayor of Sydney worried that such an approach might 'result in a trade in rats from Melbourne'. At tuppence a rat for each body delivered to a central furnace, along with other measures, including the free distribution of rat poison to councils and residents, 108,000 rats were exterminated by officials, and thousands more by householders.[7]

In a manner reminiscent of the hunt for the guilty party during the contaminated-water crisis in Sydney in 1998, the city council and the state government's Board of Health blamed each other for the outbreak. The council strengthened its milk-supply, food shop and sanitary inspections. The government undertook a massive resumption program of all privately owned and municipal wharves from Circular Quay to the foot of Darling Harbour, creating a Sydney Harbour Trust and a City Improvement Advisory Board in 1901 to rebuild the wharves and supervise resumptions, including those in the Rocks and Millers Point. The city council objected to the Harbour Trust's wide powers, especially as the trust didn't start to rat-proof the wharves until 1907 and was equally tardy in demolishing and rebuilding houses.

In 1905 the state government finally granted the city council the power to resume 'slums'. These were dwellings, mostly built between the 1850s and the 1880s, that had fallen into disrepair. Many were on tiny plots of land. Sometimes one dwelling had been built in the backyard of another, or just tacked on to an existing dwelling. The city historian Shirley Fitzgerald has observed that such was the council's 'enthusiasm' for slum clearing that it exercised 'powers which might astonish present-day planners. There was little attempt to define a slum area or to provide for any objections from interested parties, and almost no recognition that the renters who lived in the areas had any rights at all.'[8]

More than 700 houses were resumed in Ultimo, around the Belmore Markets (opening up the approaches to Central Station) and in the Haymarket, to make way for new market buildings. By 1912, 7000 people, some of whom were described by the city health officer as an 'undesirable class of tenants', were displaced but the 1905 legislation did not require the council to provide new workmen's dwellings. Few of these people moved to more salubrious suburbs, because as one council alderman later admitted 'they went across the street into another municipality, and got into the same condition again'.[9]

Cartoonists had a field day with the plague, identifying all manner of culprits. While the plague could be ignored by a public more interested in the Boer War and the coming of federation, it did give reformers and town-planning advocates additional ammunition in calling for state government intervention and sweeping municipal powers. The words 'beautification' and 'improvement' were in the air. John Daniel (Jack) Fitzgerald, a Shellharbour-born compositor, who had been active in the 1890 maritime strike, emerged as both a critic of Sydney and a champion for its improvement. A founding member of the Labor Party, Fitzgerald travelled to England in 1890 to gain support for the strikers and to pursue his interest in municipal socialism and urban renewal. Editor of the *Freeman's Journal* (1899–1904), alderman on the Sydney Municipal Council (1900–04) and a member of the NSW bar, Fitzgerald, who wrote in a lively, informed and committed fashion, became the leading spokesman for municipal reform and town planning. In *Greater Sydney and Greater Newcastle* (1906) he argued the case for united municipal government on the British model. The following year a new illustrated monthly journal, the *Lone Hand*, published his 'Sydney, the Cinderella of Cities', one of the most telling articles ever written about the city's 'civic anarchy': 'Sydney, so full of contrasts—contrasts of wealth and poverty, of palace and slum, of commercial concentration and efficiency, with civic ineptitude and dismemberment—will repay study,' he wrote.

There have been many attempts to replan Circular Quay. In 1909 planners had to grapple with its role as a ferry and tram terminus, as well as providing a rail link.
Royal Commission on Sydney Improvement, plan no. 26, *NSWPP*, 1909

Fitzgerald welcomed the appointment, in May 1908, of a Royal Commission into the Improvement of City and Suburbs presided over by the new lord mayor of Sydney, Thomas Hughes, who had led a deputation to the state government to create just such a commission. Engineers, architects, the clergy, trade unionists and many other citizens gave evidence. As Fitzgerald wrote:

> Everyone admits that Sydney has outgrown her plan (if her casual growth can be called a plan), as a child outgrows its swaddling clothes. Visitors

> from abroad wonder that the great city managed to get through its work as one of the world's greatest commercial entrepots and goods-distributing centres in the face of its hilly contours, its narrow streets, its huddled plan, the comparative inaccessibility of its harbour front, the want of adequate means of communication and of transportation between its outlying boundaries on the north, south, west and east ... Sydney is choked.[10]

Fitzgerald looked to Europe and particularly to Paris for inspiration about city improvement. He regarded Paris as a 'wonder city' that had evolved from a choked rabbit warren 'to the most beautifully ornate and spacious city in the whole world'. He admired the great straight avenues, the parks, gardens, squares, monuments and fountains but he also liked the short streets of 'exquisite design'. The royal commissioners shared such sentiments. Their plans included avenues and squares, monuments and grand buildings, including Sir John Sulman's design for a six-storey semicircular colonnade at Belmore Park and Norman Selfe's Venetian-style edifice at Circular Quay.

Front cover *Rickard's Realty Review*
January 1910

Most of the commission's proposals for city beautification concerned the area from Central Station to Circular Quay. The Sydney Harbour Trust was belatedly tackling the wharf areas but no organisation had shown much interest in cleaning up the eastern approaches to the city. The commissioners recommended the widening of Elizabeth, Oxford and William streets. For the suburbs they advocated better transport, favouring a bridge between Sydney and North Sydney but deferring the tunnel recommended the year before by the Royal Commission on Communication between Sydney and North Sydney. Mindful of the success of the London Underground and the Paris Metro they recommended the construction of an underground railway loop for the central city, the development of new suburban lines and the electrification of the suburban rail system.[11]

The royal commission delivered its report in June 1909, when, according to the city council's surveyor, 'Sydney [was] being practically rebuilt'. Real estate agents relished the challenge. In November Arthur Rickard launched his *Rickard's Realty Review*, a monthly magazine 'devoted to your interests and ours'. Born in rural New South Wales in 1868 of Cornish parents, Rickard, like most of his generation, left school at 13. After a series of jobs in hardware and wholesaling he set up his own wholesale grocery firm. Accused of supplying foodstuffs infested with weevils to local asylums, Rickard turned to real estate. Operating from a handsome sandstone establishment in Pitt Street, Rickard told the readers of the first issue of his *Review:*

> At the present time Sydney is growing as is no other city south of the line. Everywhere warehouses, shops, offices and good homes are going up as if by magic. Railways and tramways are being extended and pushed out on all sides. People are flocking into Sydney and every year this increase represents the population of a small city ... Land that was bought but a few years ago at shillings per acre is now being sold at pounds a foot.

With characteristic hyperbole, Rickard claimed that he sold more land than 'any other firm' in the nation, a claim that could just as readily be made by some of the city's other large agencies, including Richardson & Wrench and Hardie & Gorman, which had been breaking up estates in the eastern, southern and northern suburbs long before Rickard went into business. These agencies had been creating new suburban subdivisions for decades.[12]

Fuelled by rapid population growth, the subdivision and building boom saw Sydney spread out along the rail and tram routes. Steam trams were gradually replaced by electric-powered trams. The expansion and conversion were paid for by the state government, which owned the tram system as well as the railways. By 1914 the inner northern, eastern and inner western suburbs all had tram services, which extended as far as Chatswood, Ryde and La Perouse, as Map 2.1 shows.

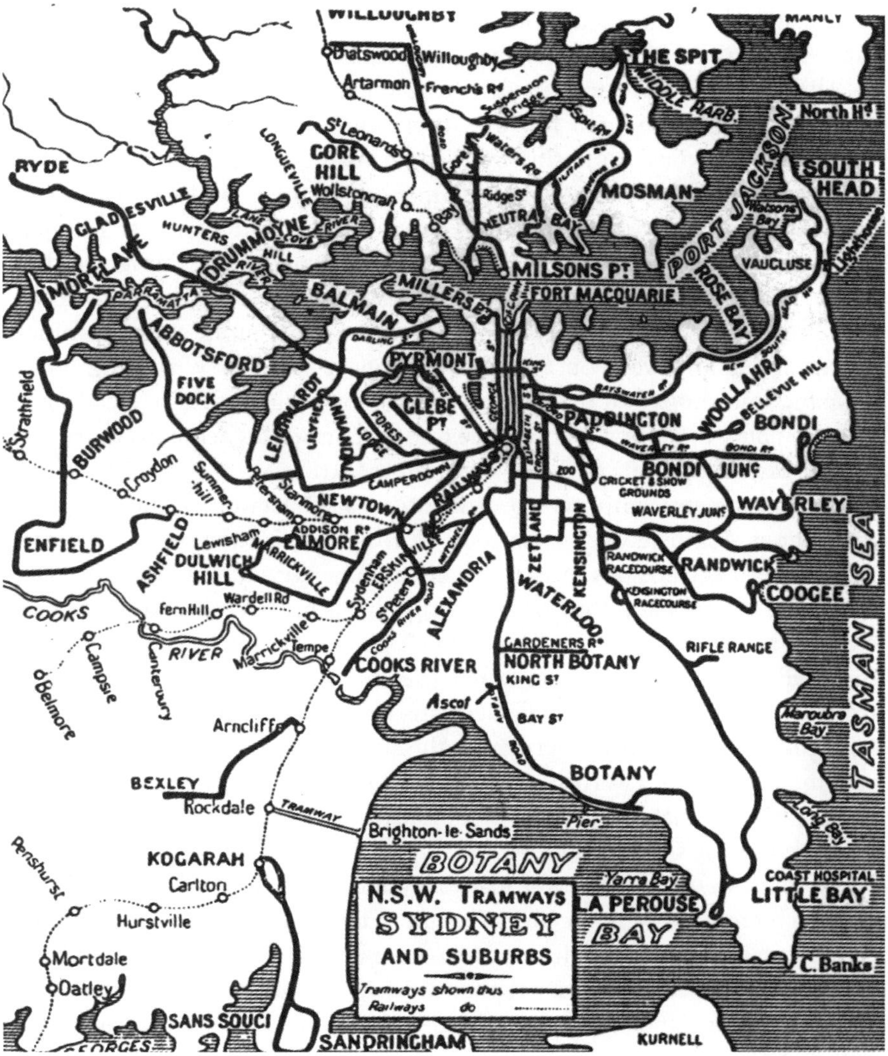

Map 2.1: Sydney's tram and rail system in 1914, claimed, along with Glasgow's, to be the finest 'on the planet'.
NSW Government Tourist Bureau, *Trips Around Sydney*, 1914

The Story of 25 Eventful Years in Pictures
Odhams Press, London, 1935

The Great War

When Britain declared war on Germany on 4 August 1914, Australia followed suit. Thousands volunteered to join the Australian Imperial Force (AIF), while ships of the recently formed Royal Australian Navy were placed under the control of the British Admiralty. On 18 August students from Sydney Grammar cheered troops as they marched past the school, while the schoolboy editor of their magazine, the *Sydneian*, contemplated the effect of the war on examination results 'if it lasts until November'.[13] On 25 April 1915 Australian troops stormed ashore at Gallipoli, where they established a beachhead despite resistance from the Turks. In the absence of any state or federal government attempts to direct economic activity to the war effort, the real estate industry continued to go about its business.

The NSW Conservatorium of Music opened its doors in May 1915 in Governor Macquarie's old horse stables near the Domain. In August the NSW State Trawling Authority unveiled an Australian first, air conditioning for its window display in a Sydney fish shop. By the end of the year almost 8000 soldiers had died. In February 1916, 5000 AIF troops near Liverpool called on other AIF troops to join them in a demand for shorter working hours; 15,000 troops mutinied. The Liverpool troops were bored, especially as they had to put up with a 'dry' canteen at the Casula camp. Some commandeered trains and went on a day-long rampage in Sydney, stealing liquor, breaking into shops and maltreating people. One solider died in a clash with military police at Central Station. The troops returned to their barracks the following day after threats of discharge from the AIF.

An internment camp, set up in late 1914 at Holdsworthy under the War Precautions Act, held over 5000 men of a variety of European backgrounds, including Australians of German descent and the crew of the *Emden*, crippled by the cruiser *Sydney* off the Cocos Keeling Islands in December 1914. The overcrowded conditions at the camp were much the same as the AIF camps that surrounded it, except that internees were locked behind barbed wire and prison life took its psychological toll. Not all Germans were interned but parents did warn their children not to speak German in the street or at school. This did not prevent the principal of Liverpool Primary School calling one child 'Kaiser Bill' in front of his classmates.[14] Readers of the *Bulletin* were regularly confronted with Norman Lindsay's cartoons of the evil hun. Posters exhorting citizens to invest in war loans were plastered over many a building and railway station.

War memorials were erected as a sign of loss and distress in suburbs and country towns. Among the first was the memorial in Balmain, unveiled on 23 April 1916, which recorded the names of 38 dead along with the words 'peace, honour, empire and liberty'. In Manly a 35-foot Corinthian column was unveiled on 14 October 1916, with a globe on top showing Australia, New Zealand and the word 'Anzac'. The granite base provided plenty of space to be filled later with the names of the Manly dead. Most other suburbs also erected memorials, although the majority were not unveiled until the early 1920s.[15]

As the war moved to France, Australian casualties mounted. A referendum on forcing conscription abroad, held on 28 October 1916, saw Victoria, Western Australia and South Australia with majorities in favour, while New South Wales, Queensland and South Australia returned majorities against. The largest single block of 'no' votes then, and at a second referendum in December 1917, came from Sydney, which had been the centre of a strike by railway and tramway workers that started on 2 August 1917 against the high cost of living caused by the prolonged war. The strike, involving almost one-fifth of the Sydney workforce, continued until mid-September. Strikebreakers, who included boys from some of the city's leading private schools, were rewarded with certificates by Premier Fuller's Nationalist government.[16]

Sydney Mail, 1916

When the Great War, the war to end all wars, ended on 11 November 1918, of the 330,000 Australian troops, 60,000 were dead. Influenza developed among returning soldiers at the Quarantine Station at North Head. By late January 1919 the worldwide 'Spanish flu' epidemic began to claim lives, with New South Wales the site of half of the 11,500 deaths in Australia. Many schools, libraries, churches, theatres, picture shows, hotels and racecourses were closed.

Garden cities and the failure of public housing

With the end of the Great War and expectations of an improved standard of living, the demand for better housing grew in Sydney, where well over half the population were tenants. But obtaining a deposit, let alone a mortgage, remained beyond the means of most people, and the building industry took some time to regain prewar levels of activity. Demands for better housing in Sydney were nothing new. The 1908–09 royal commission had recommended that the government should remodel 'slum' areas and acquire land for workers' housing in the suburbs. The preference for house and garden found expression in the Labor-sponsored Daceyville Garden Suburb in Randwick, a model development initiated in 1912. The impetus for a model suburb came from the Labor treasurers C. Carmichael and J.R. Dacey. Dacey told Parliament that the government wanted to 'create an Australian model in providing homes for the people in the shape of a garden city'.[17]

Architect and town planner John Sulman (1849–1934) from George A. Taylor *Town Planning in Australia* Sydney, 1914

The garden city concept, a way of giving new life and direction to suburban growth, emerged in Britain in the late 1890s. In 1903 its energetic exponent, Ebenezer Howard, formed the First Garden City Company to put these ideas into practice, and the planning and construction of a small city began at Letchworth, about 60 miles from London. Work on the best-known garden city development, the Hampstead Garden Suburb of London, followed in 1905.[18]

On the death of Dacey, J. D. Fitzgerald became chairman of the Housing Board and, with the architect John Sulman, produced a futuristic plan for Daceyville. Structured around an axial vista terminated by a School of Arts, the suburb was to be flanked by a 32-acre park.[19] The Daceyville settlement still exists, a series of charming brick and wood bungalows amid the worst excesses of the boom in flats of the 1960s. Unlike the post-Second World War products of the NSW Housing Commission, they have a pleasing diversity of style and outlook. Daceyville remains a working-class enclave, housing people in similar circumstances to those for whom the 1913 Labor government originally intended it.

Labor and non-Labor interest in Sydney's housing problem was further stimulated by the report produced in 1913 by Professor Irvine on workingmen's housing in Europe and the USA. Irvine's ideas were acceptable to the non-Labor politicians because he argued that public housing should pay its way, and not be mere charity.[20]

During the First World War another scheme of public housing, the Matraville Soldiers' Garden Village, was launched with voluntary labour and a gift of 72.5 acres of Crown land. The land covered 'the waste sandhills beyond Daceyville' and by 1921 *Building* magazine could report 'a beautiful

Dacey Garden Suburb
First Australian Town Planning Conference and Exhibition, Adelaide, 1917, Plate 61

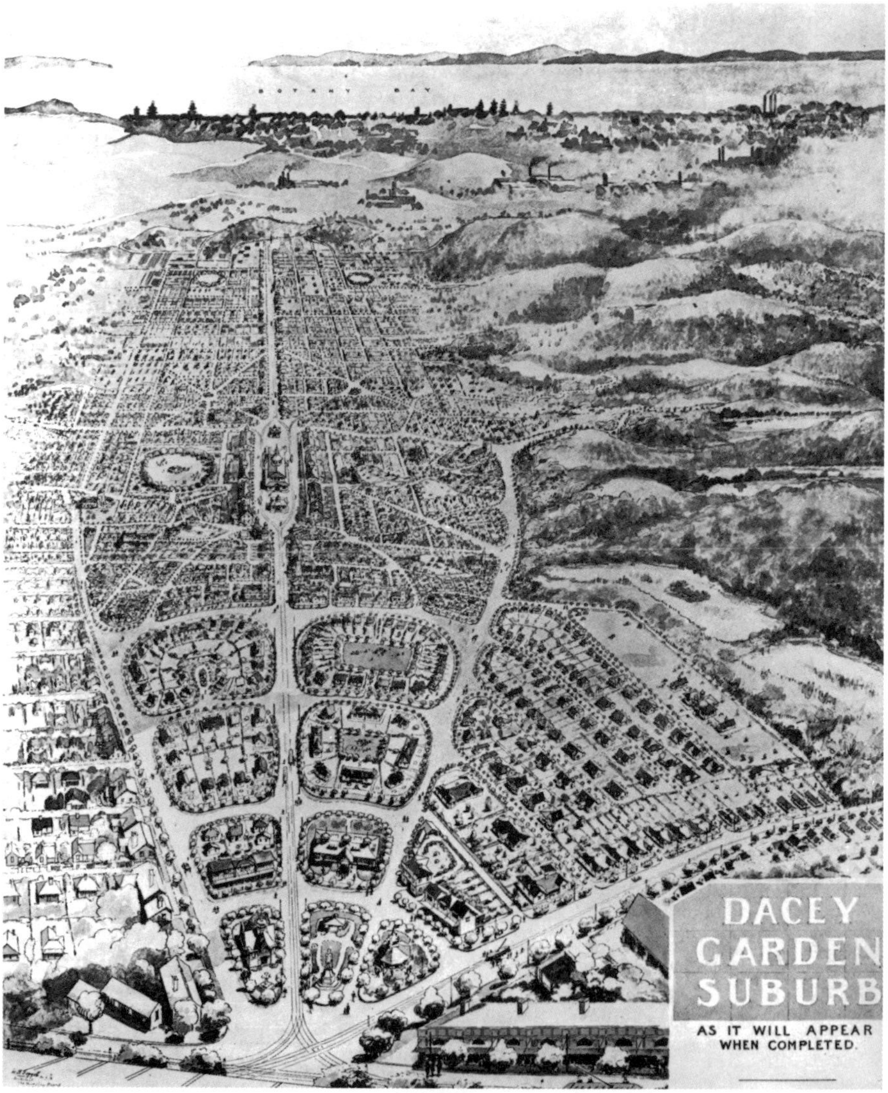

suburb with 67 cottages of varying designs'.[21] The all-rental village (which finally comprised 93 cottages) was eventually transferred to the State Housing Board. Apart from constructing Daceyville and administering the Matraville village, the Housing Board built houses at Bunnerong and Gladesville. Its only other major project was a group of houses at Stockton in Newcastle.[22]

Sydney's housing shortage soon drew the attention of Dr J.S. Purdy, appointed metropolitan medical officer for health in August 1913. Purdy served with the AIF throughout the First World War and returned to Sydney to find a 'house famine'. He explained that 'the undoubted overcrowding ... had resulted from the comparatively little building done during the war and the tendency to crowd people into tenements, flats and houses sublet to families'.[23] In Purdy's view:

> private enterprise in the building trade has not catered for that large section of the community which struggles along on a weekly rent, and suggests that there is a large field for national or community building to cater for the satisfactory housing of the people.[24]

Recommendations such as these produced little response. In April 1920 the *Shire and Municipal Record* reported that 'councils have displayed no eagerness to take advantage of the provisions of the new Local Government Act [1919] in relation to the erection of dwellings'. Lane Cove Council showed no interest, and Annandale Council said there was insufficient land in its municipality.

The private-enterprise housing boom of the 1920s had no parallel in the public sector. Even the Daceyville scheme did not progress as quickly as had been hoped, and with the death of Fitzgerald in July 1922 it lost its staunchest and most influential parliamentary supporter. The Housing Board, which since 1919 had lent funds for housing, was disbanded by the Fuller non-Labor government in 1924, allegedly on the grounds of faulty administrative arrangements and an inability to pay its way from rental income. In any case, the scheme was unpalatable to a Nationalist government that became increasingly laissez-faire in its outlook as its ex-Labor members died or, like former Premier Holman, faded into obscurity. The Housing Board had erected 818 houses (over half at Daceyville, which was never completed), and made advances on 516 others, the outstanding accounts being passed over to the State Savings Bank.[25]

The failure of the Housing Board proved a substantial blow to the cause of public housing in New South Wales and may well have been a factor in dissuading the Lang Labor governments of 1925–27 and 1930–32 from such ventures. These governments preferred to concentrate on encouraging home ownership. Despite his avowed enthusiasm for a better deal for working men, Lang himself had a real estate agency at Auburn: his experience led him to favour home ownership rather than public rental housing. The government-owned banks, the Commonwealth and the State, were expected to lend to reliable working-class purchasers. Many working-class households joined ballot and sale societies, rather like a lottery, with the lucky few winning a deposit; households contributed on a regular basis and those who won a deposit could then borrow the remainder of the funds from a bank or building society.[26]

By 1924 the only public housing under construction in Sydney was under

Way's Terrace, Pyrmont
Photograph by John Storey, 1978

the auspices of the city council. Labor lord mayor Gilpin emphasised that 'the shortage of houses was so great that it could not be met by private enterprise', while James Peddle (of the architectural firm Peddle and Thorpe) stressed that the council flats would be almost like a 'cottage home'. Gilpin also went on record as preferring 'commodious houses' and hoping the state government would legislate to enable the city council 'to go outside the City area, where the land was not so dear'.[27] The Dowling Street flats were opened in June 1925 and the Way's Terrace flats five months later. High on the tip of the Pyrmont peninsula, Way's Terrace has spectacular views over Darling Harbour and the central city area. Only one other block was built by the city council, the Alexandra group at Pyrmont Bridge Road, Camperdown. This block of 22 semi-detached cottages, designed by the council architect, opened in November 1927. All three blocks were rented to council employees and all three were in poor, Labor-controlled council wards.[28]

J.S. Purdy hailed the Sydney City Council's 'workmen's dwellings' proposals as 'a splendid lead to other authorities'.[29] None, however, took up the cause; nor were any more schemes forthcoming from the Labor council. The council was dismissed by the Bavin Nationalist government in 1927 and replaced by three commissioners before being placed under the control of the anti-Labor Civic Reform group, where it remained until 1948.

These few projects of the Housing Board and the Sydney City Council were the sum total of all public housing in Sydney in the 1920s. The prewar reformist movement petered out, non-Labor parties at state and municipal level lost interest, and the Lang Labor government of 1930–32 became entangled in Depression politics. Renewed interest in public housing had to await the Depression-stimulated protests of middle-class slum reformers in the mid-1930s, but even then the stress was as much on knocking down 'slums' as providing public housing. Not until the McKell Labor government launched the NSW Housing Commission in 1941 did support for public housing strengthen.

Metropolitan health and hygiene

Large-scale systems of food distribution are necessary to the survival of any big city. As the population grows and the suburbs spread, food has to be procured further and further from the city. With the completion in the 1880s and 1890s of much of Sydney's public transport system, the spreading suburbs forced market gardening and dairying to move to outer areas.

The main centre of metropolitan fruit, vegetable and fish distribution at this time was in the central city at the Belmore markets. Part of the site is now Belmore Park at Central Station. By the early 1900s conditions at the Belmore markets had become 'intolerable' and in the wave of city reform that produced the 1908–09 royal commission the markets were moved to a large site near the Darling Harbour railway goods yards west of George Street. A series of handsome brick buildings, together with banana-ripening towers and loading bays, appeared in the Haymarket between 1909 and 1914. These buildings were to perform their function for six decades, until the markets were moved 10 miles out to Flemington in 1975.[30]

In 1912 a royal commission into food supply and prices of meat, fish, fruit and vegetables recommended the creation of a single market authority and advocated concentrating 'slaughtering [of beef] for metropolitan consumption in one publicly managed institution'. The commission identified 48 abattoirs in the city and suburbs: the largest was at Glebe Island; Enfield, Mascot and Hornsby each had five; Granville, Liverpool and Prospect four. The Labor government created the Metropolitan Meat Industry Board in the same year, with responsibility for a new, much larger metropolitan abattoir at Homebush that would displace the Glebe facility. The meat authority went beyond mere regulation in establishing its own processing plant, which soon had a virtual monopoly of slaughtering in Sydney.[31]

Even after the rebuilding of the wharves, J.S. Purdy, as metropolitan health officer, had to exercise viligence throughout the city. The wharves and warehouses of Darling Harbour, with the Town Hall in the background.
NSW Government Printer, c. 1923

Recommendations for a single authority to control milk distribution in place of municipal supervision dated back at least to the royal commission into food supply. A similar proposal came in the NSW Board of Trade Report of 1923. In the following year J.S. Purdy argued that it would 'be possible by amalgamation of the four leading milk companies, whose headquarters are practically contiguous ... to eliminate a certain amount of competition, especially in distribution'.

The Milk Board, established in 1929, set up a metropolitan milk distribution district and a producing district, the 'milk zone'.[32] The quality of supervision increased rapidly. As Frank Clune observed in his book *Saga of Sydney* (1961), gone was 'the old-type dairyman who milked a few cows in a ramshackle shed in an outer suburb, and supplied his "round" of customers with milk in billycans from a horse-drawn cart'.[33]

The Milk Board's 1932 annual report identified 517 'dairies' in the metropolitan area. By 1940 the number had dropped to 289. Most of these 'dairies' were for distribution rather than production: in 1928 one Mosman dairy claimed to be the only one in its municipality to 'enjoy the privilege of ... keeping cows'. Efforts to improve the quality of the milk supply helped to eliminate the suburban dairy; but few proprietors suffered, for much of their property became prime residential land.[34]

Although the job of supervising the milk supply was taken from municipal authorities, they retained the power to enforce health standards in food establishments, and health officers could order the closure of unsuitable premises. In 1924 J.S. Purdy, who was city health officer as well as the metropolitan medical officer of health, supervised 21,321 premises (including houses, office buildings and factories), 241 restaurants, 217 tea-rooms, 950 milk vendors, 85 fruit shops, 65 fish shops and 101 butcher's shops in the City of Sydney.

One of his chief concerns was the 'rat-proofing of basements and kitchens'. Another outbreak of plague, introduced to Brisbane and Sydney in 1921 by rats carried on the ship *Wyreema*, resulted in 67 deaths. Although only 10 of these were in New South Wales, the outbreak served as a reminder of the vigilance needed to maintain the health of the city. In 1924, 11,351 premises were visited by the city council rat-catching staff and 8018 rats caught. In contrast , there were only 132 investigations of 'smoke nuisance' in 1924.[35]

The council regularly targeted restaurants. In 1920 Purdy ordered 32 restaurants to be closed because they were 'structurally' unsuitable. In 1921 there were 13 closures, 14 in 1922, six in 1923 and eight in 1924, while in 1922 and 1923, five fish and chip shops and one butcher's shop were shut down.[36] Like all big cities, Sydney had to deal with garbage disposal. As brick pits and quarries were in active use, it was hard to find repositories for garbage. Purdy observed in 1920 that:

> The garbage of Redfern is deposited on a racecourse near South Sydney Hospital, that of Paddington near the Hampton Oval, and that of Woollahra on Bellevue Hill, 'The Dress Circle of Sydney' according to some house and land agents ... The City of Sydney, North Sydney, Marrickville, Leichhardt and Balmain are alone in possessing incinerators ... no other method than incineration should be tolerated in a great centre like the Metropolis of Sydney otherwise it is impossible to combat the rat and fly nuisance ...[37]

The Sydney Municipal Council built its first incinerator on resumed land at Pyrmont in 1910. Plans for a new incinerator at Moore Park were abandoned in 1932 following protests by residents, and a site was chosen adjoining the old plant at Pyrmont. Designed by Walter Burley Griffin, it opened in 1937. Of his other municipal incinerators, for Leichhardt, Randwick, Ku-ring-gai, Glebe and Willoughby, only the last survived (to become a restaurant).[38]

Hospitals were operated by the churches, particularly the Catholic Church, and the state government. In 1918 one politician claimed that 'there is hardly a public hospital in the City of Sydney today that is not shockingly overcrowded'. Yet only two public hospitals were established in Sydney in the

1920s, the Rachel Forster Hospital for women at Redfern (1922) and the Canterbury Public Hospital (1928). The areas best served by hospitals in Sydney were those nearest the central city, where government and philanthropic bodies (including the churches) had created a conglomeration of medical facilities. Elsewhere, hospital building lagged far behind suburban development. The western suburbs were without a maternity hospital in the interwar years and, with the exception of Canterbury, no hospitals were built there until 1941, when the massive Concord Repatriation opened. The northern suburbs fared a little better, with Hornsby Hospital opening in 1932 and Ryde District Soldiers Memorial in 1934, while the Eastern Suburbs Hospital at Waverley received its first patients in 1935. The western and southern suburbs were also worse off for state government-funded baby health centres than their northern and eastern counterparts. These centres were first established in 1914 and by 1939 there were 57 in the metropolitan district.[39]

Public health facilities in Sydney in the interwar years were far from adequate: state and local governments were more interested in exercising regulatory powers than in funding hospitals and health centres. The Australia-wide influenza epidemic of 1919, the recurrence of plague in 1921, and a large outbreak of gastro-enteritis in 1929 (when 300 babies were admitted to the Royal Alexandra Hospital for Children) all served as reminders that the health services of Sydney could be improved.

Purdy realised that health problems could not be solved in isolation. In 1925–26 he served as president of the Town Planning Association of NSW, pointing out the 'crying need for some co-ordinating authority which will at least make a regional plan of the area and not allow the indefinite continuance of the present topsy growth of the metropolis'.[40] But too much of the onus rested with enthusiastic reformers such as Purdy; when he died in 1936 the Health Department lost interest in taking a metropolitan perspective.

Local government and town planning

Local government has been relatively weak in Australia, its characteristic feature being, in R.N. Spann's words, 'the attempt by higher authorities first to persuade and then to require local groups to accept financial and administrative responsibility for certain bread and butter tasks'. Unlike in Great Britain during these years, education, police, housing and transport were state rather than local government responsibilities.[41]

Politician and town planner John Daniel Fitzgerald (1862–1922). *Second Australian Town Planning Conference and Exhibiton,* Brisbane, 1918

The NSW Parliament passed a Local Government Act in 1906, establishing the major principles of the modern system. But the act soon exhibited a number of defects, and by 1910 both Labor and non-Labor parties and the Local Government and Shires Association agreed that amendment was necessary. Political differences about the franchise provisions of a new act prevented the repeal of the 1906 legislation for some years.

J.D. Fitzgerald became minister for Local Government in the Holman Nationalist ministry in November 1916. Fitzgerald and John Garlick, who later became the under-secretary of the Department of Local Government, had attended the inaugural meeting of the Town Planning Association in

1913. According to William McKell, minister for Local Government 1930–31, Fitzgerald and Garlick were jointly responsible for drafting the 1919 act.[42] Fitzgerald spoke persuasively to the Legislative Council—which usually emasculated any legislation that threatened the rights of private property—of the improvements the new act would bring:

> the control of new roads, subdivisions and building—and with that improvement the power to control the number of houses per acre that may be erected in a residential area ... the building provisions ... will enable us to have town plotting or planning on scientific lines ... if a council declares a district a residential district no one will be able to intrude into that district.

Mindful of the ultra-conservative nature of the Legislative Council, Fitzgerald pointed out to his colleagues the perils of industrial location in fine residential areas, citing the North Sydney Gas Company and the Burwood brickworks as examples. The latter, he said, when 'put right down in the centre of a beautiful district [would] destroy land values and the amenities of the residents of Burwood'. Those brickworks are admirable, 'as they give profitable employment to both capital and labour, but if we had a system of planning they would have been placed in a suitable locality'. The suitable locality, though Fitzgerald conveniently did not mention this, was invariably one of the working-class inner suburbs, such as St Peters, Botany or Mascot.

Fitzgerald used the examples of North Sydney and Burwood to argue 'for planning the whole of the great territory of Sydney so that we shall have our factory annexes, our residential zones, our shopping zones and our recreation zones'. The possibility of protecting the residential amenity of their middle-class suburbs appealed to the Legislative Councillors, and these provisions were passed.[43]

The Labor opposition objected to the amount of power the bill delegated to the minister for Local Government. The Member for Granville since 1913, J.T. Lang, who had twice served as mayor of Auburn, complained that 'the whole of the power is taken from the electors and aldermen and placed in the hands of the Minister ... In the first fifty clauses of the bill power is placed in the hands of the Minister no less than thirty-six times.'[44]

Local councils resented the degree of control retained by the state government. As the *Shire and Municipal Record* remarked in December 1919:

> the substance of power has been withheld from them [local governments] although they have been given the shadow. Under the new bill even the price they are to charge for emptying garbage tins is to be fixed from Sydney ... Once upon a time a council used to make its own by-laws. It now accepts all these made for it in Sydney and incapable of amendment unless the central administration consents ...

The *Record* did not oppose the expansion of powers available to local government, only the fact that the powers and their implementation were dictated by the state government:

> Suppose for example such places as Sutherland, Manly or Blue Mountains Shire decided to adopt some comprehensive scheme, borrowed from the English holiday resorts, of boosting their areas ... adopting somewhat the

tactics between enterprising subdividers of a big estate and the management of a White City [tennis courts in Sydney] ...

Instead councils were 'tied down' by 'strict legislative enactments'.

To counter such criticisms, the Department of Local Government quickly produced a series of bulletins to establish the usefulness of the act and the department. The first, released late in 1919, was *Town Planning*, written by Sulman with an introduction by Fitzgerald. It included sections on 'Planning a New Town', 'Canberra, an Example', 'Design of Daceyville' and, of greater relevance to local councils, 'Playgrounds, Parks and Gardens' and 'How to keep a Town Bright, Clean and Healthy'.

The power to declare 'residential districts' quickly became the most popular provision of the act. Randwick Council was one of the first to take advantage of the new provision: in June 1920 it prohibited 'noxious trades and advertising hoardings' from sections of its municipality.[45] In the following month the Municipality of Strathfield proclaimed a residential district where the erection of any building for the use of 'trades, industries, manufacturers, shops and places of public amusement' was prohibited. Sulman observed in his 1921 book *An Introduction to Town Planning in Australia* that 'some councils have already begun to make use of the act's clauses, especially in connection with the proclamation

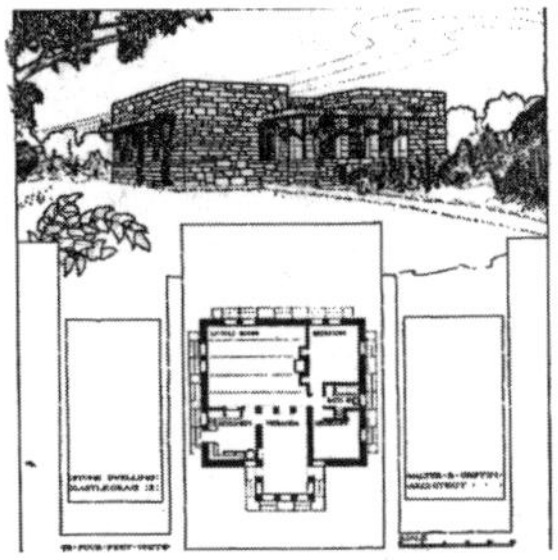

Castlecrag house

Castlecrag Homes, Greater Sydney Development Association Ltd, c. 1928

'Castlecrag architecture has struck a distinct bold note in Australia. In place of the high peaked tile roofs — a foolish perpetuation from countries where falls of snow demanded such precautions — the handsome landscape style, with its stone walls and flat roofs, has been introduced, in harmony with the great amphitheatre of stone and forest.'

Castlecrag Homes, Greater Sydney Development Association Ltd, c. 1928

of residential districts'. Willoughby Council applied the residential zoning powers in Walter Burley Griffin's 'picturesque waterside suburb' of Castlecrag, planned by the Greater Sydney Development Association (a group of land developers catering for a more sophisticated middle-class home market) as a 'first-class, safe-guarded, homogeneous, residential waterside suburb'. Castlecrag remains today as the Griffins planned it, 'safeguarded' against the encroachment of industry and working-class neighbours.[46]

The new powers granted to councils under the Local Government Act were welcomed in many quarters. The *Sydney Morning Herald* local government columnist wrote that the operation of the building regulations section was:

> not confined to the wealthier houses but is even more marked in what might be termed artisan suburbs and towns ... ten years ago ... the terrace house as a home for the working man was then almost the rule ... In those days the jerry builder employed his evil devices in secret. Now he has to expose all his tricks beforehand to ... council meetings ...[47]

This commentator underestimated the opportunities for corruption in local government decisions and the increasingly prominent role that real estate agents would play in local government affairs. Jack Lang was but one of many local estate agents who stood for municipal office, sometimes as a stepping-stone to higher positions, but often for the influence and access to information it provided on planning and zoning decisions.

Some sectional interests were less than happy with the new regulations. The president of the Master Builders Association told the *Sydney Morning Herald* in August 1925 that:

> Sydney cries aloud for homes and more homes for its workers of every class ... building, health and other regulations make it impossible to erect a home at a figure that had any possible relation to the average worker's resources ... It was [once] possible ... to put up a dozen brick terrace homes on the minimum frontage required for half a dozen detached cottages. Right away, the biggest individual item—the land—was cut in half ...[48]

The housing problem, he emphasised, was practically wholly a matter of finance. The Master Builders Association was especially unhappy with regulations that specified a minimum lot size of 2500 square feet for a dwelling. Yet it is important to note that only the builders—not, in general, the real estate developers—were complaining. The Greater Sydney Development Association was quite happy with its 'homogeneous' project, protected by council legislation, whereas agents who did want to sell land for other than residential purposes found willing councils in areas such as Alexandria and Marrickville, where industry and not residents were the major ratepayers.

Nor were the Master Builders averse to government intervention when it helped their cause. Indeed, their president called on the state government to amend the railway suburban scale and to introduce weekly tickets on the trams in order to keep down travelling costs and thus assist the workers to live in the less congested areas, where land was cheaper.[49]

Some complaints against the act and its enforcement were less self-interested than those of the Master Builders. A columnist writing in the monthly

Australia magazine under the name Real Estater, for example, pointed out that 'in their desire to prevent overcrowding some municipalities have gone to extremes and will not permit the resubdivision of allotments that are really too big for anybody except a man of means to build on'.[50]

The Local Government Act strengthened councils' powers to regulate building and subdivisions and gave them the power of resumption, often used by councils in the 1920s to aid in beautification schemes, to provide more parkland and to establish golf courses. Woollahra Council acquired 35 acres of Chinese market gardens to create Woollahra Park. From the point of view of the rate-payers of Woollahra, the removal of the Chinese gardeners improved the residential respectability of the area.

Not all beautification schemes involved resumption, though the opportunities provided by the 1919 act certainly gave councils more confidence to undertake such schemes. 'Rising suburban land values' and the proliferation of subdivisions in the 1920s considerably increased the opportunities for raising rate revenue.[51] Schemes included constructing surfing facilities at Bondi, beautifying the Spit Bridge surrounds after its completion in 1924, and constructing the promenade at Balmoral Beach, completed in 1930.

Among local authorities 'beautification' proved more popular than 'conservation' as that term is now understood. In 1925, for example, the Mosman Council took over from the Ashton Park Trust an area of 10 acres of natural bushland at the top entrance to Taronga Zoo Gardens to be 'beautified'—in other words, to be turned into recreational parkland. A year earlier, a correspondent writing in praise of a *Sydney Morning Herald* article on 'Sydney's lost beauty' claimed that municipal councils would not use their powers against 'land speculators' and 'other vandals'.[52] The correspondent did not observe that the vandals were sometimes the councils themselves.

For the Town Planning Association of NSW the 1919 act did not go far enough. They welcomed and indeed claimed credit for the town planning clauses, but pointed out that:

> as these are optional it will be necessary to have an act similar to that in Great Britain, making obligatory a definite regional survey of a town or area, with a scheme laying down the main arteries of traffic, the resumption of congested areas, definite housing schemes, adequate provision of parks and playgrounds, and other amenities ...[53]

Despite inadequacies, the 1919 act was a great improvement on previous legislation. It gave local councils the power to regulate the development of their own areas, but how they proceeded depended on the social class of the area, the views of ratepayers and the size of the rate revenue. The act did not provide state government funds: it was concerned with regulation only. Although it enabled councils to set down guidelines for suburban development, they proved inadequate, and local government remained ill-prepared to cope with the building and subdivision boom of the twenties.

Improving the metropolis was no easy task. The original impetus for most improvements came from the prewar reform movement. Fitzgerald saw the 1919 Local Government Act through Parliament but failed to establish public housing on a sound footing; Purdy's success rested on the use of regulatory powers. J.J.C. Bradfield was the only town planning advocate to get the government to fund new infrastructure. Indeed, the building of the Sydney Harbour Bridge and the underground railway were the most obvious signs of city improvement in the 1920s. Further reforms were stopped by the Depression and then another world war. By this time, the greatest impediment facing the planners of the Cumberland County Council was the haphazard suburban development of the 1920s, a decade in which enthusiasm for expanding the metropolis exceeded interest in improving it.

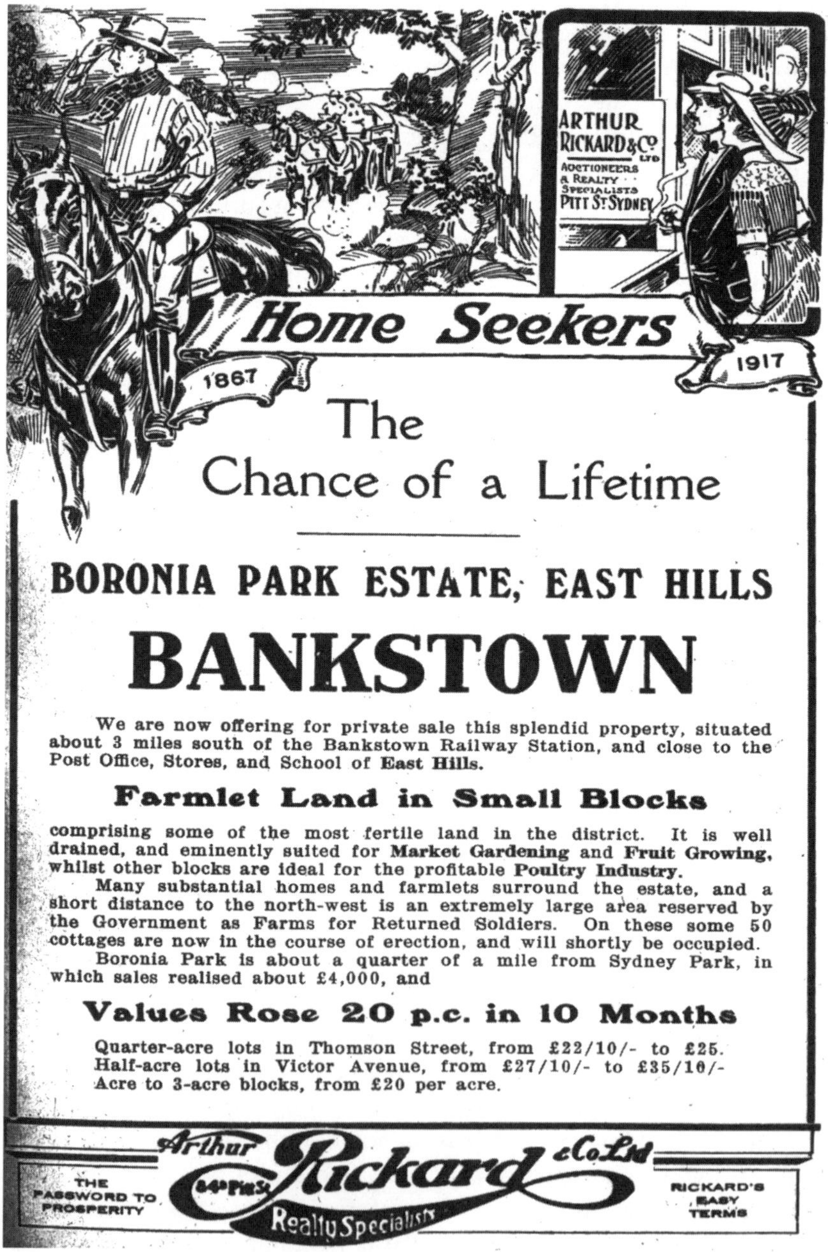

The pioneers of 1867 give way to the home seekers of 1917. Subdivisions continued throughout the war years.
Rickards Realty Review, November 1917

CHAPTER 3

Over once lovely hills

There is something brutal about the way cities expand into their hinterland. Anyone who has seen native forest flattened for housing blocks or even an old orchard carved up knows that the coming of new houses is often tinged with regret for the former landscape. In inner Sydney, by 1900, signs of the 'very thick wood' that confronted Arthur Phillip's landing party were hard to find, except around those harbour foreshore areas that had been reserved for military or naval purposes. But on the north shore, especially around Mosman, a great deal of bushland survived, with minimal foreshore development other than boatsheds and ferry landings.[1] This landscape had captured the attention of the Heidelberg School of artists, including Tom Roberts and Arthur Streeton, since the days of their artists' camp at Little Sirius Cove in the 1890s. Streeton and Roberts depicted the extraordinary mix of dwellings, wharves, industry and houses to be found around the harbour. They juxtaposed harbour waters and bushy headlands with the city beyond. By the 1920s Streeton's paintings reflected the spread of the red tile roofs of bungalows over what one commentator called 'once lovely hills'. Streeton also captured, in sympathetic pastel colourings, the coming of blocks of flats to the harbour foreshores.

Terrace balcony filled in with roofing iron, Surry Hills, c. 1930
Sydney City Council Archives.

In the central city and the inner suburbs the landscape had been transformed by successive waves of building. Wooden and stone dwellings, some substantial and some ramshackle, had given way to single- and double-storey terraces. Some were well built, many shoddily built. Most had their own walls, but houses were sometimes erected between existing dwellings, appropriating their walls, merely adding front and back walls and a roof.[2] During what J.S. Purdy had dubbed the 'house famine' in 1920, the balonies of thousands of larger terrace houses had been filled in to accommodate the many lodgers and family groups that these dwellings now catered for. Parts of Sydney were extraordinarily overcrowded.

More dwellings were built in Sydney in the 1920s than in any previous decade of the city's history, a record unsurpassed until the 1950s. The 1920s consequently played an important role in determining the nature and direction of Sydney's suburban growth. The building boom of 1912–14, when an average of 8740 buildings were completed annually, had ended with the outbreak of war; in the years 1915–18 the annual figure fell to 5220. Yet in spite of wartime losses, this was a decade of high population growth, as Table 3.1 shows. With the increase in occupied dwellings failing to keep pace with population growth, the number of persons per dwelling rose in the decade 1911–21.

The building boom of the 1920s took some time to gain momentum because wartime shortages inflated the cost of building materials (see Table 3.2).

Table 3.1: Population and dwellings, Sydney 1911–96

Year	Sydney's population (000s)	Occupied dwellings (000s)	Average number of persons per dwelling
1911	667	130	5.2
1921	994	198	5.4
1933	1224	388	4.3
1947	1484	379	3.9
1954	1863	517	3.6
1966	2447	731	3.3
1976	2767	977	2.8
1986	3364	1140	2.9

Source: Commonwealth censuses. The metropolitan definition used here differs from that used for the Sydney/Melbourne comparison in Table 1.2

Table 3.2: Index of new building projects in Sydney 1919–32

Year	Index
1919	68
1920	83
1921	72
1922	71
1923	99
1924	104
1925	96
1926	103
1927	106
1928	108
1929	100
1930	60
1931	16
1932	6

Base Year 1929 = 100
Source: C B Schedvin, Building and the Trade Cycle in Australian Cities Between the Wars, Paper presented to the 35th ANZAAS conference, Brisbane, 1961, 4.

Nevertheless, journalists conscious of the boom atmosphere in the USA were quick to identify similar signs in Sydney. On 3 January 1922 the *Sydney Morning Herald* proudly announced to its readers that the population of 'Greater Sydney' had reached 'More Than a Million', the first Australian city to do so. 'However much critics may deplore the phenomenal metropolitan aggregation of the population ...' said the *Herald*, 'most of the city dwellers will glow with a pardonable pride on seeing the giant strides that Sydney and its immediate suburbs are making.' Despite the protestations of rural dwellers, Sydneysiders were proud to be living in Australia's largest city. The new housing took many forms: older residential suburbs were filled in, new ones were established, a large subdivision investment market developed, and retail and office building expanded in the city centre. Government departments and public utilities were under pressure to keep pace with these developments.

Buying a house and garden

Suburban expansion—its pace and excitement—was made much of in the Sydney press of the twenties. Most newspapers ran a weekly real estate and building column and offered advice to prospective house and land purchasers. Typical of the times is the following item from the *Evening News* of 25 August 1920:

> Now that the weather is warming up a resumption of sub-division sales is imminent. Agents are already arranging for what many believe will be a record season ... The demand is here already. Whatever may be said of the improvidence of the Australian, he nevertheless has sufficient commonsense to acquire his own home or at least strive hard for it.

The ideal of owning one's house and garden was not new: what was new was the number of vested interests that promoted it. In 1918 a conference of the Master Builders Association was told that home ownership would enable 'the workers' to obtain 'a stake in the country'. The same speaker told the conference 'We cannot wonder at some of the bitterness that exists among the workers when they are so poorly housed.'[3] After the sectional bitterness of the conscription campaigns and the sharpening of class antagonisms during wartime strikes, the middle-class rhetoric of having a 'stake in the country' was harnessed to help the real estate and building industry. 'Real Estater', writing in *Australia* magazine in July 1924, asked: 'What is it that drives many along the road of home buying? Well, mostly, it is the high cost of rents'. Then there were those indefatigable advertisers, the real estate agents.

Most people could be convinced that the whole community benefited from increasing home ownership, especially when those homes were in the healthy surroundings of the expanding suburbs. No longer would the working class have to live in crowded inner-city terraces. Builders, real estate agents, and prospective home buyers were all in favour of the house and garden, but there was at least one group who felt left out in the rush—the architects. In September 1921 the professor of architecture at the University of Sydney, Leslie Wilkinson, complained in *Building* magazine:

> It is estimated that fully 70 per cent of the houses erected today are produced without reference to the profession. Until this state of affairs is altered and until the public appreciate the difference between the beautiful, the good and the horrid, admirable work will continue to be a rarity.

In the same year the state government established a Board of Architects, of which Wilkinson was a member, to regulate the profession. By January 1927 there were 671 registered architects with the 'requisite qualifications'.[4]

Australian Home Builder, March 1924

Plebeian builders and owner-builders were the bane of the architects. Most house designs in the twenties were the work of such people, often copied from plans in magazines such as George and Florence Taylor's *Building* (founded 1907), the *Australian Home Builder* (1920s), *Home* (1920–1942) and Florence Taylor's *Commonwealth Home* (1925–30).

Commonwealth Home, February 1925

The most common house design of the twenties, the 'Californian bungalow', can still be seen in such suburbs as Lane Cove, Auburn, Ashfield, Rockdale and Randwick, but in all of these its dominance is now challenged by the home unit. Not everyone was happy with the spread of the 'bungalow', as *Australia* magazine commented in October 1924: 'One red tiled roof house is much like another red tiled roof house. For this the builders must not be blamed. Buyers—especially women buyers—are very conservative and a speculative builder runs a deal of risk if he departs from the "usual" ...'

'Red tiled roofs' reappeared in the writings of another critic, for whom salvation lay in such planned architectural developments as Walter Burley Griffin's Castlecrag:

> One looks across to a desolate monotony of red roofs where modern Mosman has swept devastatingly over once lovely hills. Close at hand Willoughby spreads, in the unrelieved ugliness of closely packed houses, towards Castlecrag. One gets an impression of Mr Burley Griffin as a successful modern Canute holding back the advancing tide of ugliness.[5]

Griffin's flat-roofed houses were constructed of stone: no red tiled roofs here, and as much bushland as possible was preserved.

The aesthetic ambitions of most house and land buyers were easily satisfied. They were more concerned with the prosaic side of finding and buying what they could afford, the availability of public transport, water, gas, electricity and, for the wealthier or more fastidious, piped sewer. People attempted to choose an area and a dwelling within their means, but as 'Real Estater' remarked in 1924, 'perhaps the greatest factor in the high cost of homes is the desire of everybody to live in a cottage that costs more than he (or she) can afford'.[6]

The cost of both new dwellings and land usually reflected the social standing of an area, but other factors such as the availability or shortage of new blocks and the commercial strategies employed by large landholders also affected the price. The average cost of new dwellings in Woollahra in 1919, when average annual male earnings were £200, was £1200, compared to £1100 in Mosman and Vaucluse, £700 in Randwick and £640 in Willoughby.[7] By 1928, the decade's record year for building, average annual male earnings were £267 and dwellings in a middle-class suburb such as Mosman cost an average £1692, in working-class Bankstown £585 and in mixed-class Canterbury £869.[8] The range in the unimproved capital value of a home site was even greater, from Woollahra at £1142 to outer-suburban Holroyd at £111.[9]

Building societies, trading banks and government authorities provided home finance for those who could find a substantial deposit. The state government's most significant contribution in the interwar years was through the State Savings Bank, which made an average of 2600 housing loans for new and existing dwellings annually in the 1920s, with a peak in 1928 of 3018. The average loan was about £400, at interest rates that varied between 6.25 and 7.00 per cent, to be repaid over 30 years for brick dwellings and 20 years for wooden dwellings. The bank would not advance more than three-quarters of the value of the property.

These loans were of little use to low-income earners. In 1928–29, according to *Employers Review*, the official organ of the Employers Federation of NSW, fully employed male factory workers earned an average of £200 per year. Given unemployment levels of up to 11 per cent, many households had much less income than this. One of the cheapest suburbs to build in was outer-suburban Bankstown, but even there homesites could rarely be had for less than £100, while the average cost of building a home in 1929 was £585.[10] Most working-class families were unable to afford a deposit on the land, let alone pay the State Savings Bank interest. Between 1921 and 1933 advances were made by the State Savings Bank for approximately 28,000 new houses in New South Wales, about 17 per cent of the new dwellings in the state over the period.

The federal government provided housing for ex-servicemen through the Commonwealth War Service Homes Commission, founded in 1918. By June 1929 loans had been made for 11,170 houses in New South Wales; almost half were for existing dwellings. Despite such policies, there appears to have been no marked increase in home ownership in the 1920s. At the 1921 census, 41 per cent of Sydney's dwellings were owned or being purchased; 12 years later, at the 1933 census, 40.5 per cent came within this category. This figure would certainly have been higher had the Depression not intervened, but the 1920s fell far short of the rapid increases in owner occupation of the 1950s. Owner occupation varied considerably within Sydney. At the 1921 census the highest

FACING PAGE
Commonwealth Home October 1925

"OWN YOUR OWN HOME" NUMBER

3D

Please note address:
20 LOFTUS ST., SYDNEY.
Or Box 2663 G.P.O., Sydney

Registered at the G.P.O., Sydney, for transmission by post as a newspaper.

3D

THE COMMONWEALTH HOME

OWN A BIT OF THE LAND YOU LOVE

Incorporating "THE PROPERTY OWNER" (Weekly)

Incorporating "THE SOLDIER" (Monthly).

No. 921—Vol. XXXII | SYDNEY, FRIDAY, OCTOBER 9, 1925 | PRICE THREEPENCE

"THE HOME"—The Chief Call in the Federal Fight

THERE'S NO PLACE LIKE HOME

IF YOU BUT OWN IT

£20,000,000 FOR ENCOURAGING AUSTRALIAN HOME BUILDING

The most important plank of the Prime Minister's platform is "£20,000,000 for Homes for Workers". It follows the creed this journal originated, that the best way to stem any "tide of Communism" is to encourage every Australian to "own a bit of the land he loves and own a home on it". If the Labour Party is opposed to Communism it should adopt the same creed.

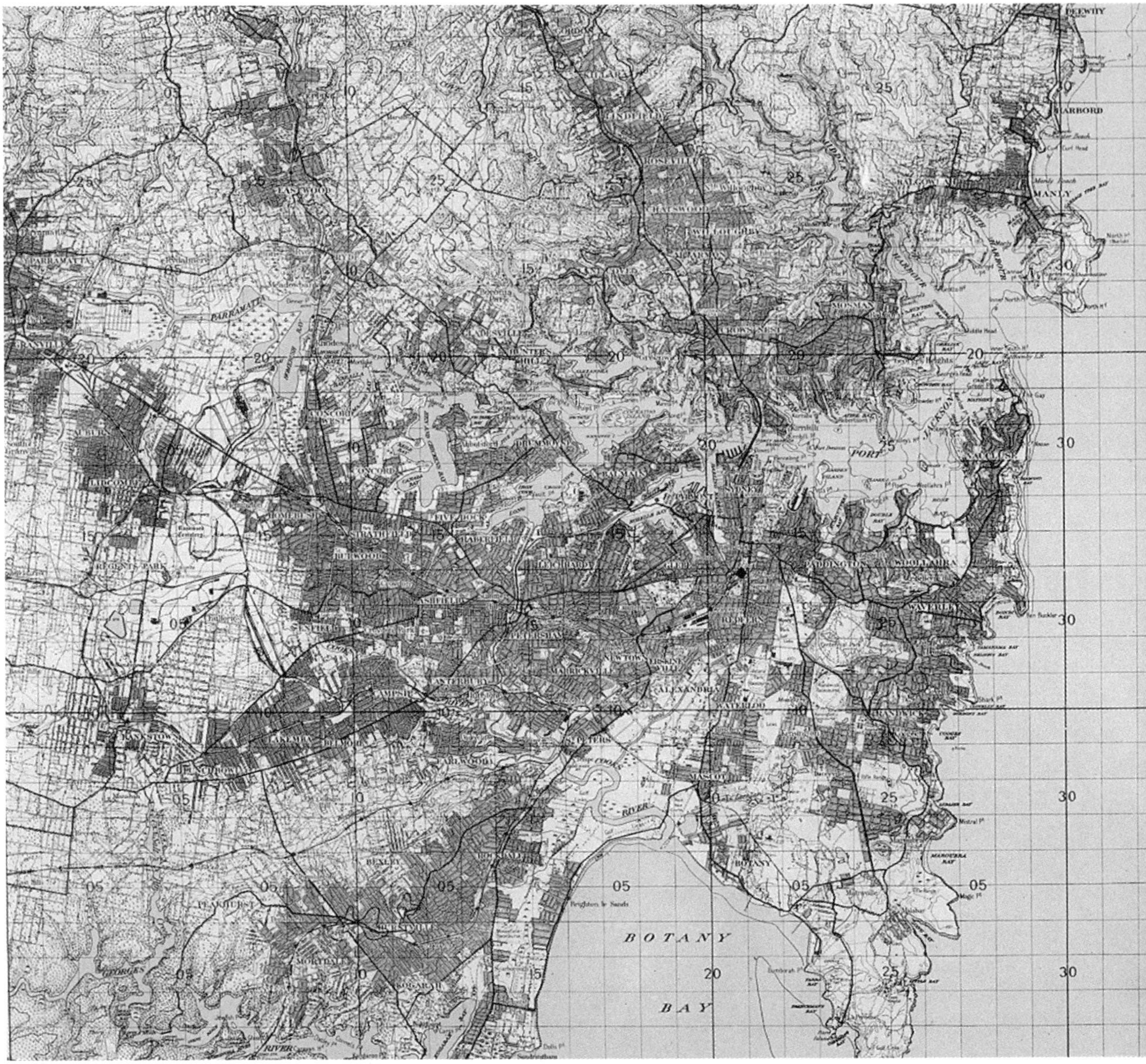

Map 3.1: Sydney and suburbs in 1933.
This army survey map, compiled in 1933, shows that urban development stayed close to the railway lines and the tramways, reaching out along the north shore line, the Ryde–Carlingford line, to the west beyond Granville, to the south-west and the south.

levels were to be found in outer-suburban working-class areas such as Canterbury (71 per cent owner-occupied) and middle-class areas such as Ku-ring-gai (73 per cent). At the 1933 census the respective figures for these suburbs were 60 and 68 per cent. One possible explanation for the greater decline of owner occupation in Canterbury is that more mortgages may have been foreclosed in less well-off areas.

Villages to suburbs

In the 1920s most new householders aspired to a house and garden beyond the inner terrace suburbs, which were substantially built up by the turn of the century. At the 1911 census over one-third of Sydney's population continued to live in the City of Sydney and the adjoining municipalities of Alexandria, Darlington, Erskineville, Glebe, Newtown, Paddington, Redfern and Waterloo, areas where terrace housing predominated. By 1921 only 23 per cent lived in these areas and by 1933 the inner suburbs' share of Sydney's population had fallen to 16 per cent. Most population growth in the twenties occurred between three and 13 miles of the city centre. With the exception of Waterloo, all of the inner municipalities lost population between 1921 and 1929. Other suburbs within three miles of the city centre to lose population were Annandale (-3 per cent), Balmain (-9 per cent), St Peters (-1 per cent) and North Sydney (-2 per cent). The largest absolute fall in population was in the City of Sydney, from 103,160 in 1921 to 90,879 in 1929.

The public transport system made possible suburban growth beyond a three mile radius of the city. Residents within six miles of the GPO had the advantage of a close network of tram services for the relatively short journeys to the city, and some suburbs within this radius were also served by train. At a time when the city centre provided well over half of Sydney's total employment and the biggest concentration of shopping and entertainment facilities, access to public transport was an important consideration in choosing a house. But travelling time meant few people were prepared to live more than 13 miles from the city centre, despite tempting real estate advertisements and the existence of railway stations at regular intervals further out.

Almost 40 per cent of Sydney's population growth between 1921 and 1929 took place in the western and south-western suburbs, slightly less than 25 per cent in the eastern suburbs, around 17 per cent in the southern suburbs and the remaining 19 per cent north of the harbour and the Parramatta River.

As a result, the shape of Sydney changed markedly. In 1920 settlement still clung close to the rail and tram networks. Within six to 13 miles of the city most urban settlements still had the appearance of villages. The local shops and most houses were within easy walking distance of a railway station, ferry wharf or tram stop. Between villages were isolated dwellings, some the residences of market gardeners, some built in the hope of greater privacy, most built to escape the higher land prices of the village centres. In an age when car ownership was largely restricted to the middle class, these households had to rely on horse and cart or, increasingly, the private bus for transport. By the end of the decade these houses were becoming less and less isolated, market gardeners were tempted to sell up and move to the outskirts of the city, and the once separate villages were joining in an octopus-like suburban conurbation.

Western suburbs: paspalum and poultry farms

The housing boom in the western suburbs created two distinct bands, one following the rail stations from Strathfield to Granville, the other along the stations from Canterbury to Bankstown. Canterbury and Bankstown saw the largest proportional increases in population in the 1920s. These two large municipalities shared one-fifth of Sydney's population increase during the decade, and the eight municipalities in the Drummoyne-Strathfield-Granville grouping accounted for another one-fifth.

On 5 January 1926, under the heading ROSY PROSPECT FOR SUBURBAN BUILDERS, the *Daily Guardian* noted that 'the Canterbury district again heads the list for the building record'. And within Canterbury the locality that showed the most 'phenomenal progress' in the 1920s was Earlwood. A typical advertisement of this period was for 'The Pines Estate':

> The Estate is on an outstanding plateau embracing most extensive panoramic views, 2 minutes from the motor 'bus route, 8 minutes walk from the tram terminus. It is close to the shopping centre and schools and adjacent to the proposed route of the Tempe-East Hills Railway ... Gas, water and electric light are available on the Estate.[11]

As with the northern suburbs, the advertisement relied partly on a railway line-to-be: this one was actually built, and opened four years later, in 1931. Sewerage didn't rate a mention, for there was none.

The lack of sewerage in Canterbury–Bankstown was not for want of lobbying. The state member for St George pointed out in December 1920 that the Campsie, Belmore and Bankstown sewerage extension 'is a very important work, because something like 50,000 people are located in the suburb named, and are absolutely without sewerage connections'.[12] A slight improvement did occur in Canterbury during the decade, from 13 per cent sewered in 1920 to 29 per cent in 1929. Bankstown fared less well: in 1929 there were still no properties connected to the sewer. The older established suburbs in the Drummoyne to Strathfield band were better sewered but Lidcombe, Auburn and Granville were still virtually without sewerage in 1929, and only partially by 1939.[13] Such problems were not, however, even hinted at in Auburn Council's 1928 publication *From Bushland to Throbbing City*:

> Fifty years since Mills and Pile made the first land subdivision! Today, a throbbing, teeming suburb! Half a century of unbroken progress! ... electric-lighted streets and the thousands of neat, comfortable homes stretching ... in all directions ... Travel along Parramatta Road ... watch the smoke rise from towering factory chimneys ... see the new factories rearing businesslike heads to the sky ... you will imagine you have discovered some rising Manchester or Birmingham in this new land ...

Hospitals and schools were other publicly funded services that took time to

catch up with population increases in the new suburbs, which had a high proportion of families with young children. Canterbury had to wait until 1918 for its first high school, and even then it was temporarily housed in primary school buildings. After many deputations the school received its own buildings in 1925. By 1927 it accommodated 581 pupils and extensions were opened in September 1933.[14] Canterbury's first public hospital, a long, one-storey building at Campsie, opened in 1928; Bankstown had to wait another three decades until 1957.

The market gardens of Abbotsford can be seen in the middle ground, with farm houses built between the 1890s and the 1920s. The spread of suburbia can be seen on the ridge beyond.
Mitchell Library, small picture collection, c. 1933

The suburban development of Bankstown dates from 1909 when the Belmore to Bankstown line opened and subdivisions first started in earnest. A fillip for the area came in 1923 with the opening of the Chullora railway workshop and the provision by the railways of electricity for domestic purposes. In 1924 a signal workshop and in 1926 an electrical shop were added to the Chullora works. The line was electrified in 1926, was extended from Regent's Park to Villawood in 1924 and four years later from Bankstown to Regent's Park. Apart from the Chullora workshops, the main industries in Bankstown in the twenties were those associated with urban development: bricks and tiles, ice, plaster and motor coach works. Yet Bankstown could double its population and still retain vast acreages of 'paspalum and poultry farms'.[15]

EASTERN SUBURBS: APARTMENTS BY THE SEA

Unlike Canterbury–Bankstown, the eastern suburbs (the municipalities of Randwick, Waverley, Woollahra and Vaucluse) were generally well built up by 1920. Moving to a new home in the eastern suburbs was a very different experience from trying to settle in the west. Many new householders in the east moved into existing dwellings while most fresh recruits to Canterbury–Bankstown, and to other newly developing suburbs to the south and north, were either building their own or becoming tenants in newly constructed bungalows. In the interwar years landlords still found it worthwhile to build detached houses as well as flats for rent: half a century later, high interest rates and the demand for accommodation near the city or close to public transport would mean that the overwhelming majority of new rental dwellings were flats.

A growing number of flats accounted for some of the population increase in the eastern municipalities of Waverley and Woollahra as 'historic estates', according to the 1923 *Eastern Suburbs Guide*, were 'cut up and resold as building allotments'. Apart from some lavish homes in Vaucluse and Bellevue Hill,[16] most bungalows built in the eastern suburbs were in Randwick, including the public housing projects of Daceyville and the Matraville Soldiers' Settlement.

A major bar to Randwick's suburban progress, and one that greatly irked the council, was the Randwick Rifle Range, which separated the northern and southern halves of the municipality and could 'be subdivided into at least 3000 blocks'. The council tried to persuade the federal and state governments to let them do just this, but to no avail; the southern half of the municipality remained largely unsettled throughout the twenties.[17] Nevertheless, in 1923 the *Eastern Suburbs District Guide* could proudly boast that Randwick had 'the largest population, largest park area and largest revenue of any municipality outside the city of Sydney'. Notwithstanding the rapid increases in Canterbury's population, Randwick could still make these claims in 1929, with a lead of 3000 over its nearest rival in the population stakes.

One advantage of the eastern suburbs, in addition to their proximity to both the city and the beaches, was that they were relatively well sewered. The residents were fortunate to have been the beneficiaries of the late nineteenth-century movement for sanitary reform.[18] Waverley and Woollahra were connected to the Bondi Ocean Outfall Sewer as early as 1889 and by 1920 over 90 per cent of properties in both suburbs were sewered. In Vaucluse less than 30 per cent were sewered, but by 1929 the figure had risen to 94 per cent. Sewerage provision lagged slightly in Randwick in the twenties, with its greater population increase and greater size, but 98 per cent of properties were sewered by 1939. The 'dunny man', a common sight in many suburbs, disappeared from the east.

Southern suburbs: bayside resorts and red-roofed 'villas'

In the interwar years the southern suburbs were referred to as the suburbs on the Illawarra line. During the twenties most houses in this area were within a mile or so of the stations on the southern railway line, except for a narrow strip along the shores of Botany Bay served by trams and buses. Real estate agents embraced

Como in 1908. While actively marketed by real estate agents before and after the Great War, suburban subdivisions did not cover Como's hills until the 1920s.
Samuel Wood postcard series, 1908

the railway electrification of March 1926 because it would 'enhance values'.[19] In 1926, 4,363,313 tickets were sold at Rockdale, 600,000 more than at any other suburban railway station. Between 1921 and 1929 Rockdale's population increased more in absolute terms than that of any other southern suburb.[20]

One of Rockdale's attractions was its bayside resort of Brighton-le-Sands, launched in 1886 with the opening of the New Brighton Hotel, with its ballroom, skating rink and private seabaths. The baths were closed in the twenties and replaced by a municipal complex in 1928.[21] Opened up for residential development before the First World War, Rockdale's take-off really dates from the twenties. In 1925 Sir Arthur Rickard's real estate firm advertised residential allotments on the Hoon Estate, 'within a few minutes of Brighton-le-Sands, on the [steam] tramway route from Rockdale, and served with direct de-luxe motor bus service to Sydney'.[22]

The St George area obtained its first permanent gas supply from the Australian Gas Light Company in 1887–88, and privately generated electricity, for lighting purposes only, in the early 1900s. In 1922–23 the St George municipalities became the first in Sydney to utilise a provision of the 1919 Local Government Act to amalgamate as a 'county council' for the purpose of providing electricity to their area.[23]

Sewerage connections, provided by the state government's Metropolitan Water, Sewerage and Drainage Board, lay outside the control of local authorities, and were the cause of many complaints. In 1920, 62 per cent of properties in Rockdale, 46 per cent in Bexley, 6 per cent in Hurstville, 22 per cent in Kogarah and none in Sutherland were sewered. Four years later a local parliamentarian complained bitterly because no action was being taken to increase the coverage.[24] Sutherland remained without sewerage until well after the Second World War.

More disconcerting for residents of Sutherland was the absence of piped water.[25] Sutherland's population had grown to 10,000 by 1928, yet only 123 houses had 'town water'. The area had to wait for the much-interrupted construction of the Woronora Dam (1927–30, 1941), storage reservoir and pipelines to replace household tanks with a regular water supply.[26] With their backyard toilets and tank stands, houses in many of Sydney's far-flung suburbs had more in common with those of country towns than with city dwellings.

One advantage that Sutherland had over its neighbours on the northern side of the George's River was a vast area of parkland. The railway line from Sydney to Sutherland was constructed in 1884–85 and a year later a station was opened at the Royal National Park, which had been dedicated in 1879. In contrast, the councils in Bexley and Kogarah, along with Bankstown, Dundas, Granville, Mascot and Liverpool, were severely criticised in 1925 by J.S. Purdy for having reserved less than 10 per cent of their area for parks and recreation. Purdy argued that the only way these areas could be saved 'from falling into the condition of the older portions adjoining the city' was by 'purchasing land on the periphery as playing areas in advance of population'.

Sutherland Shire's main claim to fame, the ocean beach resort at Cronulla, boomed after the completion of the steam tramway from Sutherland railway station in 1911. The area received another transport fillip in 1929 with the opening of the George's River road bridge, which replaced two steam ferries.[27] In 1939 the steam tram was replaced by an electrified railway line from Sutherland to Cronulla. Teenagers and families flocked to the beach and to Cronulla's other attractions, including cinemas.

Northern suburbs: North Sydney to leafy Warrawee

The northern suburbs caught the popular imagination in the twenties during the construction of the Sydney Harbour Bridge, which began in 1925. J.J.C. Bradfield, the chief engineer of the project, predicted that the north shore would eventually carry a population of one million.[28] The bridge gave a great boost to real estate agents. On May Day 1925 the *Labor Daily* carried an advertisement for the 'Rising Model Harbour Suburb' of Northbridge, 'fast being built upon'. The agents promised that the 'Sydney Harbour Bridge will bring Northbridge within ten minutes run from the City by car, and a little longer by rail'. To inspect the land, however, one had to 'take boat to Milson's Point, then Northbridge tram to terminus'.

Northbridge was part of the municipality of Willoughby, in which more new houses were erected in 1922 than in any other municipality except Canterbury and Randwick. With real municipal one-up-manship Willoughby council's annual report for 1923 asserted that Canterbury was:

> recognized as an industrial suburb in which a more modest class of dwelling is erected, while Randwick has the great added advantage of having fine surf beaches at its front door. As an ideal residential suburb, however, neither of the suburbs compares with Willoughby, which is destined to become the most important in the Metropolitan Area.[29]

But the prediction did not come true. By 1929 Randwick (75,899) and Canterbury (72,340) were still more populous than the municipality of Willoughby, whose population reached 40,176 in 1929. Randwick accounted for 11.5 per cent of Sydney's population increase during 1921–29, Canterbury 16 per cent, and Willoughby 5.5 per cent. As in other developing areas in the twenties, Willoughby's citizens were concerned about lack of sewerage. In 1922, 60 per cent of the municipality was still without sewerage.[30] In July 1924 a local parliamentarian alleged a 'serious menace to health' in large areas of Hunters Hill, Ryde and Chatswood (in the Willoughby municipality) 'where the pan system of sanitation is in vogue'. The secretary for Public Works, R.T. Ball, replied that the problem would be solved by the extension of the northern suburbs ocean outfall sewer.[31] Sewerage connections increased with the opening of the ocean outfall at North Head in 1930. By 1939, 97 per cent of Willoughby, 91 per cent of Lane Cove, 67 per cent of hilly Ku-ring-gai and 61 per cent of Ryde properties were sewered.

The uneven pattern of development was evident in the northern suburbs. In older municipalities such as Mosman, where the population was not increasing rapidly, a process of filling in the remaining housing sites continued, mostly in the less accessible locations, for example around Middle Harbour. The municipalities of Manly and North Sydney were in a similar position, well built-up by the twenties and with population growth slowing. Manly's early growth had been promoted by the ferry service to Circular Quay established in 1854, which made it possible to live in Manly and work in the city. The ferry terminal became the transfer point of the tram (and later bus) routes north to Narrabeen, but Manly remained a satellite village until the next suburban boom, in the 1950s.

In the 1920s the Shire of Warringah, more than Manly, benefited from the promised improvement in transport services. Some of these, such as the Spit Bridge over Middle Harbour (1924) and the Harbour Bridge (1932), were actually carried out; others, such as the Narrabeen railway, ultimately proved illusory. Unlike the contiguous urbanisation to be found in North Sydney and other harbourside suburbs, Warringah's urban pattern was more attenuated. Even in 1927 it was still 'a number of small settlements' comprising weekend cottages and small-scale agricultural land uses. As the Sydney journalist Charles Whitham wrote in 1927:

> There are some areas of good land, which are utilised for dairies, orchards, market gardens, poultry and flower farmlets. A large proportion of the

Northbridge, a substantial farm house at Roseville, and The Spit on Middle Harbour, before the First World War. All three areas were subdivided by the 1920s and well built-up by the end of the 1930s, although more difficult harbourside sites awaited the suspended concrete floors of the 1950s and 1960s.
Postcards c. 1905–10

houses are of new-fangled fibro cement construction, and many of them don't profess to be more than weekend cottages.[32]

Closer to Manly, the pattern was more urbanised. Harbord, Brookvale and Dee Why were 'now looking like places of permanent solid homes, and land values in these localities [were] rather high'. Improvements in transport were the key to these developments, especially the rapid growth of the private bus system. Companies in Manly-Warringah advertised 'comfortable buses' to every residential area.[33] Lane Cove saw its population increase from 6000 in 1919 to 14,660 in 1929. With Bankstown and Canterbury, it was one of the few Sydney suburbs to double its population within the decade, though the latter two saw much bigger absolute increases. But as Whitham pointed out:

> Although the Municipality [Lane Cove] has an average of five people to the acre, there are not five people on every acre ... Two-thirds of the area is unenclosed bushland, some of it very rocky and precipitous. There are spots around Tambourine Bay where one can stand at night, and see no friendly house or street lamps. If it were not for the reflection in the sky, there is nothing to indicate proximity to a great city.[34]

Contrasting with Lane Cove, which relied on a tram line to the city via St Leonard's station and Crows Nest, were the settlements in the shire of Ku-ring-gai, where the houses clung 'closely to the railway' and no house was 'more than half a mile from open bushland'. Around the railway stations were usually shops, though Killara and Warrawee had none and Wahroonga only 'a few very apologetic stores'; the inhabitants of the shire got 'most of their supplies from Sydney', according to Whitham.[35]

Apart from the north shore line, only one other railway line runs north of the harbour and the Parramatta River, that from Ryde to Hornsby. Again the settlement clung relatively close to the line, although a tramway from the city to Ryde via Drummoyne and Gladesville enabled some spread. Development in Ryde itself was hampered by the inadequate punt service over the Parramatta River between Ryde and Concord. In a rare show of initiative for a Sydney municipality, Ryde Council decided to raise money for a bridge, and construction took place between 1933 and 1935.[36]

Some prewar villages succumbed to suburbia in the 1920s. Suburbs within a three to seven mile radius continued to consolidate; beyond that point nodules of settlement reached out along the old and new railway lines. For many, the twenties offered the chance or at least the dream of a move to the new suburbs. The mood of the time may be reflected in the speculations of the failed orchardist in Christina Stead's novel *Seven Poor Men of Sydney*, as he is forced to seek employment as a storeman in the late 1920s:

> He leaned his head on his hand in the hot sun-ray that came through the chimneys of the warehouse and invented plenty of easy tricky schemes by which he could make money ... [and] buy a cottage with a half-acre of ground up on the North Shore or over in the new suburbs by Balgowlah. His wife and he went there on Sundays inspecting new sub-divisions.[37]

Many of Sydney's smaller shopping centres—especially those that have escaped being incorporated into giant suburban shopping malls—still retain the character of the twenties. They remain dominated by narrow, two-storey shops in liver-coloured brick, built either just before the First World War (in which case their balconies sometimes have a stylish 'art nouveau' swirl), during the war or, more often, after it. At one time the proprietors lived above these premises, whether rented or owned, but now the top floor is more often than not used for storage or let to residential tenants.

Shopping strips were usually to be found near a railway station (Auburn and Epping), ferry wharf (Manly) or major tram stop (Neutral Bay and Bondi Junction). All the basics were there: draper, mercer, estate agent, hairdresser, bank, unlicensed 'tea rooms' (rather than the more middle-class 'restaurants', which were concentrated in the city proper), butcher, laundry, garage (with petrol pump on the pavement), newsagent, fruiterer, bootmaker, cake shop, chemist, grocer, confectioner, florist, fish and chip shop, dentist, tobacconist, medical practitioner (usually in a private house converted for the purpose), a primary school and a local pub. Pubs were more numerous in working-class than middle-class areas (where the 1919 Local Government Act gave councils the power to restrict certain types of buildings). Churches, on the other hand, were fairly evenly spread, although they tended to adjoin rather than be in the town centre, those with the largest following — the Anglicans and Roman Catholics—having the best, which usually meant the highest or most prominent, sites.

Larger centres also offered at least some of the following: a Masonic Hall (many of these temple-shaped structures, like those at Crows Nest and North Strathfield, were built in the twenties), a cinema (increasingly popular as the decade progressed), a skating rink, billlard saloon, undertaker, tailor, solicitor, watchmaker, milliner, police station (often in the front of the residence), a School of Arts, the Returned Services League hall and, occasionally, a high school.

Very few municipalities had their own libraries, so most people had to rely on the popular private lending libraries such as the NSW Bookstall Co. library. Even as late as 1947 there were only eight municipal libraries in Sydney.[38] Most town centres lacked not only libraries but baby health centres and kindergartens. Baby health centres were concentrated, like the much less numerous kindergartens and day nurseries, in the inner city 'slum' areas.[39]

The most common commercial building of the interwar years, the 'milk bar', could be found on residential street corners as well as in town centres. Local milk bars doubled as general stores but in the major shopping strips they were sometimes glamorous chrome parlours offering offering ice creams and sodas. Town centres of the twenties often looked very drab compared to the nearby residential streets. While the streets of the new suburbs reflected the more spacious American styles in domestic housing, the town centres were still strongly influenced by English commercial buildings. Most had few trees and the predominant ribbon development maximised contact between pedestrian and vehicular traffic, which increased rapidly throughout the decade. In contrast, many suburban streets boasted wide nature strips dotted with palms, trimmed English hedges or native gums. As the gardens of the newly developing suburbs took shape—often against great odds, for the sandstone substrata of Sydney produced poor soil—the gulf between drab town centre and tree-lined residential street increased. That dominant housing style of the twenties, the Californian bungalow, is today frequently hidden by decades of garden growth.

Subdivision for speculation

Two basic forces lay behind the subdivision boom of the 1920s: demand for land from prospective home owners and demand from wishful thinkers or speculators. Both were encouraged by the real estate industry and large suburban landholders seeking to make quick profits. Land subdivision could be a most lucrative business, especially in the days when developers were not required to provide fully made roads with kerbing and guttering and had no responsibility for providing other utility services.

A land subdivision boom was nothing new to Sydney. With the railway and tramway expansion after 1880, more and more areas were brought within easy reach of the city. The depression of the 1890s stopped development for a time but, as economic conditions improved and the fashion shifted from terrace housing to detached bungalows, a subdivision boom really started in earnest.

The decline of the terrace and the rise of the semi-detached house or bungalow coincided with the development of what could be a powerful Australian ideology: that the best kind of living is to be had in a private family house on its own block of land, even if that block of land is relatively small and the family home looks much like every other house around it. This ideology and the desire for quick profits fuelled the subdivision boom of the twenties.

The First World War was an unexpected interruption to the boom, but when hostilities ceased the subdivisions began anew. The first year of peace proved to be a year of 'record turnover,' according to *Smith's Weekly*, with 'many suburban subdivisions offering'. All this was achieved despite 'heavy calls on investors for War and Peace Loans, a severe drought and the severe brake put on business by the influenza epidemic'.[40] The new year saw a barrage of subdivision advertisements. Arthur Rickard and Co. started the ball rolling with their CHOICE SEA-SIDE SITES where, significantly, the stress was on 'owning your own lot' rather than owning your own home, a more expensive proposition. Rickard's advertisement included subdivisions at Woy Woy (on the Brisbane Water north of Sydney), Mona Vale (in Warringah), Bondi, Cronulla and Como (the latter two in Sutherland Shire). Only one of these subdivisions, Bondi, could honestly purport to be for 'residential' as distinct from 'week-end' use, as it was within half an hour's tram ride of the city. The Como subdivision, offering 'a fine residential and week-end property' was actually 20 minutes' walk from the station and a 45-minute train ride from town, and the advertisement neglected to mention the absence of town water. Mona Vale was a little more accessible, with a 'tram from Manly to Narrabeen, thence by regular Motor Service'. Woy Woy's

FACING PAGE
Rickards Solar System included land throughout the metropolitan area, as fair afield as Riverstone and Ingleburn, both miles beyond the urban fringe. He also sold land in the Blue Mountains and in Gosford/Wyong.
Rickard's Realty Review, June 1924

accessibility was similar to Como's, and a motor launch was needed to show prospective buyers the property.[41]

Arthur Rickard and Co., 'Realty Specialists' of 84 Pitt Street, Sydney, were probably the biggest speculative subdividers of the time. A knighthood in 1920 'in consideration of his war service' proved an asset to business. By 1926 Rickard was also a director of eight other companies and had become widely known as a 'land subdivision expert' and one of Sydney's best-known and most successful businessmen. He lived on the upper north shore line.[42]

Rickard adopted a four-pronged approach to the subdivision business: 'sea-side sites' for holiday-makers, 'weekenders' for investment, 'market gardening farmlets' for the productively inclined, and 'homesites' for those who wished to own their own. Each type had its own specially designed advertisement: RICKARD'S FARMLETS, for example, assured prospective buyers that market gardening produce could be SOLD AT HIGH PRICES. A subdivision of 2.5–9.0 acre blocks at Mortdale close to the George's River was allegedly 'very suitable for orchards and poultry-raising', while 1.0–2.75 acre blocks at Blacktown were said to be suitable for mixed farming, vegetables and fruit-growing. Some of the farmlets were as distant as Ingleburn on the Campbelltown line and Bargo between Picton and Mittagong.[43] A more direct variant of the market gardening advertisements read MAKE MORE MONEY, PIGS ... It is not possible to determine whether such advertisements precipitated an upsurge in pig and market farming, but the fact that Rickard continued this approach suggests an element of success.[44]

The final advertisement in the Rickard portfolio was aimed at seducing those working-class readers who lived in the inner suburbs away from such 'over-populated districts' where they were 'always liable to a big increase in rent'. Rickard and Co. offered land enabling them to build RENT FREE homes of their own. The land was £1 down and 10 shillings monthly, in 'healthy growing localities' that readers were told were 'most suitable for your requirements' and in which 'your investment must eventually show you a handsome profit'. Localities included Auburn, Bankstown, Clyde, Hornsby and Lidcombe.[45] Rickards were adept at using the rhetoric of small business to lure their working-class clients into substituting hire purchase for rent.

Rickards' many competitors developed their own advertising angles. On the day Rickard and Co. offered their 'Choice Sea-Side Sites' another city firm, H.W. Horning, promoted a subdivision at Como, which they chose to call 'The Coming Suburb'. If the northern suburbs were preferred, Horning offered Great Mackerel Beach, Ku-ring-gai Chase, 'the only REMAINING BEACH ON PITTWATER, and facing its GOLDEN SANDS are the splendid blocks included in this subdivision ... a DELIGHTFUL CHANCE TO THE CITY WORKER'. A close reading of the fine print would have informed the average city worker without a car (when the car was virtually the preserve of the middle class) that the combination of train or tram, motor bus and launch necessary to reach the subdivision would take two to three hours each way.

While investment was not the only reason for buying land, it was certainly a factor at the back of many people's minds, reflecting the fact that the

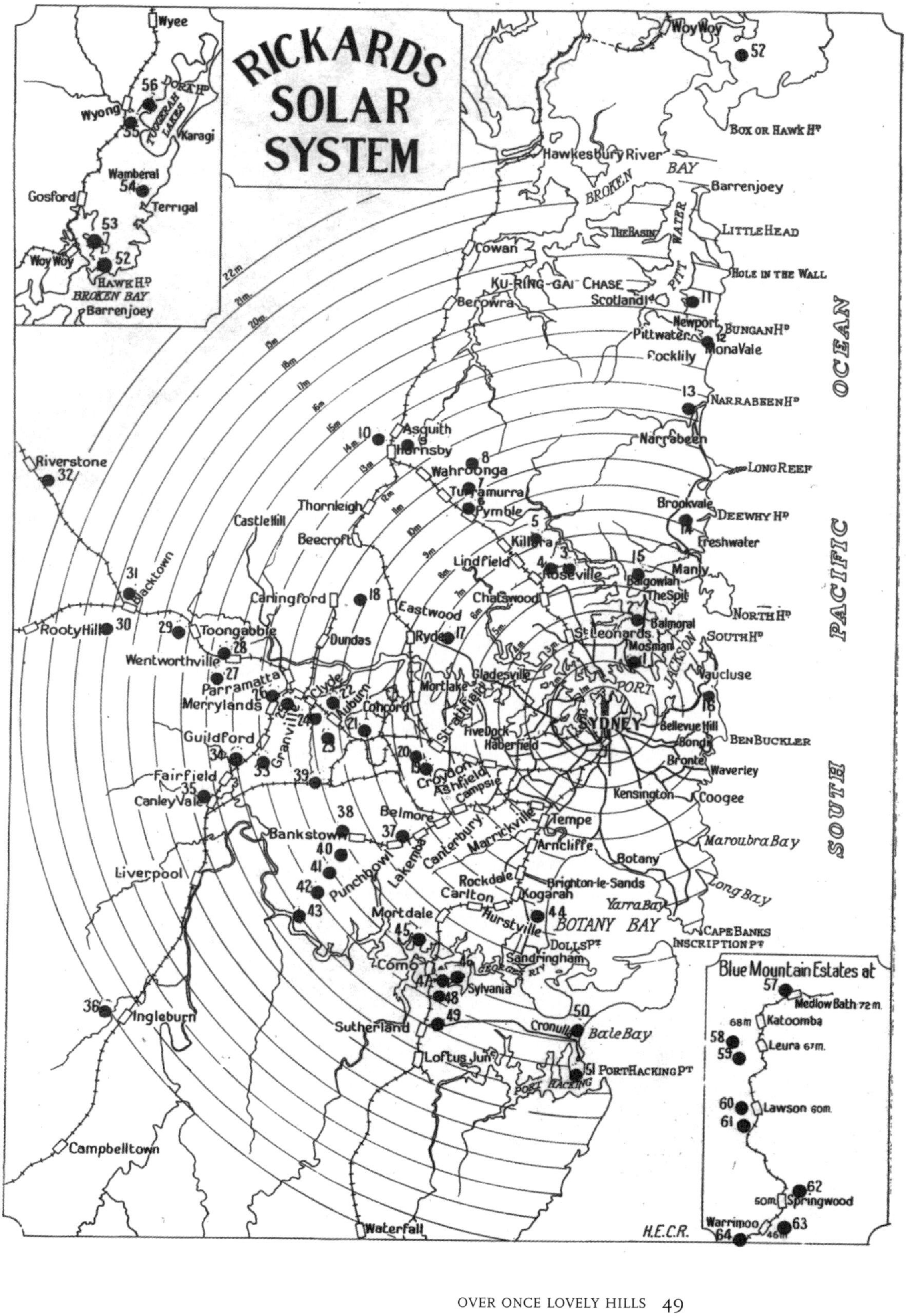
RICKARDS SOLAR SYSTEM
Wyee
Wyong
Karagi
Wamberal
Gosford
Terrigal
Woy Woy
HAWK HD
BROKEN BAY
Barrenjoey
Box or Hawk HD
Hawkesbury River
BROKEN BAY
Barrenjoey
THE BASIN
PITT WATER
LITTLE HEAD
Cowan
HOLE IN THE WALL
KU-RING-GAI CHASE
Scotland Id
Berowra
Newport
Pittwater
BUNGAN HD
Mona Vale
NARRABEEN HD
OCEAN
Narrabeen
LONG REEF
Asquith
Hornsby
Wahroonga
Turramurra
Pymble
Riverstone
Thornleigh
Castle Hill
Brookvale
DEEWHY HD
Freshwater
Beecroft
Killara
Lindfield
Roseville
Manly
Balgowlah
The Spit
Blacktown
Carlingford
Eastwood
Chatswood
Balmoral
NORTH HD
Rooty Hill
Toongabbie
Dundas
Ryde
St Leonards
Mosman
SOUTH HD
PACIFIC
Wentworthville
PORT JACKSON
Parramatta
Clyde
Auburn
Merrylands
Concord
Mortlake
Gladesville
Vaucluse
Granville
Strathfield
Five Dock
Haberfield
SYDNEY
Bellevue Hill
Bondi
Guildford
BEN BUCKLER
Bronte
Waverley
Fairfield
Croydon
Ashfield
Campsie
Canley Vale
Kensington
Coogee
Belmore
Tempe
Bankstown
Canterbury
Marrickville
Maroubra Bay
SOUTH
Lakemba
Arncliffe
Liverpool
Punchbowl
Botany
Rockdale
Brighton-le-Sands
Long Bay
Carlton
Kogarah
Yarra Bay
Mortdale
Hurstville
BOTANY BAY
DOLLS PT
CAPE BANKS
INSCRIPTION PT
Como
Sandringham
GEORGES RIV
Sylvania
Ingleburn
Sutherland
Cronulla
Bate Bay
Loftus Jun
PORT HACKING PT
PORT HACKING
Campbelltown
Waterfall
H.E.C.R.
Blue Mountain Estates at
Medlow Bath 72m.
Katoomba
Leura 67m.
Lawson 60m.
Springwood
Warrimoo

purchase of a house and land was likely to be the largest capital outlay most Australians ever made. A writer in *The Australian Home Building and Real Property Annual* of November 1922 observed:

> There is a revival of building in Sydney, but it is not yet proportionate to the city's needs ... Present conditions in the building trades do not, however, discourage investment in home sites. It is recognized that suitable land is a limited quantity, that everywhere its value is likely to rise, and that it can be held with advantage, while a further reduction in building outlay is awaited ...

Richardson & Wrench, one of Sydney's biggest real estate firms, waxed explicit about an estate at Canterbury in 1925: 'Your last opportunity to invest or speculate in Sydney's most progressive suburb'.[46] Plainly home-buying was not always at the fore of that agency's appeal, despite a claim by the firm's historian that it has been 'controlled by men with business ideals of the highest level ... acting only as commission agents and not speculators'.[47]

Among the most shady deals were those promoted by newly formed companies such as Greater Sydney Estates Ltd in 1927:

> A GARDEN SUBURB INVESTMENT. REMARKABLE PROFITS FOR SHAREHOLDERS. It is a well-known fact that more profits have been made from real estate investments in Australia ... than have been paid in dividends by the combined public companies.

The firm said that it had acquired land at Narrabeen, 'ten miles from Australia's busiest metropolis', but while Narrabeen might have been 10 miles from the metropolis as the crow flies, it was 16 miles by nearest direct road route. The *Sydney Morning Herald*, which carried this advertisement on 14 December 1927, had already informed its readers through a series of specially commissioned articles three months earlier that Narrabeen was 'the out post of Sydney's development along the coast'.[48] Unperturbed by evidence to the contrary, Greater Sydney Estates made clever use of Dr Bradfield's prediction that:

> within the next twenty years the unimproved capital value of North Shore property will exceed that of the city, and that this will be mainly due to the fact that the bridge will afford the Northern Suburbs adequate road and railway communication with the city. As a result of the Bridge, Dr Bradfield concluded, it has been estimated that the population of the Northern Suburbs will be at least 290,000 in 1931 ...

The advertisement also implied that Bradfield guaranteed the 'proposed' electric railway to Narrabeen, and concluded: 'Large fortunes have been made by people who have been awake to the opportunities, and whose successful results have proved their confidence in the growth of the city fully justified.'

The most questionable project associated with the subdivision-for-speculation boom was the railway line from Kingsgrove to East Hills, begun in the late twenties and opened in December 1931 in the midst of depression. The East Hills line was part of the original 1915 Bradfield Plan, as was the promised line to Narrabeen. It was said that the line was built to serve the interests of several of the city's largest real estate agents, including Sir Arthur Rickard, who apparently lobbied successfully within the Nationalist Party for its construction: land owners stood to gain a fortune when the area became accessible and hence subdividable. Certainly Nationalist Party members welcomed the line. J.G. Arkins, Nationalist member for Rockdale, claimed in 1928 that it would 'open up a huge area of land for housing purposes'.[49] P.L. Cantwell and Co. of Pitt Street pointed out that 'intending investors on the new railway from Tempe to East Hills have an excellent basis for judging the prospects from the remarkable progress of Bankstown'.[50]

The lack of demand for housing in the areas served by the railway showed up on its opening. In 1932–33, the first full year of operation, only 31,000 tickets were sold at the terminus station, an average of 88 passengers a day. In that same year, many Sydney suburban stations had ticket sales of from one to four million, and few stations within fifteen miles of the city (as East Hills was) had sales of less than 500,000. In the mid-thirties the East Hills line had the distinction of being the only line where eight consecutive stations beyond Kingsgrove each sold fewer than 100,000 tickets annually.

While real estate agents were pleased with the remarkable progress of Bankstown, a local historian claims that subdividers 'ran amok' in the late twenties, charging 'excessive prices'.[51] It is difficult to estimate how many of the East Hills line subdivisions actually sold, but there was certainly a glut. The amount of subdivided land in the Bankstown municipality (defined here as vacant land with water connection, the closest surrogate available) more than trebled during the decade, at a time when the number of occupied properties in the area little more than doubled, to 4692. In 1920, 40 per cent of blocks with water supply were occupied but by 1929 only 32 per cent were occupied.

The only other municipalities to have more subdivided land than occupied properties were Sutherland and Warringah, two areas that figured prominently in the sales promotions discussed in the preceding pages. But the excess was not nearly so spectacular. In 1920, 47 per cent of blocks with water supply in Warringah were occupied, and by 1929 this had increased slightly to 48 per cent. In any case, in 1929 it had only 4282 vacant blocks compared with Bankstown's 10,115. Figures for Sutherland are not available before the coming of town water in the thirties, but in 1939 homes were built on 47 per cent of the 9534 blocks with water. As these figures demonstrate, beyond their town centres these suburbs were often sparsely settled, with isolated houses surrounded by acres of vacant allotments.

In Canterbury, the number of vacant blocks with water available actually fell in the twenties. Occupied properties increased from 7820 in 1920 to 18,420 in 1929, while the number of vacant blocks fell from 4439 to 3924. Many blocks had of course become available in the intervening years but, unlike in Bankstown, most of the blocks had been built on because Canterbury was closer to the city centre.

The number of vacant subdivided lots with water supply rose from 50,657 in 1920 to 75,539 in 1929. In the areas examined here, most sales were for investment and speculation rather than for home building. No doubt much of the boom can be explained by what Leonie Sandercock has termed 'the national hobby of land speculation'.[52] In the twenties the subdivision boom was promoted by real estate firms, sometimes acting for themselves but more usually for large suburban landholders.[53] That agents invested heavily in sales promotion can be seen from the range of newspapers in which they advertised: the *Sydney Morning Herald*, the *Daily Guardian*, *Smith's Weekly* and the *Labor Daily* have all been cited here. It is impossible to determine how many people were taken in, but the depressed thirties gave them little chance to profit from their investment. Many people paid rates on vacant land worth much less than they paid for it.

A subdivision boom began again in the years after the Second World War, but the amount of subdivided land was never as far ahead of housing completions as it had been in the twenties, thirties and forties, and much of the building in the latter two decades was on land subdivided in the twenties.[54] By 1959 there were only 35,150 vacant watered blocks in Sydney, so the subdividers had to go much further afield than Warringah and Sutherland. Up and down the New South Wales coast they did just as much damage.

The nature and the impact of Sydney's subdivision boom of the twenties has been best summed up by the authors of the *County of Cumberland Planning Scheme Report* in 1948—they had to cope with the results:

> Electrification of suburban railways in 1926 and the growth of motor transport meant a far wider choice of residential areas. On the pleasant slopes and in the rural valleys—anywhere within walking distance of fast transport—land speculation was rife. In remote areas, too, where there was any chance of profit, lots changed hands. Some of the land was bought by genuine home-builders: much of it was bought as an 'investment'. Those who acquired lots believed that the value would automatically increase as their neighhours improved the locality for them. Land subdivision was little more than a gamble, in which profit, not housing needs, was the first consideration. This speculation did not result solely from action by land owners. Very often investment value of the land was enhanced by the provision of railways, tramways, water, sewerage and electricity without there being any coordinated relation with real needs.[55]

The Roaring Twenties?

In 1918 C.J. Dennis's Digger Smith returned home, seeking:

> *The chance to live a clean, straight life,*
> *A dinkum deal for kids an' wife ...*

Yet 'The Roaring Twenties', the title of Jack Lindsay's autobiography of literary life in Sydney, have been characterised as a decade devoted to 'the search for pleasure'.[56] Was it pleasure that mum, dad and the kids found in the move to the suburbs? What sort of pleasure? It depended on where one could afford to buy a house or land, and having done that, how much money was left over after mortgage payments.

One day in 1924, Susie Button, the wife of a young teacher in Brian James' novel *The Advancement of Spencer Button*, had some wealthy acquaintances over for afternoon tea. The Shaw-Wilsons arrived from their home on the upper north shore line in a 'late model car'. It was a 'cordial visit on the surface, but stiff, starchy and formal underneath':

'What a nice place you have here, Susie, so handy and all that.'

That handy street in Stanmore was pure, unadulterated, nearer suburbia, and that was what Mrs Shaw-Wilson meant. Quite incidentally it slipped out that the Shaw-Wilsons had ... one of those new-fangled refrigerators (not a mere ice chest), and Mrs Shaw-Wilson found the Electrolux a boon ... [S]he did love trees and lawns, and wouldn't like to live anywhere but in Warrawee.[57]

After the Shaw-Wilsons leave, Susie, voicing her husband's thoughts, says 'We must get a car.' 'Yes, Susie ...' he replies, 'I'd like to get away from here too; somewhere on the North Shore Line.' The Buttons eventually get their car, enabling a return visit to the Shaw-Wilson's without loss of face. But Spencer and Susie unconciously create resentment among their own circle of acquaintances:

Spencer's colleagues at school were not pleased with Spencer's car, which they somehow considered a personal reflection upon themselves ... But however strongly the rest felt about it, Spencer's buying of a car set the fashion. Soon half a dozen of the staff sported cars, and a line of cars appeared each morning under the brush-box trees or the big fig-tree. They stood with their sterns pointed towards the yard—like a line of horses eating out of the feedtroughs.[58]

For most families in the twenties, buying a car was well beyond their means. It has become a cliché to see the 'roaring twenties' in terms of 'the young man in the T-model Ford speeding at nearly 50 miles an hour towards destruction'.[59] This may have been the style of the carefree, wealthy young, but it was not the style of the masses.

In contrast to car ownership, electricity did become an integral part of many households during the period. By 1929 there were at least 164,805 'retail consumers' of electricity in Sydney at a time when the city had 289,828 occupied properties.[60] But in most homes electricity was used only for lighting and small appliances; gas continued as the most common cooking fuel until the mid-sixties.[61] Electrical appliances such as vacuum cleaners and refrigerators did decrease drudgery for the few housewives who could afford them, but refrigerators did not become widespread until after the Second World War. The most common—as well as the cheapest—electrical appliances in the inter-war years were irons, toasters and jugs: the popularity of these appliances in Sydney was reflected in increasing employment in the electrical appliance industry for both men and women. Faced with a gradual decrease in the availability of servants (as a proportion of the population) middle-class housewives welcomed the new appliances and the trend to more efficient kitchens.[62]

The Australian Gas Light Company was still advertising the All Gas Home in 1922, including gas cookers, coopers, irons, bath heaters, gas fires and gas lighting. *Home* September 1922. Electricity suppliers, including the many local councils, began an aggressive marketing campaign in the 1930s. Manly Municipal Council ran this image of the happy housewife in its *Manly Diamond Jubilee, 1937*

Electricity itself continued to be treated with a sense of novelty. When Manly Municipal Council celebrated its Jubilee in 1927, 'thousands of residents and visitors gathered to watch his Excellency the Governor switch on the Jubilee lights which transformed Manly into a city of a million twinkling globes of red, white, blue, green and amber'.[63] And it was electricity and skyscrapers, a combination new to Sydney in the twenties, that made the central city such an exciting scene at night:

> The skyscrapers in the business heart of the city tower up in the distance beyond Circular Quay ... At night it is all changed to a veritable fairyland. Coloured lights blaze in all directions; scores of ferry-boats, each with a band on board, flit to and fro across the harbour like glow-worms; brilliantly-lit mail steamers thread their way carefully up to their berths; electric trams and motor cars on the crests of the hills add their moving lights to the scene.[64]

Many employees during these years did not have the security Spencer Button had in his teaching job. Unskilled workers often experienced intermittent employment: unemployment never fell below 5 per cent, and in 1925 and 1928 rose as high as 11 per cent. With at least one in 10 wage and salary earners out of work for some period in the twenties, the ability to enjoy the new but costly technological luxuries was limited. Picture-shows were one mass diversion of the twenties most people could afford, and they became by far the most popular form of entertainment. By 1921 suburban cinemas were better patronised than those in the city. This was to continue throughout the interwar years.

Films were first commercially produced in Australia in the late 1890s, and by the First World War filmmaking had become a thriving industry, much of it centred on Sydney. The war proved no deterrent: 1918 saw the premiere in Sydney of such films as *The Lure of the Bush* and *Satan in Sydney*. The popularity of the pictures may be attributable to their Hollywood-style appeal—so much of what was thought fashionable in the twenties derived from the USA—and their cheapness. The average price paid for (taxable) tickets in 1920–21 was 1 shilling, and this figure excludes tickets costing 5 pence or less. In contrast, live theatres cost three times as much, dancing and skating twice as much, while the average price paid at concerts was 3 shillings and 7 pence and at race meetings 4 shillings and 4 pence.[65] And more and more of these activities took place in the suburbs, as Table 3.3 indicates.

Table 3.3: Number of taxable admissions to public entertainments in Sydney 1920–21

	City	Suburban
Picture shows	7 822 110	11 571 082
Theatres (live)	2 714 962	1 031 729
Race meetings	–	2 455 720
Dancing and skating	253 466	703 664
Concerts	146 485	54 486

Source: *NSWYB*, 1921, p 497.

Patronage of live theatres dropped markedly in the twenties, from more than four million state-wide in 1920–21 to less than 1.3 million in 1930. The decline continued in the following decade as silent films were replaced by 'talkies'. On 21 August 1929 two writers in the *Sydney Mail* bemoaned the fact that 'many of our playhouses have yielded to the dictates of progress'; even the St James Theatre had 'submitted to the indignity of "wiring"'. The authors lamented the hundreds of thousands of pounds spent on cinemas, which they regarded as 'flamboyant temples of pseudo-art, while the theatre as we have known and loved it for centuries languishes for want of support'.

Apart from such welcome diversions as a trip to the beach, the local milk bar and the Saturday matinee, most children attended some form of Protestant or Roman Catholic Sunday school, and virtually all of them attended a government or private school for 40 weeks a year. They usually spent their holidays in the confines of the backyard and the suburb as few of their working fathers had more than two weeks of annual leave. In better off households, mothers would take their children to a guest house or seaside camping ground, where fathers would join them at weekends. At school, children were introduced to key aspects of Australian society. In his 1929 school text *Australia*, G.S. Browne, vice-principal of Melbourne Teachers' College, told British and Australian children:

> In the towns and cities ... weatherboard houses ... were superseded by Queen Anne villas and brick bungalows. There has always been a marked absence of those long lines of continuous joined houses, so common in England, under the name of 'terraces'. With a strong desire for individuality, breathing space, and fresh air, the Australian has insisted on his own house, quite detached, situated in its own block of land and garden. The result is that cities like Sydney and Melbourne cover an enormous expanse of territory.[66]

Those school children who continued to live in the inner terrace suburbs in the decade (and Sydney had more than Melbourne) may have regretted, under such propaganda, that their parents were lacking either the money or the 'individuality' necessary for them to move to their own home in the suburbs.

There was another, less praiseworthy side of this ideology. In 1927 Francis Jackson, a local school teacher, complained about the suburban narrowness of most Sydneysiders:

> The education of civic pride and intelligence makes little progress in a democracy whose attention is divided between beauty competitions, the racing and betting news, and the latest of inane revues ... A citizen of London, Edinburgh, Paris, Berlin, Florence, Rome or even Melbourne on Yarra can boast of his native city with a clear pride in her beauty, traditions and integrity. A native of Sydney should be able to feel that he is one of a great community whose life contains something distinct in civic development ... There is a need for the spread of the ideals of federation in city politics to give him the wider vision which goes far beyond boosting his own suburb in order to raise land values.[67]

Suburban land values were an integral part of the growth of Sydney in the boom. If it was a 'roaring' decade, it was the roar of the subdividers that sounded loudest, a roar not everyone benefited from.

An air photograph of the Harbour Bridge from above Circular Quay in which the photographer has selected a startlingly modern pattern composed of sea and land and the shadows of steel.
Photograph by Dr George R. Hamilton,
The Second Bridge Book, Art in Australia, 1931

CHAPTER 4

Shadows behind the bridge

The dancing halls filled. Music filled the air. On with the dance—for an old year, with its unfulfilled hopes, its broken resolutions ... was dying. On with the dance ... for [the] new year ... could not be much more brutal than the one that had passed ... Midnight came. Ferry sirens rent the air, tram bells pealed a welcome to 1932, train whistles joined the chorus.[1]

Busker
Sydney Mail, 3 June 1931

So Sydney welcomed 1932. The day before had been hot and sultry: several women fainted in the crowded city stores. Relief came with a southerly change at 2 p.m. The *Herald*'s optimism was premature: 1932 proved to be the worst year of the Depression. But it was also the year of the most spectacular event in Sydney's history, the opening of the Sydney Harbour Bridge.

Most Australian accounts of the Depression start with the Wall Street crash, but there is little to suggest that the citizens of Sydney were particularly concerned about the state of the New York stock market. It was not until the enduring consequences of the Depression became obvious that it emerged as a topic of public concern. One of the best descriptions of the coming of the Depression to Sydney is to be found in Caddie's *Autobiography of a Sydney Barmaid*:

Things were getting rough [around 1930]—not only for little businesses like mine. It was just about then that people began to talk about the depression but I didn't realise what it really meant till I found how hard jobs were to get ... There was nothing but talk of lost jobs in the bar. Everyone was on edge and tempers became short.[2]

Unemployment was the most crushing aspect of the Depression in Sydney. The earliest and most marked indication was the rapid shut-down in the most visible and vulnerable of all urban activities, building construction. Sir Arthur Rickard's real estate company went into voluntary liquidation in 1930. The family's heavily mortgaged mansion, Berith Park at Wahroonga, was sold and they moved to a modest home in Killara.[3]

In no other capital city did construction activity drop off to the extent that it did in Sydney. The Melbourne-based *Australasian* commented on 2 January 1932 that 'nothing demonstrates the reduced conditions of Sydney as accurately as the figures of the building trade' (see Table 4.1). The annual report of the NSW Real Estate Institute said that 1931 had been 'difficult, harassing and embarrassing' for their members. The number of new buildings approved by municipal councils in Melbourne between 1931 and 1934 never fell below 2300 annually, while in Sydney a mere 688 buildings were approved in 1932.[4] Melbourne, the home of most of Australia's company headquarters and of the bulk of federal public servants, proved a little more resilient than Sydney, although poverty and desperation were widespread in the inner industrial suburbs of both cities.

Jack Lang, who had been premier in the 1925–27 Labor government, emerged as the dominant political figure of the depression years in Sydney and in Australia. With a tall, commanding presence, and nick-named 'The Big Fella', he caught the attention of the electorate, who either admired or loathed him. Cartoonists and caricaturists depicted him in many guises. He attacked not only the ruling Bavin government in New South Wales, but the Scullin federal Labor government, especially in July 1930 when it took advice from Sir Otto Niemeyer of the Bank of England. Lang rejected Niemeyer's call for a reduction in public spending. In the October 1930 state election, which his party won by 20 seats, he promised public works to reduce unemployment and a double payment for each family's first child. In March 1931 he refused to pay the interest on state government loans due in London. The Scullin government met the debt. Lang's subsequent actions split the state Labor Party, and were a major factor in the defeat of federal Labor at the December 1931 election.[5]

Jack Lang caricature by George Finey.
Art in Australia, June 1931

Unemployment in the suburbs

As the Depression worsened more and more businesses closed. Bakers and shopkeepers were forced to choose between longstanding customers who could still pay and those who couldn't. Employees of government departments, banks, hotels and the city emporiums were more likely to keep their jobs—even if on reduced hours—than workers in small manufacturing companies and other commercial enterprises with little capital to fall back on. Most declared themselves bankrupt. With little demand for real estate other than at bargain basement prices, their assets rarely covered their liabilities. For some in the community the Depression was a fall in the standard of comfort, rather than the standard of living. As one scholar later wrote:

> Their houses may have been smaller and shabbier but they had houses. Their clothing may have been worn, but it was adequate. Their diets may not have been as varied, but they had sufficient to eat. The true loss of a standard of living was experienced by those who lost their jobs ... The pensioners' lot was never a happy one, but they did have the certainty of an income, however small. Thousands of the unemployed had no such certainty.[6]

At a time when the metropolitan area held 47 per cent of the state's population, 57 per cent of unemployed wage-earners were in Sydney. Sydney and provincial urban centres (such as Newcastle) had roughly the same levels of unemployment: 28 per cent of male wage earners and 15 per cent of female wage earners were unemployed. Although female unemployment was less—women were often kept on by employers for the simple reason that their wages were so much lower than males—it is likely that many women who wanted a job did not even bother to register. Some female employees suffered active discrimination. On 7 March 1932 a *Herald* editorial explained the sacking of married women teachers in favour of males as 'a case of painful necessity'.[7]

Table 4.1: Index of value of building completions in Sydney and Melbourne 1929–38

Year	Sydney	Melbourne
1929	100	100
1930	60	62
1931	18	21
1932	6	20
1933	11	33
1934	28	45
1935	52	64
1936	69	83
1937	75	85
1938	87	85

Base year 1929 = 100.
Source: CB Schedvin, Building and the Trade Cycle in Australian Cities Between the Wars, Paper presented to the 35th ANZAAS conference, Brisbane, 1961, p 4.

The most palpable evidence of unemployment in Sydney could be seen in makeshift camps. All but one of these were south of the harbour on vacant crown land at Brighton-le-Sands, Rockdale, Long Bay, La Perouse and, according to the communist *Workers Weekly*, at 'other scrubby, sandy, flea infested beauty spots'. The Aboriginal settlement at La Perouse expanded at this time.[8] The only major camp to the north of the harbour was in the thinly inhabited area of Clontarf. Only one camp, at Lidcombe, was planned, being organised by the Sydney-based Unemployed Housing Committee.[9] The most famous of the camps, 'Happy Valley', at La Perouse, was described by the *Workers Weekly* as one and three-quarter miles long, with 129 tents and shacks sheltering campers from 'the southerly busters that sweep across Botany Bay'.[10] One of the campers complained of parsons 'of all denominations bribing attendance at hymn bawling meetings by hand-outs of cast-off clothing' and complimenting campers on their 'hardy pioneering spirit'.

Sir Otto Niemeyer Caricature by George Finey.
Art in Australia, June 1931

One parson who practised as well as preached his gospel was the Anglican Archdeacon Hammond. Before the Depression he had established 'Pilgrims' Homes' for homeless men in the inner city and these were enlarged in the crisis. An advocate of self-help, his most notable scheme was to build a settlement of inexpensive houses for families under threat of eviction. The houses were not for rent but for rent-purchase. The first houses at 'Hammondville', two and a half miles beyond Liverpool, were completed in November 1932; the one-hundredth cottage was unveiled in November 1937.[11] Although an impressive achievement for a voluntary agency, this example of the suburban ideal, situated miles beyond the built-up area, was little more than a utopian dream to the many thousands of homeless.

Most of them remained in the unemployed camps, like those on Botany Bay, where they had to put up with 'the passing line of cars on the roadway, 50 yards from our doors', and 'the disdainful glances of a well-fed, well-dressed bourgeois as they pass by on their way to Moorefield or Ascot race courses', as the *Workers Weekly* put it.[12]

Where did the well-fed bourgeoisie live? The municipalities with the least unemployment at the June 1933 census were the well-established upper middle-class areas of Vaucluse (16 per cent), Ku-ring-gai, Mosman (both 18 per cent) and Strathfield (19 per cent). There were only three exceptions to the class pattern of unemployment by which middle-class suburbs had lower levels of unemployment than working-class suburbs—the municipalities of Homebush, Botany and Concord.

Botany, with a male unemployment rate of 25 per cent, was much better off than other near-city working-class industrial suburbs such as Alexandria (44 per cent unemployed) or Redfern (48 per cent). The explanation for these differences lay both in the more stable local employment in these suburbs and in the movement of the unemployed to the more depressed suburbs in search of cheap accommodation. Many of the men who lived in Homebush and Concord were employed in the metropolitan abattoirs and in the Australian Gas Light Company's plant, industries less subject to retrenchment during times of depression than many of the manufacturing and building

La Perouse 'blacks camp'. August 1933

operations that provided most of the unskilled and semi-skilled jobs for workers in near-city municipalities. In Botany, Davis Gelatine's large processing plant, established in 1918 and little affected by the Depression, gave that suburb at least one stable centre of employment.[13]

The extremes of unemployment diverged markedly from the 25–30 per cent average that is usually quoted by historians. They ranged from upper middle class suburbs at one end, with relatively low rates of 16–19 per cent, to working-class suburbs at the other, 16 of which experienced over 40 per cent unemployment. The suburbs in between form a cluster, with 38 of the 56 falling between 22 and 40 per cent. While no suburb was entirely immune from high rates of unemployment, working-class suburbs suffered more than middle-class suburbs.[14] Relief work usually reflected the social character of an area. Councils in working-class suburbs such as Botany and in newly developing areas such as Canterbury and Bankstown tended to concentrate on the essentials. In those suburbs money was spent on bridges, roads and drainage.[15] The Ku-ring-gai council had slightly more high-flown aims, and in conjunction with the Main Roads Board and the state's Unemployment Relief Committee set out to ensure that 'good traffic facilities shall be available for those who are erecting commodious residences ...'. Councils in older established middle-class areas concerned themselves with recreational or scenic works: Strathfield on parks, Waverley on a 'marine drive' and Beach Pavilion at Bondi, and Mosman on the Rotunda and Promenade at Balmoral beach.[16]

Relief work in Petersham reflected the mixed class character of that area. With 9 per cent of its males earning over £260 per annum in 1932–33, Petersham was just a little below the Sydney median of 10 per cent of males earning more than that amount, while with 31 per cent unemployed among male wage earners, it was better off than many other municipalities (median unemployment 39 per cent). In 1932 the council, which had experienced difficulty in collecting rates because of 'the sheer inability of many people to pay', arranged work for 'unemployed ratepayers' who were willing to pay back some portion of their wages for overdue rates. Two years later, using state government money, the council started a more ambitious scheme that employed between 560 and 753 men on a fortnightly basis. Their tasks included basic public works such as constructing kerbs and guttering and less pressing needs such as the improvement of parks and reserves. Petersham's local historian concluded that the most important benefit of the relief works was 'the moral effect on the men employed'.[17]

Because middle-class municipalities had proportionally fewer unemployed than working-class ones, they were able to make better provision for their jobless. A survey conducted by the NSW Department of Labour and Industry in 1936 found that the average relief worker in the northern suburbs had been so employed for 21.7 months, while in the inner suburbs the average was only 10.3 months. The plight of the northern suburbs jobless was not so pressing, with lower unemployment rates and longer periods of relief work, while food relief there lasted 2.3 months on average; in the inner suburbs it lasted 14.8 months.[18]

Linking the suburbs: the Sydney Harbour Bridge

The most spectacular event in Sydney during the Depression—the one that really took people's minds off their immediate problems—was the construction of the Sydney Harbour Bridge. The popular press, the quality weeklies and monthlies and the professional journals all carried comments and pictures on the bridge's development, amply illustrated with dramatic pictures taken from every angle and at every time of day and night. Cinema and radio coverage was also substantial.[19] The bridge evoked new images. Jean Curlewis, daughter of the novelist Ethel Turner, tried to express some of them in the 'Sydney Number' of *Art in Australia* in June 1927:

> Traffic noise. Trams, ferry boats, trains. Sirens. Steel hammers clanging. Builders in the city. Building a bridge in the sea city. Thrust of girders web of girders over the sea. Memory of builders in the city ...

Nor did public interest wane in the early years of the Depression. The July 1930 issue of the Railway and Tramway journal, the *Staff,* commented that interest in the bridge 'is increasing as the structure rears its head into view of many parts of the city and suburbs and the higher lands further out'. The bridge could be seen, and can still be seen, from a surprising number of vantage points around the city and suburbs. No one doubted that it would be a magnificent structure: the enthusiasm of the business community, not least their determination to embrace the bridge as a symbol of progress, spilled over into an enormous range of advertising attracted by the Bridge Supplements in the various papers. The most pointed comment came from *Smith's Weekly,* whose cartoon 'School of Real Estate Agents Crossing the Harbour Bridge to Spawn' accurately depicted the coalition of interests of

A dogman rides a Harbour Bridge girder, above the vehicular ferries of Dawes Point with passenger ferries bound for Circular Quay in the background.
Erection Wages, 1932

property owners, real estate agents and would-be north shore dwellers.

A mammoth construction job, the bridge employed thousands of workers in dangerous conditions. Its five million rivets were all individually heated on site and beaten into the steel joists. Safety precautions were minimal and safety harnesses unknown. Thirty men died during the construction. Although a shocking toll, this figure is not much greater than the level of fatalities in the construction industry today, especially given the size and length of the job.

During the 1930s the bridge became a symbol for the city, linking its two halves, a prosperous symbol, planned in better times. It became a sign, in the midst of the Depression, that a return to suburban prosperity was possible. It was a symbol worth capturing, and Jack Lang was pleased that a Labor premier would open it.[20] Had a non-Labor government been in power it would almost certainly have invited royalty to the occasion. Such a suggestion was in fact made. In January 1932 Eric Campbell, a solicitor of Turramurra, told the Lane Cove division of the para-military New Guard organisation (which he founded in February 1931) that 'the people of NSW will not permit Mr Lang to open the Bridge' and at a meeting a few weeks later at Chatswood he suggested that royalty be called on to perform the ceremony.[21]

Journalist Colin Wills wrote a series of poems to go with Bill Pidgeon's drawings for their book *Rhymes of Sydney*, first published in 1933.

On 17 March 1932, two days before the bridge opening, *Smith's Weekly* published a cartoon with the caption 'The Man Who Beat Lang to the Tape'. On 19 March Captain de Groot, owner of a period-furniture factory at Rushcutters Bay, procured a 'decrepit steed' with the aid of the Campbells and opened the bridge on behalf of 'the decent and loyal citizens of NSW'.[22] Lang re-opened it on behalf of the people of NSW. De Groot later claimed that the *Smith's Weekly* cartoon had 'suggested the idea'.[23]

In the months after the bridge was completed, its shadow lengthened as unemployment grew and Lang's hold over the Labor Party waned. On 5 May a memorial tablet to dead bridge workers was unveiled. Eight days later the state Governor, Sir Philip Game, decided that Lang's instruction to state public servants not to pay money into the federal Treasury was illegal, and dismissed him. To the surprise of many, Lang 'stepped down quietly'. The legality of Lang's instruction was never tested in court.[24] The following day nearly 400 bridge workers were laid off; they had been taking part in the general clean up around the site since the opening.

In this turbulent atmosphere a general election was set for 11 June. Major firms used the threat of unemployment in an attempt to sway the working-class vote. On 31 May, in 'A Word With the Workers', Felt and Textiles of Australia Ltd, with factories at Waterloo and Alexandria, told its employees:

> Men, you have good jobs with good employers, who are much better friends to you than ever Lang will be. You are lucky in these bad times. There are many thousands who would be thankful to have what you have. Any one of you who risks the closing down of this factory by voting for a selfish liar and traitor is a fool.[25]

There can be no doubt that such tactics had some effect. The number of seats held by Labor in both metropolitan and country areas was more than halved. Labor dropped from the 55 seats it won in the 1930 landslide victory to 24, and managed to retain only 14 of its 29 Sydney seats.

The *Australian Worker* told its readers on 16 March 'there is a shadow behind the Bridge', 'two hundred thousand unemployed'.
Cartoon by Will Donald

Unemployment began to ease in 1933. In June that year the tide of magazine and newspaper closures was reversed with the production of the first issue of the *Australian Women's Weekly*, which sold 120,000 copies. A headline, WHAT SMART SYDNEY WOMEN ARE WEARING, was accompanied by photos of eastern suburbs socialites. The *Weekly* did not remind its readers that, as Judith Wright later wrote, 'the park benches were crowded still with hopeless workless men as grey as their clothes'.[26] Not all its readers could afford sartorial elegance so on 16 September the *Weekly* invited housewives to write in for crochet directions to make a 'Symphony of Steel' traycloth, an 'absolutely charming reproduction of the great bridge'. On 30 December the *Weekly* assured its readers that 'we can all look forward to 1934 as the best year we have had for a long time' and reported that the hotels and boarding houses at the surfing beaches were full.

Revival of a kind

'The depression was over. Money was going round again ... Lists of unemployed receded, buildings began to grow'.[27] Thus did Sydney newspaper editor Eric Baume record the end, by 1935, of the Depression in Sydney. Just as the collapse of the building industry had been a visible sign of depression, so the revival in building signalled better times. Real estate agents rejoiced: 1935 was the best year for Sydney's leading real estate companies since the boom of the twenties.[28]

NSW State election pamphlet 1932

New building was evident in both the city and the suburbs, but the suburbs were the first to benefit because investment decisions about individual dwellings did not require the planning necessary for large city projects. City building reached its lowest value in 1934, though the lowest point for building permits was 1932. Suburban building sunk to its lowest value in 1932, but permits issued began to rise again after 1931 (see Table 4.2).

With growing employment and increasing funds, home building began to

Table 4.2: Value of buildings completed and building permits issued in Sydney and suburbs 1929–40

Year	City of Sydney £000	Suburbs Permits	£000	Permits
1929	4945	78	10 617	8494
1930	2865	46	5745	2260
1931	543	20	1090	508
1932	1074	12	701	721
1933	717	34	1319	1343
1934	538	46	2617	3058
1935	1158	63	5358	4331
1936	2080	106	6648	5416
1937	1558	86	6276	5762
1938	2808	109	8210	7456
1939	2182	72	9046	6975
1940	2382	66	9614	6803

Value of buildings completed includes government buildings but building permits (issued by councils) does not.
Source: NSWYB 1939–40, pp 178–79.

revive in 1933 and the pace quickened in following years. The outward movement of young families seeking their own home and garden, a characteristic of the twenties, was resumed. Both the Labor and non-Labor parties applauded this trend. In December 1937 the United Australia Party Premier B.S.B. Stevens, outlining the proposed slum demolition and rehousing project at Erskineville, told Parliament that:

> one half of our people already have their own homes. We aim to see that proportion increase ... The average man aspires to his own home, particularly the man in poor circumstances. For the home is the cradle of our race ... the basis of family life.[29]

As in the twenties, most new houses were built in middle and outer suburbs. The pattern of new suburban housing in this decade was one of filling in: the subdivision boom of the twenties had created, by the end of that decade, over 75,000 vacant building blocks (defined as land connected to water supply). In Canterbury, the suburb to see the most house building in the thirties, subdivisions kept just ahead of building demand. In 1929 there were 4000 subdivided blocks and in the following decade 2700 houses were built. Bankstown municipality, which had a similar increase in its housing stock, had been the main area of speculative subdivision in the twenties. In the thirties the filling-in process was aided by the opening of the East Hills line in 1931, but the completion of the process had to await the postwar baby boom and the rapid increases in car ownership in the 1950s.

Although the average figure for persons-per-room in private dwellings in Sydney in the interwar and early postwar years fell only slightly (0.88 in 1921 and 0.77 in 1947), this masked significant changes in particular municipalities. In 1921 Bankstown had the highest persons-per-room average of any Sydney municipality (1.11), while Canterbury (0.96) was much nearer the average. The average continued to fall in both municipalities after this date, as shown in the 1933 and 1947 censuses (Canterbury 0.83, 0.78; Bankstown 0.93, 0.88). The highest average persons-per-room figures in the interwar and early postwar years were in the inner city and outer suburban working-class areas, the lowest in the northern, eastern and southern suburbs. Those people who moved, under the ideological supervision of the slum reformers, from the 'congested' inner city to the outer working-class suburbs often found themselves living in more crowded houses—admittedly in more rural surroundings. They were also much further from the pubs, factories, warehouses, shops, cinemas and churches that made up the inner city community. Most of the fringe areas lacked sewers, properly made roads and stormwater provisions; hospitals and schools were few and far between and, except for some within reach of the outer rail or tram networks, these areas had to rely on often inadequate private bus services.

The T&G insurance building, with its distinctive tower, was one of the few office blocks completed in the Depression. Opened in 1932, it reached the height limit of 150 feet. The War Memorial opened two years later.
Postcard c. 1936

The Metropolitan Water, Sewerage and Drainage Board caught up with some of its backlog in the 1930s, mainly because the number of dwellings in Sydney increased by only 42,000 during the decade, half the 85,000 increase of the 1920s. Baulkham Hills, Blacktown, Ermington and Rydalmere, Fairfield, Liverpool, Hunters Hill and Sutherland were still without sewerage in 1940, while only 6 per cent of Bankstown, 12 per cent of Dundas and 12 per cent of Warringah were sewered.[30] The 'dunny man' still called in these suburbs. While nineteenth-century suburbs such as Hunters Hill had back lanes, so the dunny man could visit discreetly, in the newer suburbs, whether working-class or middle-class, he had to enter via the front gate.

Municipalities differed greatly not only in the provision of services and the size of houses, but in the materials of construction. In the second half of the decade, less expensive timber-framed houses clad in asbestos-cement ('fibro') sheets became popular as a substitute for brick. A quarter of all house building permits issued in Sydney between 1936 and 1940 were for fibro or weatherboard.

In 1938 James Hardie Pty Ltd claimed that their asbestos cement factory, on 19 acres at Camellia, was 'an enormously valuable asset to the Parramatta district' and that its product 'fibrolite' was stimulating home building 'by helping to bring the purchase of homes within the reach of people of moderate means'.[31] Fibro and weatherboard were particularly popular in working-class outer western municipalities such as Fairfield and Bankstown (average cost of houses £533) but little used in Ku-ring-gai (average cost £1711), whose wealthier inhabitants preferred and could afford brick.[32]

Most houses in Sydney had electricity for lighting purposes by 1930, but gas continued as the main source of cooking energy. At the 1947 census gas was connected to 91 per cent of dwellings, and 83 per cent used it as the main method of cooking. A major campaign by suppliers to increase the use of electricity for cooking began in the thirties and produced a counter-campaign by the gas companies. In 1938 the Parramatta and Granville Electric Supply Company claimed that 'cooking by electricity is definitely cheaper and better food results from it. Your bath is ready in half the time with an electric heater ... Be modern—think electricity.' In its advertisement the Australian Gas Light Company stressed the 'continuous' 'modern' character of its product, which was 'closely linked with the advancement and betterment of this mighty community'.[33]

The biggest percentage increases in population in the decade were in municipalities with higher than average rates of home ownership. Baulkham Hills' population increased 48 per cent from 6220 in 1930 to 9190 in 1940, the biggest percentage increase of any Sydney municipality. With only 21 per cent of dwellings tenanted, it had the highest rate of home ownership in Sydney. The outer metropolitan municipality to experience the biggest absolute increase in population between 1930 and 1940 was Ku-ring-gai, gaining 5700 new inhabitants. At 68 per cent Ku-ring-gai had the fourth highest rate of home ownership. By the thirties, the interwar pattern interrupted by the Depression had been resumed: the new suburbs were peopled by home owners rather than tenants.

Most municipalities in which more than 60 per cent of dwellings were owner-occupied were on the urban fringe. The only exceptions to this were older inner municipalities: Strathfield (65 per cent home ownership) and Hunters Hill (61 per cent home ownership). There were, of course, marked differences in the owner-occupied housing areas. With an average of 0.64 inhabitants per room, the families of Ku-ring-gai were more spaciously accommodated than those of Bankstown (0.93) despite the fact that around two-thirds of the private dwellings in each municipality were owner-occupied.

Those municipalities that lost population in the interwar years had low rates of home ownership. These ranged from St Peters, where 64 per cent of dwellings were rented, to Redfern and Darlington, the municipalities whose populations decreased most during the thirties, where 90 per cent of residents were tenants. These suburbs were regarded as slum areas and were the target of a reform campaign later in the decade. Of the inner city slum municipalities, Waterloo, with only 27 per cent owner-occupied, had the highest home ownership rate, but this was still 17 per cent below the Sydney average of 44 per cent.

Another group of suburbs had tenancy rates almost as high as those of the slums, the municipalities of Waverley (71 per cent tenants), Woollahra (66 per cent) and Randwick (61 per cent). Here the explanation lay not in a deteriorating housing stock but in the boom in flats of the 1920s and 1930s.

Flats: the antithesis of suburbia

One of the most striking developments in Sydney's housing in the 1920s and 1930s and one that aroused much public debate was the proliferation of flats in certain parts of the city and suburbs. Although older structures, such as large Victorian houses, could be turned into flats, they were rarely self-contained. The blocks of flats of the twenties and thirties were double-brick walk-up structures, usually of two or three storeys, with between four and 12 self-contained flats in each block. Most of these blocks were built for and owned by individual investors; it was extraordinarily difficult to raise finance from a bank or building society to buy a flat because there was no prospect of a conventional land title. This problem was partly overcome in the 1930s by the creation of companies that issued shares in their 'company title' flats, giving the shareholder the right to occupy a designated space in the building.

The Edwardian mansions of Cremorne Point gave way to apartment blocks in the 1930s.
Postcard c. 1938

Banks still weren't keen, however, so the great majority of flats continued to be owned by investors who rented out the entire block, although occasionally a landlord would choose to retain one for his or her own residence.[34] The most notable spate of flat-building took place in the eastern suburbs municipalities of Waverley and Woollahra. In Waverley, flats as a proportion of all housing increased almost fourfold between 1921 and 1933. In Woollahra almost 60 per cent of all dwellings were described as flats at the 1947 census. In the meantime the number of flats and tenements in Sydney increased from 12,760 in 1921 to 36,057 in 1933 to 71,788 in 1947. (For census purposes, 'tenements' were rooms and apartments that lacked bathing and/or cooking facilities; the term did not include terraces or semi-detached houses.)

Contemporary observers took the revival of flat-building in the mid-thirties as a sign of a return to better times. According to one newspaper columnist, writing in May 1935, an eastern suburbs agent reported that 'a procession of builders' had decided to buy land and erect flats in his area, and that there was no difficulty in selling new blocks of flats—sometimes long before they were completed.[35] The boom in flats was accompanied by large population increases in the areas most affected. The municipality with the largest absolute increase in population in the thirties was Randwick, which gained over 10,000 inhabitants to make it the most populous suburb in Sydney with a population of 86,120 in 1940. Waverley gained approximately 9000 new residents and Woollahra 5500.

What all these areas had in common was their relative proximity to the city centre and to the harbour or surfing beaches. With the exception of Vaucluse, approximately two-thirds of eastern suburbs residents were tenants. Other municipalities that shared the three characteristics of nearness to the city centre, average or higher than average tenancy rates and a large part of their housing stock in the form of flats included Mosman, North Sydney, the City of Sydney, Paddington and Glebe.

Beyond the city centre, the only suburb that had many flats was Manly, where the percentage of flats increased from 19.5 per cent in 1921 to 30 per cent in 1933. Although Manly was ten miles distant from the city by road, it was only a 35-minute ferry ride away. While it is difficult to date the beginning of the urban commuter's flat in Manly, a 1945 survey showed that the number of employees living in Manly was almost twice the number of employees working there.[36] Most of Manly's flats were two- or three-storey walk-ups in various shades of red brick; in the 1930s elegant art deco lines began to appear. The flat dwellers included retired couples, families and single women of mature years.

Most middle-class north shore councils used the Residential District Proclamation provision of the 1919 Local Government Act to prohibit flat construction in all but a few selected areas. Lane Cove council proudly boasted in 1938 that it had 'very few flats'. The local history published in that year observed 'it might be easier to attempt to pass an Alderman through the eye of a needle than to get the Civic Fathers to relax on building restrictions'. (Its councillors experienced no such difficulty during another boom three decades later.) Trenchant opposition to flats was also adopted by councils in working-class areas, even those with a great deal of industry such as Botany, which had one of the lowest percentages of flats of any Sydney municipality.[37]

Both major political parties, the UAP and Labor, also opposed the building of flats. One opponent argued that 'the increase of population and vehicular traffic brought about by flats destroyed the tranquillity of a district', and that flats were 'unfavourable for the rearing of a family'.[38] Such complaints were the basis of opposition to the proposal by the Housing Improvement Board (established 1937) to construct a group of flats in Erskineville. Even the UAP government agreed that 'individual houses would be better', but argued that flats were the only dwellings that could be provided at a suitable rental.[39]

Despite much opposition, flat construction in Sydney in the thirties had a dramatic impact on the suburban landscape, especially in the areas where single-storey houses predominated. Flats comprised approximately 41 per cent of all dwellings built between 1933 and 1941. The scale of flat-building in Sydney was much greater than in its nearest rival, Melbourne, which gained 17,566 occupied flats between 1933 and 1947, less than half Sydney's figure. War and postwar shortages meant that most of these flats were actually constructed between 1934 and 1941.

Blocks of flats in Billyard Ave Potts Point built in the interwar years.
Postcard c. 1937

Various explanations have been advanced for why flat-building on such a scale was able to proceed despite much opposition. Robin Boyd argued later that it was 'town planners' (does he mean architects?) aligning themselves with 'the investors of depression money' that helped to overcome the opposition. There is some support for this in the activities of Florence Taylor, whose publications, particularly the trade journal *Building*, were vocal supporters of the boom in flats. While the ethos of the house and garden remained as dominant here as in any other Australian city, Sydney's reality diverged sharply. Increasing numbers of Sydneysiders lived in small flats rather than on quarter-acre blocks.[40]

Whatever the explanation, the boom in flats was so marked—over 500 blocks were constructed annually in Sydney between 1935 and 1941—and construction so unregulated, that by 1940 the NSW government was forced to introduce special building regulations. In March 1938 the Lord Mayor, Alderman Nock (of the well-known Nock & Kirby hardware store), had complained that the city council, which was not then subject to the Local Government Act, could not compel owners of flats to allow land for recreation purposes or prevent them from building on the total site area. Nock alleged that this was the cause of the congestion at Kings Cross.

Yet the flats also had their champions. The press liked to picture 'huge blocks of modern flats' with their attendant 'thronging crowds', as witness to the increasing sophistication of Sydney, and this compact form of housing had its adherents among architects.[41]

Flats were the antithesis of single-storey suburbia. They grew vertically and were located within easy access of the central city. Flat dwellers created their own communities within their individual block of flats and with surrounding blocks. In parts of Kirribilli, Neutral Bay, Elizabeth Bay and Manly almost everyone lived in flats or boarding houses. Flat dwellers, whether by deliberate choice or circumstance, were rejecting house and garden. So many Sydneysiders moved into flats in the 1920s and 1930s that this new form of urban accommodation was an important factor in containing suburban spread. The slow growth of car ownership in the thirties and forties ensured that suburbia remained contained.

Slums: 'overcrowding' at the centre

In January 1933 the *Labor Daily* informed its readers that the NSW birthrate in the year 1932 (17 births per 1000 people) was the lowest ever recorded. The drop was much more marked in the metropolis than in the rest of the state,

This photograph of Woolloomooloo emphasised untidy backyards.
F.O. Barnett and W.O. Burt, *Housing the Australian Nation*, Melbourne, 1942

and it was this that alarmed contemporary observers. The decline—and particularly the difference between Sydney and the rest of the state—made slum and housing reformers more vehement in condemning housing conditions in the inner city areas, where there was an alleged lack of necessary 'breathing space'. The South Australian journalist Paul McGuire observed that 'it is worth noticing that the best city birth-rates now are usually on the fringes where suburbs merge into the country-side and children have room to run'. McGuire overlooked the probability that the younger families of outer areas would naturally produce higher birthrates. Nor did such explanations occur to statistically naive slum reformers.[42]

In January 1935 the Protestant Churches' Debating Federation, following a lead given by the NSW Institute of Architects, forwarded a report on 'slum conditions in Sydney' to Premier Stevens. Other groups with a less altruistic interest in the subject were quick to take advantage of this new field of Christian charitable endeavour. In February the Master Builders Association urged 'a continuous and comprehensive policy for the abolition of decadent homes or decadent buildings [as] an essential part of the programme of national and State development'. In the following months the anti-slum campaign gathered force and the Labor press began to take up the issue. The Bricklayers' and Carpenters' Union came to the same conclusion as their employers had a few months earlier, and carried a resolution calling for 'an immediate campaign to abolish slum areas and to build better homes for the workers ...'. Speakers at the union meeting declared that besides providing better homes for the workers and abolishing 'city eyesores', such a scheme would assist employment.[43]

Encouraged by the support they had generated, the Debating Federation continued the campaign through radio and the press. In late July 1935 one of its members, N.H. Dick, a manufacturer and UAP member who lived in the harbourside suburb of Darling Point, wrote two articles for the *Herald* in which he urged the 'total elimination' of the slums, which he defined as the 'inner suburbs'. According to Dick, slums spread in a ring from Woolloomooloo Bay through Surry Hills, Paddington, Redfern, Newtown, Glebe, Pyrmont and Balmain, and extended south to Alexandria, Waterloo and Botany. Dick's geographical definition of the 'slums' was soon to be adopted in toto by Labor men such as William McKell who, unlike Dick, lived in Redfern, one of the condemned localities.[44]

The Debating Federation's radio broadcasts on the topic were received favourably by the Labor press under headlines such as *Labor Daily's* CHILDREN PLAY IN GUTTERS: SPEAKERS SAY SLUM AREAS MUST GO.[45] The Labor papers were joined by some Labor parliamentarians who took up slum reform because they wished the working man and his family to enjoy the same spacious suburban conditions as the middle classes. The existence of 'slums' was a physical expression of the gulf between the classes that they hoped to remove.

This desire may help to explain why McKell was so ready to collaborate with middle-class social reformers, even to the extent of advocating the demolition and rebuilding of his own suburb. McKell, an astute politician, could also see the political advantage to be gained by championing a cause that had the sympathy of the progressive middle class. This is precisely what he did in November 1935 when, as opposition spokesman, he gave an address on slums over the Labor radio station 2KY. A report of the speech appeared in the *Labor Daily* under the heading EVILS OF SLUM AREAS:

> Mr W. J. McKell, MLA ... stated that housing and slum clearance was one of the State's most important problems. The problem has become so acute, and its evil effects so far reaching, that leaders of the church, and social workers generally are becoming loud in their condemnation of Government inactivity ... It was only necessary, he said, to pay a brief visit to certain parts of the city, and the suburbs of Redfern, Paddington, Newtown, Glebe, Pyrmont, Balmain, Alexandria, Waterloo and Botany to appreciate the justice of the protests ...[46]

Erskineville Flats, indicating that children will still have room to play.
F.O. Barnett and W.O. Burt, *Housing the Australian Nation*, Melbourne, 1942

In December 1936 the Housing Conditions Investigation Committee, which included the town planner and architect Alfred John Brown, presented its report on Sydney's inner city 'slums'. The committee suggested that the 'slum problem' could be solved by demolishing and rebuilding according to specific guidelines. These included strict land use planning, possible under the zoning regulations of Fitzgerald's 1919 Local Government Act, which allowed for the declaration of residential, garden, school, industrial, shopping and sports areas. The committee put forward a proposal for a model residential area in Erskineville, consisting of two-storey flats set in gardens, which was eventually built in 1938–39.

Official portrait of the NSW Premier William McKell (1891–1985) c.1943

The main disadvantages of slum suburbs were attributed to the blighting effects of industry, warehousing, and heavy traffic, particularly around wharves. The main objections to the terrace houses (mostly built around 1870–1900) were their lack of ample gardens, their 'ugly and monotonous' appearance, their lack of adequate bathing and kitchen facilities (though most were sewered) and the fact that they were severely overcrowded.[47] Overcrowding was exacerbated by the collapse of the building industry and the inability of even employed working-class families to pay the rent for a whole house. But these circumstances were conveniently ignored by the reformers. They also ignored the fact that, as the 1933 census had shown, outer suburbs such as Bankstown and Holroyd had more persons per room than most of the inner city areas.

From the photographs in government reports condemning the slums we can see that the terraces did not have to be falling down to be condemned: most of those pictured were brick, and the backyard, not the house itself, was the common photographic target. Apart from the fact that terraces were thought to be intrinsically bad, the reformers and their bureaucratic allies seem to have been preoccupied with small disorderly backyards and untidy washing. The reformers recognised that there were reasons why people might choose to 'inhabit these slum areas'—to be near their work and 'for the companionship of old associations'—but that didn't deter them from promoting change.

The solution had two prongs: slum clearance and rebuilding in the inner areas, and new decentralised satellite towns to provide employment possibilities. The fate of the 'companionship of old associations'—the communities that

OVERLEAF pp 74–75 Cahill's promoted their restaurant chain with this map drawn by Cyril Samuels, c. 1941. An Aboriginal figure at La Perouse abuts Randwick Racecourse and the film studio at Pagewood. A Royal Sydney golfer has lost his club, while a boxer at the stadium has lost his head.

existed in the areas marked for demolition—did not concern the reformers. That most terrace houses, especially those built of brick, could be renovated and provided with missing facilities occurred to few people until the 1960s.[48]

In response to the slum reform campaign and their own belief in the advantages of suburban home ownership, Labor leaders continued to urge that the slums must go. Slum eradication found its most vocal and persistent Labor advocate in William McKell. On November 1939 he told Parliament that:

> One block of flats in Erskineville does not even make an appreciable dent in this city's slum problem ... Scarcely a day passes without the newspapers publishing some item or items relative to the appalling slum conditions ... The home life of the people is the real basis of our society ...

When McKell's party was elected in 1941 they finally had a chance to practise their own ideas about slum reform.

After 150 years: Sydney in 1938

Everyones, 18 March 1932

An opportunity to celebrate the virtues of the 'Harbour City' came during the celebrations for the sesquicentenary of European settlement in Australia, which opened on 27 January 1938 and coincided with the city's first Empire Games. The usual range of celebratory activities was organised and the usual complaints arose. The controversy over the high prices of seats for the 'pageant' was similar to the heated debate at the opening of the Sydney Opera House 36 years later. A number of local councils took the opportunity to organise histories of their municipalities while others produced pamphlets as a contribution to Australia's 150th anniversary celebrations. Lane Cove hoped that its production would help inculcate 'a greater local patriotism and civic pride', while the writer of *Back to Hornsby Week* praised the local Chamber of Commerce for surviving the Depression 'when so many similar organisations were abandoned'. Botany praised its unemployed ratepayers who worked on relief tasks in the Depression to pay off their rates.[49]

One group was less than enthusiastic about progress since 1788. On Australia Day, 26 January, the Aborigines of Australia declared a Day of Mourning for 'the 150th Anniversary of the Whiteman's seizure of our country', appealing to Australia 'to make new laws for the education and care of aborigines'. In a festive Sydney, with thousands of visitors and powderblue skies, the protesters were easily ignored.[50]

The celebrations provided an opportunity for Sydney chauvinists to praise their city. In the February 1938 issue of Sydney Ure-Smith's magazine *The Home,* Basil Burdett wrote:

> Golden beaches. Sun tanned men and maidens ... Red-roofed villas terraced above the blue waters of the harbour ... Even Melbourne seems like some grey and stately city of Northern Europe compared with Sydney's sub-tropical splendours ... There are a dozen other Sydneys at least—Sydney of the ocean suburbs, stark aggregations of brick dwellings, facing the sand and surf. The Sydney built on the sand dunes on the shores of

Home magazine's account of the eastern suburbs on the opening of the Sydney Harbour Bridge, including 'flatland', golfing, surfing at Bondi, the Coogee Ocean Pier, the City Railway and the Sydney Municipal Council's logo.

Artwork by Adrian Feint, *Home*, March 1932

CROW'S NEST
KURING-GAI CHASE
ADMIRALTY
GOAT ISD
UNDER GROUND RAILWAY
N.
W.
E.
S.
WYNYARD STN
CAHILL'S
HUNTER ST.
G P O
C.T.A. BLDG.
MARTIN PL.
GOVT HOUSE
GEORGE ST.
ROWE ST.
132 PITT ST.
51 CASTLE-REAGH ST.
ELIZABETH STREET
PHILLIP ST.
MACQUARIE ST.
KING ST.
MARKET ST.
PITT ST.
CASTLEREAGH
462 GEORGE ST.
PARK ST.
BATHURST ST.
LIVERPOOL ST.
TOWN HALL
MASCOT AIR PORT
KYEEMAGH
BOTANY BAY
PAGEWOOD

CREMORNE
MOSMAN
TARONGA ZOO
O.L
MRS MACQUARIE'S CHAIR
ROYAL SYDNEY
WOOLLOOMOOLOO
BONDI
WHITE CITY
WILLIAM STREET
KING'S +
30 DARLINGHURST RD.
CAHILL'S
STADIUM
OXFORD STREET
CRICKET
VICTORIA BARRACKS
CAHILL'S
RESTAURANTS
THE SHOW
RANDWICK
LA PEROUSE
CYRIL SAMUELS

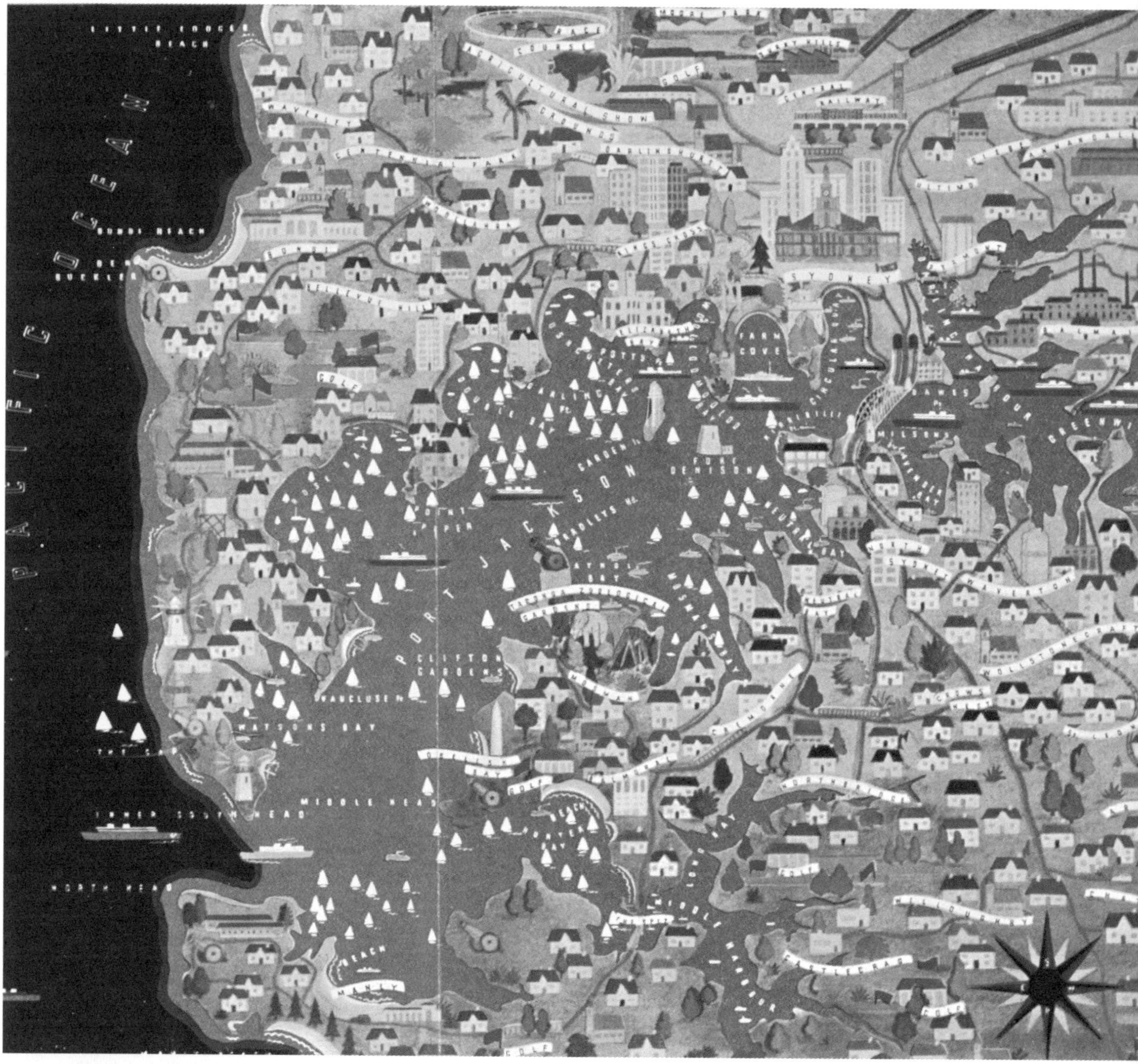

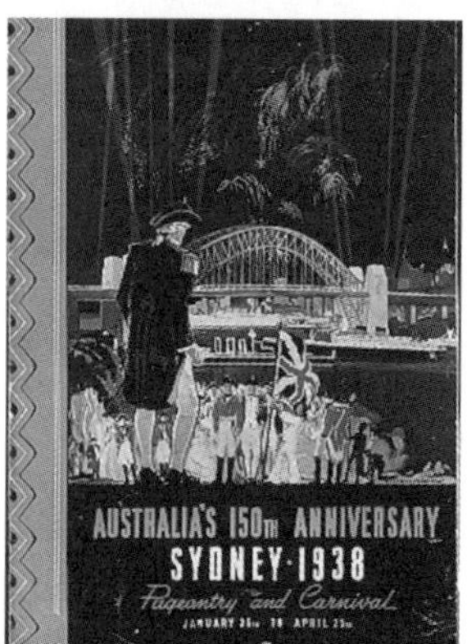

An unusual bird's eye view of Sydney, with a viewpoint from north to south, produced for this commemorative brochure, printed by Smith and Julius studios in Sydney, 1938. Houses, apartment blocks, power stations and gasometers dominate the landscape, along with the Macquarie Light House and the Quarantine Station at North Head.

> Botany Bay, the Sydney of the Northern Suburbs from St Leonards on the height over-looking the harbour to leafy Wahroonga and Warrawee, where houses dwell in acres of bushland and the streets are verdant ...

Enthusiasm for Sydney was not confined to its own residents and Burdett's themes were echoed by overseas observers. In 1939 the visiting British ballet writer, Arnold Haskell, wrote that 'life in Sydney is not a grim affair ... Outdoor pursuits are not a luxury but part of a well-ordered life'.[51] In comparison with European and North American cities Sydney's climate was very pleasant: no snow, adequate but not excessive rainfall, and most of the population within relatively easy reach of harbourside resorts, national parks and surfing beaches. Nor was it particularly expensive to get to these places by public transport. Almost all were accessible by bus, tram, train or ferry.

In 1940 P.R. Stephensen's magazine the *Publicist* published a series of articles by an American sociologist, Edward A. Ross, under the title 'A Look at Australia', based on 15 weeks spent in the country in 1938. Like Haskell, Ross noticed the importance of outdoor activities such as surfing, but he also revealed what he thought to be a seedier side of Australian urban life:

> As for the people of the Towns, one doubts their taking much thought of day-after-tomorrow. When I note the way they crowd the race tracks, bars and betting booths, the trash that they read if they read anything at all, their rapt intentness on sporting events that in a practical way can never mean a thing to them, I conclude that they are a year or two more adolescent than even average City Americans ...[52]

Ross did not approve of such working-class diversions, nor did he attempt to understand the all-male mateship culture of the ubiquitous local pub.

Arnold Haskell offered a different but equally misleading picture of Australian life: 'Unlike Melbourne, Sydney has its Cafe Society. The centre of this life is the Hotel Australia, an enormous modern hotel with five restaurants at varying prices. Everyone looks in at the Australia at least once a day.[53]' Prices at the Hotel Australia may have been 'varying' but a counter lunch in a local pub was cheaper still. Anzac Day, two-up, SP bookies and other forms of illegal gambling were more representative of Sydney society than the narrow clique at the Hotel Australia.

The insistence that all enjoyed—or could soon enjoy—the good life without much government intervention was sufficiently widespread throughout the electorate for the anti-Labor forces to prevail. The UAP fought the 1935 election with full-page slogans such as LANG IS STILL LANG—HIS BASIC WAGE THE DOLE.[54] Labor gained only five more seats than in its 1932 disaster, and only two of these in Sydney. In 1938 it gained only one further seat, again in Sydney. The UAP theme for this election was 'Hold Prosperity': the advertisement in the party magazine pictured a middle-class family plus car in a suburban setting with the growing city centre in the distance. This was a caricature of the good life: no doubt many people aspired to such a state, but for most the reality was otherwise. At the end of the thirties more than half the population still lived in rented houses, and few people could afford cars. Unemployment had not disappeared: up to 10 per cent of the workforce still went without jobs. The shadow lingered behind the bridge.

Yet the January 1939 editorial of *Building* magazine was headed AUSTRALIA IS PROSPEROUS: 'The manner in which Australia has risen from the slough of depression to achieve even higher pinnacles of progress than before the advent of this calamity has been indeed remarkable.' By that year Australian sales of the giant multinational Unilever company were 25 per cent higher than their 1929 turnover.[55] While Nazi Germany's aggressive acts often made the headlines in 1938, in January 1939 calm prosperity seemed assured. Nine months later war broke out in Europe, but it was some time before Sydneysiders realised how this second catastrophe would affect their city and their lives.

War comes to Sydney

Sydneysiders greeted the Second World War, which Australia entered with the 'mother country' on 3 September 1939, with bemused anxiety. The war certainly made life easier for newspaper headline writers: the *Daily News* of 2 December 1939 carried the following front page headlines: RUSSIANS ATTACK HELSINKI AGAIN and CROWD DANCES IN THE CITY. The second referred to the huge crowd that attended the lord mayor's annual fund-raising appeal in Martin Place, the site of so many troop parades in subsequent years.

'The Dinkum Game: AIF recruiting vans are visiting sports grounds in NSW appealing to young men to enlist.'
Ted Scorfield in the *Bulletin*, 14 May 1941

In the best traditions of concerned capitalism, the Sydney-based business magazine *Rydge's* headed its editorial of October 1939, HOW WILL WAR AFFECT BUSINESS?:

> now that this first shock of the declaration of war is gradually passing away, businessmen are confident of the future and see ahead stabilised, in fact, boom conditions ... Probably within six months it will be impossible to find an unemployed man in Australia. The large government expenditure and the boom in trade will make jobs available for everybody.

The uncertainty of the early months of the phoney war was concealed beneath a carnival spirit, illustrated by newspaper reports of New Year's Eve 1940 when, according to the *Daily News*, '40,000 revellers took complete charge of King's Cross'. Five months later France fell to the German army and Dunkirk was evacuated. Now the war began to have a more tangible impact on life in Sydney, though the battle itself was still many thousands of miles away. Demonstration air raid shelters were established in the Sydney Domain in July 1940 as a guide to those who wished to make their own. Shelters were also constructed in Hyde Park, and the unused tunnel sections of the yet-to-be-completed Quay Railway were prepared for the same purpose.

Not everyone took these preparations seriously. At the end of the year students at the University of Sydney titled their annual review '1940 and All That'. Among the cast of a satire on the League of Nations was E.G. Whitlam (later prime minister of Australia) as the British Prime Minister, Neville Chamberlain. In mid-1941 the Domain shelters were closed by barbed wire barricades as a precaution against vandals and unauthorised use.[56]

Nicholsons Pty Ltd, the publisher of this sheet music, were to be found just down George St from the Town Hall.
The AIF is Marching, 1940

The Japanese attack on Pearl Harbor in the Hawaiian Islands on 7 December 1941 took the USA by surprise. Although many had feared the prospect of Japan entering the war, the magnitude of its assault, which wiped out most of the US Pacific fleet, stunned Australians. So did the air attack on Port Moresby on 4 February 1942 and the fall of Singapore to Japanese forces 11 days later. The war was drawing perilously close to Australian soil. Four days later the Japanese launched an enormous air attack on Darwin. Then, on the evening of 31 May 1942, three Japanese midget submarines entered Sydney Harbour. One became entangled in the boom net at the entrance to the harbour and was destroyed by its crew. Another remains unaccounted for, while the third fired a torpedo at the HMAS *Kuttabul*, a ferry turned depot ship, killing 19. That third submarine was later attacked and sunk.

This 1942 guide advised servicemen and women where to get free and 'small change' meals, about cabarets, surf beaches and prophylactic ('Blue Light') centres.

Press reports of the incident were heavily censored but harbourside residents witnessed much of the action. Speculation, fuelled by shelling of Sydney and Newcastle by Japanese submarines on 7 June, became mixed with rumour and gossip. The *Australian National Journal*, a Sydney-based monthly that continued to publish through the war (on much cheaper paper), nicely captured the mood in its July 1942 issue, with a dash of racism and a droll comment on Australian cooking:

> Sydney has not been able to complain so bitterly of gloomy Sundays, as the Japs have been doing their little best to brighten things up. Harboursiders found themselves provided with ringside seats for the first show. The seeping into the harbour of midget submarines, the quick discovery of their presence, the hunt which was up in a matter of moments, their destruction and the eventual raising of the remnants from the harbour bed—this was a real show, and Sydney's first faint introduction to war. (Incidentally, the number of people who saw subs surfacing, or gliding through the water like shadows, or could practically touch them, my dear, have to be heard to be partly believed) ...
>
> Rumours are flying that at any moment foodstuffs will appear on the rationed lists, and there is much speculation as to how stringent these rations will be and what effect it will have on our kitchens. There is very little doubt that normally we have some of the best food in the world before it goes into our kitchens, and there is no doubt at all that we have some of the worst food in the world after it comes out.

Prime Minister Curtin told Australians that they might not 'be spared the horror of air raids and the threat of invasion'.
Magazine advertisment, 1942

The building revival of the late thirties had continued during the early war years. In December 1940 the federal government, under National Security Regulations, required that consent be obtained for all buildings costing over £5000. The regulations were gradually tightened and by June 1942 the limit was £25, covering repairs as well. The number of buildings completed in Sydney fell from 8138 in 1940 to 582 in 1943, impressive evidence of the power of central government to regulate an economy in times of crisis. This contraction of the building industry for all but essential government projects proved even more severe than the partial collapse of the industry in the Depression. While 528 building permits were issued in 1931, in wartime 1943 only 258 were issued.

One attack on the building restrictions came from a government member, Rowland James, the Labor MHR for the mining seat of Hunter, who claimed that the restrictions would have their severest effect on 'working-class people' who had lived for many years in shacks, bag humpies and tents. Despite attacks, the regulations were not significantly eased until August 1945 when permits were no longer required for single unit dwelling houses costing less than £1200.[57]

Most projects under way at the outbreak of war were completed despite the hostilities, but by 1942 building was virtually confined to government works. Some major projects, including the King George V hospital for mothers and babies near Sydney University, which opened in 1941, were thought integral to the national effort. Among the biggest wartime construction undertakings were the Captain Cook Graving Dock at Garden Island and the Concord Repatriation Hospital. The latter, on the Parramatta River, opened in 1942. Controversy over the siting of the dock between Garden Island and Potts Point flared in October 1940, although construction had begun in July. The location, so close to the city heart, was criticised by both Labor and non-Labor city aldermen. Objections ranged from the fear that 'the proposed site would invite catastrophe for the 100,000 citizens living in the area' to the assertion in the *Sydney Morning Herald* that:

> the dock cannot be of the slightest use in this war. They say it will take three years to build. To judge by the time needed to build the city railway and the harbour bridge, the dock will take double the three years estimated.[58]

Constructing the dock was a spectacular event in a city where most building had already come to a halt. A labour force of 3500 men reclaimed 30 acres from the harbour for the complex. 'All day and throughout the night in the blaze of myriad lights which contrasted strikingly with the blacked-out city, thousands of men laboured in a scene of almost bewildering activity.' The war in Europe was almost over by the time the dock was open for shipping in March 1945, but the British Pacific Fleet used it for the final drive on Japan.[59]

The Metropolitan Water, Sewerage & Drainage Board had assisted in the dock construction. The war had deferred work on the board's most important and ambitious project, the Warragamba Dam, a major storage essential to amplify Sydney's water supply. The city had been in the grip of an unusually dry period since 1934, and by 1937 a new weir had to be built above the site selected for the dam to supplement the inadequate Upper Nepean system.

Other wartime building in Sydney included vast munitions factories at Villawood and St Mary's, armed forces barracks at various sites, and service hospitals at Herne Bay (near Riverwood station in Hurstville municipality) and Hargrave Park (in Liverpool municipality). The Department of Main Roads and the MWSDB were both called on to aid in these projects.[60] The Wakehurst Parkway from Seaforth to Narrabeen through the sandstone plateau country of French's Forest provided the army with an alternative route to the coast. The country it traversed was largely unsettled, but today only the recreation reserve between Oxford Falls and Narrabeen Lagoon remains bushland.

As well as restrictions on building, wartime controls were extended to such commodities as food, clothing, petrol, tobacco and liquor. These items were all rationed and some were also subject to price control.[61] For the urban development of Sydney the most significant controls were building restrictions, petrol rationing (which prolonged the primacy of public transport for another decade) and rent control. The Fair Rents Act, introduced by the non-Labor state government in September 1939, was greatly strengthened by the Commonwealth Rent Control Regulations during and after 1941. One member of the Real Estate Institute of NSW complained that the regulations 'surround the tenant with protection to a degree never approached before in our history'.[62]

Produced by the Parents and Citizens Association early in 1945, this campaign encouraged school students to raise one penny for each pinhole in the sixty milestones between Tokyo and Sydney.

Rent control regulations meant that rent could not exceed that payable at the prescribed date (31 August 1939 in NSW). For premises not then in existence or leased, the prescribed date was 1 March 1945. Fair Rents Boards were set up under the Landlord and Tenant Regulations in December 1941 and they were empowered to control dwelling rents not exceeding £4/4/- per week. In March 1943 the limit was raised to £10 per week, and in June 1944 the powers were extended to all prescribed premises irrespective of rent (the only exceptions were licensed premises and holiday accommodation).[63]

Peace, and the housing shortage

The European war ended in May and the Pacific war in August 1945. 'Everywhere jubilant crowds gathered in the streets', recalled Paul Hasluck.[64] Demobilisation was not immediate, but as a writer in the army magazine *Salt* observed that

A squatter climbs in through the window of Maramonah in April 1946.
Pix, 30 April 1946

although the warships 'riding at anchor in Sydney's matchless harbour' still reminded the city of war, peace had definitely arrived. 'Expectancy is in the air ... Everybody wants to go some place soon. There is talk of big expansion, whispers of roaring days to come. Sydney is straining at the leash.'[65] And so were most of the troops: the final issue of *Salt* in April 1946 included advice on marriage and how to avoid venereal disease.

The war had a lasting effect on Sydney: it could not have been otherwise. 'For six years the whole world seemed to come to Sydney. Through its harbour portals streamed Americans, British, French—soldiers, sailors, airmen of many nations.'[66] Other effects of the war, such as the impact of rationing, were not peculiar to Sydney but, with Brisbane and Townsville, the city had experienced a much greater influx of American troops than other Australian cities. The victory was celebrated, as always, in Martin Place. Five years later the poet Kenneth Slessor wondered what it all meant:

> [T]hrough this valley of sandstone, successive columns of Australian fighting men have marched, going to the wars and returning from the wars. Here managing directors and office-girls danced hand-in-hand and tore up snowstorms of paper on what they thought was Victory Day ...[67]

The return to peace was not unplanned. A few months after the war began, William McKell, Labor opposition leader at the time, urged the necessity for social reconstruction,[68] a plea taken up by both Labor and non-Labor supporters. In 1941 Brian Penton, the editor of the Sydney *Daily Telegraph*, published his *Think or Be Damned*. I. Clunies Ross's *Should We Plan for Peace?* also appeared in 1941, while H.D. Black, a lecturer in economics at Sydney University, wrote in the *Daily Telegraph* that 'when peace comes it may be a calamity because we have done no post-war planning in Australia'.[69] In December 1942 the federal Labor government established a Department of Postwar Reconstruction, charged with preparing the way for the postwar world. One of its first tasks was to find ways of overcoming the growing housing shortage.

That shortage, and the need to eradicate inner city 'slums', were among the chief concerns of the postwar reconstruction literature. In April 1943 the federal government appointed a Commonwealth Housing Commission, which was to report to J.B. Chifley, the minister of state for Postwar Reconstruction, on the condition and future requirements of housing in the 'post-war period'.

Concern about the housing shortage had increased markedly during the war. On 27 June 1941 the president of the Real Estate Institute of NSW outlined what he saw as the reasons for Sydney's housing shortage: petrol rationing 'compelling people in outer suburbs to move closer to town', and the influx of workers from other states coming to Sydney for employment in war industries.[70] But despite their complaints, real estate agents received little sympathy, one economist from the Bank of New South Wales arguing that 'every building put up now is depriving us of bombers and tanks'.[71] This view reflected government policy. Both the private sector and the NSW Housing Commission (created by the new McKell Labor government in 1941) were severely restricted in their activities. Most of the commission's work consisted of the construction of temporary houses and hostels for the employees of munitions factories. These 'temporary' dwellings provided postwar migrants with their first taste of life in Sydney's suburbs.

The Real Estate Institute of NSW lobbied through the war years for a lifting of building restrictions as a way to ease the housing shortage.[72] In April 1943 Sir Arthur Rickard, president of the Millions Club (a group devoted to boosting population growth), estimated the housing shortage in Sydney to be between 35,000 and 45,000 houses. Sir Arthur also noted the close relationship between the social class of an area's inhabitants and the amount of building in progress.

The August 1944 Commonwealth Housing Commission Report pointed out, as the Real Estate Institute had done, that the prewar housing shortage was exacerbated by 'the practical cessation of all civil building during the war'. It further suggested that the shortage would be increased by the discharge of defence personnel, the prospect of general demobilisation, and the demand for separate dwellings due to wartime and postwar marriages. As well as constructing new dwellings, the commission also wished to make 'slum clearance' a major part of the housing program.

Hard facts on the extent of the shortage were not a feature of the Commonwealth report, on the grounds that the available information was meagre, but the NSW Labor government had fewer reservations about the lack of data and was quite happy to put a figure on the housing shortage in Sydney, no doubt in an attempt to gain increased Commonwealth aid. McKell, reviewing the housing shortage in 1946, summarised it thus:

> Taking the rate of building before the depression as 'normal'—10,000 new dwellings a year in Sydney and suburbs—we 'lost' over 45,000 new houses and flats during the depression. It was not until 1938 that the pre-depression figure was reached again ... And then came the War! This meant another six years during which house-building slowed down and then practically stopped ... In Sydney and suburbs we 'lost' during the war almost another 45,000 new homes ... The end of the war found us about 90,000 homes 'short'.[73]

The housing shortage and its causes were much discussed at the time, especially by Jack Lang, whom McKell had defeated in September 1939 for the leadership of the state Labor Party. In his newspaper *Century* (founded in 1938 after he lost control of the *Labor Daily*), Lang attacked the state Labor government for neither building houses nor granting permits to build. In questioning this policy Lang pointed to the black market in building to support his belief that more could be done.[74]

In March 1946, 600 people attended a meeting convened by 'squatters', homeless people occupying Maramonah, a 'mansion' acquired by the City Council for what is now a park at Kings Cross. The Civic Reform Lord Mayor, R.J. Bartley, a company director and resident of Vaucluse, told the meeting he regretted that the issue had become one between 'Communists and lawful authority'; a member of the Communist Party attacked the mayor over the council's park proposal. Two days after the Kings Cross occupation, ex-servicemen seized a 100-room, four-storey apartment house at Bondi, claiming that they and their families were living in conditions of extreme hardship.[75] Such actions were similar to the anti-eviction battles of the Depression years and have a counterpart in the much publicised 'Battle of Kings Cross' almost 30 years later, when police were called in to remove squatters from terrace housing in Victoria Street that was about to be demolished.

The McKell government was worried by these protests, especially at a time when Labor was facing outspoken criticism from the Communist Party, which was strengthening its position in the unions. The Labor member for Bondi, Abram Landa, opined: 'I do not believe that "squatting" ought to be allowed ... If we are going to ignore proprietary rights altogether, then the whole system under which we are living must go by the board.'[76] For humanitarian reasons, and to prevent such a situation developing, the McKell government had initiated state Housing Commission action some months before. By May 1946 the government could boast that the commission was completing new homes at the rate of 200 a month, which was more than 'all the other states combined'.[77] Finance for the new homes was provided by the Commonwealth–State Housing Agreement Act of 1945 (a direct result of the 1944 report), which made it possible for the states to undertake, for the first time, large-scale programs of welfare housing. But by 1947–48 the commission had become frustrated with the timelag in providing the facilities for its projects 'on the outskirts of the city' and began to turn more attention to the longstanding question of slum clearance.[78]

'Slum' clearance

McKell and the Housing Commission came under particularly strong pressure from the left-wing press, which became an enthusiastic advocate of slum clearance and town planning. On 31 January 1947 the communist newspaper *Tribune* complained that while thousands of workers lived in 'slums, single rooms or tents, and children are banned from school for lack of classrooms, the Sydney Turf Club, a semi-government body, is building magnificent new accommodation for racehorses at Rosehill.' There was even more class bitterness a week later when *Tribune* alleged that 'slums, squalor and suffering are the heritage which Mr McKell leaves behind him in Redfern' as he departs as Governor-General 'for the millionaire standards of Yarralumla'.

The announcement of Labor's slum clearance program in 1947 roused one critic, significantly a builder who, while accepting the conventional wisdom about inner city housing as 'slums', argued that the time for elimination was not 'opportune':

> [I]f attempted it can only intensify the housing shortage ... Most of the dwellings are served by such essentials as proper sewerage and sullage drains, gas and electricity. There may be leaking roofs, broken windows and other damage, all of which could be temporarily repaired ... Any industrious person can make almost anything into a home even without the facilities that these city slums possess ... The local municipal councils have power to compel a landlord to carry out structural repairs but apparently are not doing so ...[79]

In a subsequent letter, this member of the building trade contrasted inner city housing with conditions at the outer metropolitan northern suburb of French's Forest, where people lived 'without sanitation, in disused army camps and garages, and whole families living in one rented room'. The original letter brought a spate of replies. The town clerk of Glebe complained of 'parents attempting to raise a family in a hovel constructed 100 years ago of sand-stock bricks'. Another letter came from the superintendent of the Paddington Christian Community Centre who wrote that:

> disease, crime, anti-social behaviour of various kinds, cramped and distorted attitudes and the like can all be traced to the deplorable and depressing environment in which thousands now live. This is not to say, of course, that a new and better environment is the only solution. But in most cases the first step to taking the slum out of man is to take the man out of the slum.[80]

Such Christian socialist views prevailed, and found support in the Cumberland County Plan report of July 1948, prepared under the auspices of the Redfern-born Labor minister for Local Government, J.J. Cahill. The report condemned as slums exactly the same area that N.H. Dick and McKell had condemned in the thirties. The report also observed that:

> the extent of home ownership, generally regarded as the most effective safeguard against obsolescence, was always small. Sample surveys carried out in the Darlington and Redfern areas reveal that 95 per cent of the occupants of houses are tenants, and it is estimated that for the whole of the inner areas 92 per cent are tenant-occupied.[81]

In the next 20 years redevelopment took place on a much smaller scale than originally intended. One of the major factors in the change of direction, and one not predicted by the Cumberland Plan of 1948, was the spectacular increase in the number of owner-occupied properties in the so-called slum areas. Twenty-five years later a study of one section of Redfern found that while 6 per cent of residential properties were owner-occupied in 1947 (which corroborates Cumberland's tenancy figure), by 1956 it was 31 per cent and by 1969 had risen to 68 per cent. In these years the Cumberland Plan's main criterion for safeguarding 'against obsolescence' was met, as home ownership grew dramatically. Despite the hopes for slum reform, the main theatre of action in postwar Sydney was not demolition in the inner areas but house building in the middle and outer suburbs: it is to them and their growing population that we now turn.[82]

PERSONS
25

CHAPTER 5

Homes for the people

Much as one may love Britain, one has to admit that these days it is becoming pretty crowded, while Australia still offers the attractions of space and opportunity.

FACING PAGE
British migrants get their first look at Sydney from the *Fairsea*, 1968.
National Library of Australia

Thus were migrants lured to Australia after the Second World War, and from 1948 they came in tens of thousands. Over three-quarters of Sydney's population growth between 1947 and 1971 came from immigrants and their Australian-born children. Internal migration was of little importance: between 1947 and 1954 Sydney actually lost 42,891 Australian-born to other parts of the country, while gaining a similar number in the next intercensal period, 1954–61.[1] The proportion of Sydney's population born overseas is shown in Table 5.1.

Table 5.1: Proportion of overseas-born in the Sydney region 1911–96 (percentages)

1911	21.4
1921	20.2
1933	16.6
1947	12.8
1961	19.8
1976	24.4
1986	27.1
1996	30.7

Source: Commonwealth censuses.

Before the Second World War the state governments, with their agents-general in London, attempted to attract British migrants with the promise of sun and agricultural prosperity; after the war the responsibility for attracting migrants passed, irrevocably, to the much-strengthened federal government. The motives of the federal Labor government in fostering migration were a mixture of altruism and a desire to facilitate economic growth. 'Displaced persons' were allowed entry along with British and Continental European migrants. Labor managed to gain approval for its policy from both industry and trade unions, the former attracted by the prospects of cheap labour and the latter consenting because Australian workers were not rushing to take the manual jobs that were filled by migrants.[2]

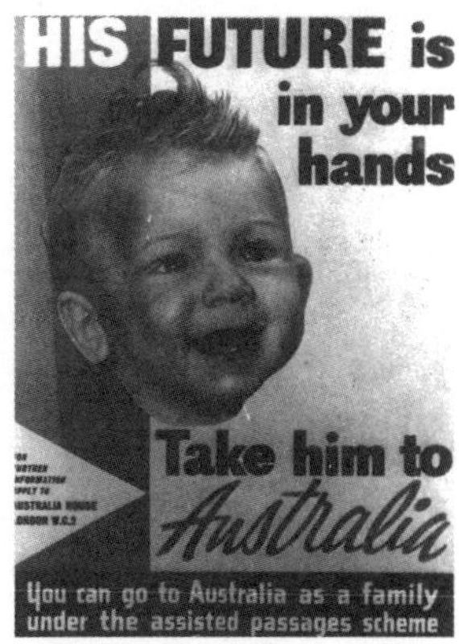

This 1958 poster aimed to get Britons and their children to migrate to Australia.

In 1947 only 13 per cent of Sydney's population was foreign-born; by 1966 the figure had grown to 22 per cent. Between those two dates the number of people in Sydney born overseas increased by 329,320, the biggest intake of immigrants Sydney ever received, much greater than those earlier peaks of 1871–91 and 1911–33. But Melbourne, with 409,724 arrivals in the same period, was the largest centre of postwar migrant settlement. In the 1980s and 1990s Sydney would become the largest centre of migrant settlement in Australia (see chapter 10), attracting over one-third of all Asian migrants. The birthplace of Sydney's population 1947–96 is shown in Table 5.2.

British migrants were by far the biggest group: at the 1966 census they accounted for 39 per cent of the foreign-born in Sydney. A typical British account of Australia promoted Sydney as 'the second white city of Empire', its Harbour Bridge a masterpiece of 'British engineering' set in a city with 'an ever-present holiday atmosphere'.[3] Potential migrants were reassured that they would not see 'our Aborigines; Abos, as we call them ... Today the Abos live in the back of beyond.' Despite the White Australia Policy, 'the individual Aussie couldn't care less whether the man working alongside him is coloured or not'.[4]

Most Aborigines lived at that time on mission stations, not 'in the back of beyond'. They did not have the vote nor did they have adequate health, housing or education. Sydney did have a small but growing Aboriginal community at La Perouse, founded in the 1880s. By the 1930s the settlement had become a well-known tourist attraction; in the words of one guidebook, 'the blacks are always ready to entertain visitors by Boomerang throwing, and they sell some cleverly-made shell work in imitation of flowers'.[5] Until the growth of Aboriginal migration to Sydney in the postwar years, Sydneysiders had been able to ignore their existence, but the growing numbers of Aborigines in parts of the inner city, especially after 1960, made white metropolitan Australians more aware that the first Australians were much more disadvantaged than the foreign-born.[6]

The migrant presence

Front cover, *Migrant Australia.*
Mills & Boon, London 1960

Migrants had a marked effect on Sydney, though at first their influence was largely confined to particular areas. Some localities, such as Kings Cross, had long been the centre of an immigrant culture, and naturally became a focal point for new immigrants. In *King's Cross Calling* two authors described the scene in 1945:

> Behind Con's shop is the most cosmopolitan room in the Cross ... Con is a Greek; his wife comes from Mount Lebanon. Over a game of poker ... are patriots from Turkey, Syria, Arabia, France, Russia, Greece, faces so representative of their countries that a casual glance will classify them ... And, threading his way through all, belonging to all yet bound to a race of his own more ancient than theirs, is that intrepid international, the Jew ...[7]

Kings Cross was also one of the settings that the Czech immigrant V.L. Borin chose for his 1959 novel *The Uprooted Survive: A Tale of Two Continents.* One of Borin's characters, arriving at Kings Cross at eight o'clock one night, saw at a glance that 'this was Europe in Australia—the shops open, the streets full of people walking nowhere and talking loudly together'.[8]

'Cosmopolitan' became a frequently used word in the postwar period, since it banished anxiety that Australian civilisation might be bland and dull. Increasingly, restaurants advertised themselves as offering both 'continental and Australian' cuisine. The influx of migrants was welcomed by some for bringing variety and tolerance to Australian life. As journalist Sarah Dunne observed in 1949:

> Little Australian children are learning and playing side by side with school fellows from many lands. Foreign voices, foreign languages are heard daily in trams, trains or along country roads. Continental cakes and foreign foods are on sale in every Australian city. European craftwork is in the shops. Australia is growing up and becoming more cosmopolitan.[9]

Not everyone welcomed the change. Epithets such as 'pommy', 'dago', 'Balt', and 'reffo' were often used to describe the new Australians, with either humorous or abusive intent. In a country that had prided itself on being 98 per cent British in origin, resistance to foreign immigrants was not surprising.[10] Even the British

Table 5.2: Sydney's population by birthplace 1947–96, as percentage of total population

	1947	1961	1971	1986	1996
Africa[1]	0.1	0.5	0.8	0.8	1.0
Asia	0.4	1.2	2.3.	n.a	n.a.
Asia, excl. China, HK, Philippines, Vietnam	n.a.	n.a.	n.a.	1.7	3.6
Americas[2]	0.2	0.3	0.7	0.7	0.9
China, HK, excl Taiwin	n.a.	n.a.	n.a.	1.0	2.9
Europe, excl. Greece, Italy, former Yugoslavia	1.0	5.3	5.2	3.4	2.9
Greece	0.2	0.9	1.7	1.2	1.1
Italy	0.3	2.0	2.3	1.8	1.5
Lebanon	n.a.	n.a.	n.a.	1.2	1.5
New Zealand	1.1	0.9	1.0	1.6	1.9
Philippines	n.a.	n.a.	n.a.	.4	1.2
UK and Ireland	9.3	8.2	9.1	6.9	6.0
Vietnam	n.a.	n.a.	n.a.	1.0	1.7
Yugoslavia, Former	0.02	0.5	1.4	1.3	1.5
All other	0.2	0.1	0.3	3.4	5.0
Not stated	n.a.	n.a.	n.a.	1.8	3.9
Australia	87.1	80.2	75.1	71.0	69.7

1 Comprises Egypt and South Africa 1986 and 1996.
2 Comprises Canada, Chile, USA 1986 and 1996.
Source: Commonwealth censuses 1947–96.

came under criticism for being 'whingers'. The English commentator Malcolm Muggeridge noted the contrast between British and non-British migrant hostels in Sydney in an article for the *Sydney Morning Herald* on 16 April 1958:

> One meets the less favoured migrants in hostels ... well run, but communal life cannot but be unattractive to families. To the English temperament particularly it is abhorrent ... most of the British migrants who have to stay in one for any length of time become unhappy, cantankerous and obsessed with nostalgic memories of their former circumstances. In the non-British hostels the mood was very different. Most of the migrants in them have come from, or have experienced, hard and cruel conditions ...

Migrant hostels were rarely pleasant environments, often consisting of barely converted wartime army huts, many of them made of arched corrugated iron. The main hostels were at Bradfield (in the south-west corner of Ku-ring-gai), Leighton field (on the Liverpool line), Cabramatta, Hammondville (on the edge of the Holsworthy military reserve) and Randwick. It was a measure of Australians' ambivalence towards migrants and the immigration program that it took so long to replace the barrack-like hostels with more attractive accommodation.

Non-British migrants were frequently associated in the popular mind with particular occupations. Some of these stereotypes were founded in statistical fact: by 1961 nearly half the shopkeepers in Melbourne and Sydney were born outside Australia. To many Australians these shops seemed like goldmines for their owners, but as James Jupp remarked in his *Arrivals and Departures*, this was only so for the very industrious.[11]

"But all I want is corn beef and cabbage!"

Emile Mercier, *Hold It!*, Angus & Robertson, Sydney, 1960

The problems faced by newly arrived migrants in Sydney were depicted in the best-selling novel *They're a Weird Mob*, which purported to be the autobiography of an Italian immigrant, Nino Culotta. The author was actually the Australian-born John O'Grady, a pharmacist educated at the University of Sydney, who took time off in 1954–55 to become a builder's labourer and bricklayer and later turned to full-time writing. Published in 1957 and filmed in 1966, *They're a Weird Mob* describes the arrival in Sydney of an Italian immigrant in the mid-fifties and his search for a job. His first employment as a builder's labourer provides vivid descriptions of life on the job, no doubt based on O'Grady's own experience. Like others accounts of the 'new immigrant arrives in Sydney', Culotta's introduction to the city is through the ubiquitous taxi driver:

> 'Kings Cross. Three bob.'
> 'Excuse me, sir, but do you mind telling me where I now am?'
> He shouted very loudly KINGS BLOODY CROSS!

New immigrant arrives in Sydney.
Front cover, *They're a Weird Mob*, Ure Smith, 1963

The problems of replying to advertisements for his first job were no easier: 'What mean these letters and figures? Are they a telephone number?' To which the newsboy replied 'Ain't a cricket score, sport ...'[12]

For social and economic reasons migrants tended to settle in particular regions of Sydney. This was especially true of Greek and Italian migrants, who accounted for 8 and 10 per cent respectively of the foreign-born in Sydney in 1966. Most Italian migrants arrived in Australia between 1948 and 1961 and congregated in the near-city municipalities of Leichhardt, Ashfield, Drummoyne and Concord, while smaller concentrations in Warringah and Fairfield were based on already existing market-gardening communities. The Greeks, most of whom arrived after 1961, tended to concentrate to the immediate south of the Italians, in the municipalities of Sydney, Marrickville, South Sydney and Botany.[13]

British migrants, 37 per cent of the foreign-born in Sydney by 1971, were much more dispersed than other immigrant groups. The majority settled on the urban fringe in every direction, while the better off were attracted to near-city middle-class suburbs. British migrants tended to avoid areas with high Italian or Greek concentrations. Meanwhile, the inner city municipalities experienced a decline in the Australian-born population, who, if they could afford it, were tempted to move to new suburban subdivisions.

In the words of Donald Horne, migrants gave Australian cities 'a much greater diversity of richness and texture' but because they and their children accounted for over three-quarters of Sydney's population growth between 1947 and 1971 they also contributed to the city's biggest problem: they had to be housed.[14] So, too, did those Australians who had lived through the war and early postwar years in overcrowded conditions.

Planning postwar suburbia

At an election meeting at Redfern Town Hall in May 1947, the former Labor Premier Jack Lang admitted the existence of 'unbounded prosperity' in the country but asked what the 'toiling masses' got out of it. 'A leaking roof', answered a voice from the hall. Housing was the overriding issue of the 1947 election. Labor Premier McGirr promised that the government would build 90,000 homes for the people of New South Wales within three years.[15] Labor won the election and remained in power until 1965. To implement its housing and planning promises the government had established a Housing Commission in 1941: in 1945 it amended the Local Government Act to establish the Cumberland County Council, which would draw up a metropolitan planning scheme.

One of the chief concerns of the *County of Cumberland Planning Scheme Report*, presented in 1948, was to set out guidelines for the orderly development of postwar suburbs. Such a grand planning exercise had never before been attempted; though differently expressed, the report's proposals were similar to those advocated by Hugh Stretton in his influential book *Ideas for Australian Cities* more than 20 years later. The tone of the report was ambitious:

> If it were said that every home should have sewerage; that it should have frontage to a street possessing a footpath, kerbing, guttering and carriageway; that the children should be able to reach their schools without being exposed to dangers on main traffic arteries; that the housewife should reach the local shop or baby clinic by a convenient walk; that the breadwinner should reach his place of employment without fatigue and at reasonable cost; that the whole family should participate in regular outdoor recreation in conveniently placed open spaces—if it were said that a home needed all these things to make it worth living in, it would not be an unreasonable demand. Yet it is surprising how many thousands of homes in the county do not possess these features or even half of them. It is the aim of the Plan for living areas, in association with other elements of the Plan, and with local planning, to provide for these things in full measure.[16]

Cumberland County Council brochure, 1946

Though not an 'unreasonable demand', it was nevertheless difficult to achieve. Many of the proposals—such as ridding Sydney of its slums—reflected the preoccupations of the interwar period, while the objections to suburban sprawl were a reaction to the virtually unregulated subdivision boom of the 1920s. The report pointed out that five large Bankstown estates, subdivided in 1923 and totalling over 4000 lots, accommodated only 110 houses in 1948, a quarter of a century later. 'Subdivided and sold on the pretext that major projects, such as new railways and tramways were to be undertaken, they remain vast stretches of waste land, useless to the holder and equally useless for farming purposes ...' The situation was worst in the outer suburbs of Bankstown, Blacktown, Sutherland and Warringah, where the number of vacant lots was almost twice the number of the existing, scattered houses.[17]

The Cumberland report also complained about the 'undesirable concentration' of employment and administration in the City of Sydney, traffic congestion in both the city and the suburbs, conflicting land uses due to inadequate zoning, and a serious shortage of open space. In place of all this the report recommended urban districts, each with a centre for business, entertainment, cultural activities, educational facilities and scope for local employment. These land uses would be allocated by careful zoning. Encircling the urban districts was to be 'a girdle of countryside', the Green Belt, which would ensure 'for all time ready access to rural surroundings'. A coordinated rail and road network would link the city with the urban and rural districts, providing for both radial and circumferential traffic.[18]

It was a brave plan, but in the 20 years after its delayed implementation in 1951 many things went wrong. The 1954 census revealed that the rate of population growth in the county was about twice that predicted in 1948. Moreover, the plan faltered because the assessments of future needs did not match the estimate of potential resources. Its implementation depended on the cooperation of other government departments and authorities, not always apparent in the actions of the Housing Commission, the Department of Main Roads and the Metropolitan Water, Sewerage and Drainage Board. These instrumentalities were among the most important forces in shaping postwar suburbia.

Building postwar suburbia

Under the state Labor government the NSW Housing Commission became a champion of suburban family house building. The commission boasted that its guidelines made it 'impossible for sub-standard conditions ever to develop' on its estates. These included minimum allotment areas of 6000 square feet, with street frontages of not less than 50 feet and distances of not less than 14 feet between adjoining dwellings. These were among the facts proclaimed in a large glossy 1949 commission publication entitled *Homes for the People*, with an introduction by James McGirr. Billed as the first 'Minister for Housing' in NSW (although a Ministry of Housing existed from July 1919 to December 1921), McGirr had succeeded McKell to the premiership in February 1947.

Front cover, NSW Housing Commission Brochure, 1949

The booklet included plans of housing-scheme layouts and homes, pictures of exteriors and interiors and construction details. Designs of cottages to cater for every family need were prepared, ranging from two to four bedrooms, to be built in fibro, brick or timber. The aim of the design was to provide 'a comfortable well-appointed dwelling for every family in the community'. 'The neatly designed floor layout is an example of basic architectural policy to plan sleeping and living quarters as distinctly definite portions of the home'. Most commission houses had tiled (rather than corrugated iron) roofs, to add 'tone' to their appearance.

The larger of the commission estates gave planners an opportunity to demonstrate many of the ideas about neighbourhood design that the housing reformers of the thirties had advocated. By 1976 the largest estates in Sydney were those planned at Villawood (2138 houses), Dundas (2558), Green Valley (6373), Lalor Park (2759), and the enormous complex at Mt Druitt (9150). They were considered to be models of their kind, with park areas, school sites and shopping centres carefully arranged. In these respects they were markedly better than most other residential areas, but the Cumberland Plan's hopes for the build-up of significant district centres were only partly realised. By 1971, employment in the two largest suburban centres, Parramatta and Bankstown, had reached only 15,800 and 12,300 respectively. Consequently many residents of planned outer-suburban estates had long journeys to work and, beginning with the recession of the mid-seventies, higher than average levels of unemployment.[19]

The backlog in sewerage services meant that some of these otherwise well-planned estates had to wait many years before 'dunny cans' were replaced by indoor toilets. Even middle-class areas such as Warringah Shire, where Frank Hardy set his novel *The Outcasts of Foolgarah*, had to wait a long time for sewerage services. They suffered when the night soil collectors went on strike and certain local notables tried to do the job instead:

> And who is that grey-haired gentleman with the Doctor Cyclops glasses and the foaming corners on his mouth, driving a night-soil cart into A Riding in broad daylight? ... There's a strike on, haven't you heard? A Communist plot to spread typhoid fever into every corner of the shire ... He'd even cart shit to foil the Communists in their dastardly plotting to end the right of all men to be unequal, especially wage workers.[20]

In 1951 just over 70 per cent of Sydney's properties were sewered, a slight fall on the figure a decade earlier. The Metropolitan Water, Sewerage and Drainage Board was unable to keep up with the suburban sprawl and by 1960–61 only 67 per cent of Sydney was sewered, leaving thousands of houses dependent on septic tanks or night soil collectors. Fifteen years later, helped by funds channelled from the Whitlam Labor government's Department of Urban and Regional Development, the board had managed to sewer 89 per cent of Sydney's dwellings.

The board, which had been forced to resort to stringent water restrictions during the war (a result of the long drought of 1936–42), made a sustained effort in the early postwar years to complete the Warragamba Dam project at the expense of most other parts of the capital works program, especially sewers. The suburbs with the largest sewerage backlog were those on the outer urban fringe.

The Housing Commission's most urgent postwar task was to provide temporary housing. For this purpose the commission negotiated with Commonwealth authorities to take over wartime establishments that were no longer needed. The largest centres were at Herne Bay, Hargrave Park and the former RAAF camp at Bradfield Park (named after the bridge engineer, in Ku-ring-gai), while others were located at Beverley Hills, Lilyfield, Merrylands, Ryde and French's Forest. Military huts at these sites were converted into temporary dwellings, and by the end of 1951 there were 2374 such 'temporary dwellings' in Sydney.[21] These settlements were popularly regarded as eyesores, and the lack of sound-proofing in the timber-framed buildings made life in the family apartments very difficult for all but the least sensitive of the occupants. But the Housing Commission seemed impervious to criticism: a July 1950 Housing Commission booklet, *Know Your Department*, stated that:

> The largest centres have, of course, retained the somewhat uniform appearance necessarily associated with temporary military quarters. The hutments, however, have been divided into two or more flats, each unit completely self-contained ... Casual visitors ... particularly if they are themselves well housed in comfortable homes in attractive suburbs, may be inclined to see only the drabness ... To see the true picture, it is necessary to place oneself in the position of the families so housed and to have some knowledge of the conditions under which they were previously accommodated.

Many of the people housed in the huts were British and European migrants. Despite the 'all-in-the-same-boat' rhetoric, some evidence suggests that social class was taken into account in the allocation of people to particular centres. Bradfield Park, for instance, was the main centre for white-collar workers, an appropriate setting given its location in middle-class Ku-ring-gai.

As the housing shortage became less acute, the settlements at Herne Bay and Hargrave Park were increasingly used for emergency housing for families suffering hardship from eviction and family breakdown. So many of the juvenile and other offenders appearing before the courts in Bankstown and Liverpool gave Herne Bay and Hargrave Park as their address that magistrates and local authorities urged that the settlements be removed. Both were later cleared and developed as permanent Housing Commission estates, but Herne Bay had such unfavourable associations that in the early 1960s the name of the locality (and its railway station) was changed to Riverwood.[22]

By June 1956 the Housing Commission had constructed 23,863 dwellings in Sydney and suburbs and 13,855 in the rest of the state. In the immediate postwar years the commission's activities accounted for almost one-fifth of all houses and flats in New South Wales. Public housing as a percentage of the total stock of occupied dwellings increased markedly over this period, from 1 per cent in 1947 to 7 per cent in 1966.[23] Between June 1945 and June 1976 the commission built 73,588 dwellings in Sydney, 6501 in Newcastle, 10,456 in Wollongong and 34,130 in towns throughout the state.

Under the provisions of the federal Labor government's 1945 Commonwealth–State Housing Agreement, the Commonwealth was to cover

Emile Mercier, *My Ears Are Killing Me,* Angus & Robertson Sydney, 1955

"It's a dream home in every way! As a matter of fact, considering the unprocurability of essential materials and the building rackets, the only way this house can exist is in a dream!"

70

the state's expenditure on housing projects. Dwellings were allocated according to a scale of 'needs', and ex-servicemen, merchant marines and their dependants were to receive at least half of all dwellings erected. A family on the basic wage paid one-fifth of the wage in rent. Up until 1956 most of the houses constructed were for rent, but a new Commonwealth–State Housing Agreement (under the auspices of a non-Labor coalition government) provided that 20 per cent of houses to be erected would be available for rent, with the remaining 80 per cent for sale on a deposit of £50 and the balance repaid over 45 years. By June 1976, 40 per cent of the 125,461 dwellings built by the Housing Commission since 1945 had been sold. The Wran Labor government, elected in May 1976, decided to charge market rents and institute a rental rebate system, with the hope of ensuring a more equitable distribution of commission dwellings.[24]

The Housing Commission's activities were subject to frequent criticism by non-Labor state parliamentarians. In November 1951 the newly elected member for Earlwood, Eric Willis, complained that the commission built too many two-bedroom homes and not enough three-bedroom ones, for which some families had waited six years. Willis wished to encourage large families because 'there is no better immigrant than the Australian baby'. Douglas Darby, the conservative member for Manly, told Parliament that young couples had been driven from the countryside because of the difficulties of finding homes and the attractions of city trade unionism, 'which permits a man to earn a great deal of money for very little effort'. In the city these young couples found themselves shunted into Housing Commission flatettes, unable to live 'a decent, normal family life' and rear 'the large families that they should be encouraged to have'. For Darby, the solution was simple: an end to government restrictions, for 'in the 1930s if a man had money and wanted to

Emile Mercier, *My Ears Are Killing Me*, Angus & Robertson, Sydney, 1955

build a house, it was not long before he had a home to live in ...'[25] In the thirties Darby had been a schoolteacher with a steady job and steady income: the plight of low-income earners was not his concern and he viewed with disfavour the activities of the Housing Commission.

Not all of the early postwar houses were built by speculative builders or the Housing Commission. Many were the result of efforts by owner-builders, not a new development in Sydney, but one that began to be measured in 1951. Some of the reasons for owner-building were outlined by Gwen Kelly in her 1957 *Meanjin* article 'Portrait of a New Community':

> The ballots of the Housing Commission left at every drawing a disappointed majority ... From this class sprang the home builder in the literal sense ... He watched the papers for the cheaper blocks of land, the division of old estates in outer Sydney, the release of areas within the green belt ... For the most part the ensuing houses were fibro constructions ... They paid rates for street lighting which was almost non-existent, and for street maintenance even though they were not likely to see kerbing and guttering for the next fifty years.[26]

The NSW government statistician's category of owner-building was relatively broad, ranging from 'the employment on wages of a supervisor, who performs the services usually undertaken by a contractor but takes no responsibility for financing the project, to the work of the owner himself who, alone or with the assistance of friends, undertakes the actual construction at weekends, during annual holidays or in other free time'. Under this definition, owner-builders were responsible for approximately half the houses completed in New South Wales (figures for Sydney are not available) in 1952 and 1953. The proportion fell steadily after this and in 1957 stood at one-third.[27]

Parliamentarians praised the owner-builders. In November 1950 the Labor member for the outer western electorate of Blacktown, John Freeman, told state Parliament that many ex-servicemen in his electorate were building houses at the weekend with the help of tradesmen mates, while 'the young wives prepare afternoon tea in picnic style'. It was a healthy picture of postwar suburbs, filled with young couples and new houses. Not even the communists could spoil it, because, according to Freeman, 'No Communists will be found building their own homes but decent Australians are getting a stake in the country, and homes built under those conditions will be an asset to the State'.[28] The spirit and activity of the owner-builders was romantically captured by Gwen Kelly in her description of life at Mt Colah on the outskirts of Sydney:

> Nights and weekends were alive with the constant beat of the hammer, the whirr of the saw, the odorous skid of the plane. When they ran out of money they built cupboards and laid bricks for their wealthier neighbours, or their wives took jobs in the stores of the nearest suburb. Their babies were conceived in garages or unfurnished back rooms, against the grand day when the whole family would move in. Sometimes two or three children had appeared before this happened, and new bedrooms or sleep-outs were carefully tacked on to the original design.[29]

Fibrocement sheeting became the most popular building material of the early postwar years, as it was cheap and easy to handle, especially for inexperienced owner-builders. Sydney became the fibro capital of Australia. Of the 58,000 housing permits granted in Sydney between 1948 and 1953, half were for fibro dwellings, nearly half for brick dwellings and just 3 per cent for weatherboard, which was a popular building material in Melbourne and Brisbane. At the 1947 census 80 per cent of Sydney's private dwellings had brick walls: at the 1971 census only 66 per cent had brick walls. Most fibro houses built in the intervening years were in the outer western suburbs, though significant numbers of fibro dwellings were also built in the municipalities of Warringah, Hornsby, Ryde, Hurstville and Sutherland.[30] Spiralling building costs in the 1950s meant that even some middle-class households chose fibro rather than brick; often it meant they could afford an extra bedroom. While most of the fibro houses were modest two- or three-bedroom homes they were usually well-sited on their blocks, with ample windows and often a pleasing outlook. Although the soil left much to be desired in some of the coastal and western suburbs settings, a determined gardener could do a lot with an appropriate choice of native shrubs. After a decade or so many of these houses had pleasant leafy gardens.[31]

Buying postwar suburbia

Home ownership in Sydney remained virtually static in the interwar and early postwar years. At the 1921 census 40 per cent of dwellings were owned or being purchased; in 1933 the figure was 40.5 per cent, and in 1947 it was 43 per cent (see Table 5.3). But by 1954 home ownership had risen dramatically to 59.6 per cent, reflecting the fact that the mid-fifties was the cheapest time between 1948 and 1968 to purchase a home in Sydney.[32] In his 1954 election

Table 5.3: Nature of occupancy of private dwellings in the Sydney region 1911–96 (percentages)

	1911	1921	1933	1947	1961	1976	1986	1996
Owned	26.4	25.1	27.3	33.3	43.7	29.2	36.2	40.6
Being purchased	4.8	14.7	13.2	9.7	27.1	35.6	31.2	23.4
Rented:								
private tenant	66.3	57.7	57.2	55.8	24.2	23.2	21.6	24.1
housing auth.					3.8	4.4	6.2*	5.6
Other, not stated	2.6	2.6	2.3	1.2	1.1	7.7	4.9	6.3
Dwellings, 000	118	173	280	325	561	973	1140	1311

*Includes 0.9 for other government agencies.
Source: Australian Bureau of Statistics, census.

policy speech Prime Minister Robert Menzies said:

> The Labor Government, when it prepared the Commonwealth–State Housing Agreement in 1945, rejected the idea that people should become, in the famous phrase, 'little capitalists'. We have always stood for home ownership ... We will require that any new [housing] agreement encourages ownership.[33]

Although they gradually affected fewer and fewer dwellings, rent controls reduced the rate of return on rental properties to landlords and effectively removed the incentive to construct new rental properties. Successive NSW Labor governments found it necessary to water down the regulations because landlords were finding it more profitable to sell their rent-controlled houses and flats than to continue renting them. In 1954 almost all the rental stock in New South Wales was controlled, but the 1961 Royal Commission on the Landlord and Tenant Act estimated that this had fallen to 20 per cent of total rental stock. A decade later, less than 10 per cent of the rental stock in New South Wales remained controlled.[34] Since then such properties have all but disappeared as their tenants have either died or moved into aged-care accommodation.

In 1946 buying a lottery ticket seemed the only way to get one flat, let alone nine.

Sun, 3 October 1956

As in the interwar years, home ownership did not follow a class pattern. The highest levels of owner-occupation were to be found in outer metropolitan working-class municipalities such as Bankstown, where house ownership increased from 71 per cent in 1947 to 80 per cent in 1971, and in outer metropolitan upper middle-class municipalities such as Ku-ring-gai, where house ownership increased from 75 per cent in 1947 to 91 per cent in 1971. The lowest rates of owner-occupation were to be found in inner city working-class municipalities such as Redfern. In between these extremes of house ownership are such middle-ring municipalities as Ryde, Parramatta, Auburn, Canterbury and Randwick.[35]

Despite decisions by successive state Labor governments to stop selling Housing Commission houses in Sydney, the ALP remains as firmly committed to the principle of owning one's own home and land as the Liberal Party. In the mid-1970s Labor encouraged house and land ownership by establishing a Land Commission with the power to purchase, subdivide and sell new housing blocks. Such commissions were set up in a number of states under the aegis of the Whitlam Labor government of 1972–75, and had their origin in disquiet over skyrocketing land prices and profiteering by land speculators. Between 1971 and 1974 the average price of building allotments in Sydney rose 80 per cent, to $18,500 per lot,[36] primarily because the demand for housing blocks was greater than the State Planning Authority's Sydney Region Outline Plan of 1968 had allowed and consequently big land developers were able to exploit a seller's market.

The non-Labor parties chose to portray the land commissions as socialist land monopolies, an absurd claim in a society where private real estate agents and developers controlled the bulk of both land and new suburban estates. In 1976 the Liberal member for the state electorate of Kirribilli, Bruce Macdonald—himself a land developer—described the Land Commission as a product of the 'socialist left headed by Tom Uren' (the federal urban affairs minister) who suffered from 'paranoia about land and property developers'.[37]

The NSW Land Commission promised by the ALP during their successful 1976 election campaign was duly set up in November of that year. While it remained firmly committed to the bipartisan ideology of encouraging home ownership by supplying serviced land at the lowest possible price, the commission was nevertheless a new departure in shaping postwar suburbia. A number of restrictions were placed on purchasers: the land could only be used to construct single residential dwellings (rather than petrol stations, for instance), individual purchasers were to complete their homes within three years, and commercial builders had to proceed within one year. The conditions of sale were designed to prevent speculation, and the commission prohibited the transfer of unimproved land.[38]

The Land Commission worked with remarkable energy and by April 1977 had released its first development of 300 blocks on the St Clair Estate, near St Mary's, at prices ranging from $8250 to $10,000. These blocks were released to a market depressed by the collapse of the land boom of the early seventies. Similar land at a nearby private development was advertised in the *Daily Mirror* of 11 November 1977 at $10,300 to $11,000. By December 1977 the commission had acquired from developers over 1200 hectares of land at Penrith-St Mary's, Campbelltown and Shellharbour (south of Wollongong), with a potential for over 9000 building blocks. All these areas were predominantly working class, for the Land Commission concentrated on reducing prices for those least able to pay. In 1976–77 almost 12,000 houses were completed in Sydney; if it had maintained that acquisition rate, the commission would have controlled about one-third of the market. 'We are the biggest real estate agents in the state,' commented Premier Wran in December 1977.[39] After the 1975 federal election the newly elected coalition government in Canberra quickly disbanded the Department of Urban and Regional Development and its spending initiatives. Nonetheless, state governments, both Labor and non-Labor, continued to intervene in the urban land market, especially when major state or Commonwealth government landholdings, such as abandoned munitions sites, became available. Such sites were seized and redeveloped in a more organised way by another federal Labor government, this time in the early 1990s, under the Building Better Cities Program, but again that program was the early victim of a change of government.

Neville Wran, born in Balmain in 1926, educated Nicholson St Public School Balmain, Fort St Boys High School and the University of Sydney. QC 1968, MLC 1970–73, MLA for Bass Hill 1973–1986, Premier 1976–1986.
Caricature by Ward O'Neil, 1978

The NSW Department of Housing, created in 1986 and combining the Housing Commission and the Land Commission, administers the Rental Bond Board, overseeing landlord–tenant relations in the state. The department continues to build a few thousand flats and houses each year. Increasingly these are aimed at particular groups, including people with various disabilities. In 1996 the department owned 130,000 rental dwellings, with 93,000 people on the waiting list. Another 38,000 households received rental assistance in the private market.

Sydney's high rents pose a particular problem for smaller households, such as sole parents, where only one member of the household is receiving income. Average household size has fallen from 3.3 in 1971 to 2.7 in 1996 and real income per household has also fallen, from $876 per week in 1975 to $786 per week in 1995 (figures in 1995 dollars). By 1995 only 36 per cent of Sydney's low-income households were owners or purchasers, while 78 per cent of high-income households were outright owners or purchasers.[40] Home ownership remains high in some working-class outer suburbs, but it is increasingly dependent on having at least two incomes in the household. Despite the historically low interest rates of the late 1990s, a growing proportion of households are likely to become lifelong tenants, whether they want to or not. The proportion of outright owners to purchasers and tenants varies over time (see Table 5.3) subject to demographic factors and economic conditions.

The new boom in flats: texture brick and besser block

Not until 1965 did the new boom in flats surpass that of the thirties. Building flats for rent (which had provided a significant part of the new dwelling stock in the prewar period) was not resumed until after 1954 when the Landlord and Tenant Act was amended to free new dwellings from its provisions. The introduction of a Strata Title Act in 1961 made it much easier for owners or investors to purchase individual flats, or 'home units' as they were increasingly called. Buyers could not get separate titles for individual flats. Banks and building societies were much more ready to lend on strata titles than on company titles.[41]

The number of flats built in Sydney between 1954 and 1973 is shown in Table 5.4. Of the 153,800 new flats, just under one in ten were built by government agencies, principally the Housing Commission of NSW. Flats comprised 32 per cent of the 469,621 private dwellings built in Sydney during that period.

Table 5.4: Flats completed at five-year intervals, Sydney 1954–73

Years	Private	Govt	Total
1954–58	1 713	1 368	3 081
1959–63	17 350	2 940	20 290
1964–68	47 682	5 234	52 916
1969–73	73 535	3 978	77 513
1954–73	140 280	13 520	153 800

Source: NSW Statistical Registers.

The high point in Sydney's postwar building boom came in 1971, with more dwellings completed than in any other year of the city's history. That year also marked a major turning point in the history of housing in Australia, because Sydney became the first city to have more flats (17,431) than houses (15,514) completed. This pattern was reversed in 1972, but then flats again took the lead. This pattern continued through the housing recession of the mid-seventies, but in 1976–77 the pattern reverted to that of the sixties with more houses (11,752) than flats (6813) completed.[42] One-quarter of Sydney's population lived in flats at the 1971 census. Sydney, more than any other Australian city, is no longer the preserve of the detached house. By 1996, one-third of Sydney's dwellings were terraces, town houses, semi-detached houses or flats (see Table 5.5). The 'home unit' terminology of the 1960s and 1970s has since lost ground to the more American 'apartment'.

Of the 430,000 people living in flats in 1971, 8 per cent lived in blocks containing only one flat, 46 per cent lived in blocks of two to eight flats, 27 per cent lived in blocks with nine to sixteen flats, and the remaining 19 per cent lived in blocks with seventeen or more flats. The towering flat blocks dominating the horizon in parts of the eastern suburbs and the lower north shore

Table 5.5: Dwelling completions in the Sydney region 1957–96

Year	Detached houses	Other (eg. town houses, flats)	Other as percentage of total
1957–61	84 000	22 000	21
1961–66	75 000	41 000	35
1966–71	87 000	70 000	44
1971–76	76 000	68 000	47
1976–81	82 000	34 000	29
1981–86	62 000	33 000	34
1986–91	62 000	26 000	29
1991–96	61 000	56 000	48

Source: Commonwealth census; M Daly et al., *Monitoring Sydney*, AHURI, Melbourne, 1997; P Spearritt and C DeMarco, *Planning Sydney's Future*, A & U, Sydney, 1998. (Dwelling completions to 1980, dwelling commencements from 1981.)

may be the most noticeable but they are not the most typical.

Until the 1980s Sydney's flats were concentrated in the eastern suburbs, along the northern beaches, and along the railway lines and arterial roads. At the 1971 census more than four in every ten flats in Sydney were in the municipalities of Randwick, North Sydney, Waverley, Woollahra, Canterbury and Sydney. In only four municipalities, North Sydney (63 per cent), Waverley (55), Woollahra (52) and Mosman (50 per cent) did flats comprise more than half of all dwellings, and in only four—North Sydney, Botany, Lane Cove and Mosman—did they account for more than one-third of all dwellings built between 1958 and 1971.[43]

Despite the importance of flats in municipalities such as Woollahra, this does not mean entire suburbs were given over to flat development. In 1968, after public criticism of some very tall projects in Darling Point, the Liberal Party-dominated 'Woollahra Action Committee' won a resounding victory in the local government elections with a policy banning development over eight storeys high. By

This photograph is taken from the first block of high-rise flats at Kirribilli, the Greenway Flats, built by the NSW Housing Commission in the early 1950s. The photograph shows a Kirribilli unchanged since the late 1930s, apart from the one new private enterprise block on the horizon.
Stanton Library, 1958

1971 a detailed code had been introduced controlling the height of flats, their floor space, site coverage, the setbacks from the street and car parking requirements. All local councils in Sydney introduced statutory regulations governing flat development, but standards varied markedly from the unsightly excesses of Randwick Council to the sedate, low-rise developments in Lane Cove.[44]

'Ar, it's not snow after all. It's only Mrs McSnurd combing out her hair'.
Emile Mercier, *Hang on Please!*, Angus & Robertson, Sydney, 1964

What was life like in Sydney's flats? In 1972 this question came under close scrutiny in a new television series, *No 96*, which purported to show life as it really was in a block of flats in Paddington. The show had a number of stock characters: an Eastern European who owned a delicatessen, working-class English migrants, two male homosexuals, a number of attached and unattached men and women, and a couple of families (spiced with occasional hints of incest), but no children younger than teenagers.[45] As an attempt to reflect the demographic reality of an eastern suburbs block of flats it wasn't too bad. The show depicted both the disadvantages of flat life—the inordinate interest in each other's affairs shown by many of the occupants—and the advantages, including the reduced likelihood of feeling the isolation often associated with suburban living. A novel based on the series includes a characteristic scene:

> 'Don Finlayson? Getting married?' Dorrie Evans' voice rose. 'Mrs. Godolfus, why wasn't I told?'
>
> 'We only found out yesterday evening. There was a small party in flat 6, which is why I have no tomato paste until Arnold visits the wholesalers this afternoon. You and Mr Evans were at your Senior Citizens' Club last night, I think.'
>
> 'Not the whole night. We distinctly heard sounds of revelry from upstairs when we returned. They could have had the decency to think our hours might be less ... We keep early hours as befits decent people, Mrs Godolfus ...'
>
> 'They have no time to arrange parties to suit everyone, Mrs Evans. Don Finlayson and his fiancee are to be married next Thursday.'
>
> 'Next ...' Dorrie's jaw dropped and her purse spilled coins all over the counter. She clutched at Roma's hand. 'Is there something else I ought to be told?'
>
> 'Why, no!' Roma exclaimed. 'You know already all there is to be told you.'
>
> Dorrie sniffed. Such a peculiar way some of these foreigners had of talk-

ing—and to be strictly honest, some of these Jewish foreigners were the worst. You never knew exactly what they meant, let alone what they were thinking.[46]

The pros and cons of living in a flat versus living in a house have been much debated in recent years and the detached suburban bungalow still has its champions, including the historian and economist Hugh Stretton and urban affairs academic Patrick Troy. They have argued cogently that 'urban consolidation' may not be the panacea for metropolitan problems.[47] Nonetheless, the continued popularity of apartment living in Sydney is more than simply a developer's plot. The demand is there, especially from younger office workers, students and retirees who want to live close to the central city free of the obligations of house and garden. Moreover, since the 1980s a lot of the demand has come from households in which the children have left home. Such households are able to sell the family home, usually a detached cottage, and move to an apartment that is often smaller than the family home but nearer to public transport and commanding a view. Sydney is a city where views count, especially of the water.

'Here's the solution for preserving the view. On every block we're going to paint the view they obscure.'
Cartoon by George Molnar, *Sydney Morning Herald*, 17 October 1959

Giving suburbia a bad name

Despite the thousands of apartment blocks built since the introduction of the Strata Title Act in 1961, two-thirds of Sydney's dwellings remain detached houses. It is these houses that make up the popular image of suburbia. The postwar suburban creations of owner-builders, the NSW Housing Commission and private contractors were not universally admired. The staunchest critic was the Melbourne architect Robin Boyd, who wrote in his 1960 book *The Australian Ugliness* that:

> The recent growth of Sydney is mainly confined to three zones. Out west, the wooden villa, or *Villawood Zone*—to use the name of one of its central districts—sweeps from Liverpool north through Parramatta. It is a fairly typical Australian working class development, repeating the dreary, ill-considered housing growth on the outskirts of every Australian town ... The Housing Commission of New South Wales, speculative builders and private owners compete with one another to reduce the bush to a desert of terra-cotta roofs relieved only by electric wires and wooden poles. The same approach extends south into the *Tom Ugly Zone* ... where the Georges River opens into Botany Bay. Here the familiar suburban techniques are more destructive because the

houses are slightly more pretentious ... The really depressing parts of Sydney, however, are in the *North Shore Executive Zone* ... beautiful country ... Out through French's Forest and along the spine above Pittwater ... [is a] wild scramble of outrageous featurism.[48]

No suburb escaped Boyd's waspish eye: his objection to suburbia was largely aesthetic, but he had no feasible proposals for how else the urban population might be housed.

Cartoon by Bruce Petty on the first edition of Hugh Stretton's classic study of Australian cities, self published in Adelaide in 1970 and later reissued by Georgian House.

The private car had made much of this postwar suburbia possible: now development could proceed well beyond railway stations, tram and bus routes. Those who could not drive or had no access to a car—principally children, housewives and the elderly—might enjoy spacious suburbia but their freedom ended there. To Sydney journalist Allan Ashbolt, postwar suburbia was not just aesthetically ugly, it was socially bankrupt. He wrote in 1966:

> Behold the Man—the Australian man of today—on Sunday morning in the suburbs, when the high-decibel drone of the motor mower is calling the faithful to worship. A block of land, a brick veneer, and the motor-mower beside him in the wilderness—what more does he want to sustain him, except a Holden to polish, a beer with the boys, marital sex on Saturday night, a few furtive adulteries, an occasional gamble on the horses or the lottery, the tribal rituals of football, the flickering shadows in his lounge-room of cops and robbers, goodies and baddies, guys and dolls?[49]

This is an absolutely classic version of the left-wing intellectual's disdain for Australian suburbia, filled with visions of false consciousness. It can be found in the twenties in the writings of such noted Australianists as Vance Palmer and it has continued as the conventional wisdom among many intellectuals.[50]

It was this conventional wisdom that Hugh Stretton so eloquently attacked in his best-selling *Ideas for Australian Cities*, first published in 1970. To Stretton, postwar suburbia meant the prospect of equality. He pointed out that land and cars were distributed more equitably in Australia than other forms of property and wealth and that the much maligned quarter-acre block was put to creative use

Table 5.6: Population distribution in Sydney 1971–2011 (percentages)

	1971	1986	1996	2011 (projected)
Inner	25	20	18	17
Middle	36	30	29	28
Outer	39	50	56	55
Total population (thousands)	2 725	3 365	3 841	4 500

Sources: P Spearritt and C DeMarco, *Planning Sydney's Future*, A & U, Sydney, 1988; M Daly et al., *Monitoring Sydney*, AHURI, Melbourne, 1997; Department of Urban Affairs & Planning, *A Framework for Growth and Change*, DUAP, Sydney, 1997, p 107.

Parkes Development was one of the contributors to, and casualties of, the mid-1970s property bust.
Sun, 8 November 1974

by most Australians.[51] Virtually every Australian backyard houses at least a gas or wood-burning barbecue, a vegetable garden, a shed or a swimming pool (its size and construction depending on the social class of the area), and many contain all of these. While the phrase 'the quarter-acre block' has come to dominate discussion about suburban Australia, the average housing block of land, especially since the war, is much more likely to be one-sixth of an acre rather than one-quarter. Until the 1980s it seemed that most of Sydney's population growth would continue to occur in the middle and outer suburbs. But by 1986 it became evident, as Table 5.6 shows, that population decline in the inner city was a thing of the past and that the proportion of the population living in the outer suburbs was unlikely to rise much further. The demand for new accommodation in the inner city was largely met by new apartment blocks and townhouses, and the conversion of factory shells and redundant office blocks to apartments.

The problem with Sydney's suburbia was not to be found in the individual homes or backyards but in the fact that so much of it was so far removed from shops, jobs, hospitals, beaches and parks. This isolation decreased with the gradual suburbanisation of work and retailing in the postwar years and the rapid increase in car ownership.

Women assembling toasters in the Australian General Electric factory at Auburn, 1933.
National Library of Australia

Chapter 6

The suburbanisation of work

As in all large cities, Sydney's economy reflects its immediate attributes, its hinterland and the changing demand and prices for goods and services in the local, national and international economy. Most of the city's early industries developed in the region between Circular Quay and Botany Bay, with the Cook's River and the Parramatta River favoured locations for a great variety of establishments, from boat builders to tanneries and textile works.

With the discovery of gold, the growth of export markets for wool and wheat, and the increase in domestic demand from immigration, Sydney, along with the rest of Australia, enjoyed a flourishing economy from the 1870s. Avoiding the worst excesses of the speculative boom that brought Melbourne unstuck in the late 1880s, Sydney weathered the subsequent depression and became Australia's largest city by the early years of the new century. Protected, like the rest of urban Australia, by generous tariff walls, most of Sydney's industrial concerns flourished. Many other industries—from brewing to the manufacture of gas from coal—did not have to bother with competition from imports. These high-volume industries demanded large local manufacturing plants, which soon established themselves as notable features of Sydney's landscape. By the 1920s the gas plants and gasometers at North Sydney, Waverton, Mortlake and St Peters dominated the surrounding landscape.

The gasometers were a direct link between the suburban economy and the home because in the 1920s gas stoves accounted for almost all home cooking in Sydney. Electricity, which gradually replaced gas as a light source from the 1880s, did not become an important source of home cooking energy until the 1950s. Nonetheless, like the gasometers, the coal-fired electricity stations were a major feature of the suburban industrial landscape. All were near water and some, including Bunnerong Power Station overlooking Botany Bay, and Balmain Power Station overlooking the Parramatta River, had commanding positions. Like the gasometers, they were evidence that Sydney was a major industrial city.[1]

The two most visually dramatic changes in the economy of Sydney since the 1920s have been the demolition of gas plants, power stations and other large industrial plants, and the rise of office blocks in a handful of major suburban centres. The demolition of the plants in the 1980s and 1990s reflects a move away from urban manufacturing to new forms of distribution: in the case of urban energy the introduction of natural gas and the ability to transmit electrical energy from power stations more remote from consumers. The suburban office centres, which have effectively created cities in the suburbs, are evidence of the seemingly inexorable rise of service industries, from banking, insurance and finance to telecommunications. Of these only telecommunications creates much demand for goods, and in any case these goods—from computers to telephones—are more and more likely to be imported than manufactured locally.

Gainful employment: mapping the city

Despite the fact that New South Wales was long regarded as a largely rural economy, Sydney has always been the largest centre of employment and industry in the state. In 1921, when the metropolis held 43 per cent of the state's population, 45 per cent of all jobs in the state were in Sydney. By 1947, 53 per cent of all jobs were in Sydney; by then the city contained half the state's population. The continuing growth of economic activity and employment enabled Sydney to support an ever increasing population. At the 1921 and 1971 censuses 45 per cent of Sydney's population were classified as 'gainfully employed': these were the people who provided the goods and services that kept the city and suburbs functioning. Those considered not 'gainfully employed' included young children, school children and housewives who received no wages.

This chapter focuses on the 'gainfully employed' because their occupations and their workplaces reflect the evolving economy of the city. This is not to suggest that those without a direct source of income do not also shape the city: their demand for goods and services and the enormous array of productive activities that take place within the home are also pivotal to the economy of the city.

One way to map changes in the metropolitan economy is to study shifts in the composition of its workforce over time. Table 6.1 shows the composition of the Sydney workforce at the 1921 and 1947 censuses while Table 6.2 shows a more detailed breakdown for the period 1954–96.The only industry type to retain a constant proportion of the workforce between 1921 and 1996 was

Table 6.1: Industrial composition of the workforce in Sydney 1921–47 (percentages)

	1921	1947
Manufacturing	34.0	37.5
Commerce (finance, wholesale, retail)	22.1	18.3
Public authorities & professionals	11.1	13.2
Transport & communication	10.6	10.1
Catering & entertainment	10.3	7.6
Building & construction	6.6	7.0
Primary & mining	3.5	1.2
Other & industry inadequately defined	1.6	5.3
Numerical total (thousands)	400	640

Sources: Commonwealth censuses; M Neutze, *Urban Development in Australia: A Descriptive Analysis*, A & U, Sydney, 1977, p 85.

Table 6.2: The Sydney region workforce 1954–96

	1954		1971		1986		1996	
Industry	000	%	000	%	000	%	000	%
Agriculture, mining	20	2.4	18	1.4	17	1.2	15	0.9
Manufacturing	310	36.1	360	27.8	244	16.7	215	12.8
Utilities	20	2.3	24	1.8	28	1.9	11	0.7
Construction	65	7.6	92	7.1	89	6.1	107	6.4
Retail, wholesale	150	17.4	252	19.5	285	19.6	332	19.8
Transport & storage	64	7.4	72	5.6	88	6.1	87	5.2
Communication	20	2.3	27	2.1	34	2.3	41	2.4
Finance, property etc	31	3.6	121	9.4	209	14.3	312	18.6
Defence and public administration	117	13.6	70	5.5	80	5.5	66	3.9
Health & education			132	10.2	239	16.4	259	15.5
Recreation, personal services	54	6.3	69	5.3	89	6.1	135	8.1
Others and not stated	9	1.0	58	4.4	55	3.8	95	5.7
Total	858	100	1293	100	1456	100	1675	100

Source: Australian Bureau of Statistics, census 1954–96. Health and education was not a category at the 1954 census.

building and construction. Manufacturing expanded in the later thirties and during the Second World War, but its primacy was steadily eroded in the post-war years, largely by its arch-rival commerce. By 1971 commerce (comprising wholesale and retail trading, finance and real estate) had overtaken manufacturing as the most important source of employment in Sydney.

Women have always played an important part in Sydney's paid workforce, accounting for one-quarter of all employed in 1921, over one-third by 1971 and 45 per cent by 1996. This growth reflected the increasing number of married women who wished, or were forced by economic circumstances, to work outside as well as inside the home. In 1920 most paid workers in Sydney were male and more than half were blue-collar workers. By 1976 more than one-third of Sydney's paid workforce were women and well over half of that workforce were white-collar workers. Twenty years later less than 15 per cent of the workforce would be engaged in manufacturing and many industries, from clothing, textiles and footwear to car manufacture, had almost disappeared.

Although economists and psychologists have studied these changing industrial structures and their impact on industrial relations, they rarely stop to consider the importance of where people work. Yet the location of people's workplaces is one of the most important parts of the urban experience: most people travel to and from their workplace 10 times a week and spend a quarter of their adult lives there. To the workers of Sydney the workplace has always been almost as important as the home.[2] To a small but growing proportion of workers—about 5 per cent in 1998—home has become the workplace. Most people working from home run one-person or small businesses, which, if they grow, may move into formal business premises. Nonetheless, at the end of the twentieth century the home emerged as a site of business activity, with Internet connections enabling the transfer of text and data as easily as from an office block.

MANUFACTURING: THE PATTERN CONSOLIDATES

Sydney's factories have rarely been sited outside the central city and the areas to its south and west. The harbour proved an effective barrier to the development of factories on the north shore, as did the hilly topography. Moreover, it was much easier to construct railways and roads on the southern side of the harbour and that was where most industrial workers settled. That this pattern had set in by the 1880s was shown in 1883 when public pressure led to the Royal Commission into Noxious and Offensive Trades Within the City of Sydney and its Suburbs. The 1889 New South Wales *Statistical Register* shows that 20,000 of the 25,000 factory jobs in the metropolis at that time were concentrated in three municipalities: Sydney (15,425), Balmain (1537) and Redfern (2822). Mosman had no factory jobs and Manly had 27. Nor did the opening of the Harbour Bridge lead to any marked change: throughout the industrial expansion of the twenties and thirties the southern and western pattern of development predominated.[3]

In the interwar years the city and the inner suburbs continued to be the heart of Sydney's industry. Government statistics for 1944–45 (the first available) showed 342 factories in Alexandria, with 22,238 employees, making that municipality the second biggest centre of industry in the metropolis after the city (with 2633 factories and 69,089 employees). Next came Waterloo with 17,227 workers, then Redfern with 15,208, Marrickville with 11,227 and Balmain with 10,170.

In 1943 Alexandria Council published *The Birmingham of Australia: 75 Years of Progress,* claiming 550 factories in its municipality. The Labor mayor of Alexandria was a railway employee, Samuel Chenhall JP, who was 'always to the forefront when the progress of the municipality is discussed'. For the mayor and his council progress meant industrial growth, without which 'Alexandria would not be what it is today'. In 1943 Alexandria was the domain of the large industrial firms that occupied more than half its land area.[4] In 1889 it had 18 factories, by 1944–45 there were 342. Throughout the twenties, thirties and forties firms such as Australian Iron and Steel, Dorman Long & Co., Federal Match Company (established 1913), Australian Window Glass (established 1930), Commonwealth Oxygen (new factory 1939), Felt and Textiles (new factory 1937), Metters (expanded c. 1935 from 18 to 28 acres), Slazengers (factory 1938) and Standard Telephones and Cables (factory 1936) invaded many of Alexandria's remaining residential areas.

Despite a declining electorate (8 per cent between 1930 and 1940), residents of Alexandria continued to vote Labor. In 1943 at least 10 of the 12 aldermen were members of the ALP and all were wage earners.[5] One of them was reported as saying in 1928:

> At the present time the number of factories exceeded 300, some of them being the largest industrial units in the State. This development was inevitably pushing back the boundaries of the residential centres, but he hoped for sentimental and economic reasons, that the old suburb of Alexandria, which provided workmen with homes near their centres of employment, would not be entirely obliterated.[6]

This phenomenon of industrial concentration in particular suburbs was often noted at the time. Those attending the 1929 exhibition by the Chamber of Manufacturers at Farmers department store could stand on the eighth floor of the building, and enjoy:

> a fine view of a score of Sydney's industrial suburbs—Alexandria, St Peters, Chippendale, Camperdown, Stanmore, Annandale, Balmain, Rozelle, and farther to the west Clyde, Granville, Auburn and Parramatta. Nothing impedes our view to the west save the Blue Mountains. Surely, from here, we can see between one and two hundred factory chimneys. What a task to visit them all! Fortunately, however, that is unnecessary, for manufacturers have come here to show us their wares ...[7]

The expansion of industry in the interwar years put great demands on those government services that served the commerce of the city (although port facilities were spared the strain because there was no marked increase in cargoes handled at Sydney between 1920 and 1950). The greatest demands were on power generation, the railway system and, particularly with the increasing use of motor lorries, the roads. A number of freight railway lines had been built in Sydney before the twenties, especially around the docks area. This system was extended in 1922 with the opening of 2.5 miles of line from Rozelle Bay to the Darling Harbour wharves. A more ambitious project was the construction of five miles of track from Sydenham to Botany, to transport coal to the Bunnerong electric power station, opened in 1929. Many firms took advantage of the line.

The factories and terrace houses of Ultimo, showing just how dense the inner suburbs were.
NSW Government Printer c. 1920

With flexible road transport meeting most of the growing needs for freight movement, no further industrial railway lines were built after 1925. The number of trucks in New South Wales increased twenty-fold between 1921 and 1939 (figures for Sydney itself are not available), while the number of cars increased only seven-fold. This trend continued after the war: the number of trucks doubled between 1944 and 1950 while the number of cars increased by 50 per cent. Trucks hastened the decentralisation of manufacturing in the postwar years.

The location of Sydney's factory employment in 1944 and factory building between 1929 and 1944 was mapped by the Department of Main Roads (DMR) in 1945. As a prerequisite to its freeway plans, the DMR became the first NSW government department to take a serious interest in land use studies. Its mapping exercise showed that the long-established concentration of factory jobs in the central city and the municipalities to its immediate south and west continued into the forties.[8]

In 1948 the first postwar oil refinery in Australia was built at Matraville by Boral Ltd with the American-owned Caltex Oil Co. as the major shareholder. In 1956 a much larger oil refinery was opened at the Kurnell Peninsula on Botany Bay.[9] The other main sector of manufacturing employment followed the river, the highway and the railway west to Parramatta. The eastern suburbs and the increasingly populous outer western suburbs of Canterbury and Bankstown had little factory employment and the northern suburbs even less. Even so, North Sydney Council hoped that its late 1940s plans to turn Ball's Head (where there was already a coal loader), Berrys Bay, McMahons Point and St Leonards into a major industrial area would come to fruition.[10]

Factory building in the interwar years followed the established pattern. One

The Australasian Society of Engineers campaigning for a 40-hour week in 1939.
ANU Archives of Business and Labour

result was that new factories could only be built in some of the inner industrial working-class suburbs if cheap rental housing were demolished. The area to suffer most was the City of Sydney, where the number of occupied private houses fell from 9783 in 1933 to 8866 by 1947. In 1947 the Communist candidate for the state electorate of King (in the central city area) alleged that homes in Pyrmont bought by the CSR monopoly would be demolished to allow the company to 'expand its factories and engineering works', while other companies were turning terraces into factories, thereby accentuating the housing problem.[11]

In the interwar years some long-established manufacturing firms took every opportunity to diversify their operations—but not, usually, their location. The oldest brewery in Sydney, Tooths, founded in 1835, established links with other brewers such as Resch's (owner of the Waverley Brewery, opposite Moore Park) in 1929 and in 1936 opened their 'Blue Bow Aerated Waters and Cordials' factory at Redfern.[12] Tooheys, the other major brewer, had its plant in Elizabeth Street, opposite Central Station.

In the early 1970s Tooheys decided it would close the medium-sized Millers Brewery at Taverners Hill near Leichhardt and its old brewery at Central Station in favour of a new brewery on a 22-hectare site at Auburn, 20 kilometres from the GPO and near the population heart of Sydney. The Millers Brewery was closed in 1977 and the city brewery in 1978, the year the Auburn plant became fully operational. The changeover from relatively labour-intensive old plants to a highly automated new plant was evidence of a wider economic trend, with the productivity of capital increasing faster than the productivity of labour. Most employees were prepared to accept a redundancy scheme offered by management and the unions, with only a few electing to transfer to Auburn. At a time when unionists rightly feared automation, it was prudent of the company to combine a new plant with new techniques rather than alter an old plant with the possibility of strike action. The Tooheys move, like that of the City Markets to Flemington in 1975, is a classic example of the suburbanisation of work in the postwar years.[13]

Manufacturing: the moving frontier

In 1945 the City of Sydney still held nearly a third of all factory jobs in Sydney, and in the early postwar years the city (on 1948 boundaries) managed to retain its manufacturing workforce. Although its share of the total Sydney workforce was declining, the big decreases only came in following years, when the absolute number of manufacturing workers fell to 115,883 in 1962–63 (32 per cent of the Sydney total).

The increasing use of trucks was gradually freeing factories from their traditional reliance on rail or water-borne transport. Passengers travelling on the main western line out of Sydney in the 1950s saw railway yards, brick pits, gasometers, wheat silos and flour manufacturers and a huge range of smaller industrial establishments making everything from toasters to shoes. By the 1980s most of these establishments would be defunct and even the NSW government's own railway workshops had begun to shrink.

The Lincoln Electric factory opened on this 16-acre site at Padstow in the late 1950s. It is typical of single-storey low factory building in the suburbs, providing ample parking space for its workers.
New South Wales: A State of Prosperity, NSW State Government, Sydney, 1960

The inner suburbs of the City of Sydney, North Sydney, Leichhardt and Marrickville made up the only region to lose both population and manufacturing jobs between 1953–54 and 1960–61. Although the next ring of suburbs lost population overall, it gained manufacturing jobs, especially in the municipalities of Botany and Canterbury, but the most spectacular growth in manufacturing jobs was in the municipalities of Bankstown and Parramatta. The municipality of Bankstown, 30.3 square miles in all, was well served by road and had large tracts of vacant flat land suitable for industry. The number of persons employed in factories in Bankstown rose from a mere 3346 in 1944–45 to 11,442 in 1953–54 (when it had the seventh largest manufacturing workforce among municipalities) to 25,159 in 1960–61, by which time it had the second largest factory workforce. Only the City of Sydney with 122,145 factory workers was more important and its numbers were being steadily eroded. The third largest centre was the City of Parramatta, where a major increase took place between 1953–54 (12,854) and 1960–61 (22,794).[14]

Like Bankstown and Parramatta, Liverpool attracted new and relocated industrial plants. David Jones moved its knitwear production from Surry Hills to Hargrave Park ('where the labour was') in 1947 while Cottee's moved a food factory from Kent Street to Orange Grove in 1962. Standard Telephone & Cable purchased a 60-acre site in 1948 and by 1958, 1300 workers were making refrigerators, radios and televisions.[15]

The decentralisation of manufacturing within Sydney slowed after 1960. A decade later the 'centre zone' (all municipalities within 10 kilometres of the GPO except Randwick) still held 44 per cent of the manufacturing workforce, while the inner and middle zones (all municipalities within 20 kilometres of the GPO) held another 46 per cent. The largest percentage increase was in the outer zone (Baulkham Hills, Blacktown, Fairfield and Liverpool), while the fringe municipalities of Windsor, Penrith, Camden and Campbelltown did not experience significant levels of industrialisation until the 1970s. Neither the Chrysler nor Ford plants promised for Campbelltown in that decade materialised, but the municipality did gain an aluminium plant, a detergent-powder plant and a number of computerised warehouses.[16]

By the 1990s the old concentrations to the south and west of the CBD, especially from Marrickville to Botany and Kurnell, still have some of the biggest manufacturing plants, alongside the Villawood–Bankstown–Liverpool region. The north shore municipalities have managed to contain most industry within Brookvale, Naremburn, Artarmon and Ryde. In the last 20 years even these industrial estates have altered dramatically, with computer companies, publishers, advertising agencies and graphics studios setting up alongside small manufacturing plants.[17]

From production to distribution

Although at least a third of Sydney's paid workforce has been in the manufacturing sector for much of this century, by no means all of these people worked on the factory shop floor. Salesmen, typists, service personnel and administrative staff were numerically greater than the factory workforce in those industries engaged in distribution as well as production. In 1933 one of Sydney's largest firms, the Australian Gas Light Company (established in 1886) employed 3000 people, of whom no more than 750 were factory workers. With a huge plant at Mortlake on the Parramatta River, the company serviced the area south of the harbour and the river. It had more than a quarter of a million customers in 1933, supplying a million residents and 2000 factories and workshops. In the rhetoric of the time, it was 'a great national bulwark'.[18]

Breweries were another industry type responsible for both production and distribution. In 1935 the Kent Brewery in the southern part of the city gave 'direct employment to business executives, brewers, engineers and numerous craftsmen, clerks, typists, lorry drivers, storemen and general brewery employees—in all some 1300 souls, comprising 61 different callings ...'. The many callings are illustrated in photographs of the staff: the all-male managerial staff are at the front of the photograph, then the female clerical staff, and behind an assortment of other male workers.[19]

Nestle's Chocolates, whose Abbotsford factory had 650 employees in 1934, was another firm concerned to point out that its operation involved much more than a few factory hands:

> But what of the people who make these chocolates? ... The pay-roll covers a remarkable variety of occupations: carpenters and engineers (for the factory has its own repair shop and case-making plant) as well as chemists, gardeners, painters, drivers, labourers, confectioners and a large administrative staff. Hundreds of families are directly dependent on the factory. Indirectly employment is provided for thousands of other good Australian workers; timber getters, farmers (for milk, honey and fruits), sugar growers, cane-cutters, printers, transport workers and operatives in almost every field of industry. The employees at Nestle's Abbotsford factory are undoubtedly a happy family.[20]

Nestle's closed its Abbotsford factory, with a commanding site on the

'Nestle's immense factory at Abbotsford, NSW, charmingly situated on the Parramatta River in the midst of 22 acres of parklike ground. The building is approx. 1,000 ft long. Here chocolate and cocoa are manufactured under ideal conditions.'
Ambrose Pratt, *National Handbook of Australian Industries*, Specialty Press, Melbourne, 1934

Parramatta River, in the 1980s. By 1999 the site consisted of expensive medium-density housing.

After manufacturing, the biggest workforce was in commerce, which accounted for about one-fifth of Sydney's employment in the interwar and early postwar years and one-third by the seventies. Retailing was the largest employer within this grouping. At June 1940 there were 25,181 male and 26,684 female employees in Sydney shops. As in manufacturing firms, however, not all these employees served on the shop floor: 61 per cent were shop assistants, 15 per cent (with a marked preponderance of women) were office assistants and the remaining 24 per cent were classified as 'other', including everyone from managers to cleaners. Slightly more than half the operators of the 18,072 registered shops in the Metropolitan Shopping District in 1940 said they had no paid employees; many shops were family-run corner stores.[21] Small and medium-sized shops (up to 10 employees) accounted for a good deal of suburban employment in the interwar and early postwar years.

Anthony Horderns Brickfield Hill store, the largest in Australia, had 1900 employees. The 21 stores in Sydney in 1939 employing over 100 people accounted for about one-fifth of all shop employees.[22] Every one of these stores was in the central city. Before the war the only suburban centres to have anything larger than a Coles or a Woolworths were Bondi, Parramatta and Newtown (Brennans in King Street). But in the postwar years there was a remarkable suburbanisation of retailing, so that by 1971 only one-fifth of all retailing jobs were in the city municipality.[23]

Apart from the retail trade, the only other tertiary industries to employ more women than men in 1947 were 'hotels, cafes and personal service', 'health and hospitals' and 'education'. With the exception of hospitals and tertiary institutions, these facilities were to be found throughout the suburbs. In clerical employment females certainly outnumbered the almost non-existent male typists, but precise census figures are not available. While employment for women in industry and commerce expanded considerably in the interwar and postwar years, paid domestic employment declined: its share of Sydney's female workforce fell from 30 per cent in 1921 to 20 per cent in 1933 and

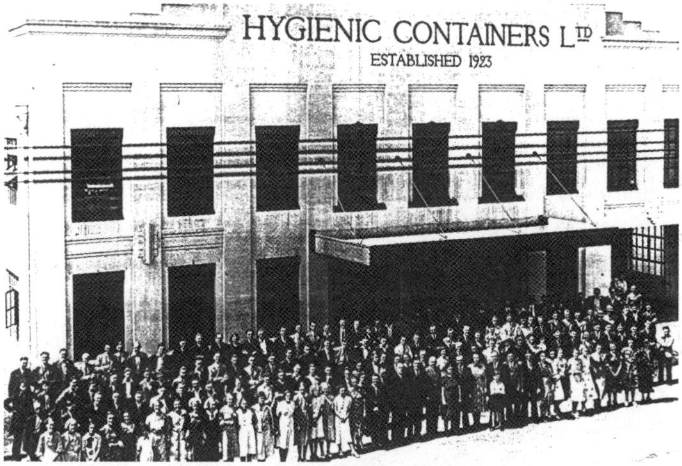

Hygienic Containers Limited started manufacturing in Alexandria in 1923, with three employees. By 1938 they had 200 employees, of whom 150 were on the factory floor and fifty in the general office. They manufactured paper ice cream dishes and spoons and paper picnic plates as well as cardboard tubes for the textile trade.
Commemorative photographic volume, 1938

approximately 6 per cent in 1947. Domestic work in middle-class households became a 'do-it-yourself' activity for women, with the aid of the increasingly popular vacuum cleaners and washing machines.[24]

New employment opportunities for women became available in industries geared to changing fashions, which were soon attracting young women from regions outside the metropolis. In Ada Holman's novel *Sport of the Gods* (1921), Cecil Eucalyptus Mapeson came on her first visit to Sydney from her country home when she was 19. She had no trade skills but soon gained a job at a beauty parlour near Hyde Park because of her good looks and because her employers could get away with offering her a pound a week. Cecil had to pretend she was 40 and that her good looks came from Madame Jardine's beauty techniques. Madame Jardine explained to her:

> [Y]ou will have a lovely frock with stockings and shoes to match, which you will put on here every morning, and Halevy, who is a kind of partner of mine, will dress your hair every morning. You will have to be at his shop in the Arcade downstairs every morning at eight o'clock. He will take twenty minutes. My clients begin to come at nine ... [Y]ou had better have a big son of twenty on a Queensland station—somewhere a good way off—and talk as maturely as you can. In some ways you do look a woman rather than a girl.[25]

Home Sept 1924, 15

'Truly Delilah was in despair, but the barber had the cunning of a serpent. "Madame must be shingled" he said insinuatingly.' Male barbers still dominated women's hairdressing in the 1920s, but by the late twenties more and more women worked in hairdressing salons.
Home, September 1924

Beauty parlours became big business in the twenties: in April 1929 the *Employers' Review* commented that the expansion in ladies' hairdressing was due to 'the modern adoption by women of short hair'. The 1930 *Sands Directory* lists 260 'ladies hairdressers' in Sydney, two-thirds of which were in the suburbs. Almost all employees in this growing service industry were women.

Males greatly outnumbered females not only in the higher paid professions such as medicine, law and tertiary teaching but also in rail transport, enlisted defence personnel and building and construction.[26] Many of these people were employed by government. In June 1947 there were 40,000 males and 12,800 females employed by the federal government in New South

Table 6.3: Employment by gender, Sydney 1991

	Male %	Female %
Managers & admin	14.0	6.8
Professionals	14.2	14.6
Para-professionals	6.4	7.0
Tradespersons	20.4	3.0
Clerks	7.2	31.5
Sales, personal service	9.6	18.9
Plant and machine operators	9.2	2.6
Labourers	12.3	6.1
Not stated	5.6	6.1
Total (thousands)	886.5	676.2

Source: C Foster, *Australian Cities*, OUP, Melbourne, 1995, p 45.

Table 6.4: Industry by gender, major industry groups, Sydney 1996 (thousands)

	Male	Female
Manufacturing	146	67
Construction	93	14
Wholesale	78	41
Retail	106	107
Transport	62	24
Finance	46	54
Property	115	97
Education	36	74
Health	36	116

Source: ABS, Basic Community Profile, 1996 census.

Wales, 117,100 males and 17,700 females employed by the state government, and 20,700 males and 1700 females employed by local government. The largest employer was the state government's Railway Department with 55,333 men and 2460 women on its books.

In the last hundred years one of the biggest changes in industrial organisation has been, in the words of the geographer Peter Hall, the 'shift of interest away from the physical process of production, and towards questions of financing, decisions to produce, and marketing: in other words, from the factory to the office'. The result has been a continuing increase in white-collar employment in the professions, in advertising, marketing and in the retail trade.[27]

Mildred, the woman on the left, is the fashion buyer while Joan is the advertising manager. Together they sell 'becoming gowns' at Curzons fashion store in Pitt Street.
Highlights of Sydney, 1950

White-collar clusters

In tiled and fireproof corridors
the typists shelter in their sex;
perking beside the half-cock clerks
they set a curl on freckled necks
...
Comptometers and calculators
compute the frequency of fires,
adduce the risk, add up the years ...

So Judith Wright depicted clerical workers in her 1966 poem 'Typists in the Phoenix Building'. By 1971 there were 163,000 females and 86,000 male clerical workers in Sydney. Almost half of these clerical employees worked in the city municipality, while North Sydney and South Sydney shared another 9 per cent. The only other Sydney municipalities to have more than 5000 clerical jobs were Parramatta, Bankstown, Auburn and Willoughby. White-collar employment remained clustered, symbolised in the office blocks dotting these centres, which in 1971 held almost 70 per cent of all clerical employment in Sydney.[28]

Professional workers were rather more evenly spread, and less than a third crowded the city municipality. The suburbanisation of professional workers is

The bourgeoisie study the baffling array of medical names in Macquarie Street.
Colin Wills and Wep *Rhymes of Sydney*, Johnson, Sydney, 1933

most noticeable in the case of the medical profession. In the interwar and early postwar years Macquarie Street—with its virtual monopoly of specialists and its adjacent Sydney Hospital—dominated specialist employment. But after 1960 medical centres funded by the specialists themselves appeared at St Leonards, Hornsby, Parramatta and Randwick.

Hospitals too were finally catching up with the population spread to the west of Sydney. The city and inner suburbs still had some oversupply, but the hospitals at Concord (1941), Bankstown (1957), Westmead (1978) and Mt Druitt (1982) were part of an irreversible trend. In 1977 Sydney Hospital gained another reprieve from closure but many other city hospitals, most notably Crown Street Womens, did not survive.

Some professionals refused to budge and still insisted that their clients trek into the city for their services. The most notorious in this group were lawyers and solicitors, two-thirds of whom continued to demand city addresses, leaving working-class suburbs such as Botany, Mascot, Fairfield and Mt Druitt almost without adequate legal facilities.[29] Women continue to outnumber men in clerical and sales employment, as well as in education and health. Substantial numbers of women are now to be found in all main occupational categories, with strong growth in the professions and in property management. While three-quarters of the workforce in manufacturing and construction are male, these are among the few industries to remain male-dominated (see tables 6.3 and 6.4).

Sydney goes to work

In 1945 the City of Sydney and the 'inner suburbs' held between them two-thirds of all jobs in Sydney, but only 28 per cent of Sydney's workforce lived in these areas. This disjunction between where people lived and where they worked resulted in the problem of what urban planners term 'the journey to work'.

Between 1920 and 1950 the City of Sydney accounted for almost half Sydney's non-factory employment. This was due to its well-established position as the centre of government, business, retailing, warehousing and entertainment. Many leading insurance firms such as the AMP and the MLC had their head offices in Sydney. All these activities generated non-factory jobs. The City of Sydney had more than twice as many non-factory as factory employees, but the ratio was reversed in the inner suburbs, which also housed a much higher percentage of their working population than the city. The percentage is impossible to calculate because the data do not reveal whether people living in a particular region worked there or not. Determining the journey to work had to wait until the 1961 census. But it seems likely that most of the inner-suburban workforce worked in their own or adjoining suburbs or in the city. Consequently they would have had a much shorter journey to work than people on the north shore and Manly–Warringah, where the ratio of 3.7 people in the workforce to each local job was the highest in Sydney.

Other areas such as outer-suburban Canterbury–Bankstown and St George–Sutherland also offered little local employment, but these suburbs

Train strikes in March 1976 created havoc for people getting to work.
Benier *Daily Mirror*, 29 March 1976

were able to provide jobs for more of their non-factory workers than the north shore or the eastern suburbs. The western suburbs and Parramatta were well provided with both types of employment. This region had long been a centre of factory employment: in the nineteenth century Parramatta had established itself as a small but separate city generating jobs in local shops and offices.

Most factory workers lived within six miles of their factory and many within three miles. About half of the inner city factory workers lived within two miles and many could and did walk. The importance of walking to work is illustrated in novels of the time, notably Kylie Tennant's *Fouveaux* (1939) and Ruth Park's *The Harp in the South* (1948). Of the rest, most lived on railway, tram or bus routes. Though few factory workers lived on the north shore, those who did lived near 'the line'. Most other workers lived near the Ashfield–Parramatta, Bankstown, East Hills or Rockdale–Hurstville lines, using feeder buses or trams if they were any distance from the station.[30]

With the exception of those who could walk to work, the journey in the interwar years by tram, train, bus or ferry was part of everyday life for all but a few workers who used private cars. The average length of a train trip in Sydney remained less than 14 kilometres throughout those decades. The people with the longest journey to work were probably middle-class business and professional workers, clerical workers and those shop assistants who had to travel from outer suburban areas to their central city jobs. The public transport routes were lucrative for newspaper sales and provided employment for news boys throughout the city and suburbs.

The dramatic suburbanisation of work in the postwar years had marked effects on the journey to work. In 1945 more than three-quarters of Sydney's

A vulnerable Sydney. The *Sunday Herald's* response to the coal strike, 3 July 1949.

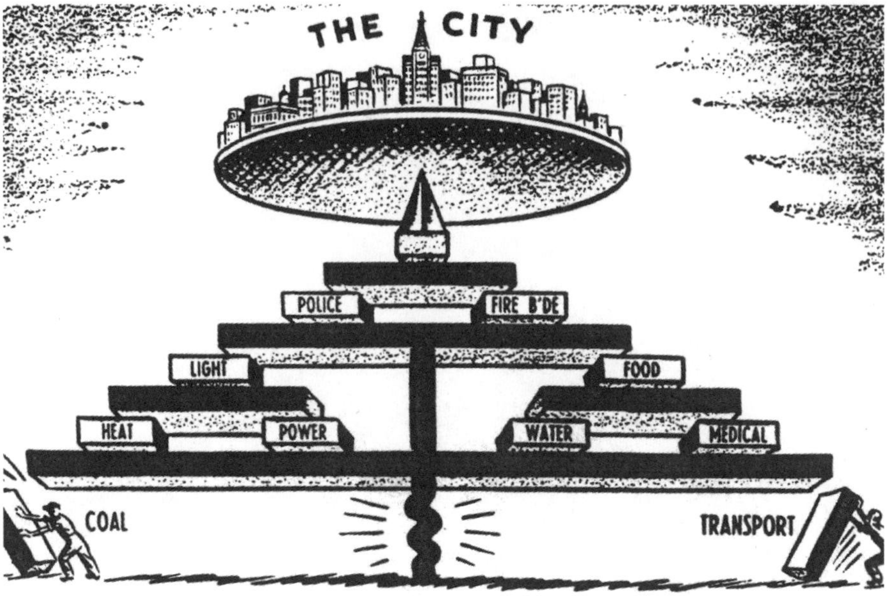

paid workforce lived within 10 kilometres of the GPO but by 1971 less than half did. Although most new jobs went to the suburbs rather than the city, the length of the journey to work did not decrease. By 1971 the median journey by train had increased to 18 kilometres, and by 1991 to 21 kilometres. Bus trips to work averaged 9 kilometres, car trips 14.3 kilometres.[31]

In 1961 the central city and the remainder of the city municipality held 26 and 19 per cent of Sydney's paid workforce respectively, but over the next decade the figures had dropped to 19 and 15 per cent, with the leeway taken up by the middle and outer ring. By 1991, 24 per cent of the workforce were located in the city, South Sydney, Leichhardt and Marrickville, 27 per cent worked within their own or an adjacent municipality, 36 per cent had to cross two or more municipalities to get to work, and 4 per cent worked at home.

That women live closer to their paid jobs than men is indicated by the fact that the average journey to work for men in Sydney in 1971 was 9.7 kilometres and for women 7.3 kilometres. By 1991 the average journey had lengthened for males to 15.4 kilometres and for females to 12.9 kilometres. The problem of the journey to work in Sydney was well summed up by Ian Manning in 1978:

> For the present ... a policy of job decentralisation to suburban centres can be expected to reduce distances travelled to work, without unduly limiting people's choice of jobs, and without depriving them of public transport ... Should a coming energy crisis increase the cost of transport, particularly the energy-intensive (private) forms of it, a policy which enables and encourages short work journeys in the present will have incalculable benefits in the future.[32]

With an average journey to work in 1991 of 14.3 kilometres, the figure for

Sydney was only a little above the average of the other four mainland state capitals of 13.1.

Holding the suburbs to ransom?

On Friday 1 July 1949, readers of the *Sydney Morning Herald* were told 'Sydney Coal Stocks Dwindling: Gas Supply Down to 10 Days'. Within a few days a strike in the NSW coalmines had made an enormous impact on the city. Two weeks earlier the communist weekly, *Tribune*, had declared that a 'huge Sydney rally' backed the miners' fight and that police had refused to allow miners to march from Central Station to the Town Hall.[33] By 29 June *Tribune* was accusing state and federal Labor governments of 'completely exposing themselves before the Australian working-class' by throwing 'their full weight behind the coal-owners against the miners'. The *Sunday Herald* had a different view: it blamed 'the communists' and carried an article explaining how a 'few wreckers can clog the works for millions':

> Sydney, as a place to live and work in, comes out rather poorly in the present crisis. A strike in a single industry has knocked the city, economically, into a very sick state ... A quality which Sydney shares with all big cities is vulnerability. As cities grow more complex their essential services get more essential and their key men more key.

The writer reminded readers of the dire results of the 1945 New York lift drivers' strike and the 1923 Melbourne police strike. The article was accompanied by a cartoon that showed transport and coal workers undermining the foundations of the city.[34]

In the following days the *Herald* reported cuts in public transport, traffic jams, reduced working hours and restrictions on gas and electricity supply. But three days later the specially appointed State Emergency Transport Coordinator claimed that 'road and rail services could keep the state supplied with essential food and materials indefinitely'. All bulk milk, petrol and meat could be supplied by oil-fuelled locomotives. Meanwhile, the courts had given state transport departments the right to stand down employees without pay during the coal crisis.[35]

The crunch came over the provision of gas. On 13 July the *Sydney Morning Herald* editorial warned that 'in five days time the greater part of Sydney may be without any gas at all'. The newspaper adopted a two-pronged approach to the crisis, attacking the alleged 'communist inspired' strike and publicising its effects on 'the masses'. One reporter found 'plenty of hungry people in Sydney industrial suburbs last week ... Soup kitchens were back again in seven or more suburbs for the first time since depression days'. The Alexandria branch of the Sydney City Mission complained that they had not had sufficient public support for their soup kitchen: an explanation could be found on the notice-board of St Silas' Church of England in Alexandria, which juxtaposed the two biblical texts 'The labourer deserves his wages' and 'If any will not work let him not eat'.

Although the impact of the strike was most severe in the industrial sub-

This Liberal Party pamphlet gives their version of why they won the 1949 federal election. The Liberal–Country Party coalition managed, with a few close calls, to stay in power until December 1972, by providing most of the people with jobs, cars and home ownership.
Liberal Party, *Popular Pictorial*, Sydney 1952, La Trobe Library

urbs, all Sydney was affected. There were long periods without gas, at a time when more than 80 per cent of households relied on gas stoves; electricity was 'rationed' to one light in each household and blackouts were frequent; there was no hot water in the thousands of flats that depended on coke-fired boilers; tram and train services ran on reduced schedules.[36]

Employer representatives stressed the domestic impact of the strike. The executive director of the Building Industry Congress claimed that every extra day of the strike meant 'the loss of 80 homes, one and a half million bricks, 135,000 tiles ... 2000 tons of cement and 39,000 square yards of asbestos cement sheets'.[37] Such claims struck a sensitive chord in a public desperately short of housing.

On 27 July *Tribune*, which had been almost silent on the effects of the strike on life in Sydney, reported that 'Bosses Panic as Strike Core is Stronger in 5th Week'. The following day, 'troops in trains, lorries and buses left Sydney for the northern and western fields to work the open-cuts. They were armed with sub-machine guns and rifles ...'[38] The Chifley federal Labor government, under pressure from the press and its own nervousness about 'communism' as the December election approached, had called in the troops. The NSW miners were the last to go back, on 15 August, after a seven-week stoppage. Chifley lost the December election—not, according to one voter, on his use of troops but because people resented going without cooking fuel and heating.[39] Opinion polls at the time showed a growing resentment against rationing and the miners. The strike affected most aspects of life in Sydney, but the damage was not permanent; the city continued to function.

The occupations of Sydney 'breadwinners' were indeed interdependent, as the manufacturers had claimed during the strike. Sydney offered more job opportunities than any other place in Australia, but a strike in a key industry could affect them all. Although it didn't actually take place in Sydney, the strike resulted in lay-offs in the transport and manufacturing industries and created hardships in the home. Significantly, however, the suburban middle class with their central city jobs were more seriously affected than industrial workers, who tended to live nearer to their factories.

In later decades increasing car ownership dulled the impact of public transport shutdowns. City workers organised car pools and, despite mammoth traffic jams, did eventually get to work. Moreover, the suburbanisation of work meant that the car, given a city-centred public transport system, had become the major form of transport for the journey to work. The real beneficiaries of this process were not just the workers (they may have got to work a bit faster, but the costs of car ownership were high and rising) but also the new- and used-car dealers (and their suppliers) who lined the major arteries into the city. The 'Magic Mile of Motors' on Parramatta Road was one of the more notorious examples of this development.

Continuous employment and productivity were represented as vital to individual and metropolitan welfare by both the Labor and non-Labor parties. Labor-dominated local councils encouraged industrial growth in their areas. The non-Labor parties and their supporters, while sometimes advocating unemployment as a tool of economic management, adopted a conciliatory but threatening approach in their election literature. The Liberal Party was forced to support the full-employment policy enunciated by its Labor rival.

The full employment policy was not seriously questioned again until the recession of the 1970s. By November 1977 the unemployment rate among Sydney's workforce had reached 7 per cent, the highest since the 1930s. As usual, working-class suburbs were hit harder than middle-class ones: in 1977 Liverpool had the highest unemployment rate in Sydney and Hornsby the lowest. A new twist in the seventies was that the unemployed were disproportionately young, with almost one-third of Sydney's unemployed under 21. In the December 1977 federal election the ALP campaigned strongly on the issue of unemployment while the Liberal–Country Party coalition tried to minimise its importance, arguing that inflation was the real barrier to economic recovery. The ALP's decisive defeat at that election was interpreted by many journalists as a sign that the electorate had lost interest in the plight of the unemployed.[40]

Job losses and downsizing

The suburbanisation of work from the late 1940s to the early 1970s took place in a full-employment economy, in which unemployment never rose above a couple of per cent. Most manufacturing firms benefited from high tariff walls, and the state government remained a major employer of labour. With the gradual reduction in tariff protection from 1974, the increasing productivity of major Asian manufacturers and the inexorable rise of labour-saving devices from robots to computers, the nature of employment changed dramatically. Australia's domestic market was simply too small to support the manufacture of many white goods and telecommunications products. Televisions, telephones, refrigerators and stoves are increasingly supplied by Asian and European manufacturers. Televisions, proudly manufactured in Australia in the 1950s, are now all imported. Australia never developed even a toe-hold in the manufacture of computers, all of which are imported from

Bunnerong Power Station, built by the Sydney Municipal Council in 1929, lay idle in the 1980s, eventually falling to the demolishers.
Photograph by John Storey, 1988

the USA, Europe and Asia. Most textile, clothing and footwear factories simply couldn't compete with Asian suppliers.[41] Hundreds of thousands of manufacturing jobs were lost in Australia's cities. Between 1971 and 1991 Sydney lost 140,000 manufacturing jobs compared with Melbourne's loss of 100,000 but, as P. Murphy and S. Watson point out, the impact on unemployment in Sydney was less marked because its economy was 'more diversified', giving it a 'greater potential for job growth'.[42] Sydney attracted many more international bank and finance headquarters than Melbourne, along with head offices for computing and media companies.

In the 1980s Sydney saw an extraordinary number of industrial closures, including the GMH plant at Pagewood (1980), the Unilever plant at Balmain (1988, once the largest soap manufactory in the southern hemisphere), the State Abattoirs at Homebush[43] (1988, the administration building has been preserved as a PR office for the Olympic site) and the Chemplex plant at Iron Cove (1989).

The size of the workforce in those manufacturing plants that managed to survive fell sharply, and 'downsizing' in some labour-intensive industries, especially the government rail system, was also severe. In 1988 State Rail in New South Wales had 37,000 employees, by 1997 there were just over 9000.[44] While some tasks have been contracted out, this reduction is indicative of the decline of traditional forms of employment.

The largest single sites of employment in Sydney are no longer railway workshops, car plants, food production companies, engineering works or even the wharves (the site of a bitter industrial dispute in 1998), but five-star hotels, universities and hospitals. The traditionally labour-intensive sectors of the economy have been transformed by modern technology. Mechanisation, automation and new storage and handling facilities (from container ports to centralised warehousing systems) have seen many blue-collar tasks and jobs disappear forever.

The AGM glass factory in South Dowling St. Opened in the 1930s, the plant closed in the 1980s, to be replaced by apartment blocks ten years later.
Photograph by John Storey, 1988

In 1986, 137,000 Sydneysiders were looking for work, representing an unemployment rate of 8.6 per cent. At the 1991 census 180,000 people were unemployed (10.3 per cent of the workforce) while by 1996, in better economic times, the number of unemployed had fallen to 135,000 (7.5 per cent).[45] The psychological and economic impact of unemployment cannot be overestimated, especially as these unemployed are living in Australia's most expensive capital city, with the highest rents and the highest housing prices.

Throughout the 1990s the suburbs to suffer most from unemployment were the western suburbs of Fairfield, Blacktown, Canterbury, Bankstown, Campbelltown, Penrith, Parramatta and Liverpool, which had well above average rates of unemployment. In some sections of each of those suburbs more than one-quarter of the workforce were without employment, and in the case of people aged 15–19 the unemployment rate was as high as 40 per cent. Over half of Sydney's unemployed youth lived in those eight suburbs.[46] The consequent social problems of lack of self-esteem, vandalism, boredom and drug abuse are obsessively documented in newspapers, to the extent that in her book *Out West* Diane Powell has identified a vicious cycle of western-suburbs stereotypes exacerbating undoubted social and economic problems.[47] While unemployment is less marked in middle-class suburbs, a combination of downsizing, contracting out and the regular culling of workers (so-called 'voluntary redundancy') has also taken a toll on some once-safe professions, from accounting to teaching.

The range of jobs open to Sydneysiders was one of the advantages that accrued to residents of Australia's largest city. But within the range there was a hierarchy dependent on education, skill, luck, gender, ethnic background, the state of the economy and capital accumulated, if any. A person's job affected most aspects of urban life, including where he or she could live (depending on wealth, location of workplace and availability of public or private transport) and his or her access to the good things in Sydney.

BEX
GOWINGS
BILLIARDS
ROLLS
PINES PAWS
BEANS

CHAPTER 7

Public transport and the rise of the car

FACING PAGE
Bernard Hesling, *Sydney Observed*, Sydney, c. 1950

Public transport made suburban Sydney possible. From the 1880s, expanding rail and tram networks brought the people of the surrounding settlements into closer contact with the city. A person no longer had to live within walking or cycling distance of his or her workplace.[1] The public transport system enabled more and more Sydney residents to move into well-spaced detached homes spreading around suburban railway stations. But since industry and commerce continued to be concentrated in the city centre and in the nearby suburbs where the lines converged, public transport became the vital link between home and work for an ever-increasing proportion of the population.

THE BRADFIELD PLAN

The basic pattern of Sydney's rail and tram networks took shape before the First World War. In 1909 the Queensland-born engineer John Job Crew Bradfield (1867–1943), who had been educated at the University of Sydney and joined the NSW Public Works Department in 1891, put forward his scheme for the construction of a city underground railway. Three years later, Bradfield was appointed engineer-in-charge of the newly created Sydney Harbour Bridge and City Transit Branch in the Public Works Department. His fame and influence grew. In 1915 he submitted his *Report on the Proposed Electric Railways for the City of Sydney*, which recommended a city underground railway, a bridge crossing, and electrification of suburban rail lines.[2]

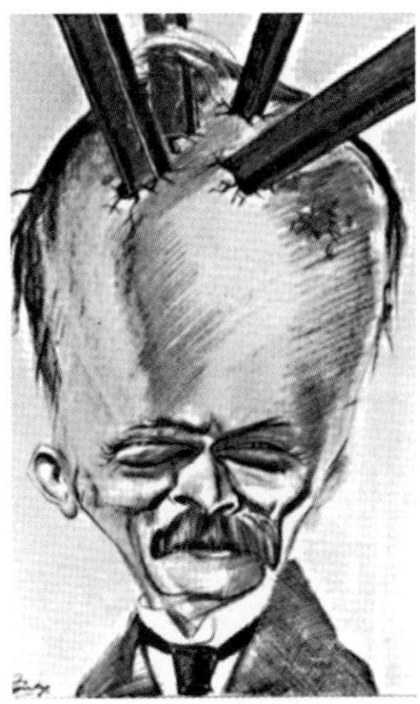

J.J.C. Bradfield, the government engineer in charge of the Harbour Bridge and underground railway, by George Finey
Art in Australia, June 1931

The electric railways legislation went through Parliament in 1915. Appointed to the Legislative Council in that year, J.D. Fitzgerald argued that underground railways were a necessary part 'of the development of great cities all over the world. In Sydney we have a city which has now a population of almost 800,000.' The Sydney Harbour Bridge Bill encountered a different fate, primarily because it did not reach the Legislative Council until April 1916. As concern for war finances grew, the Harbour Bridge became another war casualty. But Bradfield's scheme received its biggest setback in June 1917 when Cabinet decided to discontinue the city railway after the collapse of the financial agreement with the London-based Norton Griffiths Company in March 1917.[3]

Nevertheless, at the outbreak of war Sydney had a public transport system that adequately served most parts of the metropolis. The only important tram lines built in the 1920s were in newly developing areas: Hurlstone Park to Canterbury Station and Maroubra Junction to Maroubra Bay in 1921, Military

Road to Balmoral Beach in 1922, and Undercliffe to Earlwood in 1924. By 1926 Sydney's tram track reached its maximum extent of 179 miles.

In the years after the decision to postpone the city railway, Bradfield mounted a publicity campaign in support of his scheme. He took every opportunity offered, starting in Adelaide with the first Australian Town Planning Conference in October 1917. Here he first described the coalition of interests he invoked in subsequent years. This coalition included 'workers' who, he argued, would benefit from the proposed railway system because it would enable them 'to reside further afield and enjoy fresh air and sunlight'; property owners and local governments, because they would benefit from increased land values and increased rates; and the 'future', because by the year 1950 Sydney's population would 'on a conservative basis reach 2,226,000'.[4]

In September 1922 the Bridge Bill, reintroduced by the Nationalist secretary for Public Works, R.T. Ball, drew bipartisan support. Jim Dooley, leader of the Labor opposition, told the House: 'I am in favour of the construction of the bridge ... when ... trains are running over the bridge, some of the finest residential country within twenty minutes of the city will be opened up.'[5] The *Labor Daily*, writing after the event and conveniently forgetting the arguments of Labor members themselves, had a more cynical view of the reasons behind the passing of the Bridge Bill, pointing to 'the influence of home owners and land speculators in the charming and healthy northern suburbs (and) ... the rising importance of members from the northern side of the Harbour in the inner workings of the Nationalist Party and the necessity to placate them'.[6] Labor was soon ousted even from such traditionally working-class areas as North Sydney.

The main opposition to the bridge came from the country-oriented Progressive Party. According to one of its parliamentarians:

> it is a wrong thing to build the city railway and the North Shore Bridge when we want railways outback ... the North Shore Bridge would undoubtedly confer a great benefit. I recognize it as a necessary work, but it is not so vital to the progress and well being of New South Wales as the rural works which I have mentioned.[7]

The Progressives chose not to question the bridge or the Bradfield plan as such, but to query where the money was spent. Their criticism left unruffled the basic consensus between Labor and the Nationalists, and even between country-based members of those parties, such as Dooley (Bathurst) and Ball (Murray), that the bridge must be built.

Excavation work began for the city underground railway in 1923. Crowds gathered to watch the huge excavations and tunnel building in Hyde Park. The opening of the St James and Museum stations and the new section of Central Station at Chalmers Street took place in 1926. The railway and tramway staff magazine the *Staff* wrote that 'Swarms of interested mothers and fathers, together with their children, thronged the platforms and stairways examining Dr Bradfield's super Christmas box to the public.'[8] No other Australian city, not even Melbourne, could boast an underground railway. While tiny in comparison to the grand undergrounds of London, Paris or New York it nonetheless held out the promise that Sydney might one day be a world city.

Because it did not involve the construction of new track, Bradfield's electrification program may not have been as expensive as his other proposals, but it did require the purchase of new rolling stock and conversion of the old. The electrification of the Illawarra line was completed in March 1926, and that of the Canterbury line six months later. Further electrification was completed in subsequent years—the North Shore line in 1928, and the Sydney–Parramatta, Granville–Liverpool, Lidcombe–Cabramatta and Strathfield–Hornsby lines in the following year.[9] (See Map 7.1.) On the new suburban routes soot-creating steam trains disappeared, but people living on the main long-distance lines into Sydney were not so fortunate. Households abutting the major freight routes had to put up with smoke residue in their houses and on their washing well into the 1950s.

The electrification program culminated in the opening on 19 March 1932, amid great ceremony, of the Sydney Harbour Bridge and two more of the city underground stations, Wynyard and Town Hall. Ticket sales at the new stations were high, demonstrating the demand for the city underground. By 1939 a clear hierarchy of stations had been established on the city loop line, with Wynyard and then Town Hall as the main stations where shoppers and workers entered the downtown section of the city. Both these stations were placed astride the ridge running between the commercial and the warehouse/docksides of the city. St James, opposite David Jones' retail store, was on the edge of the commercial sector, separated from the warehouses and wharves of Woolloomooloo by Hyde Park; Museum, under Hyde Park, was also on the edge of the commercial hub.

The only other new railway lines built in the interwar years were Kingsgrove–East Hills opened in December 1931, and Sutherland–Cronulla, opened in December 1939, both a boon to speculative subdividers. In December 1931 C.A. Gregory, secretary of the Modern Transport Federation of Australia, a lobby group favouring private buses and opposing the state-run tram and train systems, queried the East Hills line on three grounds: an 'officially estimated' annual loss of £60,000, the absence of an inquiry into alternative forms of transport such as the omnibus, and the rise in the 'market values of the contiguous land ... many times greater than before the line was begun'. A Maroubra reader, replying to Gregory's letter, said that the loss was justified because the line was of a 'developmental nature, and the fact that land values have increased enormously proves its developmental value'. Gregory replied tellingly:

> If the improvement of land values (mostly speculative) establishes the 'developmental value' of the East Hills line ... it certainly does not relieve the taxpayers of the burden of the losses incurred. There would be some point in the increased land values argument as justifying the building of more non-paying lines if the Railways Department, and not land speculators or large holders, received the advantage of the increment, or if it went to the State through a betterment.[10]

This issue—the relationship between the funding of urban infrastructure and the financial gains from higher land values—arises every time a major rail or road investment is made.

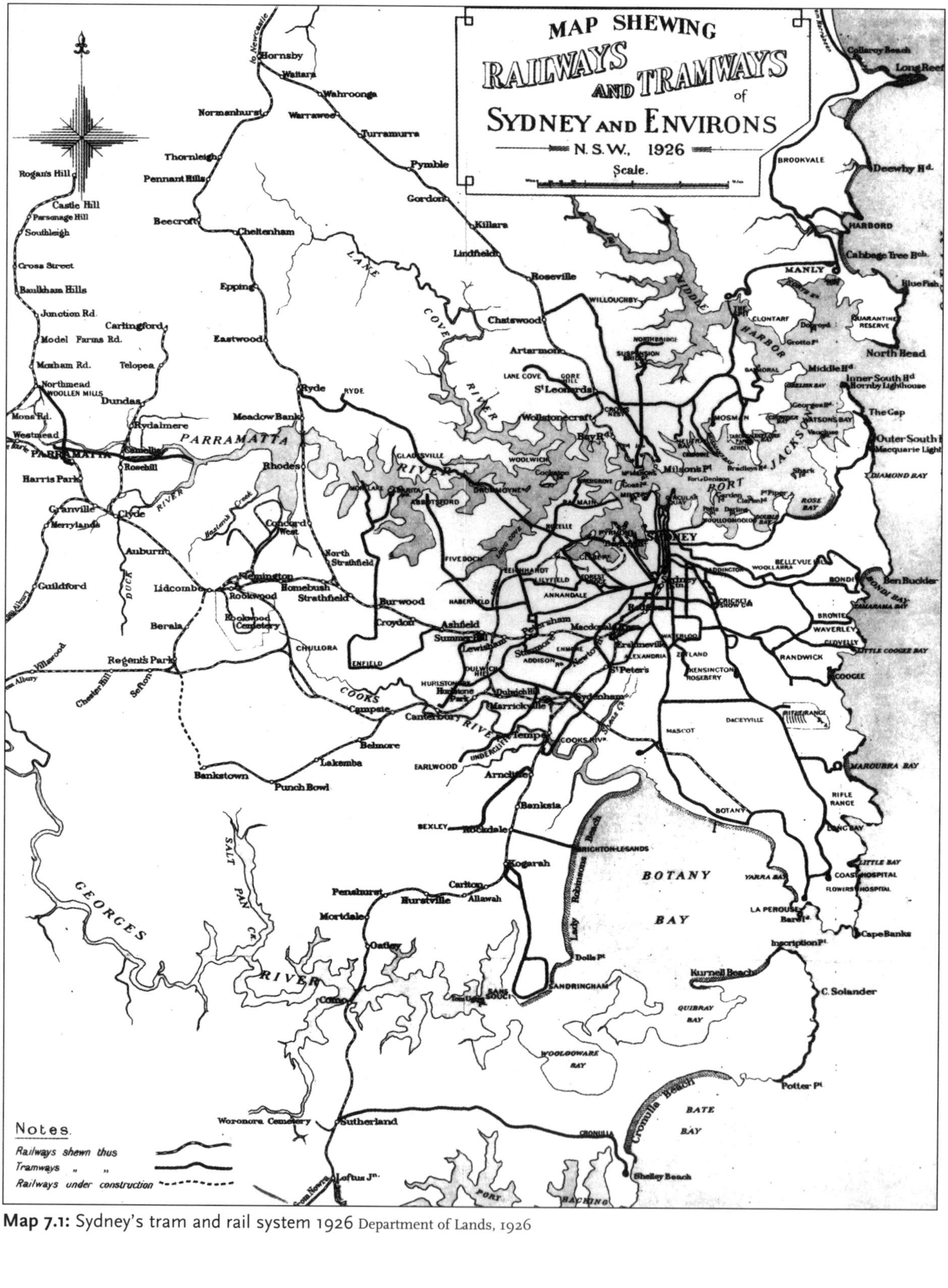

Map 7.1: Sydney's tram and rail system 1926 Department of Lands, 1926

Passenger numbers for the Bradfield plan were predicated on assumptions about Sydney's population growth based on migration and birthrates at the time. Like most metropolitan boosters around the world, Bradfield did not foresee the Depression nor the consequent drop in the birthrate. Migration did not surpass the level of the twenties until after the Second World War. As one historian put it, Bradfield's scheme was 'a system designed to carry 733 million passengers per annum by 1950, which actually carried only 230 million and which consequently constituted a financial burden which the NSW Railways could have well done without'.[11]

Front cover of John E. Webb's farewell booklet after 48 years as a Sydney journalist.
Publicity Press, 1956

Despite the excess capacity in the rail system, politicians still lobbied for the completion of various parts of the Bradfield plan. Among the main projects urged in the thirties were the Eastern Suburbs Railway, the St Leonards to Eastwood Railway, and the completion of the city loop to include Circular Quay. The failure to complete the loop, which remained two dead-ends, proved a popular subject of debate and ridicule and a boon to cartoonists. The magazine *Australian Industry* pointed out in April 1935 that the tunnel between St James and Circular Quay, completed 17 years earlier, remained 'dark, lonely and deserted':

> No train has ever run through it. The money laid out in its construction has just about doubled itself at compound interest ... The tunnel, however, is not entirely unproductive. They grow mushrooms in it ... Thus a true primary producing industry has been introduced into the heart of the City of Sydney.

The Labor member for the inner city seat of King, Daniel Clyne, could not dismiss the subject so lightly:

> The tragic circumstances at Circular Quay are astounding. There has been a spoliation of business and land values ... The beautiful Sydney Cove looks as though it has been shelled by enemy guns. It has been shelled, but it has been by the Stevens–Bruxner Government ... [there remains] an arch bearing the inscription 'City Railway, 1918', as a monument of ineptitude, neglect and twenty years blundering incapacity. The country party has a dominating influence in the Cabinet and is delaying the construction of the railway ... it has the plans and specifications prepared years ago by Dr Bradfield, but the work has not been carried out ...[12]

Clyne may have been correct to point his finger at the Country Party—and certainly its role in diverting funds to rural areas would support his accusation. But his own party also failed to act, for they had held office on three occasions since 1918. The Second World War put paid to any Labor plans to complete the Circular Quay station until the 1950s, 40 years after Bradfield's original proposal.[13]

Ferries

Sydney's spectacular harbour lends itself to waterborne transport of people, goods and vehicles, and ferries have long been one of the city's most distinctive features. The harbour and its ferries were pivotal to a number of novels and stories of the interwar period, including Eleanor Dark's novel *Waterway*

Map 7.2: Sydney Harbour, showing resorts and ferry services 1938

(1938). One of Dark's characters, Lady Hegarty, always boards the ferry with a feeling of relief, because 'for the next three quarters of an hour she had nothing to do but sit still and watch the harbour':

> The tall Norfolk pines still stood in the garden of Admiralty House, and the little steps which had intrigued her as a child still led down to its wharf and the deep water, golden-green over the yellow rocks.
>
> Lawns and trees sloped to the harbour edge on Kirribilli Point, but there were more flats and fewer houses than when she was a girl ... The bays swung into the land down the long northern shore, Neutral Bay, Shell Cove, Mosman, Sirius Cove, Clifton Gardens; the red roofs of the houses and the mingled greens of gardens and bushland came down to meet the grey of the rocks at the water's edge ...[14]

The ferry service from Circular Quay to Manly had started in 1854 and most other ferry services in Sydney also date from the latter half of the nineteenth century. The ferries serviced the mighty and the lowly, from the residents of the grand harbourside mansions to the tenants of the modest workers', cottages to be found at Watsons Bay and Lavender Bay. Passenger figures for Sydney ferries were first made available in 1904, a year in which ferries carried 19 million passengers, compared with 30 million carried by rail and 131 million by tram. Ferry patronage did not increase as rapidly as other forms of public transport: by 1923 rail passengers had more than trebled to 113 million, tram passengers more than doubled to 317 million, but ferries had barely doubled to 40 million.

Sydney's ferries reached their peak annual patronage, 47 million, in 1927. That year the city witnessed the greatest disaster in the history of its harbour when 37 people—including many schoolchildren—were killed in a collision between the Watsons Bay ferry *Greycliffe* and the Union Steamship Company's liner *Tahiti,* bound for San Francisco. Many of Eleanor Dark's leading characters in *Waterway* found themselves on the fateful trip. Some survived, some did not:

> At one moment there were quiet and thoughts, and the noise of water and the throb of engines. And the next a siren scream so shatteringly close, so madly urgent, that the heart stood still under the shock of it; and then only shrieking and shouting and chaos, the bright harbour no longer a picture for you to gaze at, but a menace, a terror, death waiting ... The steel-plated bow of the liner, biting into the wooden superstructure of the ferry, was turning her over and ploughing her along through the churning water. She turned slowly until her keel-plates showed above it, and all the time her terrified passengers fought upward from the slowly submerging side, clinging desperately to seats, posts, railings, clutching at each other, trampling on each other in their frantic efforts to keep out of reach of the rising water. The *Neptune,* still carried forward by her own impetus, bit deeper and deeper, cutting through the ferry amidships as if she were no stronger than a matchbox, until at last she was completely severed, and the two halves floated away to the north and south of the liner ...[15]

The *Daily Telegraph* took the ferry disaster as an opportunity to point out the dangers of harbour traffic congestion and to reflect on the future role of the ferries:

> As the suburbs on the North Shore continue to expand, attracting new harbour

Manly pier.
Postcard, 1909

ULYSSES OF THE KOOMPARTOO

Colin Wills and Wep, *Rhymes of Sydney* 1933

> passengers with each development; as the overseas shipping grows in number and tonnage with the rapid progress of the whole State, the congestion of traffic along the harbour routes becomes more intensified with every passing month. The completion of the North Shore Bridge will minimise the difficulties and reduce the dangers ... Will not the continued increase of population and advance of sea borne trade still make harbour transport an enormous business, even when the bridge is finished ...[16]

The bridge had certainly helped to reduce harbour congestion. The number of ferry passengers (including those using the vehicular ferry) fell from 43 million in 1931 to 20 million in 1933, the 1905 level. Although some of the decrease may have been caused by the Depression, passenger numbers only rose to 28 million by 1939.

Most of the ferries that plied the harbour until the 1960s were built between 1910 and 1928. The 1300-passenger ferry, *Bellubera*, still on the Manly run in the early 1970s, was built in 1910 by Mort's Dock Engineering Company at Balmain. Other ferries still in use in the early 1970s included the *North Head* (1913) and the *Baragoola* (1922), also built at Mort's Dock, and Sydney's largest passenger ferry (1781 capacity) the *South Steyne*, which came from Scotland under her own steam in 1938. The *South Steyne*, burnt out in 1974, withstood various plans to turn it into a waterborne fun park. It eventually succumbed to this fate in the 1990s, and is now permanently housed at Darling Harbour as yet another eatery in that palace of fast food and tourist prices.

By the 1960s, ferry passenger traffic was shared almost equally between the Port Jackson and Manly Steamship Co. and Sydney Harbour Ferries Pty Ltd. Before the bridge opened, Sydney Harbour Ferries Pty Ltd—with their passenger service and their vehicular ferries—accounted for 85 per cent of all ferry journeys in Sydney. Ferry patronage was subject to a number of constraints, including the size and speed of the ferries and the population of the harbourside localities and their immediate hinterland. The main exception was Manly, where a bus and tram terminus adjoined the ferry wharf and passengers came south from the northern beaches. Buses and trams played an important role as feeder services for the ferries. Hundreds of guesthouses were located within easy reach of ferry terminals, and in the interwar years these same areas proved popular for new blocks of flats. Kirribilli, Neutral Bay, Cremorne and Manly were all popular with flat developers and with tenants.

Like travel on other forms of public transport, ferry travel increased substantially in the war years, to a peak of 37 million passengers in 1945. After the war it declined continuously until 1963, when it stood at 11 million, and has since increased slightly. Thirteen million people travelled by ferry in 1997. Harbour travel received a fast and fashionable boost in the mid-sixties with the introduction of two hydrofoils on the Manly run. But despite the 15-minute turnaround, their carrying capacities of 72 and 140 passengers respectively were no match at peak hours for the 40-minute turnaround, 1500-passenger vessels. Eventually, though, all these grand vessels were phased out. Jet cats now offer a speedy trip to Manly, and the low-wash 'River Cat' catamaran services Parramatta.[17] A score of conventional ferries still ply the main routes. They are pleasant vessels but have none of the grandeur of the big boats of the past.

The harbour and its ferries are part of the city's imaginative life. Ferries feature in countless children's stories and in television series such as *Water Rats*. Apart from visitors to the zoo and Manly, the bulk of ferry passengers, whether from the north shore, Parramatta, Hunters Hill or Balmain, reflect the class structure of the suburbs they come from—the middle-class harbourside settlements where views equal money.

A main harbour ferry trip is a telling way to appreciate Sydney's history, environment and sense of place. Generations of Sydneysiders have reflected on points in their own lives, as well as on the life of the city, on a ferry trip, whether as a regular part of their journey to the city or a special weekend outing. The ferries have also become popular with international tourists, placing Sydney, along with Venice, New York and Hong Kong, as a city best viewed from the water.

Buses or trams?

In the years after the First World War, motor vehicles had a continuing impact on Sydney's public transport system. Cars, for the few who could afford them, provided an alternative to train or tram travel but much more significant incursions were made by buses, which were flexible in a way fixed-track trams were not. By 1929, 612 private buses carried 90 million passengers annually. The issue of buses or trams became the major transport debate of the interwar years. The inroads made by private buses drew the ire of the unions and management involved in government transport services. In 1924 a correspondent of the *Staff* asserted that:

> [private] buses are run only when there is paying business to be had. People whose work requires them to leave home early in the morning or travel late at night know that it is the tram and not the bus on which they can rely to carry them. This constitutes the difference between a public utility and a profit making concern.[18]

The chief concern of this correspondent was with shift workers, and in this respect the argument was probably accurate. But what this writer, the transport unions, bureaucrats and many politicians continued to ignore throughout the twenties was that private buses did in fact meet a demand not catered for by other transport modes. Both routes and stopping places could be altered, an enormous advantage in a period of haphazard suburban growth when population density could vary enormously within and between suburbs. Neither the tram nor the train offered such flexibility.

The fall in tramway patronage after 1928 and the steady growth of the private bus industry increasingly worried the Labor Party and the transport unions. In April 1930 a committee of the Metropolitan Provincial Conference of the ALP reported on the 'Nationalisation of road transport conveying passengers and goods', with the aim of combating 'the propaganda cry of "Scrap the Trams" so often raised by privately owned motor competitors'. The committee

Buses trams and cars in Kings Cross.
Postcard, c. 1948

claimed that under a nationalised system the public would receive 'better treatment, greater convenience and cheaper travelling'. Its complaints that buses ran 'during favourable weather conditions subject entirely to the licensee' and that they might be abandoned at will were similar to those made in the *Staff* six years earlier. One of the committee's key arguments for retaining trams and restrictions on private buses was that trams could carry more passengers. (The greatest number ever carried on one day was 1,367,568 during the visit of the British Fleet in 1924.) But the best argument for the trams was their ability to move a Randwick Racecourse crowd of 92,300 in half an hour: 'over 2300 fully loaded buses' would be required to shift the same crowd.[19]

Even with the onset of the Depression, Sydney's private buses carried five million more passengers in 1930 than they had in the previous year, at a time when patronage on other forms of public transport, particularly trams, was falling rapidly. This development, and pressure from transport unions expressed in the 1930 committee report, led the Lang Labor government to institute stiff taxes on private buses. Private bus operators retaliated in the May 1932 election by openly aiding UAP candidates, but on the accession of the UAP–Country Party coalition, Colonel Bruxner (minister for Transport)—to the dismay of private bus operators—decided to start a state bus service. The first government bus service commenced in Newcastle in September 1932 (private buses had also been successful there) and in Sydney in December 1932.[20]

Buses replaced the 1.5 mile Hurlstone Park to Summer Hill tram line in July 1933, the one-mile line from Ryde to Ryde railway station in March 1934 and the half-mile line from College Street Junction to Woolloomooloo Bay in July 1935. By 1935 the debate underwent a fundamental change: no longer was it private buses versus government services, but government buses versus government trams. The buses had supporters on both sides of Parliament but most of the debate at this time centred on whether trams caused more congestion on the roads or not, rather than the financial merits of the two modes of transport.[21]

Though he was not 'anti-tram', Colonel Bruxner did attempt to rationalise the two systems. In July 1937 an electric trolley bus system replaced the Kogarah to Sans Souci tram and in August state bus services were extended across the Sydney Harbour Bridge. This was the thin end of the wedge: in September 1939 the first major replacement occurred, when the Spit to Manly and Narrabeen tramline, 8.5 miles long, was closed in favour of buses. Between 1940 and 1945 tram passenger numbers rose to an all-time high, reaching almost 400 million in 1945.[22]

Bruxner by George Finey.
Art in Australian, June 1941

It proved a short-lived boom: in the postwar period buses again made their presence felt, and with the easing of the petrol situation passenger numbers increased dramatically. From 1949 onwards they were aided by the rapid closure of the entire tramway system by a Labor government under pressure from the National Roads and Motorists Association (the NRMA, founded in 1923) and in response to the advice of its senior transport advisors that economically and technically buses were better than trams. By 1961 trams disappeared from Sydney's streets, with only disused lines and tramway properties as a reminder of their former importance. These included special tram-only routes, such as the one running parallel to Anzac Parade, and tram depot sites. Most of the latter were taken over by buses, but the most famous, at Bennelong Point on the harbour, decried as an eyesore for many years, became the site of the Sydney Opera House.[23]

In the USA the removal of trams was a more obviously conspiratorial affair. There, in the interwar years, oil and motor interests bought up private tram companies with the sole intention of closing them down. In New South Wales, a more subtle coalition of the NRMA and British engineering experts hired by the Labor government achieved the same effect. All the major British cities eradicated their tram lines in the 1950s and all Australian cities, except Melbourne, followed suit in the 1960s. In Melbourne a combination of many more 'rights of way', where trams had their own separate section of roadway, plus the strident leadership of Major General Risson, head of the Melbourne and Metropolitan Tramways Board, saved that city's trams. Their future is guaranteed because of their status as one of Melbourne's few distinctive icons.[24]

Trams in George St.
Postcard, c. 1952

On 25 February 1961 the *Sydney Morning Herald* announced 'Today a Part of Old Sydney Will Die':

> [T]he city's most characteristic, most criticised and most loved form of transport will have disappeared forever ... It will be hard to imagine Sydney without trams. Once it had the second-largest tramway system (after London) in the world. For 80 years and more trams carried Sydney people to the races, to the beach, to the zoo, to the Show, the cricket and the football and to work. The trams themselves ... were noisy, draughty and cumbrous, neither particularly attractive nor particularly comfortable. Yet they were homely and dependable and, in an age before the streets were being slowly strangled to death by private cars, reasonably punctual.

After a 36-year absence Sydney welcomed trams back to its streets in 1997, when a light-rail service aimed at both city workers and tourists opened between Central Station and Wentworth Park in Glebe. Using abandoned goods rail lines, it is certainly more sensible than the absurdly gimmicky and strikingly ugly monorail, a forlorn attempt to link the Central Business District with Darling Harbour. Like the monorail, the new light rail also services the Star City Casino, so it could be that the monorail's days are numbered.

Travelling public

The cost, quality and frequency of public transport has been a recurring issue in NSW politics, not least because the government owns most of the system. Class and party differences were apparent in a debate on the condition of railway stations in October 1922. Labor opposition leader Jack Lang began by saying, in true populist style, 'It is we members of Parliament who associate with the people, who travel in the same trains, who pass through the same barriers, and who suffer the same affliction of having to show our tickets three or four times to officials in one journey.' He went on to make accusations about 'elaborate railway stations' in suburbs such as Strathfield:

> which of recent years have been the places of residence of Ministers of the Crown and Railway Commissioners. They are well catered for, but the moment you leave those aristocratic centres you strike a station like Flemington, which I suppose returns to the Commissioners more revenue than any other station in Sydney.[25]

Sir Charles Rosenthal interjected that most of the revenue at Flemington came from stock being transported to rail yards, challenging Lang with the quip 'you do not want elaborate platforms for stock, do you?'

Hop off here for surplus stores,
Curios and crays,
  Life assurance,
  Wife assurance,
Lingerie displays.
Pitt Street.
Colin Wills and Wep, *Rhymes of Sydney*, 1933

The Auburn railway station, in Lang's own electorate, was described in 1928 as the Cinderella of the main suburban line, 'absurdly inadequate for a town of this size' and still lighted with gas. 'This neglect is the more amazing in view of the fact that Auburn is stated to be the fifth greatest revenue-producing station in the State!'[26] In contrast were the stations of the North Shore line, with attractive, well-kept gardens, the products of intense inter-station competition.

Those least served by public transport were the residents of the outer western suburbs, not all of whom lived within easy walking distance of a station. Of these residents the least likely to have access to cars were young people and women. In their novel of wartime Sydney, *Come in Spinner*, Dymphna Cusack and Florence James described the plight of one such commuter at the appropriately named 'West Hills' station:

> Guinea walked along the barren platform of West Hills station. The westerly hit her face like a blast out of a furnace and the grit oozed into her sandals. 'Jeepers,' she groaned, 'fancy having to walk a mile in a wind like this' ... Half a mile off she could see the square fibro house set among straggling trees at the top of the hill.[27]

Among the complaints, the most vehement were undoubtedly those concerning fare rises. On 10 January 1920, *Smith's Weekly*, with a fine tinge of

Table 7.1: Public transport use in the Sydney region 1947–96

year (June)	rail	govt bus	ferry	private bus	public transport trips per capita
	Passenger journeys (millions)				
1947	245	496	32	68	496
1957	249	293	17	77	310
1961	238	249	13	60	243
1966	242	232	13	94	229
1971	239	208	15	111	204
1976	178	166	10	103	151
1981	208	171	13	65	143
1986	216	175	18	48	136
1996	256	177	14	na	na

Notes: Figures for private buses are not reliable as they have not been compiled consistently. The 1986 figure is an estimate.Source: Annual reports of State Rail Authority, Department of Motor Transport, and Urban Transit Authority.

class consciousness, denounced a 20 per cent increase in train fares: 'what does it matter to [Premier] Holman travelling comfortably and free in a state motor car?' On 23 March 1926, the *Daily Telegraph* complained that:

> The cost of city and suburban transport in Sydney is a cruel exaction upon every worker, and especially every family man, who does not own a motor car and cannot afford a taxi ... As the population of Sydney has increased, train and tram fares have increased also, when the growing business should have made the inclination the other way ...

One reason for the *Telegraph's* complaint was that two tram sections in Sydney cost 50 per cent more than they did in Melbourne—threepence instead of twopence—even though Sydney had out-stripped Melbourne in 'population, commerce and public activities'. Whatever the merits of the comparison with Melbourne, the paper's claim that the cost of public transport in Sydney was 'a cruel exaction upon every worker' was somewhat exaggerated. Contrary to popular belief, the real cost of public transport (measured as a percentage of the average male wage) decreased for all transport modes over the period 1914–76.

In June 1976 the incoming Wran ALP government tried an unusual experiment when it introduced 20 per cent cuts in train, bus and ferry fares. It was only the second across-the-board cut in NSW public transport fares, the first being in 1933 amid a much more serious depression. The condition and cost of public transport proved to be one of the central issues of the 1976 state election campaign and helped Labor win the crucial seats of Gosford and the Blue Mountains.[28] The fare reduction did not lead to a spectacular increase in patronage—because demand for existing public transport is largely 'inelastic' (see Table 7.1).

The ALP also promised to spend $200 million over five years to upgrade the state's rail track. A dramatic illustration of the need for such a program—

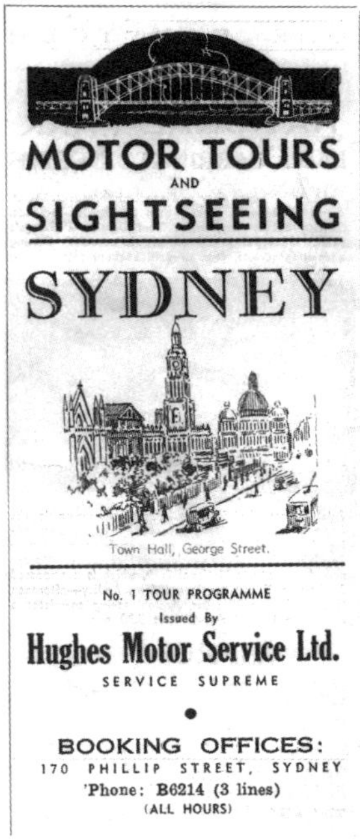

Hughes Motor Service offered half-day tours of Sydney's beaches and day tours to the Blue Mountains, Jenolan Caves and the Hawkesbury River.
Front cover, brochure, 1938

and evidence of the more than 20 years of neglect by previous governments—came on 18 January 1977 when an electric train left the track at Granville, dislodging a pylon of the road bridge, which collapsed, crushing two carriages and killing more than 80 Blue Mountains commuters. The worst public transport disaster in Sydney's history provided immediate stimulus for the Wran Labor government's expenditure on track upgrades and new rolling stock, including the distinctive double-decker carriages that started to appear on high-density suburban routes in the early 1970s.

Along with fares, which remain static as a proportion of average incomes, strikes have always been among the most popular complaints about public transport. But in the interwar years such strikes were uncommon. When the Australian Tramways and Motor Omnibus Employees Association carried a strike resolution in January 1947, the communist newspaper *Tribune* claimed that it was the first for 30 years. 'Premier McKell's neglect of bus and tram men's just demands ... is the cause of the strike which took all trams and buses off Sydney streets.'[29] Although most members of the public grumbled about strikes, they had little option but to walk. But in the 1950s and 1960s a partial alternative presented itself: the private car.

The car in Sydney

A transport revolution began in Sydney in the 1920s. It was perhaps not as important as the changeover from a walking-distance to a public-transport city in the 1880s, but it was just as visible. Before the First World War the streets of the city and the suburbs were the preserve of two modes of transport: the tram and the horse-drawn vehicle. In 1911 there were only 3978 motor vehicles registered in the whole of New South Wales (separate figures for Sydney are not available). By 1916 there were 14,973; by 1921, 33,214; and by 1926, 127,160. The motor car had come to stay. On 2 July 1923 a survey of all vehicles passing 61 checking points in the city between seven a.m. and six p.m. was carried out by the Police Department for Dr Bradfield. Motor vehicles were more numerous than horse-drawn conveyances: the survey totalled 40,253 motor wagons and trucks, 50,333 motor cars and 58,436 horse-drawn vehicles.[30]

Nevertheless, some horse-drawn vehicles remained. Many suburban bread carters and milkmen were still using horses after the Second World War because only one person was needed to operate the service whereas truck delivery required two.[31] Horse-drawn carts were part of the aural landscape of Sydney. In Jon Cleary's novel *Just Let Me Be*, first published in 1950, his main character, Joe, recently demobbed, started work as a milk carter in Sydney's eastern suburbs rather than returning to art school:

> Joe turned into the milk yard. It was approached through a long lane from the street and was, in effect, an island surrounded by a sea of houses. People all over Coogee and Randwick had been dealing with Seager's Dairy for years, but nine out of every ten had no idea of its location ... The lights were on, and as Joe came into the yard he could see the long lines of cans standing on the loading-dock ... Joe waved to the yard checker,

Early postwar traffic on Pyrmont Bridge. Most of the cars and lorries date from before the war. Horse-drawn carts can be seen to the bottom left of the photo.
Sydney City, John Fairfax and Sons, c. 1948

> Monty Simmons, said hello to a couple of the carters, and went over to the stables ... He loaded his tanks and backed the cart into the dock ... The cart bounced across the slight dip of the gutter, the milk slapping in the tanks, then it was rolling down the street, the horse's hoofs beating a percussive tattoo in the dark silence ...[32]

With declining use of horses and horse-drawn vehicles, stables gradually gave way to facilities for the motor car. Kerb-side petrol pumps appeared in Sydney in the early 1920s, to be followed later in the decade by drive-in filling stations. Most petrol stations built in the interwar years had workshops or a residence directly above the petrol pumps, and hence took up much less land than the postwar, single-storey variety. In 1940 Drummoyne proudly claimed to have 'the world's largest filling station' at the corner of Parramatta and the Great North roads. This petrol station had at least 23 pumps, closely packed together in contrast to modern station layout, and providing every available brand of petrol.[33]

Since the solid rubber or pneumatic tyres of motor vehicles need better roads than the steel wheels of horse-drawn transport, the government was under pressure to improve the state's roads. There had been strong demands for a board of roads as early as 1912 and the National Roads Association (established in 1921 as a forerunner of the NRMA) complained bitterly that motorists were not giving adequate support to its demands.[34] Legislation to establish a Main Roads Board was introduced by the Fuller Nationalist government in August 1924 as a pre-election measure, supported by Lang's Labor opposition and by Colonel Bruxner, who called it 'a non-party measure'. Particular mention in the debate was made of the motor truck. T.D. Mutch, Labor member for the industrial electorate of Botany, pointed out that motor lorries were increasing at a faster rate than cars. To Mutch the replacement of horse-drawn vehicles was a foregone conclusion, but he also cast doubt on the role of the railway. 'We are now beginning to ... realise that the railway is hopelessly unable to cope economically with such traffic as can well be carried by the average motor truck ...'[35] His opinion was echoed two years later by Bruxner:

> We are in an age of motor transport and whether it will injure the railways or not we must keep pace with the desire of the people and the advancement of civilization. In the interest of those who prefer to convey their goods by motor lorry it is the duty of the Government to see that the roads are made trafficable ...[36]

The impact of the motor lorry had been noticed as early as 1922. On 3 June a *Daily Telegraph* journalist wrote of Sussex Street: 'Thousands of tons of produce are daily carried in rumbling lorries through a densely congested thoroughfare, and at times an appalling state of affairs exists in the vicinity of some of the wharves.' By the late twenties the motor truck had become the dominant form of goods carriage in Sydney's suburbs. In Auburn in 1928 one could 'watch the hundreds of lorries thundering past, laden with spoils from the roaring factories'.[37] The proportion of trucks to cars rose continually between 1916 and 1950; in 1916 'Vans, Lorries etc' comprised 5 per cent of all motor vehicles in NSW; by 1921 the figure was 11 per cent, by 1929, 19 per cent, and by 1950, 37 per cent.

But until the Second World War most interurban carriage continued to be the province of the railways, although ships were responsible for some goods traffic with the other capital port cities. Consequently, firms in the interwar period were still tied to the city core for shipments to and from other regions. This tie was weakened after the war when improvements in trucks and intercity highways meant that road transport could be used for long distances.[38]

Throughout the twenties the motor vehicle continued to attract attention and excite public discussion. The number of vehicles in the County of Cumberland increased more than threefold between December 1919 and December 1925, to 36,978. A *Truth* editorial of 26 December 1926 reflected public attitudes to this increase:

> Everybody realises that Sydney has outgrown itself; that the congestion in the streets is such that something will have to be done, and done at once. The motor car is an absolute necessity of modern life, and it must be accepted. It is part and parcel of a day's work in the city. Without it progress would be retarded ...

At this time the problem of traffic congestion was mainly identified with the central city area. *Truth*'s solution was the creation of 'vast central parking space'.

The Main Roads Board did not prove a conspicuous success in solving Sydney's motor traffic problems of the twenties. Between 1925 and 1928 most of the board's activity in Sydney involved filling the missing links in the main roads system. This road system was of a radial and circumferential type because 'the dominance of the centre of the metropolitan area was never questioned'.[39] Such an approach added to the congestion in the city centre. The Main Roads Board was also hampered by 'inherited financial liabilities', delays in getting approval to appoint staff and difficulties in settling who should undertake the roadworks.[40]

The principal reason for the Main Roads Board's relative inaction in Sydney was that in its first four years of operation only 27 per cent of funds were spent in the County of Cumberland, at a time when that area held almost half the state's population. In contrast, local councils in Cumberland contributed almost as much to constructing and maintaining main and secondary roads as councils in the rest of the state. This pattern of expenditure was fostered by Country Party pressure but also continued by Labor governments. Between 1925–26 and 1954–55, the Main Roads Board and its successor the Department of Main Roads (created in 1932) spent £91,372,997 in the rest of the state and only £23,911,473 in the County of Cumberland.[41] In an attempt to counter criticism, the Main Roads Board established *Main Roads*, a monthly journal, in September 1929. In the first issue an officer of the board argued that the separation of the Cumberland and Country Main Roads Funds provided 'a definite safeguard ... to prevent either metropolitan or country interests predominating in the distribution of Main Roads Revenues'.

Cars became too much of a luxury for many people in the Depression: the number of registrations fell drastically and did not regain the 1929 level (170,000) until 1935. Despite the drop in motor vehicle registrations, traffic congestion remained. Most attention was focused on the central city area, and on 4 January 1935 the motoring writer of the *Sydney Morning Herald* revived the agitation for parking stations, citing British and American evidence that the construction of parking stations could be profitable. A correspondent to the *Herald* noted that:

> Sydney is a dead end. There are only five streets that can carry passenger traffic, i.e. King, George, Pitt, Castlereagh and Elizabeth. Every vehicle entering the dead end—Circular Quay—by any of those streets must, in effect, leave by the same route and that is the main cause of the traffic congestion. Sydney, with the possible exception of New York ... is the only big city in the world so disadvantaged ...[42]

With the traffic debate came mounting concern about the increasing road toll. The number of persons killed by motor vehicles in the Metropolitan Traffic District increased from 36 in 1921 to 144 in 1926, reflecting the increase in the number of cars, while the number killed by trams remained relatively static, 10 in 1921 and 11 in 1926. Motor vehicle fatalities decreased with the reduction in car registrations during the Depression, but the lull was short-lived: the number killed in the County of Cumberland increased from 205 in 1935 to 304 in 1937. In those and most other years more people were killed in the county than in the rest of the state, even though the population in the two areas was roughly equal.[43]

A similar rise in accidents occurred in Britain in the interwar years and William Plowden, taking account of the cost of cars, labelled the culprits 'middle-class killers'.[44] Given the cost of new cars in Australia in the late 1930s (most ranged from £300 to £500) and the average male wage (£250 a year in Sydney around 1937–40), Plowden's phrase may also be applicable here. The

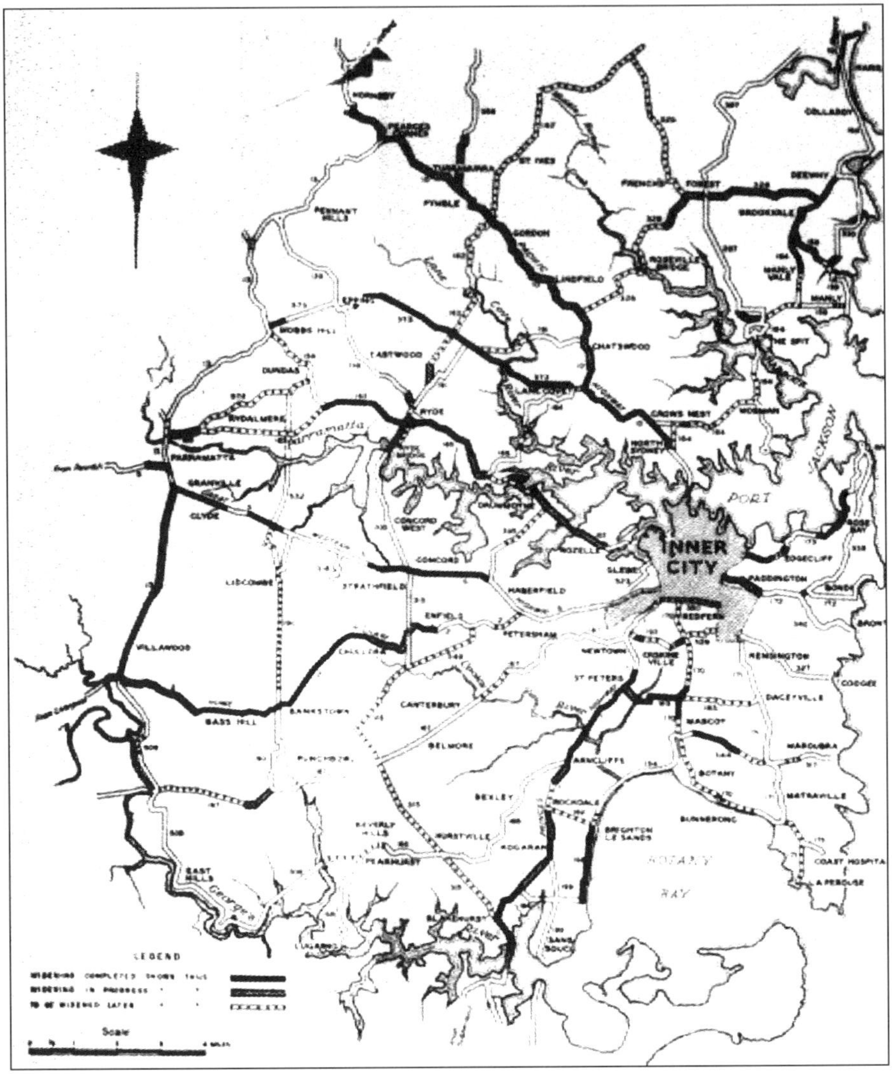

Map 7.3: The Sydney road system in 1957.
Department of Main Roads, *Annual Report*, 1957

NRMA, a vocal representative of the state's motorists, had its own views on who was to blame for traffic accidents. In 1939 the general secretary of the association attacked Sydney pedestrians in *Truth* newspaper for being 'practically uncontrolled, reckless and heedless of authority. Driving about Sydney and the suburbs is fast becoming a nightmare, and those in charge of motor vehicles have a nerve racking task.'[45]

More concerned with traffic congestion than with fatalities, the president of the NRMA, one-time Labor Prime Minister J.C. Watson, urged the 'appointment of a central body to investigate arterial roads and evolve a general plan for the future.' The Country Party minister for Main Roads, Bruxner, said that his department already had an arterial road plan for Sydney and that finance was the only problem. The reason the plan had never been published was because speculators would buy land through which the road was to pass. A day later the 'secret map, showing routes of all future road development' was shown to members of the NRMA. Bruxner regretted the move: 'now I'll

Table 7.2: Modes of passenger traffic in the County of Cumberland 1946–47

Passenger mode	Total daily journeys	(%)	Passengers entering City of Sydney during morning peak period	(%)
Ferry	90 000	(3)	13 000	(4)
Air	1 800	–	330	(1)
Rail	660 000	(22)	121 000	(38)
Tram	1 370 000	(46)	120 000	(37)
Bus	487 000	(16)	41 000	(12)
Private vehicles	384 000	(13)	26 000	(8)
Total	2 992 800	(100)	321 330	(100)

Source: Cumberland County Council, *County of Cumberland Planning Scheme Report*, CCC, Sydney, 1948, p 153.

have every real estate pirate in the State running under my neck'.[46]

Until the mid-thirties the Department of Main Roads confined its activities to filling gaps in the main roads network and to widening these roads. But after that date a more definite planning philosophy began to emerge.[47] The man most directly responsible was the University of Melbourne-educated H.M. Sherrard, who joined the Main Roads Board of NSW in 1926 as an engineer. By 1943 the department had resumed work, interrupted by the outbreak of war, on Sydney metropolitan road planning. Some indication of the department's thinking at the time can be gained from their self-indulgent war history, aptly titled *Bulldozer*, published in 1945 with an introduction by Premier McKell, who wrote:

> The Master Plan for the Metropolis, excluding the actual City of Sydney, assumes a large increase in Australian population ... our City of the future can contain 4,000,000 people ... There does not seem to be a fantasy in the contingency for which the DMR prepares already ... [There will be] express ways for Commuters, in a hurry between the heart of Sydney and the outer suburbs, which will not confuse local traffic ... Without disclosing why, the Department quietly has to obtain by resumption and purchase the ribbons where it will build for the benefit of everybody, without benefit to the Opportunist ...[48]

After the war the Department of Main Roads carried out an origin and destination survey of road traffic around the city core, recognising 'that by reason of petrol rationing traffic flow was not normal'.[49] Table 7.2 shows the continuing predominance of public transport in the late 1940s, particularly in the peak-hour period.

In 1946–47 only 8 per cent of peak hour passengers into central Sydney came by private car and only 13 per cent of all trips were by car. The use of the private car for the journey to work to the city centre was greatly restricted by the limited parking: 3000 off-street parking places and 4000 kerbside positions, the latter often subject to time restrictions.[50] But the pattern was changing, not so much for peak hour travel as for total daily journeys. Motor vehicle usage was

Freeman's Garage opened on Parramatta Road in the 1930s. When this photograph was taken by John Storey in 1980 the garage had yet to change to self-service pumps.

encouraged in June 1949 when the High Court declared the Commonwealth government's petrol rationing regulations invalid, but rationing was reimposed in November 1949 by agreement between the Chifley Labor government and the states. The Liberal Party's promise to abolish rationing undoubtedly increased its appeal among the lower middle-class at the 1949 election.

Although it maintained petrol rationing, the Chifley government also pursued the production of an Australian-made car. From the twenties federal governments sought to establish vehicle manufacture in Australia, but by the outbreak of war the highest Australian content was 42 per cent in General Motors' Chevrolet. This same firm finally produced a car made entirely in Australia, but without Australian ownership or control. When the first Holden came off the General Motors Holden assembly line in Adelaide in November 1948 it was hailed as 'Australia's Own Car'. Chifley presided over the unveiling, setting the foundation for a postwar Australian economy that was to revolve increasingly around the car industry and its by-products. In the suburbs the most immediately visible impact was the spread of service stations, which took over corner blocks on major roads, often involving the demolition of between two and four houses.[51]

PUBLIC TRANSPORT: DECLINE AND REVIVAL

Despite the continuing importance of public transport in Sydney after the war, especially for the journey to work, the system was neglected: railway rolling stock was not replaced and trams, as we have seen, were phased out completely by 1961. Only the bus system was refitted with substantial numbers of new vehicles, and these shared the roads being improved or built for the private car. Patronage of trains and buses in Sydney rose until the large fare increases of 1956. Bus patronage revived a year after the fare increase, but train patronage did not. Buses also gained patrons from the closure of the tramways but by 1963 patronage on buses began to fall.

Table 7.3 shows the decline of public transport and the increasing importance of the private car in Sydney in the 25 years after the war. It is an approximation only, because the data come from different sources, and private vehicle trips in 1960 are based on an assumed number of trips per car. From Table 7.3 and Sydney Harbour Bridge crossing data we can be fairly certain that the number of trips by private car overtook those by public transport in the early sixties.

The car had become a necessity for most suburban households, though even in 1971, one-quarter of all households in Sydney—especially flats near the city centre and on the railway lines—had no car. Nonetheless, by the 1971 census, half of all households in Sydney had one car and a quarter had two or more. This rapid increase spelt doom for public transport as a self-financing operation, leaving those who were captive to it—particularly children, the elderly and many unemployed—worse off than before. But despite increasing car ownership there were two kinds of trips where public transport remained the dominant mode of travel: the journey to work in the central city (because of traffic congestion and severe restrictions on parking) and the journey to school. Public transport use in Sydney between 1947 and 1996 is shown in Table 7.1.

Changing transport patterns, changes in the location of employment and the increasing size of Sydney all affected the journey to work. Between 1929 and 1941 the average daily train journey in Sydney increased from 7.5 to 9 miles.[52] With the spread of Sydney, the median journey to work by train increased to 11 miles by 1971, while the median journey to work on buses was 3.7 and in private vehicles 6.1 miles. That the current journey to work by private vehicle is shorter than the average daily train journey in the interwar years results from two factors: the postwar decentralisation of employment and the fact that a car enables more direct cross-suburban travel than a city-centred public transport system.[53]

The only new railway station to be built in Sydney between 1939 (the completion of the Cronulla line) and 1979 (the completion of the Eastern Suburbs Railway) was at Circular Quay, planned between 1909 and 1916 and opened 40 years later. The commissioner for Railways said at the opening of the Quay station that the Eastern Suburbs line 'could be finished in two years if enough money was available'.[54] First mooted in the 1880s, this line had been promised almost every decade since. On 14 December 1931 the *Labor Daily* said that

Table 7.3: Annual passenger trips, Sydney 1946–71

Year	Number of private vehicles	Trips per private vehicle	Public transport passengers (millions)	Private vehicle passengers (millions)	% of all trips by private vehicle	Trips per person public and private***
1946–47	178 695*	780	850	140	13	667
1960	514 017	1000**	585	514	47	493
1971	1 050 800	1220	505	1281	72	644

*This assumes that 55 per cent of registered private vehicles in NSW were in the County of Cumberland (see P.N Troy, Urban Road Planning in the Australian Context, Urban Research Unit seminar paper, 1968).
**Calculated by multiplying number of private vehicles by an assumed number of trips per private vehicle.
***Calculated by dividing all passenger trips by Sydney's population. The fact that trips per person fell between 1946 and 1960 may suggest that the assumed 1000 trips per private vehicle in 1960 is an underestimate. On the other hand the 1960 figure basically reflects the substantial drop in public transport patronage, particularly the removal of trams. One car trip may well have replaced a public transport trip involving two modes (and hence double counting), for example, tram and train, bus and tram.

Sources: Cumberland County Council, *County of Cumberland Planning Scheme Report*, CCC, Sydney, 1948, p 153; Sydney Area Transport Study, Sydney, 1974; *NSWYB*, various years.

the Lang government would create jobs for between 2000 and 3000 men on the Eastern Suburbs Railway. Lang was dismissed a few months later and nothing more happened for 15 years until another Labor premier, McKell, promised 19 new stations for the eastern, south-eastern and southern suburbs, a fair class spread.[55] Construction on McKell's proposed railways ceased in 1958 after more than £4 million had been spent on building and right-of-way acquisition.

The Eastern Suburbs Railway (but not the other proposed railways, which would have served working-class suburbs) received a new lease of life in a Liberal election promise of 1965. Non-Labor won the election (having been out of office since 1941) and proceeded, after many delays, to build a portion of the railway. Although the decision to build the railway can be explained in terms of the social class of the areas served, it was an odd promise: a decision taken amid a car boom that no one then questioned.

Over its long period of office, 1941–65, the Labor administration had been at least as pro-car as the Liberals. Responsibility for the planning of the Warringah Expressway through North Sydney (which involved the demolition of hundreds of rented terraces that housed the remains of the North Sydney working class) lies with the Labor minister for Local Government and Highways from 1959 to 1965, Pat Hills. The expressway, completed in 1968, serves the predominantly middle-class north shore, but it did not solve peak-hour traffic congestion. Leading businessmen (who command garage spaces in office towers) still twiddle their thumbs in the half hour it takes to traverse the half-mile before the bridge, the harbour tunnel (completed in 1992) not withstanding. Labor's efforts in the three decades after the war were well summed up in the phrase 'development without improvement', even for the middle class.[56]

Labor had been warned. In 1958 the County of Cumberland Council noted its concern about freeways in its *Economics of Urban Expansion*:

> As the number and use of private cars increase, congestion and parking difficulties become more acute. Remedies in the form of expressways, parking stations and control are expensive and (according to overseas experience) merely intensify traffic and parking problems by encouraging even greater use of private transport ... From the community's point of view, the cost of dealing with an ever increasing flow of private transport is high; with the present means of financing major road works, these costs are prohibitive.[57]

Two years earlier the Cumberland planners had been even more explicit when they reproduced in their magazine *Civic Development* an American cartoon showing a car devouring a city.

The Department of Main Roads ignored such warnings. Together with oil and car industry interests, it effectively became yet another lobby group for the private car. The department clung persistently to its 1945 expressway master plan, which its commissioner from 1953 to 1962, H.M. Sherrard, saw as its 'major contribution to town planning in Sydney'.[58] Despite the grand expressway plans the Department of Main Roads' principal achievement in the 1950s was a series of road widenings, as shown in Map 7.3. Apart from road-widening, freeways in outer-suburban areas, the Cahill (1962), Warringah (1967) and Day Street (1972) expressways, a tunnel under Kings Cross (1975) and a drastically amended western distributor, all the department could show for the expressway part of its master plan, 30 years later, were large swathes of red and white hatching on planning maps, some thousands of acquired properties and about a thousand demolitions.

Following American forecasting models, the Sydney Area Transportation Study team, established in 1971, advocated expressways remarkably similar to those of the 1945 master plan. That more expressways were not built in Sydney in the three decades after the war was due as much to Country Party pressure to minimise spending in Sydney as it was to the activities of resident action groups. The Country Party had starved Sydney of road funds ever since the Main Roads Board was set up in 1925; had they been more generous about funds for urban public transport, some good might have resulted. The federal Labor government of 1972–75 temporarily saved Sydney from being overrun by expressways by refusing to fund them, and in 1977 the state Labor government announced that most of the DMR's planned inner city expressways would be scrapped. The announcement drew the ire of the Liberal opposition and of the NRMA, but was popular among those whose homes had been under threat from the expressways, in some cases for over 30 years.[59]

A joint venture by Transfield and Kumagai. Publicity for the tunnel stressed that it would have little impact on the environment, to counter local protests about automotive pollution, especially in North Sydney. Unlike the Harbour Bridge, its builders pointed out that 'no houses or private property will be destroyed or resumed.'
Transfield Kumagai brochure, 1987

Since the mid-1980s there has been a resumption of expressway building; the sole concession to residents has been the installation of noise-deflecting devices. As state governments struggle to finance the insatiable demand for new road infrastructure, more and more developments are being privately funded, usually on the basis that the roadway will eventually revert to public ownership. The 2.3 kilometre Sydney Harbour Tunnel, for example, opened amid fanfare on 30 August 1992. Thousands of people walked through the tunnel, festooned with corporate ads for banks and cosmetics, making its private-enterprise underpinnings obvious. Wholly owned by its builders, the Transfield-Kumagai group, and administered by the Road Traffic Authority, successor to the Department of Main Roads, the tunnel was partly financed by bridge and tunnel tolls ($57 million in 1995–96). It will revert to public ownership in 2022. Backed by their mayor, Ted Mack, residents of North Sydney bitterly opposed the tunnel on the grounds of both pollution and increased traffic. Their protests were to no avail.

In a city where bridges have great iconic value, the new Glebe Island Bridge, an elaborate suspension bridge opened in 1995, remained within the ambit of the

Road Traffic Authority, which assisted in the coffee table homage to its construction by the Sydney photographer David Moore. To secure the bridge's iconic status, the government renamed it the 'Anzac Bridge'. In contrast, motorways, which like tunnels are rather prosaic constructions, are increasingly being left to the private sector. The M2 motorway, a tollway between North Ryde and the Old Windsor Road, opened in May 1997, did not live up to its owner's expectations of traffic volume, so the developer had to advertise its merits in the press. It is difficult for state and local governments to allocate resources and plan transport infrastructure when individual roads become marketing brands for their shareholders, and when the companies make the decisions on access and entry points based on maximising profits, not community need.[60]

Signs of life

Given the shape of Sydney, with its waterways, harbours and bays, and the fingers of development to the north, the west and the south, the public transport routes—especially rail—continue to influence commercial building and, just as importantly, residential rebuilding on existing sites. The vast majority of Sydney's flats, apartments and town houses, new and old, are near public transport, and 16 per cent of Sydney households do not have a car (see Table 7.4). Although only a little over one in five people now use public transport to get to work in Sydney, that is almost double the proportion who use public transport in Brisbane and Melbourne. In the other capital cities less than one in ten people use public transport to get to work.

Because Sydney's public transport system remains pivotal to the city, it continues to receive support from the electorate. The political parties are therefore obliged to invest in its upkeep and expansion. As Table 7.1 indicates, there was a modest increase in public transport patronage in the 1980s and 1990s. Traffic congestion in Sydney is so severe during peak times that public transport patronage will continue to increase, not least because of the introduction of 'rapid bus-only transitways' in western Sydney over the next decade, linking suburbs now without adequate public transport to the fixed rail system.

Table 7.4: Number of vehicles per household, Sydney 1996

No. of vehicles	Households (000s)	Percentage of households
0	205	16
1	543	41
2	377	28
3 or more	124	9
not stated	79	6
total households	1328	100

Source: Australian Bureau of Statistics, Basic Community Profile, ABS Sydney Statistical Division, 1996.

Staunchions for the Western Distributor, above the disused railway yards of Darling Harbour.
Photograph by John Storey, 1977

The changing pattern of weekday journeys (1946–91) and the mode of travel to work in 1991 are shown in tables 7.5 and 7.6. On any workday in Sydney about 200,000 people use a train to get to work, 131,000 use a bus and 9000 go by ferry. The role of rail and bus in both the journey to work and the journey to shop has led to bus–rail interchanges at most major regional centres. Most of Sydney's regional centres are served by both rail and bus, the main exception being Brookvale, which is bus only.

Conscious of the need to create a more efficient city, governments once again invested in rail infrastructure during the late 1980s and the 1990s. A link line between East Hills and Glenfield, completed in 1987, made Campbelltown more accessible on the rail system. A new rail link between Merrylands and Parramatta, opened in 1996, provides direct services between Campbelltown and Penrith, effectively linking the western and south-western sectors of Sydney. In 1996 work began on a new southern railway line to connect the city centre with Mascot airport and on to the East Hills line. To be opened in time for the Olympics, this rail connection will mean that Sydney is Australia's only metropolitan airport with quick public transport access to the city centre. A new spur rail line to the Olympic site at Homebush, opened in 1998, services a variety of sporting and exhibition functions, including the Royal Easter Show, relocated from its traditional home abutting the Sydney Cricket Ground.[61]

Table 7.5: Passenger journeys, Sydney region, by mode of transport on an average weekday 1946–91 (percentages)

	1946–47	1981	1991
Bus/tram	62	7	10
Rail	22	6	16
Ferry	3	0.4	0.6
Private vehicles	13	87	73

Source: P Spearritt and C DeMarco, *Planning Sydney's Future*, A & U, Sydney, 1988, p 50; Census of Population and Housing 1991. These figures exclude walking, bicycling and 'not stated', and are approximations only.

If you travel around Sydney by rail today you see a very different city from the city you see if you use the motorways that are increasingly vital to cross-metropolitan trips. On the train you still get a sense of the two Sydneys, the public transport city and the car city that has grown up alongside it. Travelling out on the line to Strathfield you see the grand icons of the public transport city—Central Station and the nineteenth-century suburban stations beyond. Because you are often elevated above the roadway you also see into the front and back yards of nineteenth-century housing, Edwardian bungalows and the blocks of flats that have increasingly clustered around the inner railway networks since the early 1960s. By the 1990s some of the three-storey walk-up blocks from the 1960s were being demolished to make way for monster apartment buildings of 10 storeys or more.

Table 7.6: Mode of travel to work, major centres 1991
(Cycling and travel on foot make up some of the remainder.)

Destination	Percentage using bus, train, ferry	Percentage using car (driver/passenger)
Sydney CBD	65	23
Parramatta	25	59
North Sydney	45	42
St Leonards/Crows Nest	26	59
Chatswood	30	52
Blacktown	15	65
Bankstown	16	66
Penrith	8	69
Hornsby	20	56
Liverpool	13	69
Campbelltown	9	69
Sydney metro area	20	60

Note: On average 0.52 per cent of work trips were by cycle, and 4.5 per cent were on foot.
Source: Department of Urban Affairs and Planning, *A Framework for Growth and Change*, DUAP, Sydney, 1997, p 122.

The Sydney you see from the motorways appears to be faster and slicker, unless you have the misfortune to encounter an accident or are trying to enter or exit a motorway in the morning or evening peak. The motorways carve their way through the suburbs—much as the railways did when they were first built. But unlike the railways the motorways often produce an enclosed landscape. Concrete sound buffers and other anti-noise devices, including cuttings, remove the car traveller from the surrounding environment. There is no prospect of getting off at the next station—the motorways are expressly designed to limit your exit and entry options. In doing this they are beginning to change our perceptions of Sydney—it has become territory to be travelled through, not savoured.

Sydney's harbour and rivers create difficulties for its transport system. Bridges have to be rebuilt. This photograph, taken in 1936, shows the original Gladesville Bridge, replaced in 1966 by a concrete arch bridge.

Chapter 8

Residents and ratepayers

FACING PAGE
Many parts of Sydney have competing land uses within close proximity to each other. This photograph of part of Lakemba, taken by John Storey in 1977, shows an army base, complete with tanks, in the foreground, a number of 1960s blocks of flats, some remaining interwar bungalows, a Catholic Church, topped by Our Lady, one high-rise apartment block, and an array of industry in the background.

The *Sydney Mail* told its readers on 6 July 1901 that 'In municipal matters,, 'we are some years behind the progressive cities of Europe and the United States.' This statement confirmed the judgement of Sidney and Beatrice Webb who, during a short visit to Australia three years before, had compared the local government of Sydney to that of London before 1885. They had advocated the establishment of a metropolitan organisation for Sydney on the lines of the London County Council. In the same year, 1898, the town planning advocate J.D. Fitzgerald, recently returned from a visit to England, addressed the Sydney Toynbee Society on 'Municipal Statesmanship in Europe' and attacked the lack of interest in municipal affairs in Australian cities. The movement for municipal reform gained some support in 1900 when two Greater Sydney conferences were held but they foundered because the first, with a majority of city aldermen, favoured unification of the 40 municipalities, while the second, with a majority of suburban aldermen, favoured a federation.[1] Despite the certainty of Australia having its first federal government the following year, such conflicts were to bedevil attempts to establish a metropolitan government for Greater Sydney.

Fitzgerald kept enthusiasm for Greater Sydney alive by publishing a series of articles in the Sydney press. He drew his ideas together in the book *Greater Sydney and Greater Newcastle* (1906), which advocated united city government on the British model. Appearing before the 1908–09 Royal Commission into the Improvement of City and Suburbs, he reaffirmed the need for a Greater Sydney council. But the commission was little interested in reforming the government of Sydney. When the Labor Party gained office in New South Wales for the first time in 1910, its platform included a unified Greater Sydney. A Greater Sydney Convention bill was introduced in 1912 but, in the face of opposition from the Legislative Council, the government decided to appoint a royal commission instead, which met the following year. The commissioners, including Fitzgerald, recommended a rather watered-down version of a Greater Sydney council, but the bill foundered in 1915 because the opposition would not countenance the Labor government's determination to end the property franchise and substitute one person, one vote.

When Premier Holman left the Labor Party over conscription to lead a new Nationalist government in November 1916, Fitzgerald became the first minister for Local Government. By this time he had learnt, through bitter experience, the difficulties facing Greater Sydney proposals. In August 1918 he told the National Debating Club:

> nearly all the efficient Governments of the world have grappled with and

solved the problem of the world's great cities ... [London] has the great and efficient London County Council. Paris, Berlin, Vienna have single councils; the great American cities the same. [Sydney, by contrast] has no central council to undertake the tasks of the city as a whole ... The government of Sydney is divided among fifty-three civic bodies, viz., the City Council, forty-eight Municipal Councils, and four Shire Councils. This subdivision of civic power and responsibility is unique in the world's experience. Everywhere in the world we find civic unification for public benefit. These fifty-three Little Sydneys are incapable of co-operation.

One consequence was that councils had to be 'assisted in their civic tasks by statutory boards', which added another handful of organisations to the myriad local authorities.[2]

Fitzgerald failed in his attempt to revive interest in Greater Sydney government but he was instrumental in the passage of the 1919 Local Government Act (see chapter 2). With Fitzgerald's death in 1922, Greater Sydney lost its most important advocate: without him there was no one of sufficient influence to capitalise on the establishment of Greater Brisbane in 1924.[3] Fitzgerald's 'Little Sydneys' had not only kept their power base intact, but their actual powers, particularly in town planning, were now enshrined in his 1919 Local Government Act.

In 1950, when *City of the Sun*, a photographic tribute to Sydney was published, the Sydney Town Hall, at 187 feet, was still the City's tallest building.
Pix magazine, April 1952

Property versus people

After the 1930 election the Labor Premier Jack Lang demoted his former minister for Justice, William McKell, a political rival, by appointing him to the less senior portfolio of local government. Anxious to re-establish his position in the party, McKell decided to tackle again the problem of metropolitan government, which had been part of the Labor platform for some years.[4] Earlier attempts had failed on the question of adult franchise and on the abolition or amalgamation of municipalities. The biggest stumbling block was the City of Sydney municipality.

Council elections in most working-class municipalities were dominated by Labor candidates, while candidates in middle-class municipalities rarely claimed an overt party-political allegiance (although many had links with the main non-Labor party of the time). The City of Sydney municipality was different. There, from about 1918, two distinct political parties emerged, Labor and Civic Reform. Despite a plural franchise for property owners (allowed to vote in every ward in which they held property, while tenants or lodgers had only one vote), Labor managed to gain and retain a majority on the council in 1923. In classic Tammany Hall style, some Labor aldermen and council officials became embroiled in bribery over the letting of a contract to the British engineering firm Babcock and Wilcox for equipping the Bunnerong electricity power station on the shores of Botany Bay. The incoming Nationalist–Country Party coalition government of 1927 used this as an excuse to suspend the council and appoint commissioners in its place. The Civic Reform party was returned to office when council elections were resumed in 1930.[5]

Into this atmosphere McKell introduced his Greater Sydney Bill, which was vehemently attacked by the Civic Reform lord mayor, Alderman Jackson:

> [T]he bill will take away the management of the city from the financial, commercial and rate-paying interests. The right to select the government of the city will be handed over to what are largely nomadic *residential voters*, who, as a general rule, *do not appreciate how the city affects them* ... If the suffrage is to be universal, as I understand, on top of the existing suffrage, the representation of the commercial and ratepaying interests will be practically negligible, probably only 10 per cent ... [emphasis added].[6]

A majority of Legislative Councillors agreed with Jackson's views on the franchise and the bill was defeated.

The franchise issue again sparked controversy in the debate on the Sydney Corporation Amendment Bill in May 1934. One non-Labor member, L.T. Courtenay, wrote to the *Herald*:

> How absurd is the present position in the city council will be shown by the following comparisons. In the Phillip Ward, which I represented in the City Council ... A. Hordern and Sons had one vote for the immense property they own running from Pitt St to George St. In the People's Palace opposite in Pitt Street there were 58 lodgers enrolled ... not paying one tenth of the rates paid by Horderns ...'[7]

Lang attacked the proposition that only property owners would be allowed to vote with a mixture of populism and Sydney chauvinism:

> We take great joy in every step that tends to make Sydney the greatest city in Australia and one of the greatest in the world ... [This bill] will destroy the fame and reputation and the cleanliness and the good name of the city of Sydney ... [by taking] away from the people of Sydney a franchise that they have enjoyed over 30 years ...

He went on to remind his listeners that the introduction of the so-called 'lodger's vote' in the early 1900s was a direct reaction to the bubonic plague that swept the Darling Harbour wharves area at that time. McKell's attack on the bill was less eloquent but better argued:

> My contention is that many lodgers have a greater interest in civic government and civic affairs than a large number of owners. What is the respective position of each? A man owns a property in the city. He may not be a resident of the city but may live on the North Shore line or somewhere else. His only interest in the city may be the property he owns there. On the other hand, lodgers are residents of the city ...[8]

In singling out absentee owners living in upper middle-class suburbs, McKell may have been thinking of the Civic Reform mayor of Sydney in 1934 and 1935, Alderman A.L. Parker, who lived at Waitara on the North Shore line.[9]

The conservative *Sydney Morning Herald* predictably supported property owners against residents: 'Instead of allowing those who paid the city rates to elect the council controlling the expenditure of them, 'the lodger vote' was introduced, which gave every irresponsible bird of passage a voice in the administration of the municipal funds which other people had to provide ...'[10]

The bill's passage reinforced Civic Reform's hold over the council and the lord mayor's chair was occupied by a succession of the city's leading businessmen, all of whom lived outside the city municipality. The mayor in 1938–39, N.L. Nock, managing director of the Nock and Kirby hardware emporium and director of David Jones Ltd, lived in wealthy Vaucluse.

Civic Reform found a useful ally in the Sydney-born F.A. Bland, who was appointed to the foundation chair of Public Administration at the University of Sydney in 1935. In October 1935 Lang alleged that Bland's appointment was evidence that 'Sydney University is fast becoming an adjunct to the anti-Labor political parties'.[11] Bland had already made himself unpopular with Labor in 1932 when he attacked McKell's Greater Sydney Bill for 'an exaggerated belief in democracy':

> If we restrict the citizen to putting a cross against the name of a candidate for ... election, we shall not only be likely to destroy his interest, but we shall obviously play into the hands of the groups which flourish on machine politics ... [T]he effect of ... the extended franchise which was proposed, would have been to hand over the management of the wealthy city area to the Labor Party ... the management ... of town and regional planning demands expertise.[12]

Bland's views were no doubt coloured by the Bunnerong scandal; his suspicion of corrupt Labor machine politicians was widely shared. Eric Baume, editor of the Sydney *Sunday Sun* 1932–38, wrote that in Sydney bars around 1930 you would hear amid laughter that you could buy for ten pounds a member of the Upper House, for five pounds a member of a certain Labor executive, and for a mug of beer sections of the Sydney City Council.[13] The replacement of Lang by McKell as leader of the Labor opposition in 1939 marked a desire on the part of the Labor party to clean up its tarnished image and to distance itself from the bitter factional disputes of the 1930s.

'Good government' and suburban loyalties

On the return of Labor to office in 1941, Premier McKell intimated his intention to revive the Greater Sydney Bill. Its provisions were to include the amalgamation of municipalities, the extension of the boundaries of the City of Sydney and the creation of a Greater Sydney Council. The *Sydney Morning Herald* supported the move in an editorial: 'As things are at present, Sydney is not a city in any truly organic sense, but rather a mere aggregation of municipalities ... It is a melancholy reflection that forty years of agitation and discussion have failed to do for Sydney what was done for Australia by the federation of independent colonies.'[14]

The Second World War delayed action on the bill, but in June 1945 the government appointed a royal commission to reorganise local government boundaries to secure 'proper, economical and efficient Local Government'. In his detailed study of the Greater Sydney movement J.D.B. Miller concluded that the report brought down by the commissioners in April 1946 'was one of the least informative documents of the many that have been written about metropolitan government in Sydney. The three Commissioners ... were unable to agree on boundaries and presented three separate recommendations.'[15]

The government adopted the recommendation of one of the commissioners to form eight 'cities' in the county: the first to comprise the whole of the harbour foreshores, the eastern suburbs and the southern suburbs around Botany Bay (a population of 1 229 635), while the other seven 'cities' were to be centres for suburban expansion in the form of satellite towns. The Local Government Association condemned the scheme as unwieldy while the Sydney City Council, 'enlivened at the prospect of incorporating 38 municipalities within itself', approved the plan. Under pressure from the Local Government Association and the Liberal Party, the government produced a compromise plan of 16 cities, which passed through the Legislative Assembly in October 1947, despite the leader of the opposition's claim that 'the centralisation inherent in the bill will create a happy hunting-ground for the socialist, the bureaucratic official and the Communist'.[16]

Although the bill encountered some opposition in the Legislative Council, a compromise was eventually reached. The 67 shires and municipalities in the county were consolidated into 39. The municipalities incorporated within the City of Sydney—Alexandria, Darlington, Erskineville, Glebe, Newtown, Paddington, Redfern and Waterloo—were thought of as 'slum municipalities'. All were geographically small but with the exception of tiny Darlington they had sizeable populations (see appendix). Despite this they were unable to fight the amalgamations because their local councils were under the thumb of the Labor Party machine. Their main consolation was that with their votes Labor would be able to oust Civic Reform from the Sydney Town Hall. The bill also brought the Sydney City Council, which now covered 11 square miles, under the Local Government Act for the first time.[17]

Glebe Town Hall, St John's Road. Opened in 1880 and photographed in 1887.

The political landscape of inner Sydney had changed forever. The Labor-dominated town halls that had held sway over the inner suburbs lost power, prestige and influence. All the municipal councils had been major employers for garbage collection, infant health, roadworks and other municipal activities. The deals or understandings between individual councillors, the local Labor branches and the firms whose factories dominated these suburbs had to be recast with the power brokers now headquartered in the Sydney Town Hall. The industrial firms still had to be taken seriously because they were the most important and most visible rate payers. With well over half the dwellings in the inner suburbs tenanted, owner-occupier ratepayers were not a particularly influential force.

Most other amalgamations also involved predominantly working-class areas (the municipalities that resulted are shown here in italics): *Auburn* and Lidcombe; *Botany* and Mascot; Annandale, Balmain and *Leichhardt*; *Parramatta*, Granville, Dundas, Ermington and Rydalmere. The few amalgamations of middle-class areas were accepted, especially if the result was socially homogeneous. Thus the amalgamations of *Burwood* with part of Enfield and *Strathfield* with another part of Enfield went relatively smoothly, as did Vaucluse with *Woollahra*, Bexley with *Rockdale* and Eastwood with *Ryde*. There was muted opposition when the residually middle-class

Petersham was forced to amalgamate with working-class St Peters and *Marrickville*. In 1948 the Petersham council's local historian, in a handsome valedictory volume, regretted 'that the name Petersham with its historic interest and associations has not been preserved ....'[18] The council had recently completed a magnificent art deco style Town Hall, which became the handsome quarters of the new Marrickville municipal administration.

Both Labor and non-Labor gained in the amalgamations. The ALP was assured of a city council with a permanent Labor majority; the opposition was secure in the knowledge that none of the middle-class municipalities where its members resided would be called upon to contribute rates to the Labor-dominated industrial suburbs. But the amalgamations fell short of the ambitions for 'eight cities' and were scarcely significant as a move towards metropolitan government.[19] Nonetheless, these amalgamations took place over four decades before more draconian amalgamations in Melbourne. There, tiny Labor-controlled inner city municipalities managed to survive until the early 1990s. The amalgamations in Melbourne were carried out by a Liberal–National coalition government that managed to force even middle-class suburbs together. Sydney, by contrast, retains many small middle-class municipalities.

In 1968 the City of Sydney's boundaries were again restructured, this time by a non-Labor government anxious to return control of the city to the pro-Liberal Civic Reform group. The Askin coalition government sacked the council and moved the boundaries back to their traditional limits. Broadly speaking, the pre-1948 municipalities of Paddington, Newtown and Glebe were absorbed by Woollahra, Marrickville and Leichhardt respectively, and the old municipalities of Redfern, Waterloo, Alexandria and Erskineville became the municipality of South Sydney.[20] In 1982 the Wran Labor government reversed the situation yet again, amalgamating South Sydney Council and all its councillors with the Sydney City Council, creating a right-wing Labor majority.

This majority was not to last. City voters were becoming disenchanted with the two-party system, turning instead to independent council candidates. The fear that this might take the lord mayoralty from Labor saw the Unsworth government sack a Labor-dominated city council in 1987. An inquiry into the council, set up by the Greiner Liberal government in 1988, recommended a much smaller city, with a franchise biased towards non-resident ratepayers. On the implementation of this plan, the remaining residential areas were combined into yet another South Sydney council. The pro-Liberal Civic Reform group lost control of the council in 1991 and an independent, Frank Sartor, became lord mayor, the first time there had been an independent mayor since early in the century. As the historian of the Sydney City Council, Shirley Fitzgerald comments: 'These expansions and contractions of the city boundaries have reflected party political battles for control of the inner city, and have not involved any serious attempt to create either a Greater Sydney or a local boundary that coincided with any genuine community of interests.'[21]

Sydney's municipal and shire councils were not renowned for their enterprise and rarely contemplated entering the housing market, even though most councils held significant land or property that was suitable for housing.

Town planners and councillors confer about the future of Hurstville.
Pix magazine, April 1952

The only housing built by local government authorities consisted of a few blocks of flats erected by the Sydney City Council in the twenties, and 600 houses by Ryde Municipal Council between 1946 and 1952.[22] Such examples of municipal initiative were rare in Sydney and as state instrumentalities such as the Housing Commission expanded their activities, local government retreated to its traditional housekeeping role. While councils provided sports grounds and libraries, other facilities were more likely to be offered by schools, churches or clubs.

The frequent abuse of metropolitan planning intentions by local councils suggests that they may not be the most appropriate agency to deal with planning matters, but as the planning historian Leonie Sandercock points out: 'The question of what development matters should be left to local councils has never been satisfactorily resolved, partly because it is not easy to decide which decisions have purely local impact as distinct from those which may have metropolitan significance.'[23]

The state government, moreover, has absolute power to dismiss councils for malpractice or inefficiency, and has done so on occasion.[24] Councils are not, therefore, their own final authority but rather administrative agencies operating under the state's Local Government Act and its regulations. Nonetheless, in the 1980s and 1990s some councils became property developers in their own right, often combining community facilities, such as a library or a sports centre, with retail properties leased on the open market.

Local government likes to think of itself as close to 'the people'. In 1951 the NSW Local Government and Shires Association, in a pamphlet on *Regional Councils*, claimed that any system of government 'should give the maximum opportunities to participate, and local government does just that ...'. Voting figures in municipal elections suggest otherwise: before compulsory voting was abolished in 1968 the turnout of voters was about 70 per cent; after abolition, voting dropped to about 30 per cent. Municipal elections were the only time when most people had an opportunity to influence suburban government, but it was influence at the small scale, which may help to explain low voter turnout. For participation to be worthwhile, big issues must be at stake. Decisions about major urban changes are, by their complex and intermunicipal nature, not very susceptible to local-level participation—consequently most decisions affecting Sydney were taken by state politicians, senior public servants and private entrepreneurs. In the absence of a Greater Sydney government some other tool of coordination had to be found; that tool was a metropolitan plan.[25]

THE FAILURE OF CENTRAL PLANNING

Retreating from the Greater Sydney idea at the end of the war, McKell's government introduced a Local Government (Town and Country Planning) Amendment Bill in 1945. The formulation of a metropolitan planning scheme for the County of Cumberland, embracing metropolitan Sydney and its surroundings, came to be regarded as a practical means of achieving some of the ambitions of Greater Sydney without having to create one metropolitan government.

The bill originally provided for a County Plan to be prepared by the Department of Local Government with the assistance of a Planning Advisory Committee, a proposal vigorously opposed by the Local Government Association. The association pressed for a second-tier local government body to prepare the plan and the government responded by creating the Cumberland County Council (CCC), made up of ten members, one representing the Sydney City Council and nine elected by constituencies of from five to twelve local councils. The legislation allowed three years for the preparation of the County Plan; the Cumberland County District was promulgated in July 1945 and the elected councillors held their first meeting in November that year. Peter Harrison, an architect and town planner who served on the council's staff from 1946 to 1950, later wrote that the council, while 'only a shadow of the ideas for a Greater Sydney Administration ... did give some promise of the first comprehensive consideration of the metropolis and its physical development'.[26]

The council mounted a publicity campaign to encourage public discussion and participation. Brochures produced by the council rivalled the earlier propaganda of the slum reformers in their colourful before-and-after contrasts. On the front cover of a 1946 pamphlet prepared for general distribution by the Cumberland County Council, mum, dad and their children get a chance to escape from terrace houses, heavy industry and gutter playgrounds to a salubrious suburban utopia. The campaign certainly had an effect: planning became a frequent topic of discussion in most newspapers and magazines. In April 1947 Jessie Street's *Australian Women's Digest* carried an article titled SYDNEY PLANS AHEAD—TO 2000 AD:

> The 1742 square miles of the County of Cumberland is the largest area in the world controlled by any town-planning body. Keynote of the policy is to preserve all that is good in the County and eliminate all that is bad. By

> July, 1948, it is to produce a master plan which will deal with all problems such as traffic, slums, wider streets, housing, new shopping centres and industrial areas ... It does not propose to make a plan and impose it on the people. Citizens are invited to act on the planning committees which are being set up ...

The council's publicity induced great hopes of what a master plan could achieve, and a simplistic dichotomy between 'good' and 'bad'. The invitation to participate in the plan was taken seriously, especially by those who thought their interests might be jeopardised, and 3500 objections were received when the plan was exhibited in 1948. Increasingly the County Council came to be regarded by land owners and local government as an agency of the state rather than as a representative of local interests, while the state government eventually found the council's freedom from direct ministerial control to be an embarrassment.

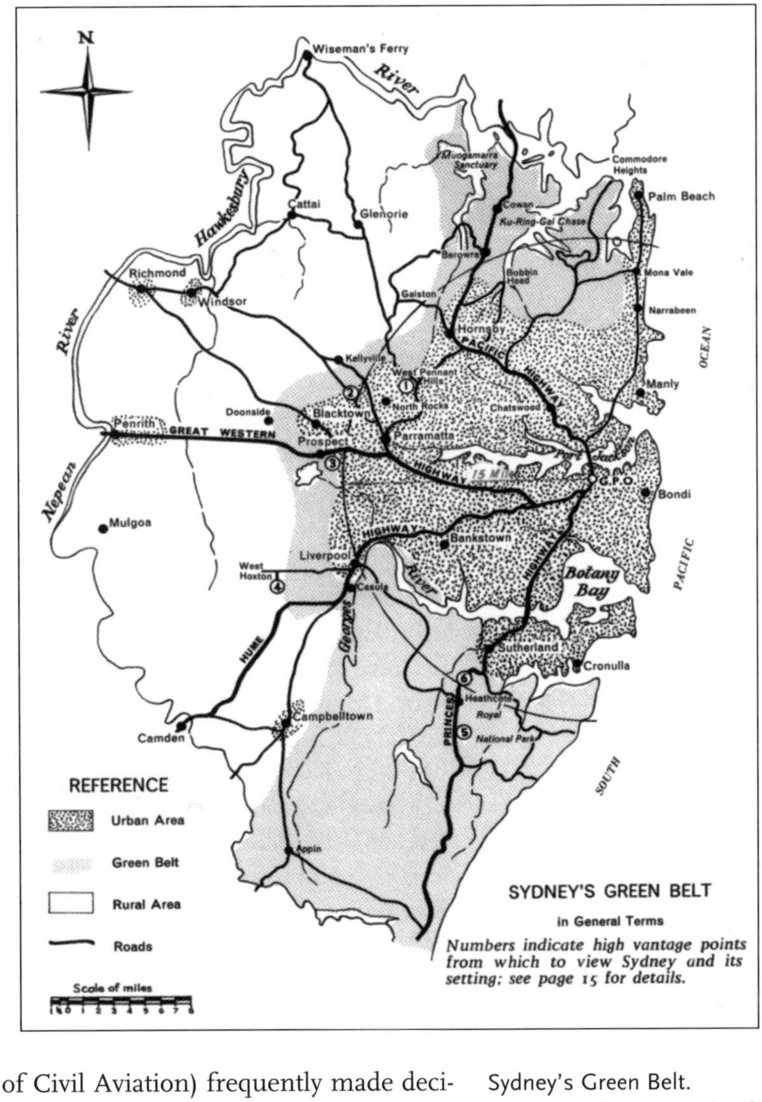

Sydney's Green Belt.
Cumberland County Council, 1963

The Cumberland County Council plan recommended that open spaces and routes for new roads be acquired, at an estimated cost of £15.7 million. McKell sought financial aid from the federal government but in December 1950 Prime Minister Menzies refused assistance to the county scheme on the grounds that it was not the concern of the Commonwealth. This stance was taken despite the fact that the Commonwealth was a major land holder in Sydney (controlling large parts of the harbour foreshores for defence and quarantine purposes, along with army bases and munitions plants), that Commonwealth immigration and economic policies had a direct impact on the city's growth, and that Commonwealth authorities (such as the Department of Civil Aviation) frequently made decisions affecting Sydney.

Presented to state Parliament in May 1951, the Cumberland County Council Planning Scheme became law the following month, the first metropolitan plan ever to become a statutory document in Australia. The three years that had elapsed since the scheme was submitted to the minister had seen considerable

'How delightfully simple! We just push the Green Belt further and further out. It can go on for ever.' Pat Hills and the Cumberland County planners confront the future.
Molnar, *Sydney Morning Herald*, 23 December 1959

SMH 23 Dec 1959

intrusions into the Green Belt and Open Space Reservations and had 'diminished whatever modest status the council had enjoyed in the hierarchy of public authorities concerned with metropolitan affairs'.[27]

The only body with cause to be grateful to the council was the Metropolitan Water, Sewerage and Drainage Board, whose massive backlog of works was eased by the restraint imposed on continuing suburban scatter by green-belt zoning. Most government departments were not cooperative. The Department of Railways virtually ignored the council's plan by refusing to build new lines, while most other departments consulted or ignored it as they saw fit. Major issues were frequently determined by Cabinet: in 1953, for instance, the minister for Local Government suspended part of the County Plan so that a Caltex oil refinery could be established on the Kurnell Peninsula, an area zoned as Open Space.[28]

A more serious suspension of the County Plan came in December 1959, when the Labor minister for Local Government and Highways, Pat Hills, released 50 square miles of the Green Belt for development. Hills' decision was 'a triumph for developers' but the Water Board found that it could not provide water or sewerage in the areas proposed for release. The subsequent deadlock was resolved in the 1963 legislation that set up the State Planning Authority; from then on all subdivision applications were referred to the Water, Sewerage and Drainage Board and subdividers had to contribute to the cost of the board's works. The inability of the CCC to resolve this deadlock contributed to its abolition.[29] According to Peter Harrison, the County Council:

> never became part of 'the ring' of departments and authorities where the workings of the apparatus of government, whether in conflict or in co-operation, are dealt with by unwritten understandings and personal or official relationships acquired over time. Its staff was not recruited from

the public service and remained outside it ...[30]

The council's greatest problem was that it had no option but to use the tool of town planning as a substitute for Greater Sydney government and the tool was too weak for the task. This same problem has dogged the activities of the county's many successors, the State Planning Authority (1964–74), the State Planning and Environment Commission (1974–80), the Department of Environment and Planning (1980–87), and the Department of Planning (1988), which received the additional responsibility of 'Urban Affairs' in 1995. Nevertheless, the County of Cumberland Planning Scheme was, in the words of the lawyer J.G. Starke QC, 'a milestone in Australian planning law. It has provided and will continue to provide a standard-setting scheme of general value and significance ...'[31] The Cumberland Plan remains the most important document to guide the growth of Sydney in this century. Later schemes—the Sydney Region Outline Plan of 1968 and the Metropolitan Strategy of 1988—were not accorded statutory authority, merely indicating a preferred direction for urban development but leaving the primary responsibility for land use zoning with local councils.

A Greater Sydney authority can only come about if the state government, headquartered in Sydney, relinquishes most of its power, and as Ruth Atkins observed in 1966:

> to ask for a real metropolitan governing body, with its own departments, its own budget, its own elections, its own officials and elected members, would be to ask the State Government to give up the heart of its empire to ... what would almost certainly become a rival control. Moreover, any allocation of funds or tax resources would be likely to force the State Government into politically uncomfortable open and obvious allocation as between 'metropolitan' and 'non-metropolitan' claims.[32]

In the 1980s and 1990s municipal reform lost steam. The Local Government Act of 1993 was an uninspired revision of the 1919 act, requiring councils to value their infrastructure, including roads, sporting facilities and other municipal property. The state government increasingly used land-specific statutory authorities to implement its more grandiose schemes. The Wran Labor government and its minister for Public Works, Laurie Brereton, created the Darling Harbour Authority in 1984 to give Sydney a festival market place, a convention centre and a casino. In the process they took planning powers away from the Sydney City Council

The Metropolitan Strategy of 1988 was revised in 1996 to produce a new strategic planning document called *A Framework for Growth and Change*. This 132-page report was the least impressive metropolitan planning document produced in Sydney in the twentieth century. Its aims of 'a healthy and sustainable environment', 'a competitive and adaptable economy' and 'liveable neighbourhoods' are remarkable only for their blandness. The quality-of-life rhetoric that pervades the document and the half-hearted 'action plan' that accompanies it show just how far state governments have retreated from attempting to articulate a vision for Sydney.[33] In the late 1990s the vision passed into the hands of the Sydney Olympics organising committee, real estate corporations and advertising agencies. They may not have been deciding where the next subdivisions go, but at least they projected an image of the city, which is more than the government seemed able to do.

From smoke nuisance to pollution control

A movement for sanitary reform and public health in Sydney gathered strength in the latter part of the nineteenth century. Its principal achievement was the Public Health Act of 1896 and the creation of a number of statutory bodies, including the Board of Health in 1881 and the Metropolitan Water, Sewerage and Drainage Board (MWSDB) in 1888. The act gave the Board of Health important powers over public sanitation. The authorities had regulatory powers and in the case of the MWSDB its own source of income, rates for water, sewerage and drainage services. The MWSDB invested in new water mains, drainage and ocean outfall sewers.[34]

Although pollution caused occasional comment in subsequent decades it was usually thought of in such terms as 'noxious trades', 'dust' and 'smoke nuisance'. The ecological consequences of air and water pollution were little realised. In 1955 the ALP government appointed a 'Smoke Abatement Committee'—the title is indicative of attitudes at the time—but a Clean Air Act was not passed until 1961, with the Air Pollution Control Branch created a year later. The power of the Maritime Services Board to curb oil pollution on navigable waters was not strengthened until 1960.

Despite a dramatic improvement in water supply and storm water and sewage disposal, Sydney's environment continued to deteriorate. The MWSDB simply could not keep up with the unchecked expansion of the urban area. Many of the new subdivisions of the 1950s and 1960s had town water but were unsewered. By 1959 two-thirds of Bankstown and almost half of leafy Ku-ring-gai remained unconnected to the sewer mains. Gradually the night soil collectors were replaced by septic tanks. Their installation became an industry in itself throughout outer-suburban Australia and in most coastal settlements. The 'tanks' were actually porous, so the waste water dissipated while solids accumulated in decomposing form. The water table in septic tank areas became extremely polluted. Between 1958 and 1970 over 100,000 septic tanks were installed in Sydney, more than 11,000 in 1964 alone. One health officer wrote in 1959 that 'Perhaps the greatest problem which confronts many Councils in the unsewered areas is the disposal of sullage waters. This, because of the non-absorptive qualities of the soil in most of Sydney, is extremely difficult.'[35]

While improved sewage disposal in the 1970s and 1980s was welcomed by councils and residents collectively, individual residents who owned or were buying their houses were not so enthusiastic. They usually had to pay a substantial compulsory levy to connect to the MWSDB's sewage disposal system, particularly irritating if one had paid for a septic tank only a few years earlier. In such an instance the collective good of residents may not be in the immediate financial interest of individual rate payers. This concern—about who pays and who benefits from pollution control and environmental improvements—explains why major corporations and governments are often tardy in addressing such problems.

In the late 1960s 'pollution' came back into common speech. The Liberal–Country Party government finally responded to public and press demands and in 1970 Parliament passed the State Pollution Control Commission Act, the Waste Disposal Act and the Clean Waters Act. In 1971 a State Pollution Control Commission and a Metropolitan Waste Disposal Authority were set up to administer the new acts. While the creation of these authorities meant that the law of public nuisance, adopted in colonial Sydney following British precedents, had been superseded, the new authorities had neither the power nor the staff to make much impact. Subsequent legislation, including a Noise Control Act in 1975, finally gave state instrumentalities the powers and sanctions they needed. In 1977–78 there were 72 air pollution, 42 water pollution and one noise pollution convictions recorded. But with fines totalling a mere $82,000 it was adverse publicity, rather than the fine, that proved the most effective sanction. Despite fines and sanctions, Sydney still suffers from massive air pollution, principally from cars and industry.[36] Water quality has improved as the industries lining the Cooks and Parramatta rivers have either closed down or improved their waste treatment processes. The introduction of lead-free petrol has cut but not eliminated car pollution, while the increasing sophistication of air filtration systems has reduced industrial pollution. Nonetheless, air polution remains a year-round problem for the city, so that clear, breezy days are in marked contrast to the smog alert days when the metropolis is overhung by yellow haze.

'The red flags's for dangerous currents, the green for poisonous jellyfish, the blue for sharks and the yellow for sewerage pollution.'
Sprod's Views of Sydney, Kangaroo Press, 1981

Drainage and sewage disposal problems have been less easily dealt with. The problem grows exponentially with the growth of the city. The submarine ocean outfall sewers, installed in the mid-1980s, have not been as successful as their advocates hoped. Many Sydney beaches are still at the mercy of the winds and the tides; on some days it is not only unpleasant but unsafe to swim because of the city's effluent.

The bitter controversy over flat development in Sydney in the 1960s and 1970s was supplanted, in the 1980s and 1990s, by an equally bitter debate about the environmental amenity of the suburbs. Pressures mounted for 'dual occupancy': the right to erect a second dwelling on a block of land in areas dominated by detached houses. The debate wasn't just restricted to the leafy north shore; it was equally hard fought in many working-class and lower

'Suburban Sydney is largely sprawling and untidy, and the answer, of course (now that I have at last got my own cottage) is that in future, individual homes must be banned, and for sheer compactness people shall be compelled to live fuller, happier, less sprawling lives in huge blocks of well aspected flats ... slap in the middle of the picture we see ... a hero's home — for only a householder game enough to do battle with councils, covenants and local authorities can ever succeed in owning such a house.'

Bernard Hesling, *Sydney Observed*, c. 1950

middle-class suburbs. Councillors and their council staff were caught between a desire for a more efficient city—making better use of existing infrastructure—and equally persuasive arguments about preserving the character and amenity of streets and suburbs.

The bitterness, manoeuvring, humanity and power struggles of local politics are brilliantly caught in the documentary *Rats in the Ranks*, an account of the Leichhardt Council in the early 1990s. Made with the agreement of the chief protagonists, including the councillors, it shows the workings of a Labor-dominated council confronting planning issues in a rapidly gentrifying suburb. Vast tracks of harbourside land in Balmain have been vacated by industrial firms that moved their operations elsewhere or simply closed plants down. Some of the sites, including the Balmain Power Station near the Iron Cove Bridge and the Caltex plant at Ballast Point, are worth millions of dollars. The politics of land use zoning in Sydney became more complex with the introduction, by the Wran government, of a Planning and Environment Act in 1979, premised on councils making comprehensive plans for their area. Developers, on the other hand, prefer prompt spot zonings for their own sites, their primary motivation being to make a profit with little regard to the impact their development has on the surrounding area. Councils, on the other hand, need to assess traffic generation, site contamination (common on industrial sites), drainage provision, the mix of housing and/or commercial premises requested and deal with objections from local residents.[37]

The costs and benefits of 'urban consolidation', whether through dual occupancy or other medium-density housing developments, continue to be debated, especially where they intersect with concerns about the 'carrying capacity' of the suburbs.[38] Many of Sydney's services are at breaking point. Gas and water mains are over a hundred years old in some parts of the inner city and often break down. The gravity-based sewerage and drainage system is overloaded—it backs up, even in fashionable suburbs such as Kirribilli, while in the west, which is flatter, flash flooding is common, not least because some of Sydney's rainfall comes in spectacular downpours.

Environmental concerns are closely related to the taxation and expenditure patterns of the municipal economy. Every year the state government raises millions of dollars through land taxes, which go into internal revenue. In 1996–97 it collected $150 million in stamp duty on property transactions and $641 million in land tax but granted less than $100 million to local councils. Municipalities have to rely on rates to raise revenue for local services, from road maintenance to libraries. Based on unimproved capital value, municipal rates are a reasonably fair way of contributing to suburban services: the more land you have and the better the view or aspect the more rates you will pay. Until recently water rates were also calculated the same way, but by the early 1990s the corporatised water authority switched to a basic flat fee plus use-based charge, hoping to encourage people to conserve water. Water consumption did indeed drop as many households became better at curbing overuse, especially in the laundry and in the garden. Water restrictions, once a common feature of life in Sydney, are now only rarely imposed.[39]

Brochure cover, c. 1935

Property owners and public access

In the late 1890s and early 1900s yachting enthusiasts and naturalists campaigned to ensure that the harbour foreshores would be 'for the people'. Their cause was taken up by Niels Rasmus Nielsen, a Copenhagen-born cabinet maker who arrived in Australia in the 1870s. Turning to farming near Young, he became an office holder in the Australian Workers Union in 1894, then served as an MLA for Boorowa and subsequently for Yass. In October 1910 he became minister for Lands in the Labor government and the following July he led a walking party along a new path through the harbour foreshores at Mosman, from Ashton Park to Athol Gardens. The journalist accompanying the party wrote that the views:

A well-meaning town planner confronts a property developer driven by different imperatives.
Penguin Petty, Penguin, 1972

are not merely views of the harbour and the city, in themselves exquisite, but also of the beauty of nature that lies here, virgin and all unspoiled, beautiful verdure and gum trees, lovely glades and rugged, rocky scenery. It was National Park: it was the Blue Mountains, in Sydney itself.[40]

Sydney had already distinguished itself by creating a National Park to the south of the city in 1879 and, shortly after, the Kuringai Chase Park. Neither of these were protected by acts of Parliament—they were merely reservations whose size and use could be altered at governmental whim. Nonetheless, colonial and then state governments, with motives varying from 'lungs for the city' to bushland preservation and public recreation, did debate issues of public access. Nielsen regretted that previous governments had allowed such an enormous area of 'beautiful waterfrontages to be taken away from the people', and he was joined in the call for harbourside lands to be resumed by the government.

In the preceding decades most of the harbour land had been converted to freehold and purchased by shipping companies, industrial concerns and, to the east of Circular Quay, by residential owners and developers.[41] Religious bodies, government instrumentalities and schools usually got their land in the form of a Crown grant, as did the Catholic and Anglican churches (for schools and seminaries), the Quarantine Station at North Head, along with land allocated for army, naval, police and municipal use.

Parliament granted Nielsen £150,000 to spend on resumptions, and the money was spent in Rose Bay, Watsons Bay, and many parts of Mosman. Nielsen was proud of the fact that he had managed to secure 16 miles of harbour foreshore, from Sirius Cove to Quaker's Hat in Middle Harbour. Among his achievements was the resumption of Forty Baskets and Reef Beaches, the latter now famous for nude bathing (yet another example of the many public uses of public space). Nielsen also secured 40 acres to be used by a government-backed Zoological Trust, so the city zoo could be moved from Moore Park to a commanding site overlooking Athol Bay. The area now became home to a grand zoo, landscaped in the European style, surrounded by natural bushland, with public access by both ferry and tram. An area at nearby Chowder Bay was cleared, a huge harbourside pool installed, and vast sheds erected for workers' picnics.

These foreshore reservations and formal parks came at a time when Sydney's most populated areas had little recreational space. Some industrial suburbs like Botany North and Newtown had no parks at all. The creation of parks and the maintenance of existing parks lay with local councils; the 1919 Local Government Act allowed councils to consider the issue of parks when assessing new subdivisions. But in the older suburbs the only way to create parks and playing fields was to purchase land. After some years of agitation the war historian C.E.W. Bean, a devotee of 'active engagement in sports' as a key to preserving the national character of Australians, formed a Parks and Playgrounds movement. From the late 1920s the provision of parks improved markedly. Between 1940 and 1960 open space in Auburn increased from 1 per cent to 9 per cent, the biggest increase due to the Cumberland County Council's purchase of wetlands along the Duck River, which it handed to Auburn Council.[42] A later purchase by the State Planning Authority formed the basis for Auburn's Botanic Gardens, including a Japanese garden, made possible by a grant from the federal Labor government in 1973.[43] This garden did much to enhance the reputation of western Sydney, well before the state government chose Homebush as the site for an Olympic bid.

The Middle Head fortifications are now included in the Sydney Harbour National Park
Photograph by Peter Spearritt, 1998

The Sydney Harbour National Park, which began to take shape in the latter half of the 1970s, is one of the world's great urban parks. Starting from the base of Nielsen's resumptions and foreshore land purchased by the State Planning Authority in the 1960s, the National Park took in large parcels of land at North Head, South Head, Georges Heights, Middle Head and Dobroyd Head. Access to parts of the park is by car, or by boat or foot. The park offers wonderful vistas of the ocean, the harbour, the bushland and the built fabric of Sydney. The Quarantine Station on North Head is a reminder of smallpox and influenza epidemics, while the fortifications at Middle Head bear witness to the fear of naval invasion from the 1880s to the 1940s. Unlike many flatter cities, Sydney offers a remarkable mix of grand vistas and local landscapes. Its harbour, its headlands and its rivers provide a level of access to these vistas that is unusual in a large world city.

CHAPTER 9

The dress circle and the stalls

FACING PAGE
Cranbrook boys inspect the chief theatre of Australian life from their school grounds.
NSW Government Printer, c. 1938

Sydney's hills, flatlands, harbour and rivers create the potential for views and breezes, for hot suburbs and cooler suburbs. Until the 1970s everyone knew that the dress circle suburbs were to be found in the east and the north. They were above and beyond the commerce of the city centre, and the industry and hotter temperatures of the inner western and western suburbs. They were also far removed from the soap factories, paint and chemical firms, power stations and gas plants that dominated the harbour foreshore in Balmain, much of both sides of the Parramatta River, its offshoot the Duck River and the Cooks River. At a time when 'dress circle' still had the lingering sense of that part of the cinema that one attended in evening dress, while the stalls were the cheaper alternative, the class structure of Sydney's suburbs seemed straightforward. With the rapid growth of the city in the 1950s and 1960s more and more waterways were colonised by view hunters. Houses were built overlooking the George's River, from Sylvania to Alfords Point. If you couldn't see the water, the next best alternative was to abut bushland. Thanks to the Cumberland County Council's green belt, many areas to the north and north-west of the city and in the southern suburbs did just that. Modernist houses embraced the bush with large plate-glass windows, verandahs and sliding doors.

The high-rise apartments of the 1960s showed that you could rise above commerce and grime and get great views. The social structure of Sydney in the mid-1960s was brilliantly captured by Bruce Petty in the cartoon reproduced overleaf. Advances in air conditioning meant that you could create your own temperate environment. By the 1980s and 1990s stall-like localities suddenly offered dress circle apartments and penthouses. The dress circle and the stalls analogy of the interwar years had given way to a society where both locations were desirable, not unlike in the Sydney Opera House where those two seating positions command the highest seat prices. With the spate of factory closures in the 1980s (discussed in chapter 6) even the once industry-dominated Parramatta River suddenly became home to upper middle-class town houses and restaurants offering river views.

In 1930 the Australian historian Keith Hancock wrote that 'Society in Australia is not yet fixed and formalised. Men do not find it difficult to change their house or town or class.'[1] But the contemporary record often reveals a clear recognition of the existence of social classes: the terms 'working class' and 'middle class' were in common usage at the time. Some people earned more and owned more than others while some localities were more attractive and expensive than others. Many men *and* women did find it difficult to

Bruce Petty captures the wealth, the poverty, the condescension and the pretension of Sydney society in the mid-1960s. Reading from the left a prominent Sydney personality of the time, the lawyer Peter Clyne, offers to evict people in rent controlled premises, while SP bookies lurk in the background. The Point Piper Push is driving itself all the way to the north shore where the residents of Ivory Stalks 'can see the bridge'. Yachting enthusiasts doubt the pleasure of motor-powered gin palaces. Propped up by illegal gambling, poker machines (then banned in Victoria) and strip joints, Kings Cross is clearly 'no place for a Melbourne man'.
Petty's *Australia Fair*, Cheshire, 1967

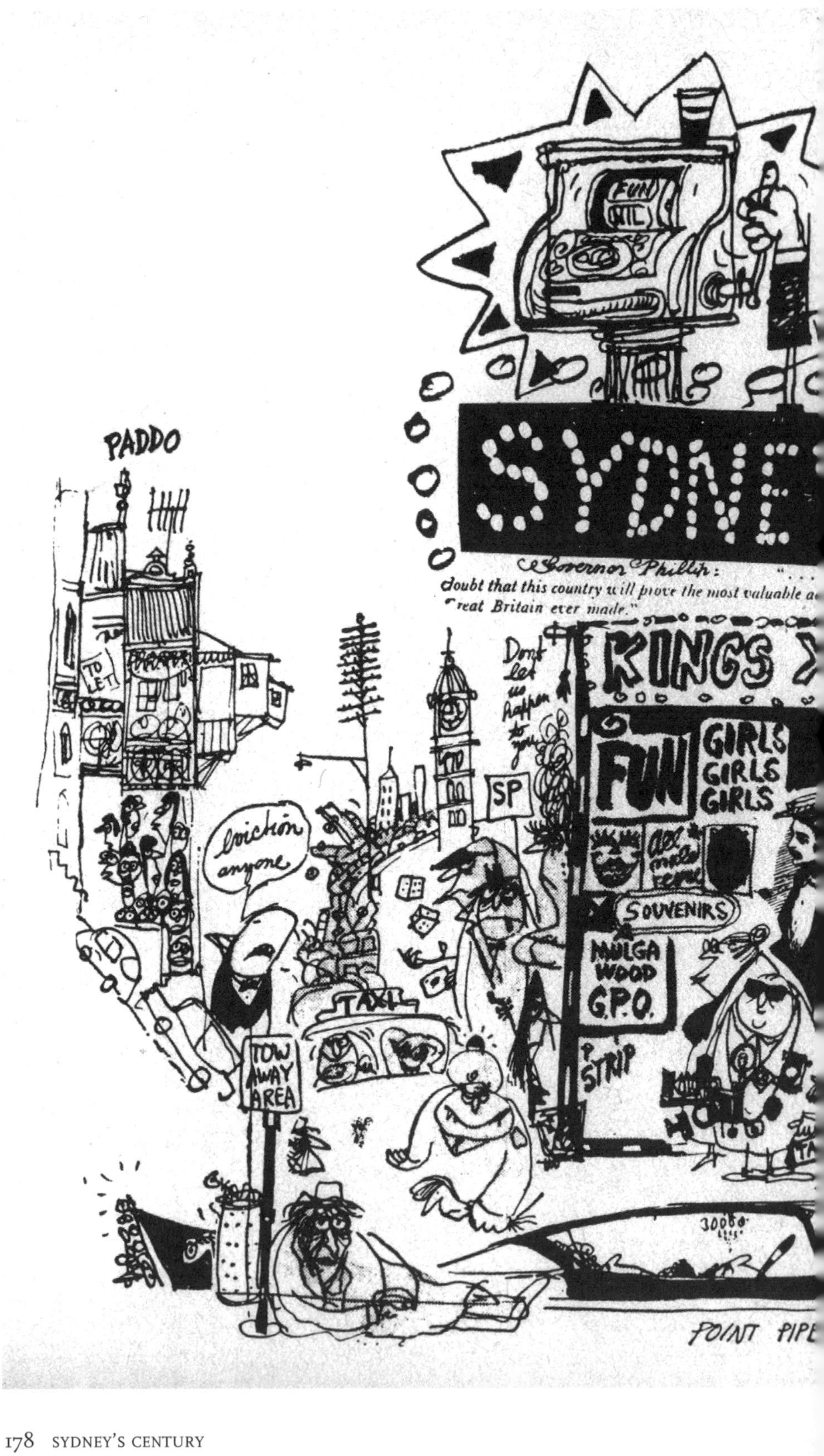

We'll call you
NORTH SHORE CULTURE
I'm repolishing an old chair
ABANDON HOPE
IVORY STALKS
HOME UNITS
I can see the Bridge
Where's the pleasure in that?
Miss Fredine Pikhe and escort at the Red White and Blue Ball held by the Companions of the Royal Commonwealth Society, the 20th Century Group of the Royal Over-Seas League and the Young Contingent of the Victoria
Petty

The terrace houses and commercial buildings of central Sydney.
Postcard, c. 1895

change their house or class. My argument in this chapter is that there exists, and existed at the time Hancock wrote, a class structure of the suburbs that was 'formalised' but not as fixed as first appearances might indicate.

Sydney's early suburbs saw landlords living side by side with tenants. Many landlords lived in one of the terraces in the terrace rows that they built. Local communities included cottages for working men and larger villas for business and professional people.[2] As Sydney grew, a pattern of land values developed that influenced which income groups could afford to buy or rent in particular localities.

The class structure of the suburbs is but one reflection of the general class structure that reaches beyond city, state and even national boundaries. The existence of social classes (or, if one prefers, social groupings) in Australia has been established as a perceptual phenomenon by questionnaire and opinion-poll data.[3] More objective measures, including the vast differences in wealth indicated by income distribution, share and property ownership, suggest that classes do exist. Social class has more ramifications than differences in wealth and power. In a large city, as Blair Badcock establishes in his book *Unfairly Structured Cities*, the social geography of urban life is a product of changing employment patterns, council zoning and the dynamics of the property market.[4]

By 1895 the compilers of guidebooks, among the city's most acute social commentators, were identifying marked differences between Sydney suburbs. As one of them wrote:

> Alexandria, Annandale, Arncliffe and Auburn are recognised as working men's suburbs, the houses being small ... Botany is devoted to factories, and Burwood and Bondi to gentlemen's residences ... Darling Point and Double Bay, which are near the harbour are ... regarded as the fashionable part of Sydney. The other fashionable suburbs are Elizabeth Bay, Pott's Point, Rushcutters Bay, Gladesville (on the Parramatta River), Point Piper, Rose Bay and Strathfield. At all the above places the houses are mostly large, and are surrounded by beautifully laid out grounds ... Mosman's Bay is a charming place on the north side of the harbour, the residences, which are mostly detached cottages, having lovely views ... Parramatta is a large business town, and the centre of a fruit growing district ... Pyrmont, St Peters and Woolloomooloo are best described as working men's suburbs. Randwick is a well laid out suburb, near Coogee with all descriptions of houses.[5]

For a suburb to be fashionable it had to be free of industry and have large houses, ample land, topographical interest and preferably views as well. No suburb more than five miles from the city was regarded as desirable unless it had good public transport, as did Strathfield with trains or Mosman with ferries. At the time the 1895 guidebook was released, the north shore line had only recently been completed, but in the following decades large houses, such as those in the eastern suburbs, Strathfield and Mosman, spread along that line, to create the longest continuous sector of middle-class settlement in Australia. Here doctors and stockbrokers, retailers and wholesalers, importers and exporters, and even the occasional teacher made their homes. The quintessentially middle-class nature of these suburbs could be seen in the clubs, churches, schools and political party branches that flourished along the line.

Occupation, income and choice of suburb

A rough occupational and income map of Sydney can be drawn using a number of measurements including income and the percentage of employers and professionals living in particular municipalities. In 1920 the Sydney Stock Exchange, the heart of Sydney's business community, had 74 members, all with offices in the central city area. Sixty-six of these gentlemen (there were of course no women) worked between 56 and 135 Pitt Street, and the remaining eight in other streets immediately surrounding the Stock Exchange.[6] *Sands Directory* of 1921 gives the addresses of 48 of these stockbrokers, none of whom lived in the city. Forty-six of the 48 lived in four distinct suburban bands: 17 in the northern harbourside suburbs from Hunters Hill to Manly, 10 on the north shore line from Chatswood to Wahroonga, seven in the eastern suburbs and 12 on the line from Summer Hill (including the off-line garden suburb of Haberfield) to Strathfield. Of the remaining two, one lived in Beecroft and one in Drummoyne. Stockbrokers, it can safely be said, were never found residing in working-class suburbs, even though a few may have been born in them.

Kurraba Point, Neutral Bay, before the coming of apartment blocks.
Postcard, c. 1933

Conversely, factory workers were not represented in stockbrokers' suburbs. Most women listed in the 1918 Board of Trade inquiry into the female living wage lived in the inner suburbs near the factories in which they worked, though a few came from as far away as Liverpool. Working-class people who wished to live elsewhere than the inner suburbs had little choice but to go a long way out; they could not afford to buy or rent in the middle-ring, middle-class suburbs. At the 1947 census the suburbs with the highest percentage of women clothing workers were the inner suburbs of Glebe and Balmain and the western suburbs of Canterbury, Bankstown, Lidcombe, Granville and Fairfield. Residential concentrations of working-class and middle-class men were more striking because the male workforce was more stratified: women, including middle-class women who sought paid work, did not have a wide range of jobs to choose from unless they had professional training or capital.[7]

The percentage of male employers by local government area and the distribution of income by municipality show a hierarchy of suburbs at the top that has remained relatively unchanged over time. Ku-ring-gai, Woollahra and Mosman were at the top of the hierarchy in 1921 and in 1971. The suburbs that now comprise the municipality of South Sydney—Redfern, Alexandria, Darlington and Waterloo—were near the bottom in 1921 and 1971, but by 1996 South Sydney, reflecting the gentrification of the inner city over the past two decades, had almost the same proportion of professionals in its workforce (29 per cent) as Ku-ring-gai, Woollahra and Mosman (each 33 per cent). These figures also reflect a dramatic shift in occupational structure, with a decline in blue collar numbers and a rise in the proportion of jobs in professional categories. Only on the outer fringe, including Fairfield–Liverpool and

Campbelltown, are there still suburbs where less than 12 per cent of the workforce are classified as professionals.[8]

The highest average weekly household incomes, not only in Sydney but in New South Wales in 1996 were Ku-ring-gai ($1225) Mosman ($1096) and Woollahra ($1030), except that Baulkham Hills, which developed rapidly in the 1970s and 1980s, came in second at $1145. Of the 14 suburbs in Sydney with the highest average income, 12 were north of the harbour; only two, Woollahra and Sutherland, were to the south. South Sydney ($644) remained near the bottom of the income scale with only Botany ($616) and Auburn–Canterbury ($593) below it.[9] These traditional working-class suburbs have housed successive waves of immigrants since the 1950s, including Greeks, Lebanese, Turks and Pacific Islanders.[10]

Class and the real estate market

Of all appeals to class consciousness, perhaps the most common is the real estate agent's For Sale advertisements. The *Sydney Morning Herald* frequently carried ads such as the following, which appeared in July 1928:

> Bellevue Hill—Luxurious New Bungalow—7 rooms, 2 garages—£4400. Fully sized tennis court. Situated on the heights in the most select residential area, surrounded by beautiful homes, this 'Modern to the Minute' bungalow will meet with instant approval ... all rooms artistically papered. Land 50 x 260 ...[11]

Bellevue Hill was and is one of the most select of the residential areas of the eastern suburbs, along with Vaucluse, Rose Bay, Potts Point and Darling Point. In 1923 the eastern suburbs were described as 'thickly populated with the prettiest houses of the middle and comfortable classes'.[12]

The north shore received similar treatment. Killara was 'one of the most sought after and exclusive suburbs', while a house in Roseville was advertised thus: '£3,250—Charming modern bungalow. Only six minutes from the station. The property is CONNECTED TO THE SEWER'.[13] The particular stress of each advertisement varied to suit local circumstances, such as availability of transport, sewerage and the like, but one feature remained constant for all these suburbs: the continual stress on class appeal.

Middle-class councils did all in their power to preserve the residential character of their suburb by excluding industry with its attendant smoke and noise. Most middle-class suburbs remained relatively free of industry. In 1947 the Cumberland County Council found that none of the harbour foreshore in Vaucluse, Woollahra, Ashfield and Mosman was alienated by industry, while 92 per cent of foreshore in Auburn, 38 in Lidcombe, 39 in Concord, 69 in Balmain, 100 in Annandale and 75 per cent in Glebe housed industry.[14] Businessmen, often aided and abetted by local councils, decided on the location of new industry but rarely lived in the industrial suburbs. In November 1941 the *Real Estate Institute Journal* reported that Mosman Council saw its suburb as:

> essentially a place where the private home type of real estate should predominate. Manufacturing premises were totally prescribed against and

"It's quite a salubrious locality. Why, you've got a germicide works one side, the hospital's at the back, and, if the worst comes to the worst, you'll find the undertaker just round the corner, right next to the morgue."

Emile Mercier, *My Ears Are Killing Me*, Angus & Robertson, Sydney, 1955

> communal buildings, such as flats, were relegated to certain defined and limited areas ... it would be wrong to erect a first-class residence in a second-class locality.

The institute commented that Mosman property had shown 'a consistency of value that should be most satisfactory to all concerned'.

In marked contrast were advertisements for inner city working-class areas. Here real estate agents not unnaturally refrained from commenting on the social character of the area: these ads lacked middle-class frills. They were usually short and packed with information. Terraces were advertised thus: 'REDFERN—Terrace of 14 houses, well built, each with five rooms, kitchen, slate roofs, good letting position, low rents. Torrens. Price £6700. Sound Investment.' Other were even shorter: 'MARRICKVILLE—three cottages—rents £221—Price only £1975'.[15] The presumably middle-class buyers of such properties did not require a social evaluation of the locality since they were not going to live there: all they needed was information on profitability.

There is other evidence to suggest that housing and land values were strongly correlated with the class of population and the land use of particular areas. One measure is the unimproved capital value (UCV) of building sites in Sydney's suburbs. UCV figures are assessed on each block of land and breakdowns for dwellings alone are not available, so to make the comparison relevant for present purposes only those suburbs that were primarily residential will be considered. The following figures are based on average UCVs for 1930, as this was the only year when the number of valuations as well as the total valuation was published. Property values in middle-class suburbs such as Woollahra (£1142), Vaucluse (£987) and Mosman (£641) far outstripped working-class (primarily residential) suburbs such as Erskineville (£193) or Lidcombe (£161). Land prices and consequently values were even lower in outer metropolitan working-class suburbs such as Holroyd (£111), Ermington–Rydalmere (£99) and Fairfield (£85). The unimproved capital value of property in an outer metropolitan middle-class suburb such as Ku-ring-gai stood at an average of £383, more than three times that in residential working-class suburbs.[16]

The value of houses followed a similar pattern to the value of land. In 1927 the journalist Charles Whitham wrote that:

> The value of property per head is greater in these northern districts than in the western and southern suburbs, the homes being of a more costly type ... [I]n 1926 ... the average value of new dwellings erected in the Illawarra and Bankstown line districts was £678, in the North Shore districts the corresponding figure was £951.[17]

When the value of land and of house was added together, the absolute extremes between middle and working-class suburbs were even greater.

Real estate advertisements often attempt to create an artificial market by using appeals to status consciousness; but because of the enormous turnover of real estate and house building the market has its own financial reality. With the exception of speculative operations and outer suburban developments, the house and land market (except in times of recession) is relatively stable. Real estate agents undoubtedly try to manipulate status appeals and stretch the meaning of phrases such as water glimpses, but the availability of finance, the quality of the immediate environment and the likely resale value of the property (itself dependent on the amenity and the dominant class of the area) have always been major determinants of price.

'With this one you get ABSOLUTELY FREE a white-ant kit, a large drum of cockroach powder, a year's supply of Ratto and a dozen galvanised buckets in case of heavy rain.'
Sprod's Views of Sydney, Kangaroo Press, Sydney, 1981

The Sydney real estate market is fuelled by a variety of interlocking demands: population growth, changes in household composition, changes in lifestyle, proximity to work and recreation, investor preferences, affordability and notions of housing as a sound asset. In the 1920s Sydney's housing stock varied from the run-down terraces of the inner city to palatial harbourside mansions, from the one-bedroom owner-built shack on the outskirts to the blocks of flats being built on the lower north shore and the eastern suburbs. These physical structures were home to a great variety of financial and living arrangements. Many of the inner city rented terraces housed more than one family, or at the very least an extended family, often with lodgers as well, while even mansions—such as Elizabeth Bay House—were sometimes converted to boarding houses and available to any paying customer.

In the 1980s, by which time the metropolis had spread to the foothills of the Blue Mountains, near-city space was at such a premium that many boarding houses were converted into middle-class apartments for purchase or rent. Some of these large dwellings had originally been built to cater for middle-class households and their servants. But during the 1980s the boarders—mostly poor adults, usually single—were evicted so that the refurbished properties reverted to middle-class occupancy, albeit with considerably less space than the original middle-class households had enjoyed. Some local councils, including North Sydney and Randwick, attempted to stem the tide of boarding house conversions, but with only limited success. The untaxed capital gains (because the dwellings had been acquired before 1986, when the Hawke government introduced a capital gains tax) were simply too tempting for landlords to resist.[18] The developers of one Neutral Bay boarding house, Rothesay, promoted its conversion with a sign proclaiming 'once the home of many, now a home for the select few'. Garages were built at the back of the property and the old bombs that once dotted the back lane gave way to BMWs and SAABs.[19]

The Ritz at Cremorne catered to short and long term guests, before being converted to apartments in the early 1990s.
Postcard, 1952

The changing class structure of Sydney real estate is not easy to map because of the many factors that impinge on it. There are only a few constants: proximity to the city centre and jobs has always been a factor in choosing housing, but this applies as much to the poor of Redfern as to the residents of Kirribilli. Harbour sites have always had a particular cachet in Sydney, but attitudes to the monetary value of views have changed over time. Many harbourside homes built between the 1860s and the 1920s still front the street, effectively turning their back on the water. Balconies and picture windows facing the water did not become common until the 1930s.

Harbourside houses and flats have not always commanded the premium prices familiar to Sydneysiders since the 1980s. The Japanese midget submarine attack in wartime 1942 and the shelling of some beach suburbs actually depressed prices for a while. Even as late as the 1980s grand houses on the upper north shore line often commanded higher prices than equivalent dwellings with harbour views. This is no longer the case. In 1998 Mosman became the first suburb in Australia where the median house price topped one million dollars. Most land in Sydney with unimproved capital value of over $1 million offers harbour or river views. Harbour mansions, priced from $2 million to $20 million, regularly feature in the property pages of the newspapers. Their prices have very little to do with an adequate rental return on the capital invested, but a great deal to do with the prestige of the owner and the prospects for capital gains in one of the world's scarcest commodities—water views in a world city.[20]

The dress circle and the stalls: images of suburban class

Any observer of a large city soon notices patterns of residential concentration and differentiation. If the city is growing, in terms of both population and physical size, there will also be pressure to change land use and structures, usually by demolition and rebuilding. In *Where to Live: ABC Guide to Sydney and Suburbs*, published in 1917, M.A. Harris advised prospective home buyers about the changing fortunes of some suburbs:

> The best residential portion of the areas controlled by the City Council are Darlinghurst, Potts Point, Elizabeth Bay and Moore Park ... [W]ith the growth of the city out towards [Camperdown] ... residences were pulled down to make room for factories ... Chippendale is another large manufacturing centre ... Surry Hills besides containing the houses of the poorer-classes, also has manufactories of every description. Woolloomooloo is also a poor class of the city having extensive wharves ...

Class consciousness also permeates building and architectural magazines. George and Florence Taylor's *Building* magazine, the official organ of the Master Builders Association of NSW, provides a fascinating commentary on builders' perceptions of suburban Sydney. The July 1920 issue carried an article on Clifton Gardens, a locality at the tip of Mosman facing Rose Bay across the harbour. 'There has grown up within the brief space of a few years, some very dainty houses ...' commented the magazine. 'The values of land in the first instance were sufficiently high to attract a class of people comfortably sit-

This palatial home at Darling Point cost £15,000. Built for Captain James Patrick, head of the shipping line, it had a swimming pool and a tennis court.
Pix, 16 April 1938

The Childrens' Evangelistic Band, open air Sunday School, Weedon Avenue, Paddington, 1937

uated in life.' From the lower north shore to the upper north shore line the story was the same. In its weekly review of 'Building and Building Land', the *Evening News* informed its readers on 25 August 1920 that:

> Killara is another Mosman, with more of the atmosphere of leisure and the environmental attributes of big homes set in spacious grounds, with gardeners trimming the hedges, and private garages in eloquent evidence of the tone of the centre ... The Killara resident has been attracted to the place because of its status. He has built a nice home, and keeps it so, because the man next door has done likewise.

In 1938 the town planner A.J. Brown built 'Fountains', a delightful home at Killara. Its many rooms and ample gardens were in marked contrast to the terrace houses of Redfern and Alexandria, many of which lacked adequate cooking and bathing facilities.

Wilson's 1924 *Guide Book to Sydney* described Alexandria as 'a manufacturing suburb with extensive brickworks and factories', while a *Sydney Morning Herald* writer said of Botany, 'over everything, the factories that crowd the district round drop terrible, choking tongues of grey brown mist'. He went on to speculate whether 'people who live in Botany and in its self sufficient shopping centres and places of amusement find all the interest necessary to their lives [and] never notice these things, but to the visitor ...'. That quotation comes from one of a series of five *Herald* feature articles on 'Sydney: A Growing City' published 6–13 September 1927. A key theme was the claim that 'of very few districts indeed can one say that they are suburbs for workers or suburbs for professional men or suburbs for wealthy men of property and business', but the 'Western Suburbs', which in the writer's definition included Ryde, Drummoyne, Gladesville and Hunter's Hill on the

'When up to £20,000 is being paid for pearl necklaces ... when furriers offer mink coats at £700 ... when men spend as many thousands as they once spent hundreds on homes ... when champagne sales boom and shops sell out of top hats — and that is the position in Australian cities to-day — then prosperity has really rounded that corner, and luxury living is back.' Australian vintners reported record sales of champagne magnums at Easter 1938.
Pix, 16 April 1938

Parramatta River, were described as places where:

> one may glimpse the towering impassive bulk of what other countries call the Great Middle Class. The Western Suburbs are their home; there they have entrenched themselves with their solid virtues, their substantial property, their sensible pleasures, their tennis and 6 o'clock dinners, their bowling clubs and lawnmowers, their parlour maids and perambulators.

That a sociologist might quibble with the population of these suburbs being labelled 'middle class' need not worry us, for the point is made that people at the time did think of suburbs and social segregation in class terms. This is more apparent in other parts of the same article, where the writer tells us that the first section of the journey to outer-suburban Ryde through 'city districts', was 'very depressing ... children sitting around on the footpaths and dabbling their feet in the drains, [it] makes your skin creep'. Drummoyne, in contrast, was depicted as having rambling gardens 'where children have no interest in the gutter'. Other contrasts he noted included the choking fumes prevalent in the inner city terrace house suburbs, which he characterised as 'slums', compared with the magnificent gardens of Vaucluse.

The fifth and last article of the series pointed out that the north shore had more attractive houses to the square mile than any other part of the city and was serviced by the tram line that ran from McMahons Point to Chatswood and the north shore line. There he found big houses and gardens devoted to the quiet settled life of professional men and superior tradesmen. The north shore was soon to become the most populous centre of middle-class settlement in Sydney, displacing the eastern suburbs. By 1927 Charles Whitham could observe that the 'burgesses' of certain districts on the north shore 'take pride in proclaiming themselves to be occupiers of dress circle seats in the chief theatre of Australian life, but this insistence would be fought by sundry swellers of Woollahra and Waverley'.[21]

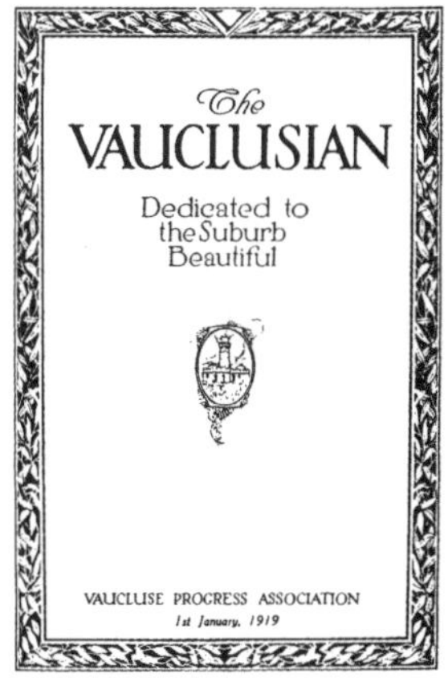

The Vauclusian, 1919

The eastern suburbs were not without their advocates. In 1919 residents of Vaucluse got together to produce a lavish celebration of their suburb in the *Vauclusian* magazine. They conducted an essay competition among school children titled 'Why I Like Living at Vaucluse': the winner, who came from Watsons Bay Public School, wrote with more than a trace of a parent's hand:

> Vaucluse, by reason of its nearness to the city, and its means of access by ferry and by tram, is a convenient place to live in. It is more or less in a natural state. The rugged cliffs and broken ground tapering down to the beautiful sandy beaches, form a picture which is always pleasing. The climate is always moderate by reason of the glorious sea breeze. When the people in the city are feeling the great heat on a day like yesterday, we in Vaucluse know little about it.[22]

Because working-class people have left fewer published records than the middle class, it is more difficult to assess their awareness of geographical class segregation. That they were aware of class is amply illustrated in labour and trade union journals, such as the *Labor Daily* and the *Australian Worker*, especially in their cartoons. More forceful evidence can be found in working-class actions, particularly strikes. There were no anti-eviction battles in middle-class suburbs during the Depression: clearly the working class and the middle class were expected to adopt different modes of protest, just as they led different lifestyles on their different incomes in their different suburbs.[23]

Redfern 'bottlo' yard. Bottles were sufficiently valuable that bottling yards employed many men to sort bottles for reuse to beer, wine and softdrink companies.
Pix, c. 1938

Terrace houses drawn by Wep for the 1961 edition of *Here's Luck* published by Angus & Robertson.

One of the classic accounts of working-class life in Sydney came from the pen of Lennie Lower. Son of an itinerant chemist, he found employment as a humorous writer, starting on *Beckett's Budget*, a Sydney scandal sheet, then moving to the *Labor Daily*, the *Daily Guardian* and *Smith's Weekly*, all of which catered to predominantly working-class audiences.

Lower's popular book *Here's Luck* traced a few months in the life of Jack Gudgeon, his wife Agatha and son Stanley, and their circle of male friends, girlfriends, relatives and enemies, from Flannery, the proprietor of the local pub, to Woggo's mob, who have scores to settle with Jack and Stanley. The denouement of the novel comes when Jack throws a party in his wife's absence, at the family home, a rented terrace house. In Jack's view, if there's no fight at a party, then the party 'isn't a success'. '[I]f modern hostesses only have the enterprise to arrange a brawl among the guests, the present boredom of the social round would not exist,' he remarks. After a brief fight and a party of strip poker, where Jack noticed that 'the girls evidently could not play poker', he retired to drink whisky from the bottle. During what is later described as 'an orgy and a saturnalia', son Stanley inadvertently drops his cigarette, setting his upstairs bedroom on fire. It takes some time for the drunken party-goers to recognise the significance of this. Jack organises for the drunks to be removed from the house, but guests are invited to stay and watch the fire:

> About fifty of the guests were sitting in a row on the kerb on the opposite side of the road, chatting excitedly ... A crowd of spectators was gathering quickly and the windows and balconies of the opposite terrace were festooned with faces ... Three fire-engines swept, clanging, around Flannery's corner and scattered us from the kerb.[24]

The fireman asks the spectators to move away, to which Stanley replieds, 'It's coming to something when a man can't look at his own fire that he started himself.' Woggo and Stanley then start to bet on whether the balcony or the roof will go first. *Here's Luck* brilliantly captures working-class disrespect for private property at a time when almost two-thirds of the population of Sydney were tenants. It takes an apparently tragic event—the burning down of a family home—and makes it the stuff of comedy, because the landlord is assumed to be the ultimate victim. In a novel published amid the Depression, when landlords were busily evicting tenants, many people thought that landlords deserved no better.

At the other end of the social spectrum stood 21-year-old Prim du Mont-Brankston, who lived in a grand house at Kirribilli with views of the bridge. She is one of the central characters in Miles Franklin and Dymphna Cusack's *Pioneers on Parade*, a comic novel about Sydney's sesquicentennial celebrations in 1938. Prim's wealthy father just missed out on a knighthood in the 1937 honours list, so Prim's mother encourages her daughter to pursue a feverish social round at the Australia Hotel and garden parties, a long way from Flannery's pub. Prim's boyfriend Greg, a doctor with a social conscience, tries to get Prim interested in the plight of slum children. For Prim:

> the memory of those narrow crowded streets with the smell of humanity heavy on the summer air, the stench of garbage and the pinched lifeless

faces of the children playing in the gutter still festered at the back of her mind. Greg should not make her do those things. What was the use? There had always been slums and poor and there always would be ...[25]

Social mobility and suburban class

Frank Clune was born in Darlinghurst in 1893 of working-class Irish parents who lived in Redfern. Educated, to primary level only, at local Catholic schools, he followed a roving career at sea and in accountancy. He was wounded at Gallipoli in 1915. His first book, *Try Anything Once: The Autobiography of a Wanderer*, was published in 1933, and in 1946 he published a second volume of autobiography, *Try Nothing Twice*:

> Down our way, in the 'Loo' and Redfern, people were too poor to pay for divorces, so the respondents fought the correspondents in the streets; but, in the precincts of the bewigged court, I realised that Potts-Pointers and Darling-Pointers also had domestic problems. They fought with money, not with fists, and the barristers did all the brawling on their behalf.[26]

By the time Frank Clune made it into *Who's Who*, in 1938, he was living in Vaucluse and was a member of the NSW Golf Club: He knew what Sydney was all about, and was a living example of social mobility. Having entered the middle class he was determined to stay there; a flow of royalties from his publisher, his practice as a tax consultant and the right address ensured that he would.

It is not difficult to find other examples of social mobility in the interwar years, but the fact is that this mobility did not undermine the class structure of the suburbs: if anything, it reinforced it. Working-class people who made good rarely remained in their home suburb, and if, like Labor politician William McKell, they did (and McKell had pressing electoral reasons to stay) they invariably moved to a better part of the suburb and bought rather than rented.

For most, social mobility remained elusive. Those who settled in the inner industrial suburbs, often living a hand-to-mouth existence, were unlikely ever to be able to save enough money to put a deposit on a house. Those who lived in small or owner-built accommodation in the middle and outer suburbs would spend most of their life paying it off. Only the lottery, the races, a booming small business or some other unexpected good fortune would enable them to buy a bigger house in a better suburb. Their main hope was that life would be different for some of their children, especially if, unlike their parents, they gained higher secondary, technical or tertiary education.

In the interwar and early postwar years there was little change in home ownership in Sydney: 41 per cent of private dwellings were owner-occupied in 1921 and 40 per cent in 1947. With the loosening of wartime restrictions and a general upturn in world trade and the domestic economy, Australia's fortunes, even for the working class, improved markedly. Many working-class servicemen had their technical college or university fees paid under a Commonwealth Reconstruction Training Scheme, and many entered the professions. It was the heyday of social mobility in Australia.[27]

Nevertheless, mobility could still be elusive. Most migrants—even those

1

2

3

4

with professional training, such as doctors—had a hard battle to be recognised for their medical, dental, legal or engineering qualifications. Working-class migrants had an even harder battle. Throughout the twentieth century a much higher proportion of middle-class than working-class children went on to higher education, increasingly the only entry point for the professions.[28]

FACING PAGE
Getting On by Percy Leason. Social mobility in five easy steps. A simple cottage in an industrial area gives way to a fine garden in a secluded middle-class suburb.
Tabletalk, 28 April 1927

Education: learning your place

The suburbs with high percentages of employers were also the suburbs with much higher than average proportions of the 15–24 year age group attending university.[29] In 1921 Strathfield, Ku-ring-gai, Mosman and Woollahra sent 5–8 per cent of their young men to the University of Sydney. Redfern and Newtown, on the other hand, though close to the university, sent less than 1 per cent of their young men to the institution that controlled access to the higher paid professions, from medicine and law to dentistry and architecture.

Males greatly outnumbered females at the university. In 1920 there were 2579 male students attending the University of Sydney and 777 females. By 1950, although absolute numbers had increased (7427 males, 1956 females) the ratio of males to females had increased from 3:1 to 4:1. In general, the suburbs with higher than average proportions of males attending university also had higher than average proportions of females attending university. Nonetheless, most middle-class young women did not get a tertiary education.

The home suburbs of University of Sydney professors were even more geographically concentrated than those of the students. Of the professorial addresses traceable for 1941, three-quarters lived in the lower and upper north shore, and the rest lived in the harbourside sections of the eastern suburbs or in Strathfield. There were a few exceptions, such as the professor of anthropology, A.P. Elkin, who chose to live at then rural Westmead, but by 1962 he had moved to Lindfield.

Protestant and independent schools were (and are) much more geographically concentrated than Catholic or state schools. In 1950, 76 per cent of all NSW schoolchildren attended government schools, 20 per cent Catholic schools, and the remaining 4 per cent attended the Protestant, non-denominational and 'other religion' schools.[30] Approximately three-quarters of all non-Catholic primary and secondary private schools in Sydney in 1950 were in distinctly high-income areas of the metropolis. Twelve were located on the railway line from Stanmore to Strathfield, 20 in the eastern suburbs municipalities of Woollahra, Waverley and Randwick (including four in Vaucluse and four in Bellevue Hill), 17 on the lower north shore from Hunters Hill to Manly and 16 on the upper north shore line from Roseville to Hornsby. Most of the remaining quarter were in four small areas, the northern beach suburbs, Epping–Beecroft–Baulkham Hills, the City of Sydney (notably the non-denominational Sydney Grammar and Sydney Church of England Girls Grammar School, Darlinghurst) and Parramatta (King's School for boys, established 1836, and Tara for girls, both Anglican). All these localities were socially respectable when the schools were founded, and most remained so.

The Old Cranbrookian, February 1954

Indeed, the presence of a Protestant school often ensured the increasing status of an area. Such was certainly true of Abbotsleigh School for girls (Anglican), founded in 1885, which moved to its Wahroonga site in 1899, when the suburb was still sparsely settled.[31] Private schools in areas that later attracted industry, such as those at Parramatta, survived surrounded by ample grounds. Even the inner city schools were not too badly off. Shore (Anglican boys), with only 13 acres at North Sydney, owned another 23 at Northbridge, so that the boys had their own private sporting space. The girls at SCEGGS Darlinghurst were among the few pupils of Protestant schools who found themselves with small school grounds at the edge of the slums, a situation the school authorities have attempted to alter by gradual purchase and demolition of neighbouring terraces over the years.

The only famous private schools in the inner west were all established in the nineteenth century: Newington (Methodist boys, established in Stanmore 1863), the Presbyterian and Methodist Ladies colleges, and Meriden Church of England School for girls, all in Strathfield. Vaucluse–Woollahra houses Cranbrook (Anglican) and Scots for boys, Ascham (non-denominational) and Kambala (Anglican) for girls. Scots' College, on the eastern slope of Bellevue Hill, reputedly owns 'the most valuable piece of suburban real estate in Australia'.[32] The lower north shore area encompasses Redlands, Queenwood and Wenona for girls, and Shore (Anglican boys), while the upper north shore line provides Ravenswood (Methodist, now Uniting), Dalcross, PLC Pymble, Abbotsleigh (Anglican girls), Knox (Presbyterian (now Uniting) boys) and Barker. Locality was important for attracting students. Cranbrook's advertisement in Wise's 1931 *NSW Post Office Directory* stated—accurately—that the school was 'beautifully situated ... overlooking Sydney Harbour'.

The contrast with state schools could not have been greater. In 1941 Brian Penton, editor of the Sydney *Daily Telegraph,* complained that the sun seldom entered the classrooms of Crown Street Public School, Surry Hills, and that it was a 'gloomy atmosphere for 1100 children, one-third of whom have only one parent or none'. Penton also drew attention to classes of 60 or more at the Bankstown Central School, 'the largest in the southern hemisphere', with 2346 pupils.[33]

Catholic schools were more numerous and more geographically spread than their Protestant counterparts, and their fees and standards varied widely. Nevertheless, the wealthier and more prestigious Catholic schools tended to be in the wealthier suburbs. Examples include St Ignatius College at Riverview (in the municipality of Lane Cove) and St Joseph's College at Hunter's Hill, both founded in the early 1880s. Also on the lower north shore are Monte Sant'Angelo Girls' College and Loreto Convent at North Sydney, while across the harbour are Our Lady of Mercy, Sacred Heart and St Mary Magdalen's, all in Rose Bay.

In his appropriately titled book *Here My Son,* a history of the (male) Greater Public Schools of Australia, the war historian C.E.W. Bean tackled the question of social background, an unusual topic for such a volume. In answer to a survey he conducted about the backgrounds of GPS boys, headmasters claimed that their students came 'from all walks of life'. The meaning of this expression is shown by the occupation of parents provided by Shore for 1947: graziers 12 per cent; professional country 6 per cent; business country 7 per cent; professional city 14 per cent; business city 52 per cent; other 9 per cent. From this and other evidence Bean concluded:

> the corporate schools draw from the professional and other more well-to-do classes a much larger percentage than do the state schools ... Needless to say boys of the labouring class are welcomed by the corporate schools if their parents can afford the cost.[34]

In the 1965 *Who's Who in Australia* just two schools, Shore and Sydney Grammar, provided 16 per cent of all NSW entries, Sydney Grammar being better represented among government officials and Shore among graziers.[35]

Some indication of the elite support of wealthy Protestant private schools can be gained by analysing the membership of Old Girls and Old Boys associations. In its school magazine, the *Weaver*, in December 1961, Abbotsleigh published a list of members in its Old Girls' Union, comprising 1578 names. A random sample of 110 revealed that 77 lived in the municipality of Ku-ring-gai, 13 lived on the lower north shore and six in the eastern suburbs. Of the remaining 14, two were at Strathfield, three at Artarmon and three on the northern beaches. Over 95 per cent of the sample lived in middle-class suburbs. While this sample is not necessarily representative of girls who attended the school, it certainly says something of the social milieu in which they moved after they left.

While private schools are to be found in all Australia's capital cities, Sydney is unique in having a relatively high number of selective government high schools, which began the practice of competitive entry by examination in the thirties. Among the more famous were Fort Street, Sydney High School and

Australian Educational Directory 1930-31

"The Census? The Census? Do you think a woman's got nothing else to do but count flamin' kids?"

Emile Mercier, *Follow that Wardrobe!*, Angus & Robertson, Sydney, 1957

North Sydney High School. All of these schools separated boys and girls on different sites, except Sydney High School where the sites adjoin. Sydney High School, located between the then slums of Waterloo, Redfern and Surry Hills to its west, and the middle-class areas of Bellevue Hill, Woollahra and Centennial Park to its east, drew a disproportionate number of pupils from Bellevue Hill. In recognition of its special status, this school was admitted to the inner circle of 'exclusive' schools, the Greater Public Schools association, in 1906.[36]

Some state selective schools, especially those of Sydney and North Sydney, attracted and retained better quality staff and substantial proportions of their students were the children of professional and business people. Such parents, if education rather than snobbery or business-network building was their prime concern, were usually delighted to get their children into these schools, because they got most of the advantages of private schools without the attendant cost. Thus the school historian who in 1962 deplored the prospect that the Wyndham scheme for reorganising education in New South Wales might lead to North Sydney Boys High losing its selectivity could proudly conclude that his school's old boys 'are to be found everywhere. Surgeons, bishops, leaders of commerce, schoolmasters, judges, scientists, public servants, actuaries'.[37] Among the 65 NSW entrants to the Australian Diplomatic Service between 1942 and 1962, 35 came from private schools, but the two largest groups came from Sydney Boys' High, providing 11, and North Sydney Boys' High, providing nine.[38] The selective government high schools, more numerous in Sydney than in Melbourne, have supplied generations of Labor and Liberal politicians and assorted professionals, giving Sydney a unique position in Australia: a government-educated elite to parallel the old school tie of the private schools. Fort Street has produced non-Labor (BSB Stevens) and Labor premiers (Neville Wran) and leading lawyers, including Justice Michael Kirby of the High Court. Labor Premier Carr attended Matraville High School while Liberal Prime Minister Howard is a graduate of Canterbury Boys High School.

Religion, ethnicity and class

Until the 1970s religion continued to be a major factor in self-perception and group identity for most Australians, irrespective of whether people attended church regularly or only for family and special religious occasions. Even children at government schools were required to state their religion and most attended some form of religious instruction at school. The great majority of adults willingly revealed their religion to the census collector. Whether you were Roman Catholic or Protestant was probably the single biggest divide in society, even more marked than your ethnic background, unless you were black or in some other way obviously not of European origin. Protestants were not allowed to be married in Catholic churches, and often vice versa. 'Mixed marriages' were frowned on.[39]

The claim that before 1939 Australia's Catholics were 'chiefly of Irish stock' has been a common one and there is little evidence to dispute the generalisation.[40] (Unfortunately the census is no help here, because Irish immigrants are lumped together with those from Britain.) The Irish background of Australian Catholics was often a topic of debate, and something the Roman Catholic Church itself felt sensitive about. In 1931 the first Catholic broadcasting station in the British Empire, 2SM (for St Mary's) went to air in Sydney. In a series of programs titled 'Radio Replies: In Defence of Religion' the Rev. Dr Leslie Rumble posed popular anti-Catholic statements and gave a Catholic justification in reply. In response to the statement 'I cannot reconcile myself to the Irish element which prevails in your Church!' Rumble admitted that 'in this country the majority of Catholics are of Irish descent' but asked: 'Is your dislike of everything Irish stronger than your love of Christ?'[41]

To establish more direct links between religion and class, it is necessary, as with education, to go to the census. In his unpublished 'Book of the North Shore', completed in 1927, Charles Whitham claims that 'about eighty-four per cent' of the north shore population were Protestant. 'The proportion of Catholics is smaller than in the districts on the south side of the harbour', he writes. 'There are a few Jews and many Scots.'[42] At the 1921 census 24 cent of Sydney's population described themselves as Roman Catholic, and another 9 per cent Presbyterian. But the percentage of Catholics went above 30 in the contiguous inner city working-class areas of Redfern, Darlington, Waterloo, Glebe, Paddington and Sydney. In her novel *The Harp in the South*, Ruth Park described Surry Hills as full of Irish people, who went there 'because they were poor'.[43] Catholics were much less numerous in Warringah, Mosman, Hornsby, Eastwood, Dundas and Ku-ring-gai to the north of the harbour and the Parramatta River, and in Kogarah and Sutherland to the south (less than 15 per cent Catholics). Suburbs with higher than average proportions of Presbyterians tended to have lower than average proportions of Catholics, and vice versa.

Anglican church at Lindfield, built in the 1930s. Wealthy, middle-class congregations have managed to retain some of their churches, although even well-heeled Anglican and Catholic establishments are finding the cost of upkeep can be prohibitive.
Photograph by John Storey, 1978

A few Jews did manage, as Whitham observed, to enter the Protestant strongholds of the north shore just as the Catholics had done. But the north shore remained, with the exception of isolated working-class areas, a home for only the most successful Catholics.[44] Most Catholics remained on the south side of the harbour, though even there wealthier Catholics could find respectable homes, in suburbs such as Waverley,

Table 9.1: Religious affiliation in Sydney 1996

	000s	%
Catholic	1137	31
Anglican	820	22
Uniting*	168	5
Orthodox	163	4
Presbyterian	123	3
Baptist	61	2
Other Christian	173	5
Islam	97	3
Buddhism	76	2
Hinduism	33	1
Judaism	31	1
Other non-Christian	16	0.4
No religion	503	14
Not stated	292	8

*Methodists, Congregationalists and some Presbyterians formed the Uniting Church in 1977.
Source: ABS 1996 census, ABS Sydney Statistical Division.

which had higher than average proportions of both Catholics and Presbyterians. This is not to say that all Catholics lived in working-class suburbs, or that all Presbyterians lived in middle-class ones: merely that the wealthier members of both denominations tended to live in the middle-class suburbs, and that a much greater percentage of Presbyterians than of Catholics had the money to settle in these suburbs. Anglicans, on the other hand, were well represented in all suburbs.[45] With the rapid decline in church attendance since the 1960s and the amalgamation of a number of Protestant religions into the Uniting Church, religious adherence has lost much of its class bite. Society churches including St Marks at Darling Point are still popular, but the nexus between religion and social class has become relatively tenuous.

The position of the Irish ethnic group as the core of the inner city working class has altered considerably since the large influx of Italians from the early fifties and Greeks from the early sixties. By this time those of Irish background or parentage were more assimilated into mainstream Australian society, while the Italians and Greeks tended to establish and remain for some time in inner suburban enclaves before diversifying into middle and outer suburbs. In this case it is undoubtedly ethnicity rather than religious adherence that is the important factor, although the two remain closely linked.[46] The same pattern of initial concentration and gradual dispersal can be seen in more recent waves of immigration from Turkey, Lebanon and Vietnam.

Church attendance continued to fall sharply in the 1980s and 1990s. Scores of Protestant churches were closed, especially after the establishment of the Uniting Church in 1977. In most suburbs only one of the Congregationalist, Methodist or Presbyterian churches survived as a church. Some became recreational halls, but many were redeveloped, as were the Masonic Halls that dotted the suburbs. At the 1996 census one-fifth of Sydneysiders said they had 'no religion' or did not bother to state a religion. (Table 9.1 shows the nominal size of religious groups at the 1996 census.) Ethnic, rather than religious background has come to be a key feature of how large immigrant cities think of themselves, but religious structures remain visible evidence in the landscape of both religious and ethnic communities. Sydney's Catholic and Protestant cathedrals still loom large in the city centre. The grander Protestant and Catholic churches in the wealthier suburbs still host many a society wedding and funeral. The sprawling suburban churches of the postwar years, including those built by the Seventh Day Adventists and Baptists, are a reminder of an era of rapid suburban growth, when churches often preceded schools and were a vital centre of community activity, as many still are. Buddhist temples, mosques and synagogues are evidence of Sydney's multiculturalism. While the mosques of Auburn, Arncliffe and Lakemba were not universally welcomed by the households they overlooked, they have survived to become central features of the suburban landscape, much like the Catholic and Protestant churches built in the latter half of the nineteenth century.

THE LANDSCAPE OF VOTING

Class differences are plainly reflected in the pattern of voting in Sydney. At the 1917 and 1927 elections the conservative party held all the seats to the north of the harbour and the Parramatta River. On the south side the Labor strongholds at the 1917 state election were the inner city industrial seats, and the outer western seats of Granville and Canterbury. The Nationalists controlled the contiguous eastern suburbs electorates of Darlinghurst, Woollahra, Waverley, Bondi, Randwick, the mid-western electorates of Drummoyne, Burwood, Ashfield, Petersham, Enmore and the Botany Bay electorates of St George and Hurstville. The pattern was largely unchanged at the 1927 election, except that Labor managed to win Hurstville with a strong personal vote for its candidate, but lost the heterogeneous seat of Paddington, which it later regained. On 10 October 1927 the *Labor Daily* editorial writer explained the outcome of the election, which Labor lost narrowly, thus:

> Labor has to rely on the class conscious industrial vote. In almost all the industrial constituencies the solidarity of Labor was never quite so pronounced. Waverley, Paddington [the electorate, not the suburb] and Randwick are not true industrial areas. They are more akin to the wealthy and near-rich areas in which Labor beats its hands against Toryism's chosen citadels in vain.

The 1930 election was a landslide for Labor, which won 55 of 90 seats and 55 per cent of the vote. All their seats, with the exception of North Sydney, were contiguous with already held Labor seats on the south side of the harbour. None of the newly won seats survived the defeat of 1932. The Sydney columnist of the Melbourne-based weekly newspaper the *Australasian* may well have predicted correctly when he claimed that elections in New South

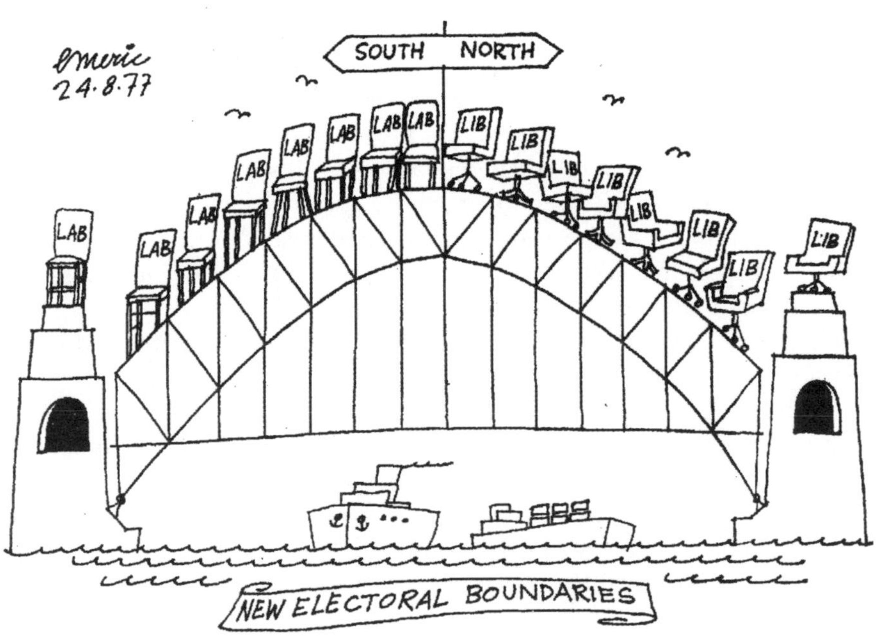

Emeric's succinct comment on class voting in Sydney 1977. Since then voting patterns have become more complex with the gentrification of former working-class suburbs.
Sydney Morning Herald, 24 August 1977

Wales are 'not decided by noisy election crowds, but by the quiet, undemonstrative middle class'.[47] AMAZING SWING IN CITY SEATS was the *Labor Daily's* headline response to the defeat. The Jack Lang-dominated newspaper sought to explain the trend, which was 'Most marked in the metropolitan area, where a big section of the dole vote, even in close industrial seats, was cast for the false promises of the anti-Labor press'.[48] The Sydney seats Labor retained in 1932 were the inner city and outer western working-class seats; this was the hard core of Labor support. At the election of 1935 Labor recaptured Arncliffe and Canterbury and in 1938 Granville.

'I'm waitin' fer me old man—he's in there gettin' televised!'
Emile Mercier, *I'm Waiting for an Earthquake,* Angus & Robertson, Sydney, 1956

Of minor political movements in New South Wales, the most colourful in this period was undoubtedly the paramilitary New Guard, which had, according to the correspondent of the *Australasian,* 'the whole-hearted approval of the solid, inarticulate middle-classes'. Until Weston Bate's 1969 pilot study, the geography of the New Guard's membership—that it was primarily a middle-class, suburban organisation—went largely unnoticed.[49]

With William McKell's election as leader of the state Labor Party in 1939, the party's fortunes improved. In the victory of 1941 the party gained as many seats as it had held in 1930—55 statewide—29 of which were in Sydney. Between 1931 and 1971 Sydney's share of the state population increased from 47 per cent to 59 per cent. More of this growing population settled in the low socioeconomic status outer western suburbs than in the suburbs to the north of the harbour and the Parramatta River. These new electorates helped to keep state Labor in power until 1965, despite a weakening leadership. Key Liberal gains in the election of that year were in the more middle-class eastern suburbs electorates such as Coogee, whose voters were attracted by the promise that they would finally get a railway. Labor subsequently modified its electoral strategy to lessen its dependence on the outer west.

Sydney's growing western suburbs electorates nevertheless proved vital to federal Labor's victories under Gough Whitlam in 1972 and 1974 and for the victories of Bob Hawke and Paul Keating from 1983 to 1993. Sydney's electoral geography is less marked now because class voting has declined.[50] The electorate no longer divides as neatly between blue- and white-collar workers, nor are there the pay differentials that often existed between industrial and white-collar workers. A growing proportion of the population works in service industries, from real estate to hospitality. Other traditional white-collar employers, such as the banks, have closed hundreds of suburban branches, making thousands redundant. The deregulation of the banking industry and the move towards privatisation in the telecommunications industry have created a new group of relatively lowly paid white-collar employees, while forcing many maintenance staff on to the dole queues. Some of the new jobs are well paid and of high status, but the majority are not.

The rich—whom we might loosely define as those households with incomes of more than $100,000 a year—still choose to concentrate in particular suburbs. Indeed only the rich can afford to live in parts of the eastern suburbs, on much of the north shore and in the gentrified parts of the inner west. Most of the houses in these suburbs cost more than $500,000, as do apartments with views. The Liberal Party still wins most of the seats to the north of the harbour and a fair swag to the north of the Parramatta River, especially in the growing north-west middle-class belt from Beecroft to Dural. The ALP still holds traditional working-class seats in the inner and outer west, even though the industrial base has declined and incoming migrant groups—from the Lebanese to the Vietnamese—have turned to all manner of occupations. Electoral volatility now has more to do with particular issues or particular groups than it did in the past. In the mid to late nineties the continuing noise issue over Mascot airport preoccupied many electors in the flight path, making this a huge issue in a number of state and federal seats.[51] In the eastern suburbs any candidate who does not take gay rights seriously—this being a major centre of gay electors—may court electoral defeat.

Health and delinquency

Just as money could buy a good education or entry to business networks via a private school, so also could it provide access to good food and health care. The connection between income and standard of health is difficult to measure, but one indicator is the incidence of infant mortality (calculated on deaths of infants in their first year per 1000 live births) by suburb. In Sydney suburbs for the four years 1930–31 to 1933–34 infant mortality varied between 87 per 1000 in the inner industrial suburb of St Peters to 30 in Mosman. Other suburbs with mortality rates in the 30–40 per 1000 range included Ku-ring-gai, Lane Cove, Strathfield and Vaucluse. With few exceptions, infant mortality in Sydney followed a class pattern, as did the location of doctors.[52] In 1953 the demographer W.D. Borrie observed that 'Congested low-income areas of Sydney and Melbourne have infant mortality rates varying from forty to as high as sixty deaths under one year per 1000 live births, which are twice as high as those in the spacious suburbs of the economically prosperous.'[53]

Although infant mortality rates have decreased spectacularly since 1900, they continue to show a class pattern. Over the period 1970–72, the municipalities with the highest rate were Sydney and South Sydney, at 27, while Mosman's was 17 per 1000. Despite the remaining difference, infant mortality rates have decreased more markedly in working-class than middle-class suburbs, thanks mainly to public hospitals.[54]

The incidence of reported delinquency followed a similar suburban class pattern. The NSW government, perturbed about rising delinquency, commissioned a study of the problem in 1940, involving 549 delinquents aged 12–17, which confirmed the findings of Shaw in Chicago, Burr in England and Barnett in Melbourne, that certain localities tend to produce more than their share of reported delinquents. In Sydney the worst localities were 'the overcrowded slum areas'. One key factor discovered was unemployment, which 'tends to be highest in the same industrial and low-rent areas where delinquency is highest': Darlington had 2.5 delinquents per 1000 residents and 51 unemployed persons per 1000 residents. In Redfern the figures were 2 and 53, in Erskineville 1.5 and 52 and in Balmain 0.9 and 26. A very different picture emerged in Vaucluse, which had no reported delinquents, Woollahra where the figures were 0.1 and seven, Strathfield 0.2 and four, Mosman 0.8 and five, Willoughby 1.0 and nine and Kur-ring-gai 0.2 and five.[55]

Such a class pattern was no doubt partly a reflection of police charging practices. Police were probably more vigilant in some areas and more concerned with certain types of offences.[56] The most common offence in New South Wales was stealing, but the next most common was being 'uncontrollable', an offence particularly subject to interpretation.[57] It may well be that police were more severe in slum suburbs than middle-class suburbs, but in any case convicted delinquents certainly followed a class pattern.

Moving up and moving down

Just as people could experience social mobility, so too could suburbs. The most dramatic changes in the class pattern of Sydney suburbs took place around 1900 and, much later, in the rising tide of gentrification since the early 1960s. In the late nineteenth and early twentieth centuries, middle-class inner suburbs such as Glebe (whose class character is attested to in its lavish 1880 Italianate Town Hall) gradually became primarily working-class residential areas. By the Depression of the 1930s, such suburbs were popularly regarded as 'slums'.[58]

It is precisely those areas—suburbs such as Paddington, Balmain and Glebe—that have witnessed a striking level of embourgeoisement since the early 1960s. Between the 1966 and 1971 censuses the percentage of professional and higher paid white-collar workers in the Sydney workforce rose by only 0.5 per cent. But in the area covered by the Paddington postcode it rose a remarkable 7 per cent, 14 times the metropolitan average, while Balmain and Glebe saw increases of 6 and 5 per cent respectively.

This complete turn around in the social status of such suburbs was much commented on by real estate agents of the time, always on the lookout for major changes in 'market preferences'. The change was also heralded by what became known in the 1960s as the coffee table book. In 1968 Ure Smith published Rob Hillier's *Let's Buy a Terrace House*, a photographic homage to the terrace houses of Sydney and Melbourne. Hillier noted that 'over the past five

In 1911, when Grace Burn drew this cartoon, ferries serviced all classes, and ferry trips started very early in the morning. Different classes caught the ferry at different times, with haute-bourgeois men going to work later in the morning, their daughters and spouses went shopping later still. By the 1980s ferries increasingly serviced only middle-class residents and tourists, so services prior to 7 a.m. were gradually phased out.
Lone Hand, 2 October 1911

or six years terrace houses have been "taken over" by authors, artists, architects and actors'.[59] The sudden rise in the price of these once-condemned slum houses excited real estate agents, owner-occupiers and investors alike.

That the process of gentrification also had political consequences was early identified by John Power in a 1969 article, 'The New Politics in the Old Suburbs'. Power noted the growth of civic action groups in Sydney and Melbourne, observing that they were stronger in the terrace-house suburbs and dominated by middle-class professionals. In Balmain the group was headed by an architect and in Glebe by a professor of fine arts; the membership list of the Paddington Society read like the society pages of Sydney's weekend newspapers. By the late 1970s the slum stigma once attached to these suburbs was replaced by the respectability conferred by lavish pictorial and textual accounts: *The Houses of Balmain* (1969), *A Place Called Paddington* (1970) and *The Architectural Character of Glebe, Sydney* (1973).[60] By the late 1990s larger terrace houses in these suburbs could rarely be purchased for less than $500,000. Only professional and business people could afford such prices. Even the rents were well beyond what most blue-collar or even clerical-income households could afford to pay.

In Peter Corris's novel *Matrimonial Causes*, set in the early 1990s, his detective Cliff Hardy visits a much changed Glebe to check out a likely source of information:

> Ferry Road follows the lie of the land, running down to Blackwattle Bay. The area was undergoing a lot of change—rusty, ramshackle factories coming down, small boatyards and workshops closing, apartment blocks rising on the sites. There were still some of the old houses, narrow single and double storey terraces jammed close together with built-in verandas and porches dating back to the Depression when rentable space was at a premium. Number 4A was smarter than most—a well-maintained terrace with two letter boxes on the gate, indicating that it was divided into two flats.[61]

The gentrification of the inner suburbs reflected a revaluing of access to the city centre and a new-found interest in the utility and renovation opportunities provided by late nineteenth-century dwellings. While invariably having narrow frontages, they were often on deep blocks, enabling incoming middle-class residents to open up what was usually the kitchen area (with an outside shower and toilet), to create a much lighter living space at the rear of the property.[62] The inner terrace-house suburbs were also close to cultural facilities, the universities (Sydney, New South Wales and the newly created University of Technology at Ultimo) and the burgeoning service industries established between the city and the airport. The fact that some of the houses, notably in Stanmore and Petersham, were under the flight path of an ever busier airport created an explosive political situation where residents objected to the growth in air traffic, largely the result of growing business and professional travel, compounded by a sharp increase in international tourism.

Topography has usually been regarded as central to the distribution of social classes in Sydney and the cost of housing and land. The housing reformer Hugh Stretton observed in 1970:

> Sydney is boxed in on three sides by the sea and two rugged coastal plateaux. Within the box, fifteen or eighteen miles square, the rich have the beautiful land north of the harbour and along as much of its southern shore and ocean coast as is not needed for merchant and naval uses. Out of sight to the south and up river to the west there is duller land for industries, rail networks and so on, with slums and suburbs for the workers and clerks ...[63]

Differences in topography were reinforced by transport. As the geographer Griffith Taylor explained, 'since railways and roads are much easier to construct on the southern side of the harbour, the industrial areas are to be found [there]'.[64] Taylor's and Stretton's comments reflect the postwar social structure of Sydney. Few foresaw how quickly this could change—and not just in the newly fashionable inner suburbs.

Along the harbour and the Parramatta River, industrial land gave way to residential development in the 1980s and 1990s. The development of Parramatta and Blacktown as major office and service centres, coupled with the redevelopment of Homebush Bay as the Olympics site and the demolition of oil storage, coal handling, munitions, gas-making and other industrial plants, from Balmain to Pulpit Point (a former Mobil depot), from Concord to Parramatta, made way for apartment blocks and town houses, many boasting water views and water access. Very few of these dwellings, especially those with three or more bedrooms, sold for less than $500,000. This was no longer working-class territory. You couldn't leave your old rowboat on the riverbank any more; marinas were provided for your smart sea-going vessel. The professional and business classes were moving back to a landscape that over a hundred years ago those of the same class found suitable as a site for rural and boating retreats. These transformations are among the most spectacular that Sydney has ever seen.

A River Cat journey from Circular Quay to Parramatta in 1998 still revealed 1950s Housing Commission houses on the northern side of the river at Ryde. Like Housing Commission flats at Manly and North Sydney, they were erected at a time when a Labor government built working-class rental accommodation with water views, without occasioning adverse comment. The old geographical class patterns were being replaced by new concentrations of wealth. But the correlation between the value of real estate and the social class of the inhabitants remained, as always, very close indeed. To afford the purchase price or high rents of Sydney's best real estate required a high income or inherited wealth.

Working-class families with one or more adults in the paid workforce could still afford to purchase fibro houses in parts of western Sydney, although even here prices by 1998 were running at $150,000 or more. Sydneysiders have got used to paying more for real estate— in poor suburbs and in wealthy suburbs—than households elsewhere in Australia. In the rental market, even one-bedroom flats in walk-up blocks of the 1960s could command rents of $200 or more per week in early 1999. Single-income families were increasingly being forced into substandard housing, including living as 'permanents' in caravan parks in the outer suburbs. The incidence of homelessness had been on the rise since the 1980s. And there was no doubting the class and income position of the homeless—they were at the bottom of the heap, whatever nomenclature one cares to use.[65]

Class markers

Class affects the social life of people at home, at work and at leisure. Class manifests itself not only in income, health and suburb of residence but in speech, dress, the ownership of refrigerators and the location of pubs and pawnbrokers. There were class overtones in McKell's attempt in June 1941 to persuade the milk monopolies to continue making deliveries twice a day, as many people were 'without refrigeration'.[66] At that time the location and number of hotels was even more important to working-class life. In 1931 Balmain had 30 hotels, while Mosman had three. Balmain had two pawnbrokers, Mosman had none, but both suburbs had undertakers. Wise's 1931 *NSW Post Office Directory* indicates that Redfern led in the hotel stakes, having the same number as Balmain but 10,000 fewer residents. Redfern had four pawnbrokers to Balmain's two, while Paddington had five. Strathfield had no hotels and no pawnbrokers, but had six private schools.

There were no pawnbrokers in Sydney beyond what were known as the slum suburbs, and the incidence of hotels was many times greater in these suburbs than on the north shore. In 1958 J.D. Pringle, the editor of the *Sydney Morning Herald*, wrote, 'In the working class suburbs wives lead home their husbands, genially or belligerently drunk, from the pubs where they have stayed too long.'[67] Pringle did not comment on the drinking habits of the Sydney middle class, but if the location of hotels is any guide, middle-class men were less subject to temptation from the rare local pub than from their own well-stocked drink cabinets. The professional classes did their public drinking in the city, and those on the north shore line could sober up on the rail trip home. Middle-class women who wished to imbibe were dependent on the resources of their own home. In the NSW liquor referendum of 1928, one-third of the voters in Manly, Mosman, Lane Cove and Croydon voted for prohibition, compared with only one-sixth in Alexandria, Balmain and Newtown.[68] There were thus differences in attitude as well as in wealth between the suburbs.

Social reformers were well aware of these differences but some believed it was possible to overcome them. In 1942 Mona Ravenscroft, a tutor in the Department of Anthropology at the University of Sydney, undertook a study of life in inner Sydney under the auspices of the federal government's post-war reconstruction committee. She reported that:

> One poignant fact, before any other, that stands out in the economic picture of working class life is this: far more money is spent in proportion to income by these people on non-essentials, such as beer, cigarettes, cakes and tawdry articles, than by middle class people ... To place these people in new dwellings and to fail to consider their emotional needs, their desire for self-esteem and independence—is to attempt to turn them into parasites ... There is a vast system of clanship ties operating in these localities, and this background, deeply rooted in tradition, is greatly valued by people in depressed areas ...[69]

Nevertheless, her survey showed that for the sake of a 'good home' working-class families would be prepared to leave the 'crowded locality', and she hoped that within a generation 'the problems of class segregation and class difference will have been banished'. It is now more than 50 years since Ravenscroft wrote that article, yet class segregation in Sydney has shown little sign of diminishing, indeed it may well be increasing.[70]

In *Waltzing Matilda* (1943), a book that proved very popular with Australian servicemen abroad, Arnold Haskell wrote of 'Rose Bay, Potts Point, Bellevue Hill and Vaucluse, the smart residential districts, with magnificent Riviera villas in their own large gardens, many of them with their swimming pools', while the north shore 'shelters a clique of its own'. 'It reads good books, patronises concerts and the safer movements in art.' But Haskell was also of the opinion that in Sydney: 'Every man has a golf links within 10 minutes of his office, a surfing beach and tennis courts. The average man can afford to yacht in the harbour.'[71] Haskell's theme of wealthy suburbs and classless recreation was reworked 20 years later by J.D. Pringle, in his *Australian Accent*:

> Sydney is ruled by three winds, which command the city in turn ... The north-eastern is a sea-breeze and is out of its element on dry land ... A few miles inland it fades away altogether, daunted by the size of the continent before it. To the western suburbs it brings no relief from the heat, but to the more favoured eastern suburbs it is a source of pride and joy; and the wealthy citizens of Bellevue Hill and Point Piper set their houses to catch it like the yachts on the harbour set their sails.[72]

Those who are not convinced by a class analysis of Sydney's suburban life may prefer to accept another construction of social reality, or to have a dual vision, as did Pringle:

> [T]here is little class distinction in recreation. The rich tend to go to the northern beaches—Newport, Avalon, Whale Beach ... Palm Beach—while the workers throng the yellow sands of Bondi, Coogee and Maroubra; but you cannot tell a man's income in a pair of swimming trunks, and the Pacific surf is a mighty leveller.[73]

As more and more of Sydney's working class were forced to live in the distant western suburbs, their access to the Pacific Ocean diminished. Forty years later the problem is no longer in choosing the swimming trunks, but in getting to the beach.

Yachts at Watsons Bay, postcard c. 1939. Until the 1970s some working-class people could still afford to rent run-down housing in the eastern and northern harbourside suburbs, so that Haskell's 'average man' could yacht in the harbour. But these suburbs have now become so expensive that only the very wealthy can afford the mooring, storage and access costs that yachting now entails.

ZONE
-1938
HERALD
WAR
IN
CH
WYLDE ST
LOVE
MAGAZINE

CHAPTER 10

Cities and suburbs

FACING PAGE
'Kings Cross is the ultimate height of heterogeneity. It is a salamagundi of caviar, truffles and fish and chips. It is a cocktail of rum, tomato sauce, raspberry vinegar and Chateau Lafite. It is a bouquet of rhododendrons, forget-me-nots, stinging nettles and pansies. Francis Broadhurst shows it above. Examine it thoroughly for types.'
Home, 1 December 1938

The city was the real and symbolic heart of Sydney. Here, on a peninsula of sandstone, rose a mass of immense buildings. The city proper covered 3000 acres, with 110,000 inhabitants in 1921. In every direction beyond lay the suburbs, with almost 800,000 people. The city housed the seat of government, the important financial interests, the major transport terminals, the largest theatres and emporiums, the cathedrals and the university. At the centre stood the Town Hall, the headquarters of the municipality and the tallest building in the city, rising 187 feet above sea level. Nothing in the suburbs could match the size or splendour of this monument to renaissance revival architecture.

But the city was more than the site of the biggest buildings. Here soldiers were farewelled and welcomed home from wars. Martin Place became the principal venue for the Anzac Day march and the War Memorial (completed in 1934, only a few blocks away in Hyde Park) assumed the role of a shrine for the commemoration of Armistice Day and other wartime events. The city also housed the Domain park, venue for Sunday afternoon orations on every imaginable topic, while the city streets accommodated everything from political demonstrations to marches of mass religious observance. For the grand procession of the 29th International Eucharistic Congress held in Sydney in September 1928 'dense masses of people poured into the city throughout the morning and took their places behind the barriers lining the route of the procession'. Enterprising youths took advantage of the opportunity and sold fruit cases for sightseers to stand on.[1]

Besides being the centre of commercial, cultural, industrial and administrative life the city had within its municipal boundaries, or immediately adjoining them, the major sporting complexes and large recreation reserves. The Domain, the Domain Baths, the Botanic Gardens, Hyde Park, the Royal Agricultural Society's Show Ground, the Sydney Cricket Ground and Moore Park (together 386 acres) were all under the administration of the Sydney Municipal Council. The 1000-acre Centennial Park (established by the colonial government in 1888) lies within the municipality of Randwick but directly adjoins the city municipality, while the Randwick racecourse is situated to the immediate south of Centennial Park. All these facilities and attractions, if not within the city itself, are easily accessible to it.

The decentralisation of the city's functions and facilities was a slow process. The Royal Zoological Society of NSW shifted its zoo from Moore Park to a site on the northern side of the harbour in 1916 partly with the aim of displaying the animals in natural surroundings. Though Taronga Park Zoo

Aerial photograph by Hall from Darling Harbour looking east, c. 1930, with City buildings rising from the sandstone peninsula.

Detail from Nucolorvue postcard c. 1958.

is located in the suburban municipality of Mosman, most of its visitors arrived and departed by a ferry service from Circular Quay, the harbour gateway to the city. Many still do.

The zoo move was unique. Although suburban councils gradually began to develop their own tourist and recreational facilities, these rarely involved direct competition with the city and never involved the relocation of a city facility. The city housed the two main museums, the Australian Museum opposite Hyde Park and the Museum of Applied Arts and Sciences in Ultimo. The state's largest art gallery, the National Gallery of NSW (founded in the 1880s), was also in the city, on the eastern side of the Domain. Most of the major private art galleries were associated with large city emporiums, including those of Anthony Horderns, Farmers and David Jones. The only suburban challenger, the munic-

ipally founded Manly Art Gallery, opened in 1930, achieved modest annual attendances of 35,000 to 39,000. The National Gallery had the overwhelming advantage of being state owned and supported: annual attendances there varied between 160,000 and 400,000, depending on the level of interest in the schools, the mood of the metropolis and the number of special exhibitions.[2]

Shopping: city versus suburbs

Until the 1960s suburban retailing operated in the shadow of the city department stores. The largest of these, Anthony Horderns, with frontages on George, Goulburn and Pitt streets, opened in 1904. The new Palace Emporium marketed itself as a 'City of Shops under one roof'. When a royal

Marcus Clark Universal Distributors, at Railway Square opposite Central Station, claimed to be Sydney's highest building.
Postcard 1905

commission considered the possibility of a Saturday half-holiday in 1909, one of the reasons advanced was that suburban shopkeepers would gain by the change because it would help to localise the trade in the various suburbs. Suburban retailers went to considerable lengths to attract clientele. A 1923 *Eastern Suburbs District Guide* advanced a number of reasons why it 'Pays to Shop in your own district':

> The local traders study your convenience; that's why they are there. You should consider this before taking your custom into the City ... It is a waste of time and money going into the City for what you can buy within a stone's throw of your door at the same price and with less trouble.

A dominant and expanding city-centred public transport system continued to deliver suburban shoppers to the city retailers. In January 1927 the *Commonwealth Home*, the journal of the NSW Town Planning Association, pointed out:

> The shortening of the time of the journey between suburban areas and the city centre consequent on the construction of the Harbour Bridge and the development of speedy transport ... may tend to restrict business development in suburban areas and concentrate same in the city, if a local spirit be not encouraged ...

To encourage such a local spirit northern suburbs businesses stressed that their goods were sold at 'City Prices'. Claude A. Willis, hairdresser and tobacconist of Military Road, Mosman, advertised 'Xmas presents of all kinds for Gentlemen at City Prices'.[3] On the bridge's opening advertising took on a more strident tone. Crows Nest firms promised 'Bridge Specials' and 'Big Bridge Week Bargains'. As the largest shopping centre to the north of the harbour, Crows Nest styled itself 'The Hub of North Sydney'. In one advertisement, Harding Bros shoe store asked readers of the local newspaper:

> WHY PAY FARES TO THE CITY? We now have the most comprehensive range of FOOTWEAR North of the Harbour at LESS THAN CITY PRICES.. . Rents, overhead and general expenses are much lower than in the City ... WE PASS THESE BENEFITS ON TO YOU.[4]

Barry Groom and Warren Wickman, *Leichhardt: An Era in Pictures: The Photography of J.G. Park.* Macleay Museum, University of Sydney, 1982

Suburban shopkeepers were subject to another threat besides the big city emporium, the chain store. The two best known, the Melbourne-based Coles chain (founded 1914) and the Sydney-based Woolworths chain (founded in 1924 in the basement of the Imperial Arcade) established substantial city premises, while plying most of their trade in the suburbs. As Coles and Woolworths were variety rather than specialist or food stores, they were not particularly threatening to other shops and were usually welcomed as adding to the status of suburban shopping strips. By the late 1930s most of the larger strips had either a Coles or a Woolworths, sometimes both. The interest of these companies in large-scale food supermarkets (which were more threatening to local stores) dates only from the late 1950s.[5]

The first threat to the local suburban store came rather from grocery chains such as Moran & Cato. Between 1931 and 1936 the number of independent grocers in the metropolitan area fell by more than one-quarter, from 3098 to 2311. Some of the decline may have resulted from the Depression

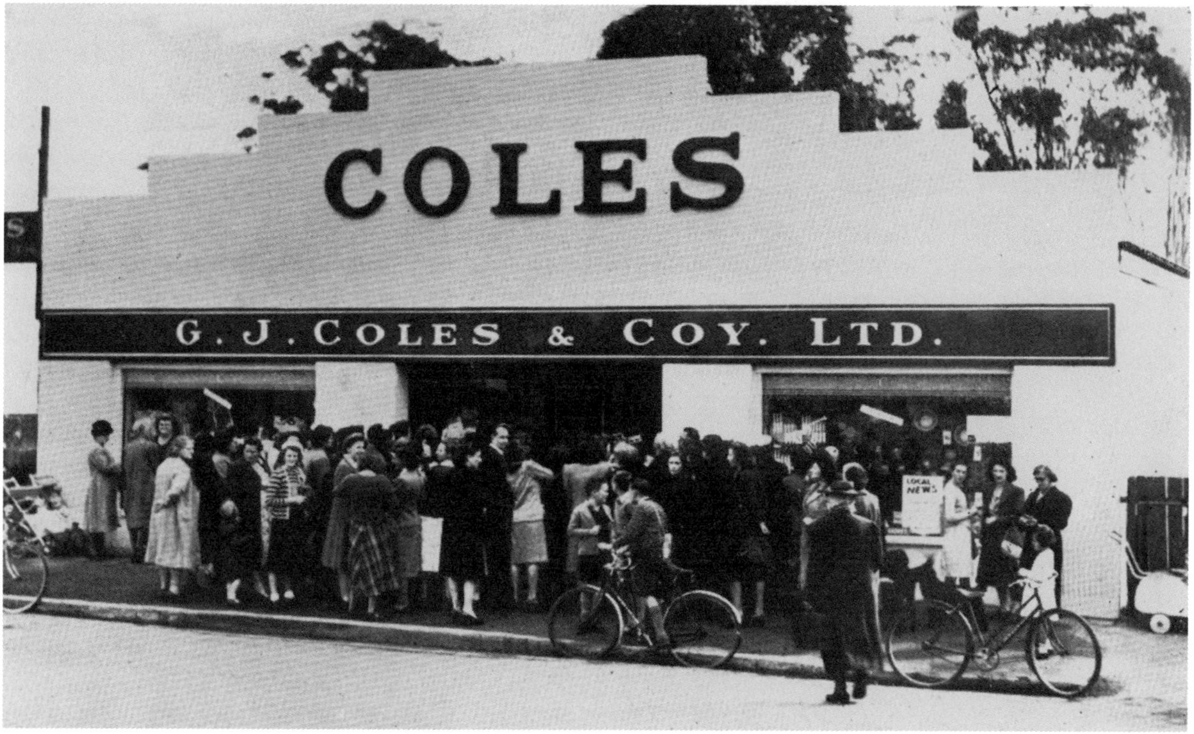

Opening day, Merrylands, 1949: one of many Coles variety stores opened in the suburbs in the early postwar years.
Colesanco, June 1949

conditions, but it also reflected an increase in chain store numbers from 157 to 415. While the chains represented only 15 per cent of all grocery shops, they handled 27 per cent of the available business. To defend themselves against such competition, 15 Sydney grocers opened as the Melray Co-operative in July 1938. As *Rydge's* business magazine commented in February 1939, this scheme avoided the impersonal pitfall of the corporate chain and enabled the suburban store to retain one of its main assets, 'the personality of the owner'.

The city dominated the wholesale markets in fruit, vegetables, meat and fish. Vegetable markets in the suburbs were rare. The North Sydney Council established a small market in 1922 but city agents, on seeing its success, prevented producers from supplying it. Randwick Council undertook a similar venture, which also foundered.[6] The main city markets were to remain in their 1909–14 Haymarket buildings for another 60 years.

Suburban shopkeepers were not alone in resenting the city centre. Grace Brothers' 'palatial premises' at Broadway (on the western outskirts), dating from 1897 but not completed until 1928–29, found it hard to compete when Farmers (1926), David Jones (1927), and Gowings (1929) opened new stores in the centre of town along the Market Street axis, handy to the new city railway stations. Grace Brothers embarked on its own elegant city headquarters in 1928, but its Clarence Street site proved too distant from the new retail core, so the company attempted to rent out the building for offices instead. In February 1933, by which time four of the city underground railway stations were operating, A. E. Grace alleged that traffic authorities were isolating the district 'from the Haymarket [south] to the City road', undermining his Broadway store. The problem was compounded by a decision to divert certain tram routes away from the area. Grace concluded that as 'customers were being taken away from the district the company had decided to bring their stores to the customers in their home districts'.[7]

The company's first suburban ventures were at Bondi and Parramatta, where existing premises were purchased in 1933. That the company would open new stores in the midst of the Depression is fair indication of its concern about the threat to the Broadway store. Grace Brothers' next wave of decentralisation did not begin until the mid-fifties, partly financed by the compensation it received after the Commonwealth government had compulsorily acquired its Clarence Street premises during the war. First used by General MacArthur as his Sydney headquarters, the building became the home of the Department of Veterans' Affairs. In 1957 new Grace Brothers stores were built at Bondi and Parramatta and Sydney's first free-standing, planned 'regional' shopping centre opened at Top Ryde.[8] As conceived in 1933 'the suburban shops would be mainly showrooms for the large emporium ... [and] would specialise in 'cash and carry' items and arrangements would be made that anything not in stock and required by customers would be immediately secured from the central shop at Broadway'.[9] Suburban emporiums to rival those of the city were not envisaged in the thirties: such developments depended on American levels of car ownership not experienced in Australia until well after the Second World War.

Grace Brothers' concern was not shared by the other big city stores. Mark Foys (opened 1909) was being lavishly remodelled to take advantage of the extra trade brought by Museum station, which opened in 1926. David Jones built its new Elizabeth Street store (on the site of the former Sydney Girls High School, relocated to Moore Park) directly opposite St James station, while Anthony Horderns refurbished its Brickfield Hill store in 1933, the very year that Grace Brothers made its decision to decentralise.[10] In 1934 David Jones, in a pamphlet entitled 'The Heart of a Great City', proudly boasted that often the number of people shopping at DJs was far in excess of a record attendance at a Sydney cricket test match, while over 5000 people were served daily in the 'Great Restaurant' and as many as 1500 could be seated at one time. Anthony Horderns also shared in the revival of trade and in June 1937 its lavish house journal, *Hordernian Monthly*, carried a photograph of a 'Great Crowd' of women 'Besieging the Hosiery and Glove Sections'.

Throughout the interwar and early postwar years the city had a monopoly on emporiums and only the city could attract enough customers to support the more unusual specialty shops. Women's clothing stores were by far the most numerous of all the specialty outlets in the CBD while second-hand bookshops, stamp and coin dealers, musical instruments, umbrella shops, sellers of military regalia, elegant restaurants and many others were to be found almost exclusively in the city. During the fifties, however, the larger suburban shopping centres of the interwar years—Bondi, Chatswood and Parramatta—began to grow larger still.[11] Most of Sydney's larger shopping strips were based around tram lines, including King Street in Newtown and Military Road, which linked Neutral Bay with Cremorne and Mosman junctions. The tram line-based shopping strips were badly affected when trams were phased out.

In the 1960s, with the ever-increasing use of the private car, drive-in, one-stop shopping centres became the order of the day. The car enabled cross-suburban travel, difficult with a public transport pattern centred on the city. With a more mobile clientele the suburbs could now attract their own department stores and specialty shops. In that decade Anthony Horderns' vast store lost customers and the country mail order section whittled away: not even a large new car park in the building itself could halt the decline and the store closed in the early seventies. Following the success of their Parramatta and Bondi stores, and the even greater success of Chermside mall in outer suburban Brisbane (1957), Grace Brothers enthusiastically eyed sites in Chatswood and Bankstown. Chatswood opened in 1961 with parking for 3000 cars. It proved so successful that its trading area was doubled in 1970. Patricia Rolfe explained the planning behind the decision to *Bulletin* readers in the issue of 19 December 1964. The 'Roselands' centre would have 255,000 people within a ten-minute drive and 459,000 within a twenty-minute one. Its 'tele-roofed, brick veneer bungalows' suggested maximum buying power. When Liberal Premier Askin opened Roselands in October 1965 he told the assembled guests, many of whom had just voted his coalition into power, that 'The million-dollar spread of merchandise under this roof brings the city to the suburbs in a glittering way that must rival even the fabled Persian bazaars'.[12]

David Jones followed Grace Brothers' example, establishing stores at Parramatta, Bankstown, Brookvale and Mt Druitt, with Farmers (bought out by the giant Melbourne Myer store chain) doing the same at Burwood, Gordon, Sutherland, Carlingford and Penrith. Sydney's central area share of total metropolitan sales dropped from 44 per cent in 1953 to 30 per cent in

Table 10.1: Retail sales or turnover as a percentage of metropolitan Sydney 1953–92

Local Government Area (LGA)	1953	1974	1992
Sydney*	43.8	13.6	12.1
Warringah	1.1	4.8	5.2
Willoughby	1.6	3.5	3.5
Ryde	1.7	2.8	2.9
Parramatta	4.2	5.4	4.1
Blacktown	0.6	3.4	4.5
Penrith	0.7	2.8	3.9
Fairfield	1.0	3.0	3.4
Canterbury	3.0	4.4	3.0
Bankstown	2.1	5.3	4.0
Campbelltown	0.2	1.2	2.9
Sutherland	1.2	5.3	4.3
Total, top 12 LGAs	61.2	55.5	53.8

*Sydney LGA in 1953 approximated Sydney and South Sydney LGAs in 1992.
Source: Australian Bureau of Statistics, Retail census.

WITH WEP WHERE IT'S WET

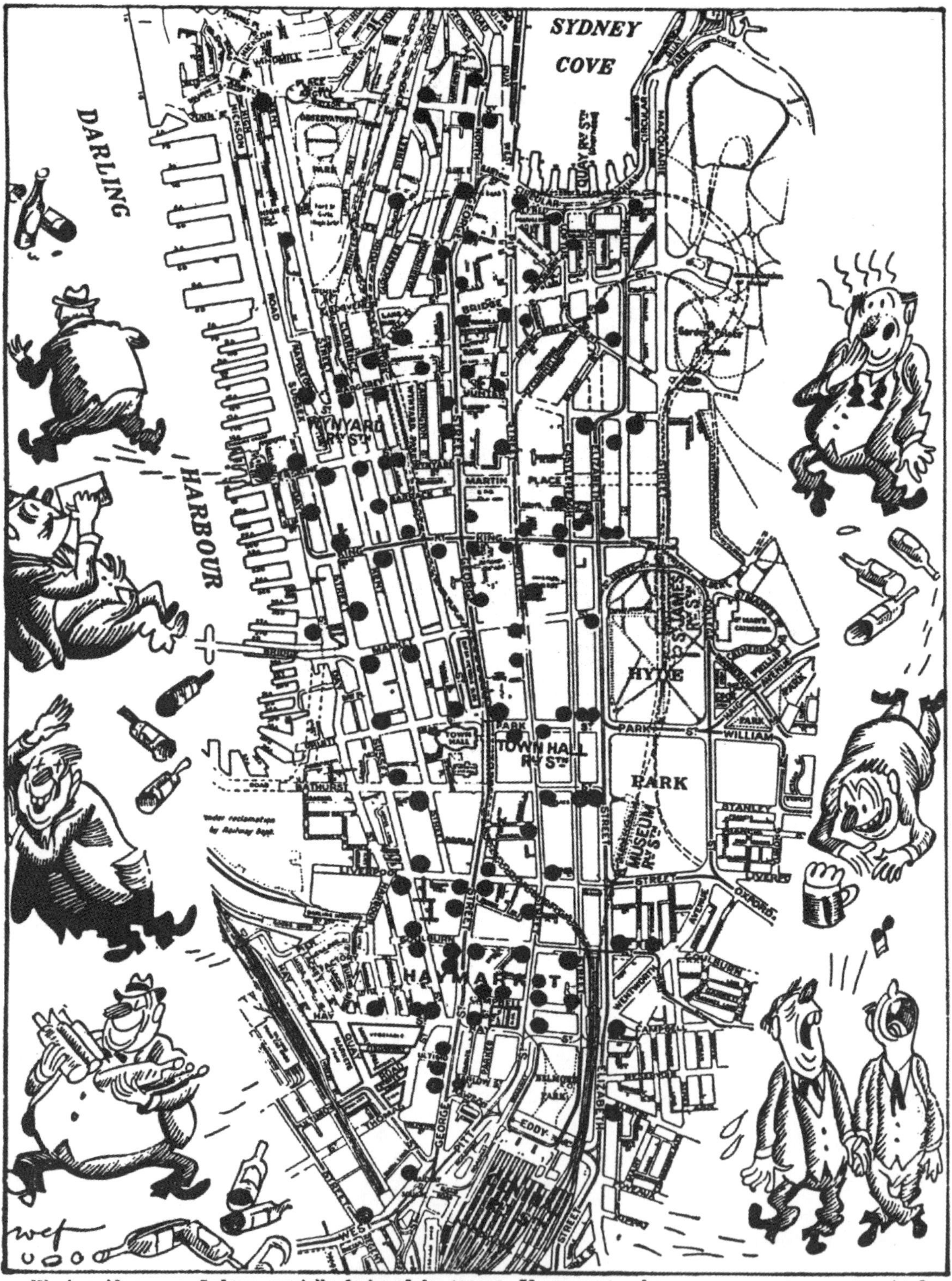

Wep's guide-map to Sydney, specially designed for topers. If any spots where you can spot are not spotted, the artist apologises. His investigations went only this far.

1961, 14 per cent in 1974 and 12 per cent in 1992 (see Table 10.1).[13] The sharpest falls occurred in the 1950s and 1960s.

The suburbanisation of retailing activity was such that the value of sales transacted in the central retail areas was declining in real terms in all capital cities except Hobart. Most of these sales were made up of clothing, drapery, electrical goods and furniture, leaving commodities such as meat and groceries almost entirely to the suburban shops. The development of suburban bulky goods strips meant that the city also lost ground in bedding, lighting, furniture, electrical and white goods. By the 1980s the big discount chains, such as Harvey Norman, and the 'category killers' (hardware warehouses, bedding emporiums) considered themselves solely suburban operators, as did international furniture chains such as Ikea, which set up at Moore Park, Gordon and Blacktown.

FACING PAGE
'Wep's guide-map to Sydney, specially designed for topers. If any spots where you can spot are not spotted, the artist apologises. His investigations went only this far.'
Colin Wills and Wep, *Rhymes of Sydney*, Johnson, Sydney, 1933

A close parallel to the outward movement of retailing was the decision, after years of debate, to relocate the city wholesale fruit and vegetable market from the Haymarket to a site at Flemington, 15 kilometres west of the city centre, adjoining the Homebush abattoirs. The new markets, opened in 1975, were almost at the epicentre of the urban area of Sydney.[14]

Pubs and boarding houses

Sydney's licensed pubs and boarding houses were concentrated in the city. At the 1933 census over half of Sydney's 632 pubs and 6278 boarding houses were in the city municipality, which then included Alexandria, Darlington, Erskineville, Glebe, Newtown, Paddington, Redfern and Waterloo. The importance of pubs in interwar Sydney is graphically portrayed in a map of central Sydney's pubs produced in 1933 by the artist 'Wep' (W.E. Pidgeon), which showed that the heaviest concentrations were around Circular Quay, the wharf and warehouse area to the west of George Street and around the Haymarket. Many of these hotels were demolished in the office boom of the 1960s and 1970s, while others succumbed to the inner city apartment boom of the 1980s and 1990s. A score or so of city pubs remain in more or less original condition with their decades-old 'play the game' beer advertisements, but with the spread of licensed restaurants and bars the pub has lost its centrality as the primary site of male drinking. The end of 6 o'clock closing in 1954, the liberalisation of drinking hours and the rise of mixed-gender drinking forced even traditionally male pubs to seek a wider clientele. Many city pubs have added a fancy restaurant to cater for the business lunch trade.

Town Hall Hotel, Darling Street Balmain in 1980.
Photograph by Peter Spearritt

Boarding houses were to be found throughout the city and the inner suburbs, from Marrickville and Waterloo to the more mixed-class areas of the eastern suburbs and North Sydney, especially Neutral Bay. They catered for all classes, but some—especially the purpose-built ones, as distinct from large terrace houses converted for the purpose—were much more expensive than others, so establishments were distinguished on the basis of cost and locality. Young women from the country or even from the suburban fringe tended to go to North Sydney or the eastern suburbs. Male apprentices could end up anywhere, from Marrickville or Newtown to Alexandria and the Rocks. The boarding houses did not serve alcohol, although many had dining rooms.

These establishments were popular settings for writers in the interwar years, including Dymphna Cusack, Ruth Park and Kylie Tennant. Many a pregnant, unmarried young woman tried to kill herself on a boarding house gas ring in their social realist novels. But it was non-fiction writers, including the journalist Vince Kelly, who described the most colourful inhabitants of the boarding house.

Around 1918 'Mrs Arnold', a woman living in Carrington Street, Wynyard Square, complained to the local police that there were 'curious goings on' in the lodging house next door to her. Sergeant C.J. (Joe) Chuck was put on the case. Chuck was faced with a dilemma—upon observation he found that while only young men ever entered this lodging house, they often came out with young women. After much detective work the truth finally dawned on Sergeant Chuck:

> Chuck realised with a shock that the 'woman' was possibly not a woman at all, but a pervert dressed in women's clothes, yet looking so much the part of the well groomed, respectable housewife that he hesitated to believe she could be anything else ... When Chuck returned to the police station his story was received at first with incredulity. A house filled entirely with sexual perverts, who were, in every other respect, living normally and honestly, posed a problem without precedent ...
>
> Chuck and his colleagues moved in and arrested ... four of them for offensive behaviour. Their prisoners gave no trouble ... When questioned, they admitted they were perverts and also that the rest of the people in the house were perverts. Three of them had been living in the 'queer house' for nearly a year.[15]

Veteran crime writer Kelly caught the terminology of the time when homosexuals were described in the press as 'perverts'. In this instance the only people to witness the allegedly offensive demeanour were the police, and they actually went looking for it.

A less mysterious but more usual experience of boarding house life is reported in Jon Rose's 1961 novel *At the Cross*, which describes a young Melbourne lad's first attempt to find boarding house accommodation in Sydney:

> I turned to look at a notice in a window. It said 'Room to let. Aussies only.' ... 'The room's fifteen bob a week, two weeks in advance, and you provide your own linen ... There's a bathroom and two lavatories.' We went back into her room and I paid her the money ... As I reached the end of the street I became terribly depressed, the room and the house were in the ugliest part of the Cross ... As I turned into the Cross proper I cheered up, after all it was only a few minutes from the centre, and it was a room of my own ...[16]

In the 1950s and 1960s boarding houses assumed a new importance as a starting-off place for recently arrived migrants. While some landladies had 'Aussies only' signs, many soon found that catering for a particular incoming migrant group could be lucrative. They were usually reliable payers and word of mouth kept the house fully occupied. The number of boarding houses in

First and Last hotel at Circular Quay photographed by John Storey in 1980, shortly before it was demolished to make way for the high-rise Quay apartment block.

the inner western suburb of Marrickville, with its large concentration of migrants, increased from 306 in 1954 to 483 in 1961. Boarding houses remain important for single men and women, especially the unemployed and the aged, and one-parent families. Many of Sydney's city and suburban pubs still provide relatively cheap accommodation (with communal facilities) on their upper floor, especially for single, unemployed men.

From picture palace to suburban cinema complex

Despite its position as the centre of commerce, retailing, pubs and boarding houses, on some other facilities the city did not have a monopoly. Before the First World War all the major live theatres in Sydney were to be found in the city and this trend persisted in the interwar years. But with the coming of the cinema the patronage of live theatres fell away. Some live theatres actually

Highlights of Sydney, Hoyt's City Theatres, Sydney, 1950

Western Suburbs Cinemas Ltd. *Guide to Suburbs*, Sydney, 1938

became cinemas, including the original Tivoli in Castlereagh Street, owned by the theatrical entrepreneur Hugh D. McIntosh. As the *Bulletin* commented on 2 October 1929, 'the Tiv can be numbered among the tragic figures that have harboured a snake in the bosom, for it was one of the first houses in Sydney to screen movies'.

There was, moreover, a major economic difference between the two forms of entertainment: live theatre required large expensive casts, and to meet the cost large audiences were needed. Cinemas were a different operation: after the initial capital expense on building and equipment, running costs were much lower and, as the cost of hiring films rose with the size of the audience, a consistently high level of patronage was not so vital to a cinema's survival. Suburban cinemas were therefore a viable proposition: suburban live theatres much less so. Sydney's first full-time suburban live theatre, the Independent (1930–77), moved from the city to North Sydney in 1939, but it was another 20 years before its example was followed, when Hayes Gordon created the Ensemble theatre.[17]

The city certainly housed the largest and most luxurious cinemas, the grand picture palaces built for the age of the 'talkies' in the late twenties, including the State and the Plaza. But by 1934 there were only 22 cinemas in the city and 115 in the suburbs, a ratio of less than 1:5. One of the largest suburban chains was centred on Parramatta and surrounding suburbs; Parramatta's 'Roxy' rivalled all but the grandest city cinemas. In 1938 Western Suburbs Cinemas Ltd announced that it dominated 'Sydney Suburbia's Entertainment Field'.

Suburban cinemas had the advantage of offering cheaper seats than their city counterparts and were easier to get to. Almost all of them were to be found on rail or tram lines. A few suburban cinemas matched those of the city in luxury and grandeur. The Cremorne Orpheum, built in the early thirties, could accommodate more than 1200 people and had the added attraction of an upstairs ballroom. Until the mid-fifties many residents of Cremorne had a permanently booked seat on Saturday nights. This theatre finally closed through lack of patronage in 1977. Ten years later, in a smaller but lavishly refurbished form, it reopened, reflecting the further evolution of cinema-going. Donald Horne, who grew up in the interwar years, wrote of the suburban cinemas:

> Since in the suburban shopping centres everything shut down at six o'clock, the packed suburban cinemas were the main opportunity for the people from a suburb to gather together and look at each other; this was the only kind of night out most of them knew. Other than these, the suburbs provided no sense of community, not even good shops.[18]

A 1951 survey of over 8000 Sydney adolescents showed the importance of cinema-going. At age 13, going to the cinema was the most popular activity for Sydney adolescents after playing sport (some of which was obligatory—the weekly school sports periods). By 18 years of age 'the movies' had become the most regular activity for boys and almost as popular as playing sport for girls.

While picture theatres, ovals and tennis courts were to be found in most suburbs, facilities for some other popular activities, such as swimming and dancing, were not. These activities often required a trip to another suburb: some of the biggest dances were held in city ballrooms such as the Trocadero, but most of the larger shopping strips also boasted ballrooms that doubled as function venues for weddings. Suburban churches were not as successful in attracting young people as the cinemas or dance halls, while Luna Park attracted a clientele far in excess of what the churches could muster even in their canvas mission tents, to be found on some of the more popular beaches during school holidays.

Logos for some of Sydney's major cinemas. *Highlights of Sydney*, Sydney, 1950

Luna Park opened in 1935 on the waterfront site formerly occupied by Dorman Long's engineering workshops. Conservationists and local residents (with concern for land values) lobbied for a park on the site; business interests prevailed and Luna Park was created instead.[19] Children and young people came by train or ferry from every suburb to this enormous playground. As Dymphna Cusack and Florence James put it in their novel *Come in Spinner*:

> The huge grotesque face of the park entrance grinned across the water ... Down both sides of the park the sideshows beckoned in brilliant electric lights ... [T]he octopus swung squealing couples on the ends of its giant arms into the darkness above the harbour ...[20]

The churches were not the only institutions to witness declining congregations in the postwar world. From the mid-fifties those temples of mass adherence since the twenties, the suburban cinemas, went into rapid decline. Suburban householders could now purchase a new domestic form of amusement, the television. No longer was it necessary to leave one's own home for visual entertainment. Regular television transmission began in Sydney in September 1956, and by the end of that year there were two commercial and one government-owned television stations operating in Sydney.[21] Because of Sydney's hilly topography, many suburbs had poor reception, including dress

Luna Park, detail from postcard, c. 1939.

Sun, 24 October 1956

circle addresses on the harbour and fibro houses in Hornsby and parts of Ryde. Towering aerials were to be seen in many localities.

City cinemas weathered the challenge of television more successfully than their suburban counterparts. While over half of the city cinemas were demolished to make way for office blocks, a few grand ones survived. Suburban cinemas, with their characteristic 'art deco' facades, were converted into furniture shops, supermarkets, warehouses or roller skating rinks. A handful made it into the 1970s to take advantage of a modest revival in cinema-going as people became increasingly bored with the poverty of television's offerings. The surviving suburban cinemas were all well served by public transport and most were within easy access of the city, such as the giant Rose Bay Wintergarden theatre, though even it succumbed to developers in the 1980s because of its harbourside setting.

Entrepreneurs' principal response to the decline of cinema patronage was to follow American trends and offer movies to the increasing number of car-owners. The result, the 'drive-in theatre', as a new concept, combined food, children's playgrounds and the privacy of the car. Originally thought to offer parents a chance to go out without the problems of finding a baby-sitter, the drive-ins soon attracted an extra clientele, the young unmarried couple. By 1957 there were eight drive-ins in Sydney suburbs. By 1974 there were twelve in Sydney; the nearest to the city was at North Ryde, nine miles from the GPO. Given the parking space required, drive-ins were one facility the city and the close-in suburbs could never provide: land was just too expensive. As patronage for the drive-in fell away and as the land value of the drive-in sites increased all of the drive-ins closed, mostly to be taken up with suburban housing.

Most of the strip shopping centres lost their cinemas sometime between the early 1960s and the early 1980s. Cinemas in major urban holiday centres, including Manly, lingered on. With both a day trip and a country holiday trade Manly's three cinemas survived until the 1970s, but all three, including the elegant Gothic-deco Odeon opposite the ferry terminal, succumbed to apartment and retail redevelopments in the 1980s. Attempts by heritage advocates to preserve these cinemas failed dismally. One commissioner on a heritage inquiry concluded that the Heritage Act was not designed to save what he called the pale suburban shadows of the great city cinemas. In losing its cinemas, some of which were grand indeed, suburban Sydney lost some of its great gathering places. While the bulk of the movies shown were American, the local cinema did engender a sense of community.[22]

In the 1970s city cinema-going revived as the cinema chains imaginatively used their sites and new equipment to create smaller venues to replace the old-style two- and three-tier cinema. In 1972 a large 1920s cinema in Darlinghurst was remodelled to create two much smaller cinemas. In 1975–76 Hoyts, one of the major cinema chains, built seven cinemas on the one site in George Street near Town Hall station. By 1974 there were 37 cinemas in the City of Sydney and 39 in the suburbs, a far cry from the days when suburban cinemas outnumbered their city counterparts five to one.

By the late 1990s, multi-screen complexes had spread to the suburbs, usually in free-standing shopping centres with up to a dozen screens. Despite the advent of television and, later, the home video, the social dimension of cinema-going still held its attraction. Once again suburban cinemas outnumbered those in the city, but this time they were to be found not in local shopping strips but in the car-based malls.

Seaside resorts: Holidaying in Sydney

Mass transport, the Saturday half-holiday and demand for Sunday outings attracted people to Sydney's seaside resorts. Ever since the founding of regular ferry services (to Manly in the 1850s, for instance) these resorts had grown in popularity. Clontarf on Middle Harbour, Manly, Clifton Gardens and Nielsen Park on Port Jackson, and other beach localities accessible by ferry were the main centres, along with the boatsheds and gardens that dotted other parts of the harbour and the Parramatta River. Many of these establishments were well-known picnic spots, for casual or organised recreational outings. In the nineteenth century the resorts offered picnic shelters, toilets and sometimes eating facilities, but they did not encourage bathing because laws passed in the 1830s prohibited bathing in the harbour or the ocean between 6 a.m. and 8 p.m. In 1903, after pressure from the proprietor of the *Manly and North Sydney News*, the Manly Council rescinded its by-law prohibiting daytime bathing. Other councils followed suit, and in February 1906 Australia's first surf club was founded at Bondi.[23] Clubs soon followed at many other southern and northern beaches.

Beach umbrellas became popular in the 1950s. Manly's ocean beach, with 1938 surf pavillion in background.
Postcard c. 1955

Saltwater harbourside pools remained popular. For many years the largest of these was the Domain Baths on the western side of Woolloomooloo, within a half-hour walk of the city centre. Opened in 1908, these baths had separate sections for men and women and a grandstand seating 1700 spectators. Demolished and rebuilt in the sixties, the Domain Baths were renamed the 'Andrew Boy Charlton' baths after a famous Sydney-born champion who, at 16, won the 1500 metres freestyle at the 1924 Olympics. For Australians of the time, Charlton was 'the greatest exponent of water sport the world has ever seen'.[24]

Harbourside and bayside municipalities were quick to follow the example of

Ferry wharf and circular swimming pool at Chowder Bay, Clifton Gardens, c. 1935. Its 'ampitheatre baths' were claimed as 'the finest in the state'.

Roseville Baths, detail from postcard c. 1940.

the Domain Baths. Shark-proof enclosures appeared at Nielsen Park, Manly, Balmoral, Clifton Gardens and Greenwich on the main harbour, Balmain on the Parramatta River, The Spit, Clontarf and Roseville on Middle Harbour, Brighton-le-Sands on Botany Bay, and Sans Souci, Taren Point and Sylvania on the George's River.[25] On weekdays the pools hosted school sports, with formal training and assessment of swimming skills. On weekends, especially in summer, they were overrun by family groups

Harbourside resorts remained popular in the interwar years. The Residential Hotel (no alcohol and therefore no public bar) at Clifton Gardens was 'close to the city, set amidst unique surroundings' with its own beach, grounds, swimming baths and natural bush. Owned by Sydney Ferries Ltd, it catered for union and company picnics. Water Board employees, butchers, bank employees and many other groups held their annual picnic at Clifton Gardens.[26]

Manly, the biggest harbourside resort, offered a harbour baths complete with grandstand and by 1933 could also claim to have the 'the largest enclosed bathing area in the world'. Promoted as both a summer resort and a residential suburb, Manly presented itself as one of 'the famous seaside resorts of the world' alongside 'Waikiki, The Lido, Coney Island and Brighton'.[27] With its central avenue named The Corso, its New Brighton Hotel and its regular Venetian Carnivals, Manly drew inspiration from the world's great seaside resorts.

The Hotel Manly, built in the twenties, became a symbol of the claim for world status when a 10-storey tower block was added in 1934. High up on the new facade a statue of Governor Phillip gazed forth over the harbour and through the heads to the Pacific Ocean. Splendid views were to be had from all points in the extension, and the building incorporated a lavish ballroom and lounges. Four years later saw the opening of a new Surf Pavilion at South Steyne. Built in brick and concrete, the streamlined modern style of the thirties, it won the Sulman medal for architectural excellence.[28]

After the Second World War Manly, like some other popular beaches, became the arena for teenage gangs. Usually they were formed into two

Coogee Ocean Pier 1928–34.
NSW Government Printer, 1928

opposing camps: in the mid-fifties 'bodgies and widgies', in the late fifties 'rockers and cools' and in the mid-sixties 'mods and surfies'. As the sociologist Dexter Dunphy wrote in the late sixties: 'For a number of teenage groups the [Manly] wharf was a setting which provided them with a social identity. The amusement pier with dodg'em cars, ferris wheels and peep shows provided varied possibilities for entertainment.' The groups kept together by strong conformity in such matters as dress. Commented one rocker: 'if he comes in a pair of tight jeans, they'd say, "Look at that kid, he looks all right." As far as the girls go, we like tight dresses. We don't like those things that trail all over the place—surfie things.'[29]

The evils of the Widgie lifestyle can be seen by their provocative stance, dress and ubiquitous cigarette.
A.E. Manning, *The Bodgie: A Study in Psychological Abnormality*, Angus & Robertson, Sydney, 1958

Manly's advantage was in being both a harbourside and a surfing resort, the two separated by a narrow peninsular. Other major resorts such as Coogee or Bondi could not play this double role but they offered similar recreational opportunities for the southern suburbs. As with Manly, particular stress was laid on accessibility from the city and suburbs. The Coogee Ocean Pier, opened in 1928, was advertised thus:

> Coogee is ideally placed for an Ocean Pier. It not only has the most beautiful beach in Sydney's Metropolitan Area, but it is the most Centrally Located Pleasure Area which can be quickest reached from the Central Railway Station and Circular Quay, the Main Sources of Metropolitan Traffic, whilst it has Direct Cross Country Access to Sydney's most thickly populated suburbs ... SYDNEY, THE CITY OF PLEASURE, has a population of over a Million and is Growing Rapidly ... It has magnificent theatres, picture palaces, omniscient halls, dancing palaces, recreation grounds but it has no ocean pier. The fact is amazing yet true ... over 26,000,000 people use the Coogee trams annually; millions of these are purely and simply holiday makers who must patronise the pier.'[30]

In 1929 the Randwick Council added an enormous shark-proof enclosure to the pier measuring 600 feet by 470 feet, to which thousands flocked. At night the enclosure was bathed in light and night surfing was inaugurated

Wep's drawing of the Bondi Beach girl with the Pavillion in the background.
Colin Wills and Wep, *Rhymes of Sydney*, Sydney, 1933

'for the first time in any part of the world'. But by 1933 the council, worried about the pier's safety, had decided to withdraw the company's franchise and tenders were called for its purchase and demolition, which occurred in 1934. Although new arrangements were made for the shark-proof enclosure, Coogee never again attracted the huge crowds of the late twenties.[31]

Like Coogee, Bondi was well served by public transport. Its elegant surfing pavilion, completed in the late 1920s, and its broad promenades were celebrated and publicised in poster art of the time. By the late thirties it was visited by at least 5 million surf bathers annually and 14 million passengers travelled there each year by tram or omnibus. While it mostly attracted day trippers, Bondi's boarding houses, guest houses and new blocks of flats also catered to city and country dwellers keen to spend their annual holidays (rarely more than two weeks) by the sea.

The increasing popularity of ocean beach surfing preceded widespread use of the car. Surf clubs were established at all the major Sydney beaches. Surf carnivals encouraged club pride and the annual carnivals with belt and boat races and march pasts. In 1935 a journalist could write of 'the boon' of Sunday morning trams and trains enabling father, mother and children to 'come down from one of the outer suburbs at the cost of two or three shillings for the party', surf and go home thoroughly refreshed.[32]

The combination of cars and the growing patronage of surf beaches began to undermine the harbourside resorts. By the mid-thirties advertisements for the Clifton Gardens Hotel had changed drastically; now its special features were extended to include ample garage accommodation, 'pre-war tariff', and only 12 minutes by car from the city via the Harbour Bridge. (The bridge caused a decline in trade for the hotel's owner, Sydney Ferries Ltd, whose ferry services suffered.) The decline was temporarily halted during the Second World War and in early postwar years as restrictions on car usage meant that most people still had to rely on public transport for their weekend recreation. But just as the 1934 extensions to the Hotel Manly symbolised the height of the harbourside and seaside boom, so the decreasing occupancy rates from the early fifties onwards symbolised its decline.

Besides the private car, postwar affluence brought another development that was to undermine seaside resorts: the private swimming pool. The two had opposite effects: the car enabled people to travel further afield and reduced their reliance on resort facilities for food and shelter; the swimming pool, like television, was a private, backyard affair. Of course, private swimming pools were not, nor ever will be, as common as car ownership. But as pollution problems sounded the death knell of harbourside and bayside public baths and made many near-city beaches (especially those near stormwater or sewerage outlets) increasingly unpleasant, the attractions of a backyard pool grew. A rash of swimming pools appeared in the well-heeled suburbs fronting onto the polluted George's River, but social class is no barrier. The same phenomenon can be seen in working-class sections of the hotter western suburbs—the pools are less expensive, but they are evident in increasing numbers nonetheless.

Although the beach resorts retained their interwar hotels in the fifties and sixties, most beach accommodation consisted of guest houses in varying levels of disrepair, and walk-up blocks of flats. Camping grounds were also popular, especially for the urban working class who had to rely on public transport and perhaps a final stint in a bus or taxi to get to their holiday destination. Tent makers catered to a wide clientele and even middle-class families frequented the camping grounds at Narrabeen Lakes, Kurnell, Sans Souci and Cronulla. Most of Sydney's camping grounds disappeared in the 1960s and 1970s, for the sites had simply become too valuable to survive the demand for housing blocks. A handful of camping and caravan establishments survive in the middle and outer suburbs, catering for domestic tourists and some 'permanents', although the latter are actively discouraged by most local councils.

Home Annual, October 1932

Grand hotels have long been a significant part of inner Sydney's image. Like other cities that grew rapidly in the second half of the nineteenth century, Sydney housed some magnificent Victorian and Edwardian establishments, including Petty's Hotel and the Wentworth Hotel. Some of the big hotels attracted a particular clientele. The Metropole, in Bridge Street, was favoured by country folk; the Australia, on the other hand, attracted the smart professional set.

Most of Sydney's big hotels were demolished in the 1960s. The loss of the Metropole, the Sydney, Ushers and the Australia meant a city almost devoid of large hotels until the Hilton, the Menzies and the new Wentworth replaced them. The first of the five-star international hotels, the Regent (1979–82) at Circular Quay, attracted a great deal of attention. While these hotels offered the elegant lobbies and restaurants of their predecessors they were also under pressure—following international practice—to take on some of the characteristics of self-contained resorts. Swimming pools and gyms became common in the larger hotels. The competition between five-star establishments is so intense that the Regent closed its doors for some months in 1999 for a complete refurbishment.

By the 1990s a shift in strategy meant that hotels were being built for specific markets. Japanese companies financed the ANA Hotel in the Rocks and the Hotel Nikko in Darling Harbour, both aimed particularly at Japanese holiday makers and people visiting on business. Smaller 'boutique hotels' also appeared. Some, like the Hotel Russell in George Street north, reused existing buildings, while others, like the lavish purpose-built Observatory Hotel, also in the Rocks, offered a swimming pool and a plethora of other facilities and services. Licensed escort agencies catered to the whims of both domestic and overseas clients; but with the spread of the mobile phone in the 1990s one is less likely to meet 'escorts' demurely waiting in expensive hotel foyers, a not uncommon sight in the 1980s.

The suburbs rose to the challenge of catering for tourists in two distinct waves of development. From the late 1950s to the early 1980s motels were established in most suburbs, particularly along major arterial roads. The Hume Highway and the Pacific Highway were early targets for motel development, especially from the outskirts of the metropolitan area to within about six kilometres of the city centre. Closer in, suitable sites were hard to find or too expensive.

The suburbs also witnessed a wave of grand hotel building not seen since the interwar years. The Travelodge at North Sydney (1979) and the Manly Pacific Hotel (1982)—one of the first hotels built since the war to have the good sense to incorporate balconies (to capitalise on its beach and ocean views)—were early examples of this trend. The Parramatta Parkroyal, the first grand hotel to be built in western Sydney, opened amid much fanfare in 1986. Since then other large hotels have been built at North Ryde (near Macquarie University), at Parramatta and at Double Bay, but only a handful rival the size, the glamour, the facilities or the views of the big city establishments. Central Sydney, including Darling Harbour and Kings Cross, remains the heart of the four- and five-star hotel trade. But this also means that the city can be a very expensive place to stay in. Only a small proportion of relatively run-down establishments offer rooms for less than $100 a night. For affordable accommodation backpackers have to retreat to inner suburbs such as Glebe and Bondi, where boarding houses have been converted into hostels, while families have little option but to go to outer suburban motels.

LIFE IN THE SUBURBS

In the 1950s suburban life continued to revolve around the home and local clubs, pubs (which often housed illegal starting price bookmakers) and churches. In the new suburbs, schools and kindergartens had to be established and they too sometimes became a focus of community life. Work life was usually associated with the city and the inner suburbs, while recreation, apart from local sports clubs and cinemas, was linked with the harbour, the ocean beaches, Botany Bay and the Blue Mountains. Few inland suburbs had municipal baths: Ryde, Lane Cove and Liverpool did not get their Olympic pools until the late 1950s.

Social life in the suburbs revolved around school organisations, such as

'Our back yard is a garden now—a place for fun and leisure'.
Australian Womens Weekly, 7 April 1954

Parents and Citizens clubs, churches and their 'ladies' auxiliaries', all-male clubs such as Rotary, Lions and the Masons, sporting organisations and the local pub. Most suburbs had their own ovals and cricket pitches. On any Saturday afternoon in summer one could see men in their 'creams' playing a leisurely game of cricket on dusty suburban ovals in the Anglo-Saxon tradition of enlightened amateurism. In winter, Rugby Union took over ovals to the north of the harbour while in the more working-class south and west, Rugby League dominated. Some children and adolescents were catered for by local boy scouts and girl guides groups and Police Boys' clubs.[33]

The decision by the Labor government in 1955 to allow sports clubs to sell liquor and then to run poker machines revolutionised suburban facilities. Until then the city had a monopoly on the classier clubs, where women were often welcome, even if only in the dining room. In many suburbs dad would be at the hotel bar and would occasionally deliver a shandy to mum and lemonade to the kids as they waited around outside or in the car. Poker machines were confined to sports and Returned Services League (RSL) clubs; hotels were excluded from this lucrative trade. Suddenly football, bowling, tennis and RSL clubs had a monopoly on a new source of revenue, and because they were community-owned organisations this money was poured into expanded premises, huge cafeteria-style restaurants, improved sporting facilities and even short-term child care. Women were welcome, and the bands, films and community activities catered for all age groups, including teenagers and the growing proportion of retired people. Church and Masonic halls became redundant. The licensed clubs became the new community cathedrals, from Balmain Leagues and Merrylands RSL to North Sydney Leagues and the Revesby Workers Club, where you could drink, gamble, eat, dance, get fit or simply chat the night away.[34]

In the 1950s the geographer A.J. Rose attempted to translate, for a primary school audience, concepts of location in Sydney into easily understandable

Father goes to work complete with hat. This family is proud of its brick house.
National Archives of Australia, c. 1955

descriptions of family life. One of his families, the 'Brents', lived in the middle-class suburb of Willoughby, six miles from the city centre. John Brent, a trading agent, had a fourth-floor office in George Street in the city, which he reached by tram rather than take his own car because of traffic congestion on the Harbour Bridge. From his office he was within walking distance of the banks that finance overseas trade and the ships that actually carry the goods. His office employed four 'girls who do the typing and clerical work' and an associate manager, an old army friend who also lived on the north shore. Two of the 'girls' in the office lived at Rockdale, eight miles to the south of the city, travelling to work by train. The junior office assistant, a woman from the country, lived in a boarding house at Cremorne and travelled to work by ferry. The senior typist shared a flat 'with two other girls' at Kings Cross, a mile east of the city; Rose describes the Cross as 'the centre for bohemian and artistic life in Sydney' where 'it is as common to hear accents originating from Europe as it is to hear the voices of native Australians'.

John Brent was a family man with three school children. His 15-year-old son Paul travelled by tram to the Church of England Grammar School at North Sydney; his 12-year-old daughter, to reach the Presbyterian Ladies College, had to travel a mile by tram to Chatswood station and then four miles by train to Pymble. Nine-year-old Sarah could walk to the local state primary school, only a mile from home. After her family had left for work and school in the morning, Mary Brent set about 'tidying the house'. 'Mary usually does the family wash on Mondays and hangs it out on the line in the backyard to dry'. About once a month Mary travelled into the city centre to shop in one of the large stores or to go to the cinema. She travelled by public transport because it was too difficult to find parking space in town. Usually, however, she drove her car to the local suburban shops or occasionally to the larger shopping centre at Chatswood where there was a wide selection of clothing stores. Mary always returned home in the latter part of the afternoon 'to prepare dinner for the family'.[35]

When this textbook was written, less than a fifth of married women worked outside the home. But this is not to say that there was nothing to do in the suburbs: clearly Mary Brent had a busy home-based life, with little help from her husband or children who travelled each day to the 'real world' outside. In the interwar and early postwar years only single women could escape Mary Brent's fate. If they were young, they lived in the suburbs and worked in the city. If they were older and allowed to make up their own minds, they could live in or near the city as well as work in it.

John Brent could share in the delights of the city because he worked there and he could afford the prices charged by the restaurants, theatres and cinemas. But many men and women who worked in the city could afford little more than a take-away lunch or a beer at the hotels that graced almost every corner block. The cleaners, tellers, lift attendants, proofreaders and waiting staff who made up much of the city's workforce knew what it was like to work in what *Building* magazine's editor, Florence Taylor, disdainfully called 'the solid and dirty environment of the city's commercial heart'.[36]

Bright lights, big city ...

> Just where is King's Cross?—or, as it is referred to affectionately by those who live there—The Cross. Can anyone say, or point to it definitely, or define its boundaries? ... Yet it is fairly safe to say that fully ninety per cent of Australians know of, or have heard of the Cross, and this also applies to visitors from overseas to these shores ... Six main arteries converge at the top of William Street, forming a large irregularly shaped space, neither circle, square nor crescent.[37]

The Cross has been a central image of city life in Sydney for many decades. Sydney writers claimed that it represented all that Australia knows of Bohemia while Sydney cartoonists delighted in depicting it as 'no place for a Melbourne man'. The Cross became a symbol for suburbanites of a life different from their own.

Kings Cross had long been a traditional centre for migrants, the 'cosmopolitan, continental part of Sydney'.[38] The concentration of immigrants in particular areas began in the 1880s and has continued ever since.[39] The Cross became known as the home for Continental Europeans. On 21 October 1929 a writer on the *Labor Daily* observed, 'the Greek plays an all important part in the life of Sydney—he practically exclusively feeds it ... No scarlet, glamorous Darlinghurst midnight revel is complete without his shining lobster ...' In 1939 Alfred Harris, a leader of the Sydney Jewish community, criticised Jewish migrants for 'congregating in or about King's Cross and Bondi, perhaps not realising that in so doing they are looked on as forming colonies which is positively undesirable'.[40]

The Kings Cross prostitute was a favourite topic in paperback fiction and for male 'humourists'. Pimps, police harassment and an equivocating state government made the reality.
George Trost, *Call Me a Cabbie*, Sydney, 1966

With its real and imagined concentrations of bohemians, foreigners, Jews, gamblers, strippers, homosexuals, transvestites, prostitutes, 'gay' bars, night clubs, illegal abortionists and other 'undesirables', the Cross continued to attract suburbanites, at least for a look. Cross champions celebrated its ambience:

> From the Loo, from the City, the suburbs, the country, going back to the Cross is going home. The yellow lights hang in the smoky air, the policeman stands in his long white coat at the Cross roads with traffic whirling around him, the youthful voices of the news-boys cut through the air like a saw. Crowds fight past, lights stream downwards from the shop windows ...[41]

One resident, the poet Kenneth Slessor, wrote of it in 1950, 'At sundown on New Year's Eve people come to the Cross from Suburbs ten miles away to stand in the streets crushed together in mass-rites, waiting for midnight to ring in the New Year ...'[42] Increasingly the Cross became a mecca for sightseers. 'They came from interstate or the Sydney suburbs and would sit at the cafes or promenade along Darlinghurst Road taking in the vivid street life.'[43] By 1965 Slessor was complaining that most of the Cross's permanent residents 'lock their doors at festival times when ... invaded by "foreigners" from duller parts of the metropolis, blowing trumpets, hurling streamers, and exploding fireworks'. After a brief heyday with Americans on rest and recre-

Colin Wills and Wep, *Rhymes of Sydney*, Johnson, Sydney, 1933

ation leave from the Vietnam War, the Cross has lost much of its allure.

In the 1980s the centre of bohemian, and increasingly of a specifically gay, sub-culture moved to Oxford Street, running from the top corner of Hyde Park to Paddington. Symbolic home to the Gay Mardi Gras, Oxford Street has recovered the pizzazz it displayed in the interwar years. The building of the eastern distributor linking the approaches to the Harbour Bridge to the airport expressway will reduce the traffic that has choked the area for years. While nearby Kings Cross retains a reputation for night clubs and bars, the centre of gravity for new year celebrations in Sydney is now Circular Quay and the nationally televised fireworks spectacular from the bridge. Adjacent to office blocks and expensive apartments, it does not lend itself to the trade in sex and drugs that still flourishes in the narrow streets and laneways of the Cross.

Hi-Spots: a souvenir guide to Sydney's night spots, back cover c. 1960.

Coming to Sydney

Like all growing cities Sydney gets newcomers from a variety of sources. Some people move to Sydney from elsewhere in New South Wales and other states; others leave Sydney to follow jobs, families, lifestyle, or cheaper real estate. The influx of British, Irish and continental European immigrants to Sydney from the late 1940s to the 1970s is discussed in chapter 5. With the gradual elimination of the 'White Australia Policy' by the late 1960s, more of Sydney's immigrants began to come from Asia. By 1996 over 300,000 residents of Sydney were Asian born, with China, Vietnam, the Philippines and Hong Kong the major sources. Those four countries between them accounted for 202,000 residents, slightly more than the 195,000 from the United Kingdom.[44]

Sydney now has a higher proportion of foreign born—30 per cent—than at any time since 1900. On the other hand, as the city grows, the proportion of the population who are either foreign-born or the children of foreign-born (second generation migrants) is starting to fall slightly, from 55 per cent in 1986 to around 50 per cent in 1996. This is because many of the adult migrants of the 1950s and 1960s are now well over 60. The death columns of the *Sydney Morning Herald* reveal the ethnic mix of Sydney society.

With 1.3 million residents of Sydney born overseas, proud claims are made for cosmopolitan Sydney, the title of a recent guide book enabling the reader to 'explore the world in one city'. Its authors, Jock Collins (of Anglo-Celtic descent) and Antonio Castillo, a Chilean-born journalist, claim that Sydney has 'a local community for nearly every team' that will march at the opening

Aboriginal flag at Mrs Macquarie's Chair, Australia Day 1988.
Photograph by Peter Spearritt

Sydney Town Hall steps, January 1999.
Photograph by Peter Spearritt

ceremony of the Olympic Games.[45] Their book traces the cityscapes, the lifestyles and the contributions of more than 70 distinct nationalities. It details the shops, the cafes, the clubs, the festivals, the religious structures and the national icons to be found in particular localities. It comes at what may well be a high point of national identification, with the collapse of the USSR and the Eastern bloc seeing a spate of new nation-states. Yet the introduction of the euro and other international trade and economic 'reforms' suggests that nationality—at least at it came to be understood in the nineteenth and twentieth centuries—might well wane in the twenty-first century.

National and ethnic groups in Sydney are much less concentrated than in many European and North American cities. The leading scholar of ethnic communities in Sydney, Ian Burnley, writes of a 'high level of population dispersal', while noting that the small, more concentrated immigrant communities in Sydney before the Second World War, including Greeks, Italian, Maltese, Lebanese, Chinese and Jews, did provide 'pre-existing anchor points' for the later influx of immigrants.[46] Nonetheless, ethnic concentrations, while not approximating the American ghettoes, have long been a feature of inner city and suburban life in Sydney. Fairfield and adjacent suburbs in western Sydney are a major place of Vietnamese settlement, especially of refugees. With its cheaper real estate western Sydney has also housed people of Spanish ancestry, along with migrants from Syria, Iraq, Iran and Turkey. Professional and business migrants from Malaysia and Hong Kong have tended to locate in the more expensive eastern and northern suburbs. Japanese migrants and business people have a penchant for Northbridge.[47]

One of the striking population movements in Australia since the 1960s has been the increase in the number of people of indigenous origin living in Sydney. At the 1986 census 18,581 Sydney residents identified themselves as Aborigines or Torres Strait Islanders; by 1996 the figure had increased to 33,606. Sydney now houses almost 10 per cent of Australia's indigenous population, and has become a major centre of Aboriginal culture, especially in dance, theatre, music and art. The main concentrations of indigenous people are to be found in the inner city areas of Redfern, Waterloo, Leichhardt and Marrickville, along with the long-established community at La Perouse and in nearby Randwick. Given the high incarceration rate of indigenous people, it is notable that 101 people of indigenous origin were in Long Bay Jail in 1996. While indigenous people live throughout the metropolitan area, their concentrations in the inner city and the outer western suburbs, often in government housing, indicates that on a common Australian measure of success—owing or buying a home—they remain markedly disadvantaged.[48] Yet for many Aborigines, leaving a mission station or a racist country town and coming to Sydney was the start of a new and better life.[49]

Office boom: Manhattan-on-Pacific

Factory employment in the city municipality fell away in the postwar years to be replaced by office employment and a succession of office building booms. At least once a decade since the late 1950s the Sydney skyline has been a flurry of cranes. A renewed faith in the worth of a city location was demonstrated in 1957 with the completion of Qantas House (on the corner of Hunter and Bligh streets), featuring a full glass circular facade, rising to the 150-foot height limit. In April that same year the Height of Buildings Act of 1912 was amended. The powerful AMP insurance company was quick to take advantage: by 1961 it was the proud possessor of Australia's tallest building, rising 26 storeys above Circular Quay. In an urban economy where land tax and municipal rates are tied to unimproved values, there was strong pressure to build as high as possible.

Circular Quay in 1905 showing the Farmers and Graziers building that was demolished to make way for AMP's first sky scraper.
Postcards, 1905 and 1962

The city had prestige value, so government and private corporations sought to make their mark there. In 1963 a 22-storey office block was opened for the federal government in Chifley Square. A revival of high-class hotel trade was indicated in the same year by the completion of the Menzies Hotel in Wynyard Square; Qantas's Wentworth Hotel in Phillip Street followed three years later. The state government and its instrumentalities also began to upgrade their accommodation. The Metropolitan Water, Sewerage and Drainage Board opened new 27-storey premises in 1965, and in 1967 the state government presided over the completion of the tallest building in Sydney, a 38-floor office tower for itself (demolished in 1997, only 30 years later, to make way for apartments). With the Manhattan syndrome in full flight, no one could retain the lead for long. The following year (1968) saw the completion of Australia Square

Tower, a 50-storey circular block, the product of a financial consortium led by Lend Lease Corporation, designed by Harry Seidler.

Primarily funded by insurance companies (particularly the AMP) and development corporations (such as Lend Lease and L.J. Hooker), this building boom was presided over until 1967 by a Labor City Council that had been in power since 1949.[50] Labor aldermen liked the city's towering skyscrapers because they were impressed by size and because rising land values added to the council's property-based rate revenue. Such funds enabled the aldermen to attend to the welfare problems of their constituents, who lived in working-class areas around the CBD.

But the office blocks failed to live up to their advocates' claims that they would bolster the city's diminishing workforce. Many of the trades and activities forced out by the office boom were labour-intensive operations, from women in the sweated clothing trades to brewery workers to employees of the PMG (post and telephone) who successfully resisted mechanisation for many years. With the breaking up of the PMG into Australia Post and Telecom (since renamed Telstra), one of the city's great land marks, the general Post Office (GPO), could be leased, in the mid-1990s, to the operator of a five-star hotel.

The State Office Block, opened in 1967 on the corner of Bent and Macquarie streets, demolished in 1997 for an expensive apartment building designed by Renzo Piano.
Photograph by Peter Spearritt

In the early postwar years the city (even on 1969 boundaries) contained more than two-thirds of metropolitan employment in commerce, finance and property, but by 1971 it held less than a third. Office employment expanded in the suburbs. By 1971 the three largest centres were Bankstown, North Sydney and Parramatta, while other suburban centres such as Crows Nest–St Leonards, Chatswood, Hurstville and Liverpool were also attracting office buildings. Despite suburban growth the city remains the prime site of new office construction, accounting for two-thirds of it between 1989 and 1997. North Sydney, at around one-fifth of the total, is its only competitor (see Table 10.2).

North Sydney, which had been in the doldrums ever since the bridge opened in 1932, became the site of a twin city. North Sydney's fortunes improved after the war because, in the words of one commentator, 'the post-war boom caused overcrowding in the city, and eyes turned northwards. Here, just across the bridge, was an area of low land values and old buildings ripe for demolition ...'[51] Served by two railway stations, at Milson's Point and North Sydney itself, the office boom began in the mid-1950s when the AMP Society built a seven-storey office block for lease. The seal of approval came in 1956–57, when the MLC insurance company chose North Sydney as the site for its prestigious head office and built what was at that time the largest office building in Australia. Golden Fleece, Ampol, British Petroleum, Phillips and many others followed the MLC's example.

By the early 1990s North Sydney had more rented office space than Adelaide and had become, in effect, Australia's fifth most important office centre. Popular with the computing, advertising, media and insurance industries, the municipality turned into a series of often ugly office blocks, beyond which lay some of the most sought-after waterfront property in Australia. The push to build Australia's tallest building now appears to have been a particular preoccupation of the 1960s and 1970s. The AMP Society finally met the

Table 10.2: Office space in major commercial centres, Sydney region 1970 and 1987

Location	1970 square metres	1987 square metres
Sydney CBD	2 137 500	3 373 000
North Sydney	223 000	700 000
Parramatta	54 800	194 000
Chatswood	38 100	203 000
St Leonards	n.a.	294 000
Hurstville	12 100	79 000
Bankstown	14 000	70 000
Liverpool	12 100	60 000
Bondi Junction	10 200	55 000
Burwood	13 300	35 000
Hornsby	12 500	33 000
Blacktown	12 100	24 000

Source: P. Spearritt and C. DeMarco, *Planning Sydney's Future,* A & U, Sydney, 1988.

challenge posed by the Australia Square Tower, and for a short time it could boast again that it owned 'Australia's tallest building':

> There's more to the new AMP centre than Australia's best view ... Australia's tallest building is well worth hard-nosed consideration by many a board of directors ... Look at the location: Sydney Cove. There's more to that than historical prestige. Sydney Cove means it's a minute walk to ferries, trains and buses. Good employees stay with companies for life for slimmer reasons than that. The centre is just three minutes lunch-time stroll from the Opera House ... sunny terraces and fine stores, eating places, coffee shops, a tavern and banking facilities ... Nobody needs to go uptown, because now this is uptown downtown. Below the terrace is parking for 270 cars ... If you would like a tour on a sunny day, or just to chat over the possibilities and the price, have your girl ring our leasing agents ...[52]

Pride of place for the AMP's second attempt at Australia's tallest building was lost within two years to a rival insurance company, the MLC, whose tower block rose 68 storeys above Martin Place. This development involved demolition of the Hotel Australia, one of Sydney's most elegant establishments, and of the Theatre Royal. The tower includes a new Theatre Royal in the basement, a concession rung out of Lend Lease and the MLC by a 'Save the Theatre Royal' group. The city lost an equally well-known live theatre, the Tivoli, in 1970, when Lend Lease demolished it for their Central Square project. The company's profit increased from $5 million in 1972 to $9 million in 1973, fell to $8.5 million in 1975 but by 1976 had recovered to $10 million. In this Lend Lease were more fortunate than many other development companies that did not survive the crash of the mid-seventies, including Mainline, Cambridge Credit and Parkes Development.[53]

While it was difficult to retain the appeal of massive blocks for long, especially in an office market that demanded ever more sophisticated cabling for

North Sydney, including gasometer, taken from the MLC tower block then under construction.
People, 22 April 1957

computing and telecommunications purposes, height remains an iconic selling point. Centrepoint observation tower with its massive turret (including two restaurants and an observation platform) became Australia's tallest structure on completion in 1980. Now marketed as 'Sydney Tower', it appears dated and requires regular refurbishment and promotion to retain its status as an icon.

If the city had continued to lose its facilities, it might have lost its attractiveness. This did indeed seem to be a risk in the sixties and early seventies, when an unregulated office boom wiped out many of the city's small and interesting trades and caused the demolition of some of the best-known live theatres. But building booms usually come to an end: the current building stock of central Sydney is the result of five substantial boom periods—around 1880–90, 1900–14, 1920–30, 1935–40, the late 1950s, 1964–75 and the late 1980s to the present. Until the 1980s the great majority of buildings were office blocks with some retail space. Since then a number of office blocks have been converted to apartments (including the IBM building) or demolished to make way for new apartment blocks. With such a large and varied building stock, rents range widely: the small and interesting trades and entertainments rightly cherished by champions of the inner city can still find relatively cheap rent and a larger clientele in the inner city than in the suburbs. But the growth of suburban centres, from North Sydney and Chatswood to Bankstown and Parramatta, has seen a city-like range of rental options spread to many parts of the metropolis.

The city's domination of the metropolis, and even of the nation, should not be underestimated, especially when it is situated on such a commanding site. The site determined the location of the Sydney Opera House, opened in October 1973; the city-centred public transport system made the Opera House at least as accessible to most people in Sydney as any suburban setting. In the past three decades the city has attracted other key facilities, such as the NSW Institute of Technology, now the University of Technology, Sydney, near

Central Station in Ultimo. The Australian Broadcasting Corporation relocated its national headquarters to an adjacent site in the mid-1990s. These institutions are more accessible to more of Sydney's population than suburban Macquarie University at North Ryde (16 kilometres from the city), where the choice for most students is between a car, which many cannot afford, or at least two changes on public transport. The decision on a site for Macquarie University, taken in the mid-sixties, was based on a sensible assessment of the direction of Sydney's population growth. The university is accessible to the growing upper middle-class suburbs to its north-east and north-west and to the working-class suburbs to its west, if one has access to a car.

During the 1980s and 1990s, investment in the city centre has taken a variety of forms. The state government has assisted in refurbishing and partly rebuilding the Rocks and Circular Quay. For complete makeovers, such as Darling Harbour, with its hotels, casino, convention centre and trade displays, the government created a separate development authority. It also paid for the refurbishment of its traditional precinct, Macquarie Street, home to Parliament and the State Library.

Office and retail development and the inner city apartment boom of the 1990s have remained the preserve of corporations. Nonetheless, both the city council and the government have often bent over backwards to foster such developments. The 'Toaster', the infamous apartment block that compromises the Opera House and obliterates views of Government House, was made possible by the city council selling the developer part of a public street and by the failure of the government's town planning regulations to prevent such an abomination. The successive planning ministers and senior government and council bureaucrats who allowed this to happen have all since run for cover.[54] It is simply too expensive to buy back a building whose apartments command prices of up to $7 million.

More and more, residents of Sydney came to appreciate the costs of providing car access between the city and the suburbs. In the early 1970s the anti-freeway movement, residents action groups and the Builders Labourers Federation's 'Green Bans' prevented some of what was best in the inner city from being destroyed.[55] In response, government authorities showed a short-lived willingness to consider the possibility of banning cars from certain parts of the city, including the creation of Martin Plaza and the Pitt Street Mall. But the rest of the central city is still overrun by traffic,

The developers of this site overlooking the Opera House originally planned to reuse the existing office building, constructed in 1956. Once its cladding had been removed, citizens could see views of the Tarpeian Way that had been hidden for many decades.
Photograph by Peter Spearritt, 26 January 1988

pandered to with 'no stopping' signs and hefty fines, which seems to be the inevitable state for Australia's largest city.

Cities in the suburbs

Sydney has always been a series of cities and suburbs. While the city centre towered above all else in both power and height, the very nature of suburban development, where formerly discrete settlements, from Watsons Bay and Manly to Parramatta and Penrith, were eventually engulfed in urban growth does not mean that they lose all their distinct characteristics, or their sense of independent urban status. Most writers on urban Australia between the 1960s and the 1980s, this author included, while rejecting the more outlandish denunciations of suburban sprawl, underestimated the resilience of local shopping strips, the staying power of community groups, the sense of place that backyard, street and locality give to people's lives.[56]

Much writing about the suburbs starts by observing their flatness, their sameness, the alleged monopoly of the 'quarter-acre block'. This is itself a misnomer, as most block sizes in suburban Sydney, even in the 1920s, were more likely to be one-sixth than one-quarter of an acre. Also, much of Sydney is not flat, with the hills, rivers, bushland, national parks and the harbour making possible a sense of topographic, even economic distinctiveness. Much of western and south-western Sydney is quite flat, but the parks, railway system, hospitals, schools and even the freeways create physical barriers and subcommunities within which people go about their home and work lives.

The physical contours of Sydney are the result of both topography and building. Until the 1950s all the tall buildings were in the city centre and even

The apartment and office blocks of Chatswood loom large on the horizon.
Photograph by Peter Spearritt, from Cammeray, 1998

Cities and suburbs from the new showground site at Homebush Bay. In the middle ground the abandoned brick pits. On the horizon, viewing from left to right, one can see the high rise of Chatswood, then St Leonards, North Sydney, and the City itself.
Photograph by Peter Spearritt, 1998

most three- and four-storey structures were to be found there or in the inner industrial suburbs, along with taller blocks of flats in North Sydney and the eastern suburbs. All the taller factories, many of which used gravity to move their products from the point of manufacture to packaging for delivery, were concentrated in industrial suburbs, from the inner city to Cook's River, Mortlake and the Parramatta River. New methods of conveying goods, made possible by electrification, meant that entire factory operations, from cigarettes and chocolate to glass and cars, could be carried out on one level. This revolution required huge areas of land, only available in the outer suburbs. The multi-storey warehouses and manufacturing plants of the inner city were abandoned for bigger sites in the suburbs. Many of these taller inner city structures still survive. In the 1960s and 1970s they became home to offices, in the 1980s and 1990s they are more likely to be refurbished as apartments.

The suburbs were also getting tall buildings. While the car-based shopping malls of the 1960s followed industrial practice, taking up huge sites for single-storey development, high land values and access to the rail network encouraged apartment developers to build 10- or 12-storey blocks in and

Table 10.3: Types of dwellings, Sydney, Melbourne and Brisbane 1991 (percentages)

	Sydney	Melbourne	Brisbane
Separate house	66.5	76.1	82.7
Semi-detached, terrace	8.9	9.6	3.0
Flat, 4 storeys +	7.1	1.4	1.2
Other flats	15.1	11.1	10.6
Other	2.4	2.8	2.5
Total	100	100	100

Source: C Foster, Australian Cities, OUP, Melbourne, 1995, p 73.

around major suburban centres. Some of these places now have multi-storey car parks, indistinguishable from those of the city centre. This policy of developing regional centres, supported by successive state governments, has produced a landscape where Sydney is now dotted with a succession of clumps of high-rise buildings. If you stand on one of the higher Olympic structures at Homebush you see a succession of cities, from the grand towers of the city centre and North Sydney to the noticeable clusters of St Leonards, Chatswood and Hornsby. From the Bankstown water tower the high-rise buildings of western and south western Sydney also greet the eye.

Tower blocks of apartments are now being built around many of Sydney's major railway stations, which usually have a bus interchange as well. New apartment block at Strathfield.
Photograph by Peter Spearritt, 1998

This spread of high-rise structures is more marked in Sydney than in any other Australian city. Table 10.3 indicates that Sydney has many more residential blocks over four storeys than other cities. These taller blocks of flats, when taken together with the office towers of the main regional centres, give Sydney the appearance of a metropolis of both cities and suburbs. While one million of Sydney's dwellings are still single-storey houses, the remaining 500,000 are two-storey houses, two-storey terraces and town houses, and apartment blocks of two to 40 storeys.

Thirty years after Premier Askin's comment that Roselands shopping mall brought 'the city to the suburbs', Sydney had become a series of cities and suburbs, reverting in a sense to its late nineteenth-century pattern where once one got beyond the inner industrial area the rest of the metropolis consisted of loosely linked towns and villages. Subsumed, it seemed, in suburbia, these have been replaced by mini-cities that owe their locality names and much of their sense of place to the first century of the city's growth.

Protesters outside the Art Deco Rural Bank in Martin Place.
Their opposition to its demolition was to no avail.
Photograph by John Storey, 1983

Chapter 11

Demolition and preservation

As it grew from almost 200,000 dwellings in 1921 to over 1.3 million dwellings in 1996, Sydney witnessed successive periods of rapid growth, followed by more modest consolidation. Over three-quarters of the dwellings constructed during those years were on land that hadn't been built on before, but the remainder required the demolition of existing structures, including houses, factories and commercial buildings. Just as Sydney has seen waves of new building, so too has it seen extensive demolition and rebuilding. The primary site of this activity has always been the central city area, where high land values and high use values have meant that retailers, wholesalers and investors in commercial property—from offices to pubs—are tempted to rebuild to maximise their returns. But even in the inner city some sites retain particular structures for decades after they have lost any social or economic utility.

While almost all structures erected in the middle and outer suburbs in the interwar years were the first on their particular sites, even here there were structures—farmers' cottages, dairies, sheds—that were demolished. And all these sites, though few recognised it at the time, had once been occupied by the Aboriginal tribes that lived in the Sydney region. Subsequent archaeological work on sites throughout Sydney, and especially around the Parramatta and Nepean rivers, has revealed relatively intensive Aboriginal occupation of many sites over thousands of years.

Outer suburban development—whether in the 1920s in Bankstown or in the 1990s in Penrith—has also seen the breaking up of often quite large landholdings. Some, dating from the 1870s and 1880s, had grand houses with vast gardens where the original owner commanded an entire valley. In the inner suburbs thousands of large houses—some of which ended their years as boarding houses or schools or private hospitals—have been successively demolished since the 1920s to make way for more modest houses or flats. In the interwar and early postwar years this was invariably for detached houses, except in near-city areas well served by trams, buses, trains or ferries where flats replaced both houses and commercial structures. A handful of other settlements, also well served by public transport, including Manly and Parramatta, experienced dramatic redevelopment in the interwar years. In Manly new blocks of flats led the way, in Parramatta big new department stores, reflecting its role as the major shopping centre for western Sydney.

In the late 1950s and 1960s almost every block of flats built in Sydney was on the site of a pre-existing dwelling, usually a detached house. When local shopping strips were redeveloped to compete with the big car-based malls, individual shops and houses made way for new supermarkets, just as they

Arthur Rickard's real estate company acknowledges, even if in a rather patronising manner, prior Aboriginal occupation of the Bankstown landscape.
Rickard's Reality Review September 1910

had for petrol stations—insatiable consumers of land—a decade earlier. In the early 1970s two semi-detached houses in Lane Cove (the author rented one with a group of recent North Sydney Boys High graduates in 1970) were demolished to make way for a supermarket. Bigger retail premises developed in all the more successful shopping centres.

Roads and bridges, to service the inexorable growth of traffic, also took their toll on grand and modest homes. St Malo, an 1850s home at Hunters Hill, was demolished by the Department of Main Roads in 1961 for the freeway linking Figtree with Gladesville, while the approaches to the new concrete bridge claimed hundreds of commercial and residential properties. More ignominious was the demolition of Subiaco at Rydalmere, built in 1836 by the architect John Verge for one of the Macarthurs. In 1961 it made way for an extension to the Rheem factory car park.[1]

The demolition of grand houses and their grounds often took place in stages. The gardens of Merioola, a vast mansion built in 1859 in Edgecliff Road, were taken up with residential subdivision in the early 1920s. The house itself was demolished for a block of flats in 1952. Between 1910 and the 1960s new blocks of flats were built on the sites of many of Sydney's stately homes. Homes with large grounds were also popular with the Department of Education, looking for sites for new schools. Ultimo House in Ultimo (built around 1805 with late additions by Francis Greenway) was demolished in 1932 to provide a site for the Sydney Technical College, while The Towers, in High Street, Penrith, was demolished in the 1940s to make way for the suburb's first high school.

By the 1990s some sites in the inner city had housed four or five different structures over 150 years. Sydney had lost so many of its grander nineteenth-century residential and commercial structures that the main reminders of that century were churches and terrace houses. Modest wooden cottages of the 1840s gave way to double brick terraces in the 1880s, which in turn were replaced, in the 1930s or 1950s with three-storey blocks of flats. Usually because they had only one owner, the blocks of flats were readily purchased and demolished in the 1980s and 1990s to create strata apartments or commercial spaces, often two or three times the height of the blocks they replaced. Ironically, the larger strata blocks may be very difficult to redevelop in the future, because scores of individual or corporate owners will have to agree. This may be just as hard to achieve as the multiple site amalgamations required for Harry Seidler's Australia Square Tower, built in the mid-1960s. Organising the demolition and rebuilding of large residential tower blocks of the 1990s, which might have 200 separate title holders, will be a logistical nightmare in coming decades, when even these structures are judged to be technologically outdated, even structurally unsafe.

Gasometer, Neutral Bay.
Photograph by Peter Spearritt, 1984

The 'megahouses' developed around Sydney harbour and in many upper middle-class suburbs in the 1990s are sometimes as large, in terms of the number of rooms, as the mansions that once commanded these sites. The difference is that these megahouses are on modest housing allotments, without the substantial grounds of the nineteenth century. The result is a series of gross structures, many of which look like they are about to topple over from a combination of ostentatious wealth and bad taste.

The building and redevelopment of commercial and industrial property follows a different trajectory to that of residential buildings. In the established suburbs land use zoning for industrial sites and commercial strips usually followed the pattern set by such activities in the 1880s and 1890s. But in the middle and outer suburbs designated areas have been specifically allocated—since the Cumberland County Plan—for industrial, retailing, wholesaling, educational, even religious uses.

The established industrial suburbs of interwar Sydney have seen spectacular changes in both their activities and their landscapes in the last 20 years. Changing technologies have enabled power generation and gas plants to be removed from the cities they serve. All of Sydney's power stations and gas plants have been closed and either reused for other purposes (for example the Powerhouse Museum in Ultimo) or demolished to make way for new commercial, residential or recreational activities. The gas plant at Manly, closed in 1938, was demolished in the 1970s to make way for a harbourside park, the gasometer at Neutral Bay remained until the late 1980s when it became the site for upper middle-class apartments offering superb harbour views.[2] Many small industries in the inner suburbs, including engineering works, paint, textile and shoe factories, have made way for offices, wholesalers or new residential uses. Most of the grander woolstores overlooking Darling Harbour have been converted into apartments.[3]

Some industrial plants were so large—the cigarette factory at Rosebery, the munitions plant at St Mary's and the CSR plant at Pyrmont—that new mini-villages can be created on such sites. In St Mary's the vast site will house a whole new suburb of 8000 dwellings along with massive wetlands allegedly creating a sustainable environment. Such suburbs, or parts of suburbs, are new creations, no longer having the stigma of manufacturing, and a new economic and social environment is enthusiastically marketed by developers. Sometimes, as in the case of the St Mary's munitions site, toxic waste has to be removed before development can begin. Apartment blocks can even be erected near noisy arterial roads as long as their views are sufficiently engaging to make them saleable in a property market where the demand for near city property appears insatiable.

The Mirvac block overlooking the new Glebe Island Bridge is just one of many instances. While property prices may fluctuate wildly, depending on interest rates and overall economic conditions, the demand for near-city accommodation remains, especially from renters in their twenties and thirties and those suburban retirees who are fortunate enough to own their own home, the proceeds of which can fund the move 'to the city'.

The old gives way to the new

Over the past 60 years both public and government attitudes to old buildings have changed dramatically. Even the meaning of the term 'old building' has altered. In the 1930s most people regarded only buildings from the convict era as old and even antiquarians had little interest in anything built after 1850. Such attitudes carried through into the postwar world. New buildings were a sign of progress. As a 'new' society, Australians longed to be thought of as modern. Cantilevered shop awnings replaced the old verandah posts on the pavement. Drive-in theatres, garages and liquor stores catered to families who were getting their first cars. The new skyscrapers, more technologically advanced than their prewar precursors, offered plate glass window views of Sydney. But the formation and rapidly growing membership of an organisation calling itself the National Trust challenged many of these attitudes. Suddenly vocal architects, historians, even society ladies and male stockbrokers became passionate about the destruction of particular buildings that took their fancy.

These changing attitudes are of particular significance in Sydney because over the last 100 years its central city and inner suburbs have been subjected to intense redevelopment pressures. Many historic structures collapsed under the wrecker's hammer, but some survived until the introduction of the *Heritage Act 1977*, which finally gave the state government the legislative power to preserve buildings. Churches, and other structures that did not have

Trafalgar, Potts Point. This post card was sent from a woman visiting Sydney to her sister in Melbourne in 1907: 'You see the front gardens go right to the sea. We have nothing in Melbourne to compare with it. I don't know how I am going to live in Melbourne after living on this glorious harbour.' Trafalgar was demolished to make way for the naval dockyard in the Second World War.

to pay their way on a site-by-site basis, including, until recently, post offices, banks, town halls and wharves, were much more likely to have survived than shops or office buildings that had passed their use by date. A look at what was demolished and what was preserved can tell us quite a lot about changing attitudes to Sydney's history and the way heritage is recycled and marketed.

Concerned that public access to the harbour was being restricted as private property owners increasingly claimed foreshore land, a state Labor government resumed some stretches of the foreshore in 1910 and 1911 (see chapter 8), along with 22 acres embracing Vaucluse House and gardens. The house, first built in 1803, was acquired by W.C. Wentworth (famous for having crossed the Blue Mountains in an early European journey of exploration) in 1829. A leading figure in the campaign for self-government for the colony of New South Wales, Wentworth turned the house into a mansion in the Gothic style, with crenellated walls, turrets, huge internal halls and suites of bedrooms. Since Wentworth was the nearest thing to a founding father that New South Wales could claim, the property was soon being portrayed by the Vaucluse House Trust as a place that could give us 'pride in our history'. First shown to the public in 1912, regular opening hours began in 1914, along with a visitors book and provision for donations to assist with upkeep. C.H. Bertie, the Sydney municipal librarian, wrote a souvenir booklet in 1917, which has been reprinted many times.

Sydney's Georgian heritage was celebrated in architect Hardy Wilson's book *The Cow Pasture Road* (1920), which painted an idealised picture of English-style villages from Parramatta to Camden.[4] Georgian architecture was also celebrated in Bertie's *Old Colonial Byways* (1928) and Quinton Tidswell's *Sydney of Yesterday* (1933), which recorded, as did the Rev. Frank Cash in his photographs, 'building after building being pulled down' to make way for the Harbour Bridge approaches.[5]

In the early decades of the twentieth century the most notable instances of demolition and rebuilding were the reconstruction of the Rocks area after the plague, the rebuilding of much of the central city and the construction of the Harbour Bridge.[6] When Mrs A.G. Foster gave a lecture to fellow members of the Royal Australian Historical Society in November 1920, entitled 'Odd Bits of Old Sydney', she explained how in the last 20 years modest shops and merchants' residences had all made way for new commercial buildings. Even the Presbyterians wanted to replace their Scots Church, erected in 1826, with a new modern structure. Mrs Foster concluded her illustrated lecture by observing: 'We all realise how rapidly the old is giving place to the new, and only by means of pictures will those who come after us know what Sydney was like once upon a time.'[7]

In Aidan de Brune's murder mystery *The Dagger and*

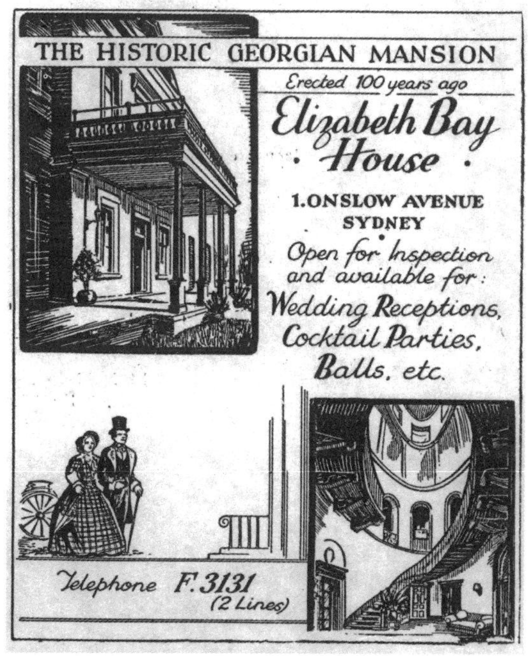

Elizabeth Bay House has had a variety of uses since the Macleay family built it in 1838. Restored to its former elegance in the 1970s, it is administered by the NSW Historic Houses Trust.
Where and how for tourists and shoppers, Sydney, 1938

Hyde Park Barracks.
Marjorie Barnard and Sydney Ure, *The Sydney Book*, Ure Smith, Sydney, 1947

Cord, set in Sydney in the mid-1920s, the main protagonist, the property developer Roy Onslay, wants to demolish some two-storey terrace houses near Macquarie Place and build a modern hotel:

> He was trying to picture the big hotel that he intended to build on the site. It would make a great improvement to that quarter. It would serve a good purpose, even if it only supplanted one of the few remaining eyesores of the city, and would certainly prove a great investment ... It would fit into the reorganisation of that part of the big city then proceeding. The lines of small shops bordering Circular Quay and the north end of Pitt Street would presently disappear; their places taken by fine office blocks. With them would go the old wooden wharves bordering Sydney Cove. The new city railway would come out of the earth under Macquarie Street and cross high over Circular Quay and the new wharves of the Ferry Companies. Away to the left would tower the vast structure of the Sydney Harbour Bridge.

Roy Onslay engaged leading architect Sir Matthew Hyston to design his new hotel. And he had no doubt that the city aldermen would agree to let him close one of their streets, enabling 'a big, modern hotel with a handsome frontage to Macquarie Place'. With 'all the overseas shipping crowding Sydney harbour' the proposition would be a 'gold mine'.[8]

In February 1937 G.H. Abbott, president of the Royal Australian Historical Society, strongly condemned the state government's proposal to demolish the Hyde Park Barracks. Designed by Francis Greenway and erected in 1817–18 to accommodate convicts, this elegant building had seen a number of uses. By 1937 it housed a series of law courts but, according to the report of the Macquarie Street Replanning Committee, was in such poor condition that 'it cannot be preserved'. The government of the day intended to sweep away Parliament House, Sydney Hospital, the mint and the barracks.

Abbott wanted the barracks given to the Historical Society to house 'historic relics', but his enthusiasm for the building was not widely shared. Eighteen months later the secretary of the Howard Prison Reform League, John B. Steel, urged the demolition of the barracks and 'other buildings associated with the early convict days'. Convict buildings, according to Steel, exercised a 'sinister influence on the community'. He told the *Herald* that 'crime had practically ceased at the Rocks since the old convict buildings had been razed to make way for the Harbour Bridge'.[9] All this might sound pretty farfetched, but Steel is merely reflecting the physical determinist attitudes so ripe in the anti-slum movement of the day, when buildings themselves, rather than the social and economic condition of their inhabitants, were identified as the chief cause of poverty and degradation. Steel drew support from a number of correspondents to the *Herald*. One wrote:

> There are no old buildings in Sydney which could be preserved on account of their beauty or even for their supposed Macquarie design. All these old barns are merely out of date and can never be antiquities. Certain old buildings at Circular Quay are certainly reminiscent of olden days, but they are useless monstrosities, just the same. Words fail to describe that shocking old Barracks at the top of Macquarie Street which is a replica of

many such buildings in England (clock and all) and which has nothing colonial about it. This place, made of brick and iron, will shortly become a menace and should be considered accordingly.[10]

Among the few supporters of the Barracks was one correspondent to the *Herald* who asked 'Where do our modern erections stand in beauty, proportion and conformity of line compared with the old Macquarie buildings?'[11] The Barracks weathered calls for demolition only because, for financial reasons, the government postponed plans to redevelop the eastern side of Macquarie Street.

Soon after the Macquarie Street Replanning Committee reported in 1936, another committee was appointed to replan Circular Quay. The government decided that the Quay railway would go ahead—to finish the underground loop—and that new offices were needed for the Maritime Services Board. When recommending that the new board building be situated at Circular Quay west, the committee did not even bother to mention that this would require the demolition of the 1812 Commissariat building or the old Taxation Buildings behind it on George Street north. Both buildings were demolished in 1939. The *Herald* reported that the protests of a handful of historians, artists and public-spirited citizens were unavailing. Journalists recorded the demolition matter of factly. One wrote of the Taxation Buildings:

> Yesterday workmen were removing the great slates, some of them 2'3" long, which the convicts wired to the roof 127 years ago. More than 200,000 of these slates are to come down, some of them 3/4" thick. Other workmen were demolishing the walls, which are 3ft thick in places.[12]

The Circular Quay committee also recommended that the bond stores on the east side of the Quay be demolished and that gardens and modern blocks of flats replace them. In fact, they were not demolished until the mid-1950s, to be replaced by modernist office blocks. Before then Circular Quay bore a remarkable resemblance to Sullivan's Cove in Hobart. The resemblance reflected similarities in the period and pattern of building, as Sydney and Hobart were Australia's first major ports.

In the 1980s and 1990s Circular Quay finally got the blocks of flats advocat-

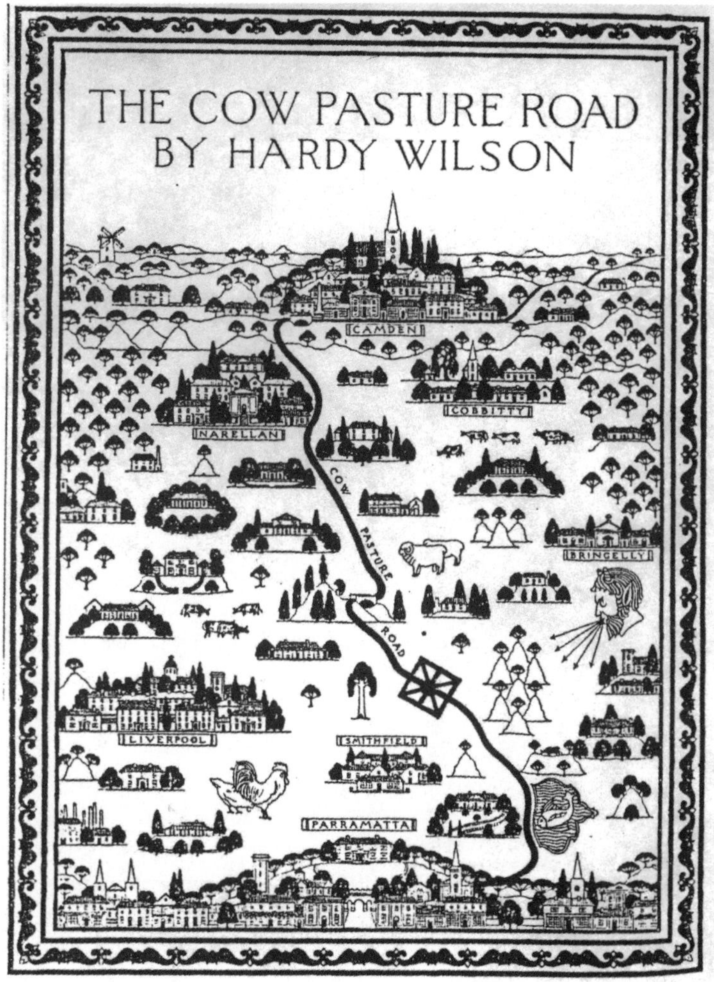

Front cover *The Cow Pasture Road* by W. Hardy Wilson, Sydney, 1920

ed 60 years ago by the replanning committee. With two-bedroom apartments starting at a little over $500,000 and a whole floor an absolute bargain at $2.1 million one can understand why the developers of the Quay apartment block, Concrete Constructions, claimed in their 1983 promotional brochure: 'The Quay is an address that many will want but few will attain.' Some Sydneysiders have even been heard to remark that they'd prefer to have the First and Last Hotel, demolished for the apartment block, back again. Instead of being home to beer-drinking labourers and clerks, the site is now occupied by some of Australia's richest people looking at Australia's most expensive view.

Quinton Tidswell in his book *Sydney of Yesterday*, Sydney, 1933, regretted that St Stephens church in Phillip Street would be demolished for the extension of Martin Place. A new church was built in Macquarie St to replace it.

The rise of the National Trust

The centre of opposition to the demolition of historic buildings moved, in 1945, from the Royal Australian Historical Society to a new organisation calling itself the National Trust (of Australia). Modelled on the British organisation of the same name formed 50 years earlier, it began with a small group of citizens who were concerned at the disappearance of 'historic landmarks'. Trust members were influenced by two important books written in the mid-1950s by the literate architect Morton Herman, *The Early Australian Architects and their Work,* which celebrated Georgian architecture and the work of Francis Greenway, and *The Architecture of Victorian Sydney*, the first Australian book to promote the architectural value of terrace houses.[13] By 1960 the National Trust had over 1400 members, 400 more than the Historical Society, which it has since out-stripped even more spectacularly. In March of that year Pat Hills, the minister for Local Government and Highways, introduced a bill to make the trust a body corporate with the aim of acquiring and preserving lands and buildings of historic or cultural interest. In the debate that followed, members from both sides of the House heaped praise on the trust as a voluntary body of well-intentioned persons. E.C. Sommerlad, MLC, a member of the council of the trust, spoke glowingly of its work. Unlike most members of Parliament—whose historic imaginations did not extend beyond a few Georgian buildings and pioneer cottages—Sommerlad argued that 'as much of our Victorian architecture is significant and as this country was settled at a later date than most other countries, it is quite appropriate that we should consider preserving historic buildings erected at a later date than 1850'.[14]

While parliamentarians on both sides urged the preservation of Sydney's 'historic' buildings, the city around them hummed with the sound of jack-hammers as builders and developers delighted in the new freedom that came with the lifting of the 150 foot height limit on new buildings. The AMP, a venerable insurance company, led the way. In the mid-1950s it acquired the Goldsborough Mort building in the Quay with the intention of demolishing it. A 1919 structure, it had few fans—though one gentleman wrote to the *Herald* claiming that it was 'one of the most outstanding buildings in our country' with 'the powerfully defiant appearance of a Renaissance palace ... its might of bulk expresses the importance of the wool industry to the development of Australia ...'[15] He wanted it declared a national monument, but it was another 20 years before the historical and architectural importance of Sydney's grand wool stores became generally recognised. On the site of the wool store the AMP planned a 26-storey structure, almost twice the height of the maximum allowed by the recently rescinded Height of Buildings Act.

By the early 1960s the central business district became a forest of cranes. The Opera House, the AMP offices and the overseas terminal were evidence of a city being rebuilt. Newspapers crowed over 'The Changing Face of Sydney' and ran diagrams of the new buildings. In May 1962 the *Herald* embraced 'New Stone for Old':

> The wreckers of buildings have carried off many a sombre sandstone structure and are now demolishing their biggest prize, the old AMP building which was built at the northern end of Pitt Street 79 years ago. This building is one of the largest of the older sandstone commercial buildings which are giving way to new buildings of lighter—and brighter—structural materials such as steel, aluminium and glass.[16]

Lighter and brighter was certainly what most Sydneysiders thought of the new developments as they travelled to the observation deck of the AMP skyscraper at the Quay to survey their city.

Nor did the National Trust seriously question the dominant ethos of redevelopment when its *Bulletin* ran an article on 'The Changing Face of Sydney' in August 1964:

> The old buildings of Sydney are continuing to topple to make way for the tall new office blocks which are so radically changing the city's sky-line. The progress of the city must of course go on and indeed many of the buildings which have been replaced are no loss.

Despite admitting that 'the city must of course go on' the trust did regret the loss of the Sydney Royal Exchange, a landmark since 1856, the loss of the old stone warehouse on east Circular Quay and it was worried that 'if the Rocks redevelopment scheme is fully implemented in its present form the historic character of this area will be completely obliterated'.

The Sydney Cove Redevelopment Authority, created in 1970 to 'restore and reconstruct The Rocks', marketed its achievement, in 1982, as 'a heritage revised'. This drawing shows cafe society flourishing where wharf labourers once mingled with sailors.
Brochure cover 1982

Others disagreed about the importance of that area, which now functions as an important part of Sydney's tourist industry. When James Wallace Pty Ltd won the contract to redevelop the Rocks in Sydney in 1963, *Walkabout* magazine described the area as occupied by 'old warehouses and nondescript factory buildings with a handful of grand sets of terrace houses, reflecting 'the pleasantly solid tastes of 19th century architects'. For the first six decades of the twentieth century the Rocks, even after the big clean up and wharf building program that followed the outbreak of plague in the early 1900s, was regarded as a slum. Most of its residents rented their terrace houses from the Maritime Services Board. The redevelopment plan provided for a series of residential blocks, offices and a luxury hotel, all overlooking the glamorous new overseas terminal opened in 1961. *Walkabout* concluded its account by observing: 'When this site, which goes back 175 years to the beginning of the first white settlement, finally yields up the last of its old houses so full of charm, Sydney will have lost much of its character, but it will have gained a waterfront gateway equal to any in the world.'

The image of the modern city captured the imagination of other writers too. In the mid-1960s a 36-year-old feature writer on the *Sydney Morning Herald*, Gavin Souter, collaborated with photographer Quinton Davis to produce a celebratory book on the Sydney that 'Sydneysiders know', 'scrutinizing back-street terraces as well as mansions, secluded bays as well as the harbour and beaches, inner suburbs as well as showplaces'. Souter wrote that:

The feverish pace of development. A new skyscraper arises on the site of the old T & G building (1929) even before it has been completely demolished. Photograph c. 1980

> Just as the inner city once seemed unlikely ever to change, now it seems unlikely ever to stand still again. The other day I counted sixteen cranes on the skyline. The upper air rings continually with the erection of girders, and somewhere a dogman is always rising overhead. It is too early yet for a final verdict on the new city, but already I prefer it to the old ... There is admittedly a sameness about the new glass boxes, an international homogeneity that fits as glibly into Sydney as it would into San Francisco or Buenos Aires, but this orthodoxy will be partly offset by the massive nonconformity of the Opera House on Bennelong Point, and in any case I much prefer the light and efficiency of the glass boxes to the sombre fussiness of the Edwardian and Victorian ages.
>
> This is not to say that I would wish to see the city lose all its brown sandstone piles. I hope that the Lands Department building with its twenty-one external statues (Sir Henry Parkes, W.C. Wentworth, John McDouall Stuart, *et alii,* all holding documents of State, or shielding their sandstone eyes against the inland sun) is never pulled down, and that Sydney's aldermen never tire of the superlatively ugly Town Hall, which was designed over a period of twenty years last century by no fewer than five different architects. I like the GPO, the clock tower at Central Station, the Customs House at Circular Quay, St James' Church and most of the other buildings designed by Francis Greenway, but otherwise I am perfectly willing to surrender everything built before 1930. Let Whelan the Wrecker do his worst.[17]

The National Trust pointed out that its efforts to 'procure the preservation of at least some of the historic features of these areas have gone down under the weight of economic considerations and high site values. Only the expenditure of very large sums could have saved them, and this money was simply not available.'[18] But the trust also had to cope with prevailing opinion; and Gavin Souter's remarks probably reflected educated opinion in Sydney in the mid-1960s. In an attempt to exercise a degree of control over unthinking redevelopment, in 1961 the trust devised a system for the classification of buildings. It hoped to convince both private and corporate owners and public instrumentalities that particular buildings were worth saving. But the trust had no teeth—it did not have the power to enforce these classifications.

Legislation to control the demolition of buildings had existed for some time but was little used. Under section 365 of the Local Government Act local councils had the power to protect, acquire, preserve and maintain places of historical or scientific interest and natural scenery. But most local councils were more interested in getting their rate income up—and almost every time a site was redeveloped its rateable value increased—than they were in preserving what most aldermen considered to be decrepit or at least old-fashioned structures. The Cumberland County Council had the power to proclaim historic buildings and prevent their demolition, but it could then be obliged to acquire or purchase the building from the owner if called upon to do so. Elizabeth Farm House and Elizabeth Bay House were among the buildings proclaimed under this ordinance but the minister for Local Government decided that it would not be appropriate for buildings owned by the government to be listed. Instead he would just have a chat with the appropriate ministers to tell them that they were not allowed to alter certain buildings in a way that might affect their historical value. Vaucluse House, Hyde Park Barracks, the Mint, Parliament House and the main building at the University of Sydney were among the few structures signalled out for listing.[19]

Pro-BLF graffiti in Woolloomooloo drawn at the height of the battle in 1973. The Wran government rehabilitated some of the houses in this area, and commissioned others in similar styles. Graffiti rarely survive for long on redevelopment sites.

Although most councils require a permit before a structure can be demolished, demolition could be done so quickly that often nobody noticed and even if they did they rarely bothered to report to their local council. The Askin coalition government, elected in 1965, was so prodevelopment that it even advocated demolition of most of the Rocks and any other part of the city where real estate developers could make a quick dollar. So irate did some members of the National Trust become that they were prepared to embrace a left-wing union with a very working-class image, the Builders Labourers Federation (BLF), to prevent mindless demolition. Much scorn was poured on this liaison by leading members of the Liberal Party and the business community, who repeatedly asked—as did the *Herald* in a series of editorials—what right one union had to decide what buildings should be demolished and what buildings should be put up in their place. None of these critics ever questioned the rights of private individuals, governments or corporations to demolish what they wanted and to build what they wanted, as long as they had the finance. They complained that the BLF was trampling on our democratic rights. What they really meant was that it was trampling on the rights of property owners to dispose of their property as they would, no matter what the consequences to the surrounding community, let alone the ambience of the city.[20]

'An elaborate piece of ironwork that once graced Observatory Hill. The Council was all for scrapping it, but there was such an outcry that they re-erected it in George St North, under the Harbour Bridge.'
Sprod's Views of Sydney, Kangaroo Press, Sydney, 1981

Demolition of the Winter Garden Cinema in Rose Bay, 1982.
Photograph by Peter Spearritt

Once Askin left the premiership the task of conservation advocates became much easier. The Liberals actually introduced a Heritage Bill in March 1976 but it lapsed. Labor won office in the election two months later, and in September 1977 introduced its own Heritage Bill. In supporting the bill, Sir John Fuller, a former minister for Planning and Environment, acknowledged that the 'general feeling seems to be that in the past we have not valued our heritage sufficiently'. Nonetheless the leader of the opposition, Bruce McDonald, pointed out that 'The Liberal Party believes firmly and fundamentally in the individual freedoms and the rights of individuals to acquire and hold private property, which should never be resumed or affected adversely without compensation on just and fair terms.' Though generally thought to be prodevelopment, McDonald also argued that local councils should be given the power to control demolitions. He pointed out that in 25 years only 16 properties had been listed under the old County of Cumberland Ordinance as worthy of preservation.[21]

The Heritage Bill tackled the problem of demolitions, not by suggesting that local government should be given more power, but by vesting in a Heritage Council the power to place Interim Conservation Orders over buildings for two years, and—after an investigation—Permanent Conservation Orders. In its first seven years of operation the Heritage Council executed 382 interim and 274 permanent orders, a vast increase on the 16 properties listed between 1948 and 1977, especially when we take into account that a single order often applies to a group of properties.[22] In April 1999 Conservation Orders were replaced with a State Heritage Register, and 1200 buildings and sites protected under the Heritage Act. A further 17,500 items were included on a State Heritage Inventory, some of which might survive if they were listed as part of a local government environmental plan. If not so listed they could be altered or demolished under municipal permit.[23]

The battle between property owners and public rights in Sydney has been a major focus of municipal and state politics for the past three decades. The demolition of the Rural Bank in Martin Place in the early 1980s is just one example of the Heritage Council's powerlessness in the face of property owners, in this case the government itself. Sydney lost most of its notable interwar cinemas between the mid-1960s and the mid-1980s, including the Winter Garden at Rose Bay, the Odeon at Manly and most disgracefully of all the Regent in George Street, where the property developer had purchased the structure cheaply, only to pull it down. Whole classes of buildings remained under threat, such as inner city hotels, boarding houses, prewar shops and a great variety of industrial buildings. It is virtually impossible to save redundant power stations and factories, no matter how grand, because they simply do not appeal to public or elite tastes. The Heritage Council and the National Trust stand as arbiters between property owners and public rights, but with limited funds they often have to let a structure go because a commercially viable and historically and aesthetically acceptable new use cannot be found.

A growing consciousness of the historical and architectural importance of residential structures in Sydney has come as much from home owners as from the National Trust and the Heritage Council. Victorian and Edwardian houses, the Californian bungalow, a variety of art deco structures, even brick veneer and fibro houses of the 1950s and 1960s have their devotees. All have been the subject of enthusiastic books outlining their architectural merits, social history and recommended modes of restoration. Nonetheless, kitchens and bathrooms rarely remain intact and many a federation-style garage has been built in front yards that were never designed to accommodate motor vehicles.[24]

The demolition for the Regent Hotel in George St.
Photograph by John Storey, 1980

TRADING OFF

Gains made by conservationists are rarely permanent. Often the same battles over the same sites have to be replayed. While most of the landscape and structures of the west Rocks, overlooking Darling Harbour, have remained with only modest alterations and additions, the east Rocks, especially where it abuts the central business district, resembles more and more the drastic redevelopment plans of the 1960s. A series of high-rise hotels (such as the Regent, completed in 1982 and the ANA, completed in 1991) and office blocks crowd the landscape. Towards the Harbour Bridge the elegant Hyatt Hotel (1989) was allowed to rise only four floors above the pedestrian boardwalk on the former site of the Sydney water police headquarters, a ramshackle structure quickly forgotten. In the process, Circular Quay has lost much of its working maritime ambience, to become yet another waterfront tourist precinct. Nonetheless, it continues to serve as an important ferry terminal for locals and tourists. Its primary attractions, the Opera House and the Harbour Bridge, seem to reinvent themselves for new generations—the introduction of the Harbour Bridge climb in 1998 is a recent example of this.

Urban conservationists in Sydney are constantly confronted with a series of trade-offs. The First Government House site has been preserved under a high-rise office tower with the postmodern Museum of Sydney as a consolation prize. The Mark Foys elegant Piazza Store, on the corner Liverpool and Elizabeth streets, was saved but Anthony Horderns, Australia's largest emporium, was demolished to make way for high-rise residential and apartment blocks. The developer abandoned the site in the 1990s, leaving the incomplete concrete lift wells standing sentinel over three devastated city blocks.

Who should make decisions about which historic structures and precincts should survive and whose interests should be represented in the decision-making process?[25] Should we accept the judgement of architects or historians about which buildings should remain? As heritage councils and committees are usually the creatures of government, they cannot always be expected to withstand powerful property interests, especially when these have the backing of the political party in power. In the battle between property owners and public rights the public, in Sydney as in all major cities, needs all the help it can get.

SPECIAL REPORT
TIME
AUSTRALIA
SYDNEY'S GOLDEN PRIZE
How Australia won the 2000 Olympics and what it means for the nation's future

CHAPTER 12

Sydney, Australia and the world

'And the winner is ... Sydney.' Those climactic words, broadcast around the world on 23 September 1993, were uttered by the head of the International Olympic Committee, Juan Antonio Samaranch. Sydney, all the world now knew, would host the Olympic Games in the year 2000. The value of the Australia dollar rose immediately, and the governor of the Reserve Bank opined that the win could help pull Australia out of recession.

At that moment Sydney received more worldwide publicity than at any other time in its history. In the late eighteenth and early nineteenth centuries the harbourside town was little more than a British outpost in the Antipodes. The discovery of gold gave Australia, particularly Victoria, a brief period in world headlines. Some notable travellers, including Mark Twain and Anthony Trollope, wrote about Sydney but, apart from its harbour and its transplanted habits, it had little claim to be unique. Although Australian cities were unusual because they grew quickly and created spacious suburbs, they were similar in architecture, transport systems and government to other white British colonial cities, especially in New Zealand and Canada.[1] Their educational, legal and municipal systems were adaptations of British practice. Their town halls and post offices were designed by British architects, their colonial and then their state governors were supplied by Britain, and they even invited members of the British royal family to officiate at their functions. Australia proudly claimed to be 98 per cent British stock, Sydney the 'second white city of the British Empire'. The decision by the Lang Labor government not to invite British royalty to open the Sydney Harbour Bridge in 1932 was atypical in a nation and a city that craved the royal imprimatur on structures and events, from the Duke of Gloucester's unveiling of the Anzac War Memorial in 1934 to Queen Elizabeth II opening the Sydney Opera House in 1973.

By the middle of the twentieth century a new international view of Australia began to emerge. And, locally and internationally, Sydney began to take a more dominant role. As early as the 1920s a German postcard manufacturer styled Sydney 'the capital of the continent'. When the American novelist James A. Michener visited Australia in 1950 his plane landed just after sunset:

> [In] the darkness, the great empty continent looms up. In the distance, a lighthouse flashes. You can feel the loneliness that engulfs this mighty land. Suddenly below you explode the million lights of Sydney. On half a hundred hillsides, down many bays, you see the brilliance of Australia's metropolis, home of nearly two million people. Few approaches to the nations of the world can be so spectacular, so portentous.[2]

While some would dispute that Sydney is 'Australia's metropolis' there is no

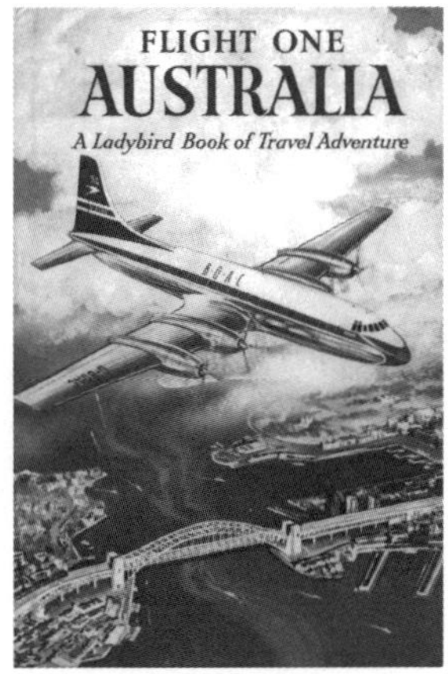

Sydney has long been the first port of call for most international visitors.
Front cover, Will & Hepworth, London, 1958

FACING PAGE
Time magazine, 4 October 1993

doubt that it has become so in the eyes of the world. Before the Second World War, when most visitors and migrants still came to Australia by ship, Sydney's claims were less obvious. Melbourne had housed the federal Parliament until 1927, when Parliament House opened in Canberra. Despite the move, the Victorian government's State Electricity Commission claimed that 'Melbourne remains the business and commercial centre of Australia' with one-quarter of the nation's factories.[3] Melbourne remained the centre of the telecommunications, banking and insurance industries, its stock exchange rivalled Sydney's and it continued to accommodate the headquarters of many federal government departments until the 1960s. Melbourne remained the major centre of heavy industry, sharing car manufacture with Adelaide. New South Wales did house the BHP steelworks at Newcastle and Wollongong, but at the time they were seen as industrial cities quite distinct from Sydney.

By the mid-1970s the six separate stock exchanges, especially the largest, Sydney and Melbourne, realised that some form of amalgamation might not only be beneficial but necessary if they were to continue as the major site for trading in shares and securities. In the early 1980s Jim Bain, chair of the Sydney Stock Exchange, was fond of saying 'It is no longer Sydney v Melbourne or Brisbane v Perth but Australia v the world.' By 1986 he recognised that 'because of the trend towards international trading, possibly on a 24-hour basis, we must give our Member Organisations the best possible facilities to compete internationally'. Screen trading had already arrived in the USA and the United Kingdom. The Australian Stock Exchange (ASX), created in 1987, incorporates each of the former exchanges as wholly owned subsidiaries. Its computer system operates out of a nondescript building in the backblocks of Bondi. One of the ASX's aims was 'to attract back to Australia some of the trading in our major listed companies which has increasingly moved to London and New York'.[4]

While screen-based trading appears to undermine the importance of particular cities in the world financial system, the information flows, the luncheon discussions and after-work drinks that are so important to business culture mean that the world's major financial centres, including London's 'City', New York, Frankfurt, Tokyo and Hong Kong have retained their preeminent status as trading centres for shares, securities, options, futures and currency. Sydney's future, not to mention Australia's, depends a good deal on whether the city's financial status is sustained in the twenty-first century. By the early 1980s Sydney had overtaken Melbourne not just as Australia's best-known and most populous city but in financial importance as well. Most new foreign companies setting up in Australia chose Sydney as their headquarters, especially banks, investment houses and computer giants such as Microsoft and IBM.[5] Sydney began to feature in a *Guide to the Business Cities of the World*,[6] while Melbourne did not.

Even Melbourne's dominance of federal politics began to falter. Melbourne had supplied most of the conservative prime ministers of the postwar era, including Robert Menzies, Harold Holt and Malcolm Fraser. Gough Whitlam, who represented an outer suburban working-class electorate in western Sydney, helped break the trend. While Bob Hawke could legitimately claim close links with three states (Western Australia, South Australia and Victoria), his successor Paul Keating was pre-eminently a Sydney character, representing another western suburbs electorate. John Howard took his Sydney roots one step further by treating his official residence in Canberra as a place to stay overnight and setting up home in Kirribilli House on Sydney's north shore, the single most expensive piece of real estate in Australia, right next door to the Governor-General (for whom Admiralty House had been purchased, from Britain, as a Sydney residence).

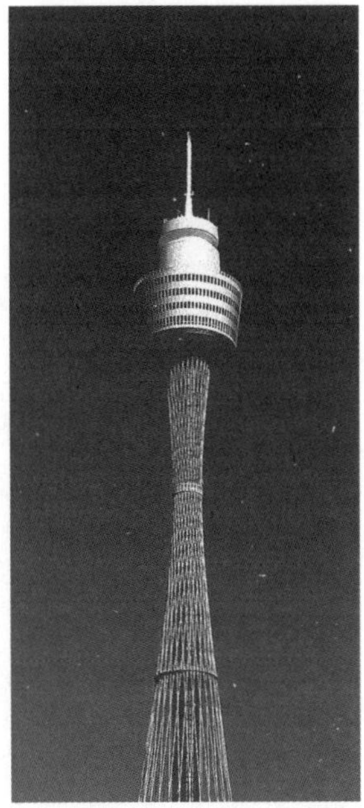

At 325 metres, Sydney Tower remains Australia's tallest structure.
Brochure 1992

Taken together with its hinterland state, Sydney regards itself as Australia's natural capital. As the mother colony, New South Wales got used to seeing itself as Australia. While Sydney lost the title of the largest city to Melbourne for the latter half of the nineteenth century, it never forgot its status as first settlement.[7] And it had much less difficulty in shaking off the convict stain than Hobart. Sydney has remained Australia's pre-eminent port for most of the last two centuries, and has the nation's busiest airport. Almost half of international arrivals to Australia enter via Sydney, which has twice as many direct flights overseas as Melbourne. Sydney attracts over two million international visitors a year, while the Gold Coast and Melbourne, the next most popular destinations, try hard to attract one million each.

Sydney is looked on with both envy and pity by the other state capitals. They envy its wealth and its world city status, but dislike its suburban sprawl and traffic congestion, though these are by no means unique to Sydney. Most international visitors to Sydney see little or nothing of the outer suburbs and can be almost oblivious to the congestion. With international hotels all directed at harbour and parkland views, ferries might appear to be the standard form of transport. The massive public investment in a rail link to the Olympic site and a direct rail link between Mascot airport and the city will give Sydney both the appearance and the reality of an efficient, modern world city that Melbourne, Brisbane and Perth will be unable to match.[8]

Sydney's roles as state capital, Australia's metropolis and world city were well tested in the 1988 bicentennial celebrations. The Australian Bicentennial Authority set up in a fancy office overlooking Circular Quay, and other states immediately suspected that its location would produce Sydney-centric celebrations. The bicentennial celebrations began in Sydney on 1 January 1988 with the unveiling of the federation pavilion in Centennnial Park and the opening of the Bicentennial Park at Homebush Bay. Sydney's eastern suburbs got their park in 1888 so there was rough justice in the western suburbs—now with 10 times the population—getting one in 1988. The state Labor government hoped that this concession to their electoral heartland, along with the opening of revamped Circular Quay and Macquarie Street, would ensure their victory in the coming election. But the failure of the Darling Harbour project to meet its January deadline did not augur well for a government about to go to the polls.

By Australia Day, 26 January, all eyes were on Sydney, whether in person or via the television, as the commemorative fleet of replica Tall Ships entered

Australia Day 1988.
Photograph by Adrian Young

the harbour. The *Australian Women's Weekly* summed up the day thus:

> WOW! WHAT A PARTY. Two million people lined the foreshores. 10 000 boats jostled for position on the water, and the eyes of the world were on us ... January 26, 1988 was a day to remember! The focus may have been on Sydney Harbour—with the royal visitors, majestic tall ships, First Fleet re-enactment and dazzling fireworks—but the celebrations were Australia's.[9]

Like the rest of the nation's Sydney-dominated media, the *Weekly* went to great pains to point out that the celebrations were a national event.

From local landmarks to national symbols

The dominant landmarks in Sydney in 1950, and even in 1960, included the Macquarie Light House, the water towers of Vaucluse and Bankstown, the power stations at Bunnerong, Pyrmont and Balmain, the Central Station clock tower, the AWA tower and the Harbour Bridge. Michener wrote that:

> Sydney is like London, but prettier. It consists of many small towns banded together in their common dependence on the harbor and on Sydney Bridge, the big, utilitarian span that links the main city with its northern suburbs. This is the national symbol of Australia, like the Statue of Liberty or the Eiffel Tower.[10]

With the exception of the bridge and the Opera House, all of Sydney's landmarks have long been overshadowed by skyscrapers financed by American junk bonds, Japanese insurance companies and Australian superannuation funds.

On the skyline of Sydney and North Sydney the names of Australian-owned companies have withered away as the big multinationals, from IBM and Zurich to Canon and Citibank, claim naming rights. Only the mutual societies—AMP, CML—still command buildings in their own right. And even here, as they turn themselves into listed public companies their local ownership dissipates. Sydney, home of the Reserve Bank headquarters, which was at the forefront of treasurer Keating's deregulation of the dollar and the banks in 1983, is Australia's first global city. The Victorian government attempted to fight back by creating the world's first ministry of Multi-Media but Sydney remains Australia's media and telecommunications capital.

The AWA Tower, opened in 1940, dominated Sydney's skyline until the skyscrapers of the 1960s hedged it in.
Detail from postcard c. 1940

The five-star hotels that dominate the landscape of Darling Harbour, the Rocks and other parts of Sydney are now all named in the multinational tradition, from the Nikko and the Hilton to the Intercontinental and the Forum. Whether they are new structures or reused historic buildings the language is always the same: international business English. It is increasingly difficult in the foyers of these hotels to remember whether you are in Singapore, Chicago, Melbourne or Sydney. The atmosphere that Michener detected in 1950 of a 'British pattern with Aussie gusto and originality' has long since gone. So has the six o'clock swill, when hotel bars ceased to serve alcohol at 6 p.m. Women have been allowed to drink alongside men in Sydney's bars for almost four decades. The bars themselves have discarded their yellow tiles for the colours and ironmongery of the licensed cafe, serving foccacia, croissants, bagels and pastrami on rye. It might not be New York or Milan, but it's a long way from time-honoured notions of Australian cuisine.

The clothes worn by traders on the floor of the Sydney Futures Exchange, by their solicitors, their spouses and their children, are more likely to be made in China or Italy than in Australia. In this regard, Sydney is no different to any other large Australian city, except that it is more expensive on almost every count: housing, rent, food, eating out or transport. In 1998 the state government, capitalising on Sydney's international status, introduced a 10 per cent hotel 'bed tax' to assist in the cost of mounting the Olympic games. Only a handful of other cities, including New York, have such a levy. Only a city confident of its domestic and international market could contemplate such a move.

Sydney's position on the east coast of Australia, half way between Brisbane and Melbourne, means that it is within a day's drive of these other state capitals. The Melbourne trip is quicker because the Hume Freeway offers almost continuous divided highway between the two cities. Its 850 kilometres are easily covered in nine hours. Over 16 million trips are made on this route each year by truck drivers, car drivers and passengers, about half the number of people who fly on all Australia's domestic routes. The Hume Corridor has become the central axis of internal Australian commerce, with warehouses for all manner of goods dotted along the route. Freeway links have reduced travel time from Sydney to Canberra to around three hours so that the national capital is fast becoming a satellite of Sydney. A 'very fast train' would only confirm this trend.

Heading north, Sydneysiders are within a day's drive of their own state's coastline and Queensland's Gold and Sunshine coasts. For weekend trips, the

The bathing pavilion at Balmoral in 1980, before megahouses and the expansion of the restaurant.
Photograph by John Storey

shape and extent of the city constrains the holiday options. Most weekend destinations take two to four hours driving time, not least because of the congestion in inner Sydney, which slows down access to those outer-suburban freeways that offer escape routes to the north, north-west, west, south-west, and the south. Whether to the Blue Mountains, Nelson Bay (north of Newcastle) or Bateman's Bay (south of Nowra), these trips are major undertakings. Sydney does not offer the plethora of holiday destinations within two hours drive of the metropolis that all other Australian capital cities can provide. Their traffic congestion is less, their real estate values are lower, their holiday accommodation costs are markedly lower and eating out is invariably cheaper, if not always better.

Sydneysiders are paying the price for living in Australia's only world city. The huge influx of international tourists and domestic business travellers sustains high hotel and cafe prices. The cafes of Bondi and Manly, once accessible to all, have gone up-market, so visitors and locals on a budget are forced back on the fast food outlets. Even the traditionally cheap Italian eateries of Darlinghurst and Leichhardt price their dishes for increasingly middle-class local residents. Public facilities such as the bathing pavillion at Balmoral Beach have been turned into fancy restaurants catering for international visitors and the expense-account set. The best reasonably priced dining-out experiences in Sydney are now to be had in the Vietnamese restaurants of Cabramatta.

In a city where the contrasts of wealth and poverty become more and more obvious, you can literally smell the money in some streets. In suburbs such as Mosman and Vaucluse it is hard to find a car more than three years old, and luxury vehicles abound. The trend to turning modest middle-class homes into what Gavin Souter calls 'megahouses' is everywhere evident. Upper middle-class business and professional people, seizing the opportunity to renovate and extend their family home, which is exempt from capital gains tax, are creating absurdly lavish mansions, where four bathrooms become the bare minimum and entertaining areas resemble the first-class deck on grand ocean liners.[11]

The residents of Sydney's megahouses and harbour-view apartments pride themselves on living in the chief theatre of Australian life. As the ferries or the River Cat pass by, the value of their own and their neighbours' properties continues to appreciate. Rarely has a city been so preoccupied with the latest sale. Harbourside streets compete for the highest price in their suburb. While vocal on the topic of the state government's land tax on household land worth more than $1 million, many are secretly chuffed to be regarded as millionaires. International film stars, media magnates, industrialists, stockbrokers, even Melbourne millionaires have their harbour views.

At the other end of the social scale are new migrants. Although they play a key role in the continuing internationalisation of Sydney, they are most likely to find themselves renting in three-storey walk-up blocks of flats built by private entrepreneurs throughout Sydney in the 1960s and 1970s. The cheapest rents in Sydney, still often $200–300 a week, are to be found in such flats and in the old fibro belt from Bankstown to St Mary's. Only a lucky few new arrivals manage to rent publically owned flats or houses. Average incomes may be low and poverty is widespread, but successive Liberal–National and Labor state governments have continued to invest in public educational facilities and to maintain the public transport system, which continues to provide access to the harbour, the national parks, the beaches and the city's other many attractions.

The Labor city-state

Political controversy in Sydney regularly flares at the local, city and state level. Sydney's local governments administer and regulate the land use of Australia's most valuable properties, along with the immediate landscape of their four million citizens. Only one council, the Sydney Municipal Council, has either the status or the rate base to take on the state government in battles over jurisdiction. Usually it loses, not least because the state government can keep altering its electoral boundaries. Much of the recent development in Sydney has taken place via purpose-created authorities such as the Darling Harbour Authority, free of local government control.

To remain in power the Labor Party, like the Liberal–National coalition, requires not only a majority of state electorates but also key sources of financial support. As the only Australian state since the Second World War in which the majority of governments have been Labor, the ALP's financial links and its financial backers invite scrutiny. The successive Labor governments that ruled New South Wales between 1941 and 1965 drew their primary support from the trade unions, from a large public sector—including the railways, the government schools and the police force—and from an accommodation with major industrial interests, especially BHP, with its plants in Newcastle and Wollongong. By the mid-1970s Neville Wran, as the new leader of the ALP, had to reformulate the party's support base. He still needed to keep industry and the public-sector unions onside, but the growing power of property interests and the rise of Sydney as a financial capital had to be added to the equation. As a leading Sydney solicitor, Wran had grown up in the business community. He had no difficulty courting the new property and banking groups. The Labor city-state he created, strengthened by its links with Paul Keating as the federal treasurer from 1983, was street wise and business savvy.[12] The NSW State Bank remained sound, unlike state banks in other Labor-run states, the State Bank of Victoria (with its reckless Tricontinental arm) and the State Bank of South Australia. The Labor regimes in those states simply didn't have the well-honed downtown connections of the NSW 'Labor right'. Although Sydney did not escape all the consequences of the early 1990s crash, when Westpac (the renamed Bank of NSW) went to the brink of being taken over because of poor risk assessment and foreign exchange disasters, it weathered the recession better than any other capital city.[13]

In a bid to clean up the illegal gaming industry, to increase state government revenue and to please some of its financial backers, Premier Wran attempted to persuade his Cabinet to legalise casinos in 1977 and 1981. Cabinet, fearing a backlash from church groups and complaints from the powerful sporting and RSL clubs, which had a monopoly on poker machines,

Under Askin's premiership 'thousands of dollars weekly in bribes and payoffs were handed over by the gambling clubs'.
David Hickie, Good Weekend, *Sydney Morning Herald*, 23 March 1985, caricature by Kantor

wouldn't agree. Wran appeared to have got his way in September 1985 when a state government committee recommended two international casinos and 18 mini-casinos. After further lobbying by the clubs, the final outcome was one privately operated casino to be built at Darling Harbour. At a time when Melbourne was also contemplating a casino it seemed obvious that no city aspiring to world status would be complete without one.

Like casino proposals elsewhere in Australia and around the world, this proposal was dogged by question marks over the proposed bidders. A Police Board report into the Hooker-Harrah bid to construct the casino found that some of its executives had been involved in 'undesirable dealings'.[14] When the Star City casino finally opened in November 1997, with 5000 staff and a building cost of $876 million, it marketed itself as a 'world class entertainment experience' where an old wharf has been replaced by 'a place where you escape from everyday life into a new realm of fantasy and fun'.[15]

The extent of corruption in the NSW police force has been a matter of legend and sometimes of record for its entire history. The prospect of judicial and parliamentary corruption has been less obvious, and usually better hidden. The corrupt practices of the NSW Premier Askin only became fully apparent after his death.[16] But in the 1980s a series of charges involving senior ALP politicians, including Premier Wran and Lionel Murphy (federal attorney-general and then High Court judge) grabbed the headlines. Part of Nick Greiner's platform in the March 1988 election was to clean up public life by establishing an Independent Commission Against Corruption (ICAC) with powers similar to a standing royal commission. It could seize documents and compel people to testify, including cross examination, 'largely unfettered by the normal rules of evidence'. The commission's early targets included National Party members in trouble over land deals (promising Crown land to developers before expressions of interest had been called for) and the ALP's failure to declare donations from the Japanese wood chipping industry.

But the commission's greatest scalp proved to be that of the Premier himself. Greiner attempted to move a troublesome former minister of Education, Terry Metherell (who had resigned from the Liberal Party but not from Parliament in October 1991), to a public sector job, but in doing so bypassed normal public sector employment protocols. The ICAC concluded that his behaviour was technically 'corrupt'. While a court later ruled that the ICAC had erred in its interpretation of 'corrupt', the Premier had already been forced by the Liberal Party to step down from office, not to return.[17] Greiner went on to become a director of dozens of major companies.

Nick Greiner's successor, John Fahey, who had played rugby for Canterbury Bankstown, managed to shield Prince Charles from a would-be assailant and to steer Sydney to victory in its Olympic bid. But this did not secure his party's re-election in 1995. As had happened when Labor went to the polls in 1988, Sydneysiders demanded more from their government than casinos and grand events. So the Labor Party, led by Bob Carr, narrowly won an election fought on a mix of issues, including airport noise, road tollways and hospital waiting lists. As always since the Second World War, the party most attuned to concerns of Sydney won the election. The July 1998 reduction in the size of Parliament to 93 seats leaves Sydney with 48, not counting the Blue Mountains, Gosford or Wyong.[18] Carr achieved a comfortable majority in the March 1999 elections, helped by the decision of the Liberal Party to change leaders just months before the poll.

Crime remained a pressing political issue during Carr's first term in office. By 1996 the Police Royal Commission under Justice James Wood, set up in 1994 because of growing evidence of corruption in the NSW police force, had uncovered protection rackets for drug dealers and other crime figures, police protection of child sex offenders, including paedophiles, and forged police time sheets. By the time the report was released, in May 1997, 640 witnesses had been examined and the public confronted with corruption on a vast scale, at least equal to that revealed in Queensland by the Fitzgerald commission in the late 1980s.

As part of the drive to bring Sydney into line with other world cities, the new government amended the Disorderly Houses Act to abolish the offence of keeping a brothel. Police could now only close a brothel if it was, in fact, run in a 'disorderly' manner. Along with the decriminalisation of homosexual relations between consenting adults in 1984, such legislation, in a climate of decreasing regulation of shopping hours, gave Sydney the appearance of being a 24-hour city. Sydney grew more famous for its Gay and Lesbian Mardi Gras, begun in modest circumstances in 1978 (including a battle with police and a number of arrests),[19] than for any other annual event. Sydney was bemused to discover in 1998 that the Mardi Gras, which has very little direct government funding, raised more tourist dollars for Sydney than did the annual Formula 1 Grand Prix for Melbourne, even though the Kennett government there spent hundreds of millions of dollars to lure the event from its original home in Adelaide.[20]

This competition between cities for events and facilities became apparent in 1995 when Premier Fahey announced three short-listed candidates to take over the Royal Agricultural Society's showgrounds in the inner east, located between the Sydney Cricket Ground and Centennial Park, to build a new film complex. Rupert Murdoch's Fox Group threatened to take their plans to Melbourne unless a greater allowance was made for an entertainment facility on the site. Fox won out, with 24 of the site's 27 acres to be for the film studio and entertainment complex, which will generate most of the cash.[21] The Royal Agricultural Society, in which ownership of the showground was vested in 1911, had to accept their new home abutting the main Olympic Stadium at Homebush.

Among the great challenges governments have always faced are natural and environmental disasters. In January 1994, after weeks of little rain, and fanned by hot winds of up to 100 km per hour, bushfires engulfed almost all of the Royal National Park south of Sydney. Four people died and over 180 houses were destroyed in the southern and northern suburbs, with fires coming to within eight kilometres of the central city. The remnants of the Cumberland County Council's green belt of the 1950s became the conduit for fires, especially in the valleys of Lane Cove and Sutherland. While the fires were modest compared to those that sometimes engulf the hills beyond Melbourne, Adelaide and Hobart (the Ash Wednesday fires in Victoria in 1983 claimed 76 lives and 2400 houses), they nevertheless received almost hysterical treatment in the national and international media. Stockholm TV showed symbolic flames licking the Sydney Harbour Bridge pylons.

Similar hyperbole greeted a short-lived pollution crisis in Sydney's water supply in 1998. Under headlines such as 'Harbour city crisis' and 'It's not Calcutta—it's Sydney', newspapers and the television gave a blow by blow description of how two parasites, giardia and cryptosporidium, had entered the Sydney system via a new private filtration plant at the Prospect Reservoir, whose owners were apparently not contractually obliged to seek out such parasites. For some weeks the entire population, including hospitals and hotels, was urged to boil all drinking water. School bubblers were shut off and supermarkets had a field day selling bottled water, thoughtfully rushed in by wholesalers from other states. When asked about the impact of the polluted water on the image of Sydney in the lead up to the Olympics, Premier Carr said, 'Forget the Olympics! Olympics or not, we ought to be able to drink clean, safe water.' Among the first to hear of the crisis was a gathering of Australia's health ministers, about to embark on dessert at a swank hotel in Potts Point.[22]

The controversy over how Sydney won its bid for the Olympics seemed less likely to disappear from public consciousness. Fuelled by allegations of special favours to International Olympic Committee (IOC) delegates to help Salt Lake City in its (successful) bid to win the 2002 winter Olympics, it was revealed that the Sydney bid team had conducted a sophisticated and targeted campaign to secure a majority of IOC votes, including the granting of favours to individual delegates. Existing and potential sponsors became nervous and the Sydney organising committee (SOCOG) admitted a shortfall in revenues. Consultants continued to claim that the Olympics would be a boon to Sydney and predicted over 250,000 visitors. Sydney's continued presence on the world stage seems assured, no matter what difficulties surround the event.[23]

Losses and gains

At the turn of the century much of Sydney was unsewered, horse dung littered the city streets, and ramshackle dwellings often housed two or more families. People then used the train or the tram to get to places beyond walking distance, and most rented rather than owned their homes: most jobs were concentrated in the city or the inner industrial suburbs. In the next three decades the suburbs expanded in every direction, but home ownership was kept in check by depression and war. Yet the general quality of housing improved and the range of household equipment diversified with the increasing use of electric appliances.

Change since the Second World War has been more rapid. With the exodus of families to the suburbs, Bradfield's railway system finally began to attract the planned numbers: the Water Board was hard put to catch up. But those parts of the Bradfield Plan that had not been built, such as the Warringah rail-

"What we should worry about is not so much the futuristic design as the fear of it being outmoded by the time they get it built!"

Emile Mercier, *Hold It!*, Angus & Robertson, Sydney, 1960

way, were abandoned because the private car—once the preserve of the middle class—became the chief form of transportation. Cars gave people greater mobility: the scope for social and recreational activities was immeasurably widened. The penalties of congestion and accidents—the toll of the road—were plainly no deterrent to an electorate in which, by 1971, three-quarters of households owned one or more cars.

The car and the truck allowed many industries to move from the inner city to the outer suburbs. Dense, multi-storey factory sites were replaced by sprawling single-storey plants. Television created new possibilities in home entertainment, while computerisation made many clerical tasks redundant. All manner of locally based groups and institutions declined: Guide and Scout groups, church organisations, the suburban cinema and the local pub. In their place came more impersonal institutions: car-based shopping malls, multi-screen cinema complexes and the licensed club, financed by poker machines. The physical quality of suburbs improved as councils insisted on kerbing, guttering and better building standards, as governments in particular built more schools and hospitals and paid more attention to the need for metropolitan planning. Home ownership increased, an important advance in a country where the dice were loaded against the tenant and home ownership was a national aspiration. But the newer and better equipped suburbs were further removed from the city and few of them could match the opportunities for education, employment, entertainment and other diversions that continued to flourish in the centre and, increasingly, in the inner suburbs.

The prospects for each suburb remained dependent on its location and the

Botany Crematorium with the striking horizontal and vertical planes of art deco architecture.
Photograph by John Storey

social class of its inhabitants. In 1970 Hugh Stretton observed that:

> As families and businesses grow, the richer ones will try to shove the poorer ones further from the good land, and from any 'city' worth the name ... But the best distributions in old Sydney would still leave a million or more too far west to enjoy the old city much, or to attract much mixed company to cities of their own.[24]

Since then a fair proportion of that million have started to create cities of their own. Parramatta, Bankstown, Liverpool and Blacktown have developed many central city facilities. University campuses, theme parks, glamorous sporting facilities, office blocks, cinemas and hospitals are now to be found in or near western Sydney's major regional centres.[25]

For many people, living in Sydney means living within easy reach of the city centre, the harbour, the rivers or the beaches. Flat building in the 1920s and 1930s catered for this, as did successive apartment booms since the 1960s. The suburban house and garden no longer has the ubiquitous appeal it held until the 1960s. Sydney offers an enormous range of housing, a range that reflects the dramatic increase in one-person and 'double-income-no-kids' (dink) households as well as single-parent ones, which have become as common as the nuclear family (see Table 12.1). It costs more to buy or rent housing in Sydney than anywhere else in Australia, so the populace has developed both a fascination for and a fear of the real estate market, which can be seen as a retirement nest egg or a source of financial stress.

While slightly over two-thirds of Sydney's population only speak English, another one million people speak at least one other language. Cantonese, Mandarin, Greek, Italian, Spanish, Vietnamese and Filipino have at least 30 000 speakers each and almost every major world language has at least 5000 speakers.[26] This not only adds to the cultural diversity of Sydney, but it means that the non-English speakers among the two million international visitors to Sydney each year don't have to go too far to find a speaker of their tongue.

Over the last three decades government agencies, including the police, have recognised linguistic diversity in Sydney, most obviously seen on beachside signs warning of dangerous swimming conditions. The tourist trade has benefited from the presence of so many resident foreign-language speakers. This level of both ethnic and linguistic diversity fascinates many Asian and European visitors to Sydney, many of whom come from much less ethnically diverse cultures. While there are obviously racial tensions and occasional flare ups, in the last 100 years Sydney has been mercifully free of racial battles of the scale seen in parts of the USA, the United Kingdom, Germany and Indonesia.[27]

In a world preoccupied with telecommunications and virtual reality, some commentators have suggested that cities will fade away and that huge collectivities of people will no longer matter. But the physical realities of our lives—birth, growth, illness, death—are not virtual. Sydney provides some of the world's most spectacular urban settings for both work and play. More and more of its harbour foreshores are accessible to the public, its ferries service both workers and tourists, its railways provide efficient transport for many of its residents and it has attempted to cater for the private car without succumbing to the nightmare of the Los Angeles freeways. Like many major cities in the United Kingdom and North America it foolishly abandoned its tramway system, once Australia's largest, and has suffered a loss of intimacy and community in many of its streets. Yet the influx of Asian migrants and finance in the 1980s and 1990s has created new forms of urban intimacy that owe more to the great Asian cities of the late twentieth century than to the nineteenth-century British cities on which Sydney and other Australian capitals were modelled. Asian-style food courts provide affordable opportunities to eat out. Like all large cities, Sydney has extremes of wealth and poverty, but there are few social problems that cannot be addressed by political parties and governments if they have the will to act.[28] Whether you wander around the outer suburb of Cabramatta, where the Vietnamese are a vital part of the community, or Australia's largest apartment block in the Haymarket called 'The Peak', where Hong Kong Chinese influence is apparent, you know you are in one of the world's great cities.

Table 12.1: Household composition, Sydney 1991 (percentages)

one-parent families	9.6
two-parent families	40.3
couples	21.8
group households	5.4
lone-person households	20.1
other	2.8
Total	100

Source: C Foster, *Australian Cities*, OUP, Melbourne, 1995, p 80.

Hong Kong Chinese influence: The Peak apartment block in Haymarket.
Photograph by Peter Spearritt, 1998

Appendix

Sydney region: Total population of local government areas (LGAs) 1921–96

LGA (date of incorporation)	1921	1933	1947	1954	1966	1976	1986	1996
Alexandria (1868)	9 793	9 018	8 060					
Annandale (1894)	12 648	12 205	12 396					
Ashfield (1871)	33 636	39 356	44 761	39 777	41 933	42 325	40 401	40 077
Auburn (1892)	13 563	20 114	21 902	47 039	48 691	47 554	47 147	50 959
Balmain (1860)	32 104	28 272	28 398					
Bankstown (1895)	10 670	25 384	42 646	102 384	159 981	155 830	151 570	157 735
Baulkham Hills (1906)	5 113	8 075	10 675	15 620	33 499	75 665	102 806	119 545
Bexley (1900)	14 746	20 539	26 862					
Blacktown (1906)	7 382	13 724	20 753	31 748	111 357	163 500	192 442	232 219
Blue Mountains (1907)	6 768	6 841	10 186	22 245	30 733	46 850	63 866	72 506
Botany (1888)	6 214	8 287	9 462	29 490	31 871	35 739	34 273	34 702
Burwood (1874)	15 709	19 373	21 734	31 341	31 843	29 045	28 556	28 579
Cabramatta–Canley Vale (1892)	3 108	6 107	10 966					
Camden (1889)	2 006	2 394	2 935	4 847	8 661	14 950	18 870	32 109
Campbelltown (1882)	2 344	2 835	3 725	9 690	25 707	53 550	121 297	143 773
Canterbury (1879)	37 639	79 050	99 396	109 871	115 802	128 669	128 502	132 360
Castlereagh (1895)	555	1 128	1 310					
Colo (1906)(g)	4 715	5 262	5 016	4 972	6 062	10 750		
Concord (1883)	11 013	23 213	29 401	28 326	27 037	24 594	23 399	23 644
Darlington (1864)	3 651	3 053	3 032					
Drummoyne (1890)	18 761	29 215	32 985	30 855	30 630	31 525	30 605	30 264
Dundas (1889)	3 523	6 017	7 635					
Eastwood (1907)	2 133	3 025	4 108					
Enfield (1889)	8 530	14 782	17 231					
Ermington (1891)	1 981	2 364	3 298					
Erskineville (1893)	7 553	6 645	6 881					
Fairfield (1888) (a)	5 303	8 709	5 987	49 027	101 226	114 581	153 522	181 785
Glebe (1859)	22 754	19 874	20 510					
Gosford (1886) (b)	15 461	19 798	18 800	25 132	42 807	75 100	109 278	144 840
Granville (1885)	13 328	19 718	26 942					
Hawkesbury (1981)(g)							43 629	57 381
Holroyd (1927)	4 356	7 993	24 129	40 385	65 983	79 867	78 237	80 470
Homebush (1906)	1 622	3 189	3 501					
Hornsby (1906)	15 287	22 596	31 816	43 730	81 170	104 080	117 565	136 746
Hunters Hill (1861)	7 300	8 989	11 497	12 571	14 233	13 017	12 271	
Hurstville (1887)	13 394	22 663	33 939	50 336	64 851	66 348	63 219	65 392
Ingleburn (1896)	545	1 881	3 270					
Kogarah (1885)	18 226	30 646	39 298	43 618	47 654	46 712	45 949	47 618
Ku-ring-gai (1906)	19 209	27 931	39 874	52 615	88 876	100 100	100 189	99 032
Lane Cove (1895)	7 592	15 138	19 817	21 806	25 109	29 332	29 113	30 107
Leichhardt (1871)	29 356	30 209	29 462	64 919	59 325	62 540	56 302	58 304
Lidcombe (1888) (c)	10 522	17 379	20 281					
Liverpool (1872)	6 302	6 315	12 642	26 610	68 959	89 656	93 215	120 197

LGA (date of incorporation)	1921	1933	1947	1954	1966	1976	1986	1996
Manly (1877)	18 507	23 259	33 455	32 473	38 141	36 705	35 730	36 265
Marrickville (1861)	42 240	45 385	46 866	78 261	76 763	87 796	81 647	76 017
Mascot (1888) (d)	10 929	14 363	17 984					
Mosman (1893)	20 056	23 655	27 562	25 909	28 136	26 810	25 781	25 468
Nepean (1906)	2 127	3 399	4 445					
Newtown (1862)	28 168	25 290	24 933					
North Sydney (1890)	48 438	49 752	60 379	56 768	51 754	48 515	49 927	53 790
Paddington (1860)	26 364	26 674	24 681					
Parramatta (1861)	14 594	18 076	20 816	76 117	106 996	131 655	130 783	139 157
Penrith (1871)	3 595	3 911	4 961	18 838	46 391	80 950	135 342	163 122
Petersham (1871)		26 236	26 941	29 451				
Pittwater (1992) (e)								51 450
Randwick (1859)	50 841	78 957	100 931	99 080	113 634	119 460	115 620	118 905
Redfern (1859)	23 918	18 834	18 637					
Richmond (1872)	2 010	2 343	3 410					
Rockdale (1871)	25 189	39 123	47 290	75 995	81 463	83 789	83 350	84 847
Rydalmere (1891)	1 981	2 364	3 298					
Ryde (1872)	14 854	27 861	36 418	54 101	81 291	89 130	89 252	92 675
St Peters (1871)	12 700	12 554	12 404					
South Sydney (1968)						33 141		82 960
Strathfield (1885)	7 594	12 147	15 751	25 829	26 704	26 299	25 662	26 044
Sutherland (1906)	7 705	13 525	29 184	65 757	134 058	156 688	175 191	194 105
Sydney (1842)	104 153	88 308	95 925	193 103	159 188	52 152	86 311	24 883
Vaucluse (1895)	3 727	7 205	9 138					
Warringah (1906)	9 643	16 054	33 176	60 239	121 819	169 913	173 941	124 299
Waterloo (1860)	11 199	11 659	11 241					
Waverley (1859)	36 797	55 902	74 800	67 474	63 607	61 724	59 847	61 674
Willoughby (1890)	28 067	42 511	51 945	52 090	54 576	51 523	51 893	53 735
Windsor (1871)(g)	3 808	3 247	3 853	9 867	9 963	18 550		
Wollondilly (1906)	5 133	6 413	7 764	11 223	11 408	15 150	24 928	33 413
Woollahra (1860)	25 439	34 727	45 122	49 073	47 326	53 207	51 057	50 169
Wyong (1946) (b)			10 095	13 187	24 727	48 450	82 638	115 999

Note

Population counts are based on existing boundaries at the time of each census. Those LGAs not showing figures after 1947 were subsumed by amalgamation in the 1948 Local Government (Areas) Act or by later boundary changes. The dates refer to the first date of incorporation; some LGAs subsequently changed from a shire to a municipality or city. The details of the 1948 amalgamations were as follows: **Auburn** absorbed Mascot; **Burwood** absorbed two wards of Enfield; **Camden** absorbed one riding of Nepean; **Campbelltown** absorbed Ingleburn; **Fairfield** absorbed Cabramatta–Canley Vale; **Leichhardt** absorbed Annandale and Balmain; **Liverpool** absorbed one riding of Nepean; **Marrickville** absorbed Petersham and St Peters; **Parramatta** absorbed Granville, Dundas, Ermington, Rydalmere; **Penrith** absorbed Castlereagh, Penrith, St Marys, one riding of Nepean; **Rockdale** absorbed Bexley; **Ryde** absorbed Eastwood; **Strathfield** absorbed one ward of Enfield; **Sydney** absorbed Alexandria, Darlington, Erskinville, Glebe, Newtown, Paddington, Redfern, Waterloo; **Windsor** absorbed Richmond; **Woollahra** absorbed Vaucluse.

(a) Incorporated as Smithfield (Fairfield) in 1888 and renamed as Fairfield in 1920.
(b) Gosford and Wyong shires were formerly shires of Erina and Woy Woy and Gosford Municipality. Figures for Gosford for 1911–47 include the total Gosford/Wyong shires area.
(c) Incorporated as Rookwood in 1888 and renamed as Lidcombe in 1913.
(d) Incorporated as North Botany in 1888 and renamed as Mascot in 1911.
(e) Pittwater formed by severance from Warringah, 1992.
(f) South Sydney formed by severance from Sydney, 1968; amalgamated with Sydney, 1982; reformed by severance from Sydney, 1989.
(g) Hawkesbury formed by an amalgamation of Colo an Windsor, 1981.

Source: Australian Bureau of Statistics censuses.

Notes

Chapter 1
The new century

1 *New South Wales Yearbook 1912*, Government Printer, Sydney, 1913, pp 73–93. There is a considerable literature on the ethnic origins of immigrant Australians and on estimating the Aboriginal population of Australia at specific periods from pre-British settlement to the present. The best starting place is W Vamplew (ed), *Australians: historical statistics*, Fairfax, Syme & Weldon, Sydney, 1987, chapters 1 and 2. See also L R Smith, *The Aboriginal Population of Australia*, Canberra, 1980; NG Butlin, *Our Original Aggression: Aboriginal Population of Southeastern Australia 1788–1850*, A & U, Sydney, 1983. See also DJ Mulvaney and JP White (eds), *Australians to 1788*, Fairfax, Syme & Weldon, Sydney, 1987, chapter 18. For an up-to-date account of writing about Aboriginal Australians see the entries in G Davison et al. (eds), *The Oxford Companion to Australian History*, OUP, Melbourne, 1998, pp 1–15.

2 *SMH*, 2 January 1901. This account draws heavily on Gavin Souter's *Lion and Kangaroo: The Initiation of Australia 1901–1919*, Collins, Sydney, 1976, pp 39–48. For a visual and textual account of the pageant see *One Destiny: The Federation Story*, CD Rom, Global Vision, Melbourne, 1998.

3 Quoted in Souter, *Lion and Kangaroo*, p 47.

4 *Bulletin*, 5 January 1901, p 24.

5 *Queanbeyan Observer*, 1 August 1905.

6 JF Fraser, *Australia: The Making of a Nation*, Cassell, London, 1910, pp 111–12. John Sulman, 'Australian Cities: their past growth and future development', *Australia Today*, 1916.

7 EW Hine, *A Parliamentary Veteran: The Honorable Richard Thomas Ball: Thirty Five Years of Public Service and Record Achievement*, Free Press, Corowa, 1937, p 34.

8 *NSWPD*, 9 May 1928.

9 DJ Merrett, 'Australian Capital Cities in the 20th Century', in JW McCarthy and CB Schedvin (eds), *Australian Capital Cities*, Sydney University Press, Sydney, 1978, pp 171–98.

10 *NSWPD*, 9 May 1928.

11 *Land*, 27 February 1931.

12 John Thomas Lang, *I Remember*, Invincible Press, Sydney, 1956, pp 360–2.

13 Gilbert Mant, *The Big Show*, Horwitz, Sydney, 1972.

14 George Forbes, *History of Sydney from the Foundation of the City in 1788 up to the Present Time*, Sydney, 1926, pp 278–9.

15 Meta Maclean, *Drummond of the Far West*, Manly Daily, Sydney, 1947, p 112.

16 GS Browne, *Australia: A General Account*, Thomas Nelson, London, 1929.

17 Peter Hall, *The World Cities*, Weidenfeld & Nicolson, London, 1966.

18 Florence Harding, A Sociological Study of Sydney's Cultural Life, MA thesis, University of Sydney, 1947.

19 Peter Spearritt, 'Women in Sydney Factories, c 1920–1950', in A Curthoys et al. (eds), *Women at Work*, ASSLH, Sydney, 1975, pp 31–46.

20 Timothy Coghlan, *The Seven Colonies of Australasia 1897–98*, Government Printer, Sydney, 1898, p 1.

21 See entries in *ADB, vol* 8.

22 *The Progress of Australasia in the Nineteenth Century*, Chambers, London, 1903, p 441.

23 Adna Ferrin Weber, *The Growth of Cities in the Nineteenth Century: A study in statistics*, Cornell University Press, Ithaca, 1967 (1899), pp 138–41, 472–3. The book opens with a comparison between the United States population in 1790 and that of Australia in 1891.

24 See Peter Harrison, 'Australian Capital Territory', in *Australians: a Historical Dictionary*, Fairfax, Syme & Weldon, Sydney, 1987, pp 25–8.

25 Builder Printing Works, Sydney, 1904, editor's note.

26 See for instance the accounts of subdivisions in M Solling and P Reynolds, *Leichhardt*, A & U, Sydney, 1997 chapter 7; T Kass, C Liston, J McClymont, *Parramatta: a past revealed*, Parramatta City Council, Parramatta, NSW, 1996, chapter 10.

27 *Argus* (Melbourne), 3 June 1911, 14 March 1912.

28 *SMH*, 4 and 31 May 1911, 5 June 1911. In the four years 1907–10, Sydney averaged 6328 shipping entrances per year, Melbourne 4915. On Sydney overtaking Melbourne as a port see G Davison, *The Rise and Fall of Marvellous Melbourne*, MUP, Carlton, Vic., 1978, pp 35–6.

29 See N Hicks, *This Six and Scandal: Australia's Population Debate 1891–1911*, ANUP, Canberra, 1978; and G Davison, 'Australia: the First Suburban nation?', *Journal of Urban History* vol. 2, no. 1, November 1995, pp 60–3.

Chapter 2
Plague, planning and the house famine

1 P Curson and K McCracken, *Plague in Sydney: the Anatomy of an Epidemic*, UNSWP, Sydney, 1989, p 168. My account of the plague draws heavily on this thorough study.

2 Quoted in Curson and McCracken, pp 170–1.

3 Curson and McCracken, p 89.

4 For an analysis of plague outbreaks in Australia between 1900 and 1925 see Curson and McCracken pp 56–7.

5 Curson and McCracken, pp 187–91.

6 On housing conditions in late nineteenth century Sydney see Shirley Fitzgerald, *Rising Damp: Sydney 1870–90*, OUP, Melbourne, 1987; and Alan Mayne, *Fever, Squalor and Vice: Sanitation and Social Policy in Victorian Sydney*, UQP, St Lucia, Qld, 1982.

7 Curson and McCracken, p 163.

8 Shirley Fitzgerald, *Sydney 1842–1992*, H & I, Sydney, 1992, p 222. See also A Mayne, *The Imagined Slum*, Leicester University Press, Leicester, 1993, on newspaper coverage of slum clearance in Sydney.

9 Quoted in Fitzgerald, *Sydney 1842–1992*, p 224.

10 *Lone Hand*, May 1907.

11 For a detailed analysis of the 1908–09 commission, see Paul Ashton, *Planning Sydney: the accidental city since 1788*, H & I, Sydney, 1993, chapter 2.

12 See subdivision and land auction indexes in the Mitchell Library; and Paul Ashton, Reactions to and Paradoxes of Modernism: The Origins and Spread of Suburbia in 1920s Sydney, PhD thesis, Macquarie University, 1999; A B Rabone, History of Richardson & Wrench Ltd, unpublished typescript, Mitchell Library, nd.

13 M McKernan, *The Australian People and the Great War*, Nelson, Melbourne, 1980, p 46.

14 C Keating, *On the Frontier: A Social History of Liverpool*, H & I, Sydney, 1996, pp 150–3. Most local histories include an account of the impact of the war.

15 KS Inglis, *Sacred Places: War Memorials in the Australian Landscape*, MUP, Melbourne, 1998, pp 109–12. See also M Solling and P Reynolds, *Leichhardt*, A & U, Sydney, 1997, pp 168–77, for an account of the war in Leichhardt, Annandale, Balmain and Glebe. It is likely that from these four suburbs alone more than 1000 men died.

16 McKernan, *The Australian People*, p 55.

17 *NSWPD*, 28 February 1912.

18 JM Simmie, *Citizens in Conflict: The Sociology of Town Planning*, Hutchinson, London, 1976; Peter Hall, *Cities of Tomorrow*, Blackwell, Oxford, 1988, p 96.

19 Robert Freestone, *Model Communities: The Garden City Movement in Australia*, Nelson, Melbourne, 1989.

20 Bruce McFarlane, *Professor Irvine's Economics in Australian Labour History*, ASSLH, Canberra, 1966; PJ Briggs, Public Housing in Sydney, PhD thesis, University of New South Wales, 1973.

21 *Building*, September 1921.

22 *Bystander*, 25 December 1919.

23 JS Purdy, 'Metropolitan Health Officer's Report for 1924', in Department of Public Health, *Annual Report*, *NSWPP*, 1924, p 112. On Purdy, see *ADB*, *vol* 11.

24 JS Purdy, 'Metropolitan Health Officer's Report for 1920', in Department of Public Health, *Annual Report*, *NSWPP*, 1920, p 45.

25 *NSWPP*, vol. 1, 1924; *NSWYB*, 1929–30.

26 Peter Spearritt, 'The Auburn Plute', in Heather Radi and Peter Spearritt (eds), *Jack Lang*, H & I, Sydney, 1977.

27 *SMH*, 5 November 1924.

28 City of Sydney Municipal Council, *Vade Mecum*, CSMC, Sydney, 1936.

29 Purdy, 1924, p 110.

30 MJ Lewis, 'Populate or Perish': Aspects of Infant and Maternal Welfare in Sydney, 1870–1939, PhD thesis, ANU, 1976; Fitzgerald, *Sydney 1842–1992*; City of Sydney Municipal Council, *Vade Mecum*, 1941; WD Scott, *Report Upon Relocation of City Markets*, *NSWPP*, 28 September 1967.

31 RS Parker, 'Public Enterprise in NSW', *AJPH* 4, no. 2, November 1958, pp 208–23; Ambrose Pratt (ed), *The National Handbook of Australia's Industries*, Specialty Press, Melbourne, 1934.

32 Lewis, 'Populate or Perish'; WE Murphy, *The Milk Board of NSW: An Outline of its Origin and*

Development, Milk Board, Sydney, 1949.
33 Frank Clune, *Saga of Sydney: The Birth, Growth and Maturity of the Mother City of Australia*, Halstead Press, Sydney, 1961, p 495.
34 *Daily*, Mosman, 18 December 1928.
35 Claudia Thame, Health and the State: The Development of a Collective Responsibility for Health Care in Australia in the First Half of the 20th Century, PhD thesis, ANU, Canberra, 1974, pp 52–3.
36 Purdy, 1924, p 112.
37 Purdy, 1920, p 60.
38 City of Sydney, *Vade Mecum*, 1941; Peter Harrison, *Walter Burley Griffin: Landscape Architect*, NLA, Canberra, 1995.
39 Thame, Health and the State, pp 221–2.
40 JS Purdy, 'Metropolitan Health Officer's Report for 1925', in Department of Public Health, *Annual Report*, *NSWPP*, 1925, p 109.
41 RN Spann, *Public Administration in Australia*, Government Printer, Sydney, 1973, p 221.
42 FA Larcombe, *The Advancement of Local Government in NSW, 1906 to the Present*, Sydney University Press, Sydney, 1978; William McKell, interview with Peter Spearritt, 26 June 1972.
43 *NSWPD*, 21 August 1918.
44 Quoted in HE Maiden, *The History of Local Government in NSW*, Angus & Robertson, Sydney, 1966, p 124.
45 *Shire & Municipal Record*, June 1920.
46 John Sulman, *An Introduction to the Study of Town Planning in Australia*, Government Printer, Sydney, 1921, p 204; *Australian Home Builder*, August 1922. See also Peter Harrison, *Walter Burley Griffin: Landscape Architect.*
47 *SMH*, 18 October 1923.
48 *SMH*, 26 August 1925.
49 *SMH*, 26 August 1925.
50 *Australia*, July 1924.
51 *SMH*, 12 March 1925.
52 *SMH*, 6 April 1925, 1 March 1924.
53 Town Planning Association of NSW, *Annual Report*, 1924.

Chapter 3
Over once lovely hills

1 See G Souter, *Mosman: a history*, MUP, Melbourne, 1994, chapters 4 and 5.
2 On housing conditions, see S Fitzgerald, *Rising Damp: Sydney 1870-1890*, OUP, Melbourne, 1987; Max Kelly, *Paddock Full of Houses: Paddington 1840–1890*, Doak Press, Sydney, 1978.
3 Dan Coward, The Impact of War on New South Wales: Some Aspects of Social and Political History 1914–17, PhD thesis, ANU, 1974, p 431.
4 *NSWYB* 1926–27.
5 *Advance Australia*, September 1927.
6 *Australia*, July 1924.
7 *Smith's Weekly*, 10 January 1920.
8 *Commonwealth Home*, January 1929.
9 Charles Whitham, The Book of the North Shore, typescript, 1927, pp 7–8, held in ML.
10 *Commonwealth Home*, January 1929, February 1929.
11 *SMH*, 1 October 1927.
12 *NSWPD*, 21 December 1920.
13 MWSDB Annual Reports.
14 James Jervis, *Canterbury Boys High School, 1918–1950*, Canterbury Boys High School, Sydney, 1965.
15 Merle Peters, *The Bankstown Story, A Comprehensive History of the District*, self-published, Yagoona, 1969, pp 64–5.
16 R Adams, *Distinctive Australian Homes*, self-published, Sydney, 1925.
17 WB Lynch and FA Larcombe, *Randwick 1859–1959*, Randwick Municipal Council, Sydney, 1959, pp 183–4.
18 MJ Lewis, 'Populate or Perish': Aspects of Infant and Maternal Welfare in Sydney, 1870–1939, PhD thesis, ANU, 1976.
19 *Daily Guardian*, 26 September 1926.
20 NSW Department of Railways, Annual Reports.
21 P Geeves and J Jervis, *Rockdale: Its Beginnings and Development*, Rockdale Municipal Council, Sydney, 1954, pp 88–93.
22 *Daily Guardian*, 26 September 1925.
23 Geeves and Jervis, *Rockdale.*
24 *NSWPD*, 30 September 1924.
25 *NSWPD*, 7 December 1920.
26 MV Aird, *The Water Supply, Sewerage and Drainage of Sydney*, MWSDB, Sydney, 1961, pp 90–3.
27 DR Kirkby, *From Sails to Atoms: First Fifty Years of Sutherland Shire 1906 to 1956*, Sutherland Shire Council, Sydney, 1970.
28 *Evening News Yearbook*, 1927.
29 *Shire and Municipal Record*, April 1923.
30 *Shire and Municipal Record*, p 389.
31 *NSWPD*, 23 July 1924.
32 Whitham, The Book of the North Shore, p 115.
33 Manly Municipal Council, *Manly Diamond Jubilee*, MMC, Sydney 1937. 1927.
34 Whitham, The Book of the North Shore, p 32.
35 Whitham, The Book of the North Shore, pp 343–5.
36 Eric Russell, *Drummoyne: A Western Suburb's*

History 1794, 1871, 1971, Drummoyne Municipal Council, Sydney, 1971, pp 213–14; P Geeves, *A Place of Pioneers: The Centenary History of the Municipality of Ryde*, Ryde Municipal Council, Sydney, 1970, pp 162–3.

37 Christina Stead, *Seven Poor Men of Sydney*, A & R, Sydney, 1934, 1965 edition pp 109–10.

38 *Sands Directory*, Sands, Sydney, 1930; and *Wise's Directory*, Wise, Sydney, 1947.

39 Peter Spearritt, 'The Kindergarten Movement: Tradition and Change', in DE Edgar (ed), *Social Change in Australia: Readings in Sociology*, Cheshire, Melbourne, 1974, pp 583–96.

40 *Smith's Weekly*, 3 January 1920.

41 *Smith's Weekly*, 17 January 1920.

42 George Forbes, *History of Sydney from the Foundation of the City in 1788 up to the Present Time*, Brooks, Sydney, 1926. See also the entry on Sir Arthur Rickard in *ADB*, vol. 11.

43 *Smith's Weekly*, 31 January 1920.

44 *Smith's Weekly*, January 1920; *Daily Guardian*, 31 October 1925.

45 *Smith's Weekly*, 24 December 1920.

46 *Daily Guardian*, 31 October 1925.

47 AB Rabone, History of Richardson and Wrench Ltd, unpublished typescript, ML, nd.

48 *SMH*, 13 September 1927.

49 *NSWPD*, 9 May 1928.

50 *Labor Daily*, 30 October 1929.

51 Peters, *The Bankstown Story*, p 65.

52 Leonie Sandercock, *Cities for Sale: Property, Politics and Urban Planning in Australia*, MUP, Carlton, Vic., 1977, p 77.

53 Richardson & Wrench, Record Books, 1920–30, ML.

54 Cumberland County Council, *County of Cumberland Planning Scheme Report*, CCC, Sydney, 1948, p 188.

55 Cumberland County Council, *County of Cumberland Planning Scheme Report*, p 27.

56 Ian Turner, '1914–19', in FK Crowley (ed), *A New History of Australia*, Heinemann, Melbourne, 1974, p 355.

57 Brian James, *The Advancement of Spencer Button*, A & R, Sydney, 1950, pp 170–1.

58 James, *Spencer Button*, pp 172–3.

59 Weston Bate, *A History of Brighton*, MUP, Carlton, Vic., 1962, p 375.

60 *Tait's Electrical Directory*, 1929.

61 Andrew Spearritt, The Electrification of the Home, BA Honours thesis, Dept of History, University of Sydney, 1983.

62 EA Boehm, 'The Impact of Electricity', *Economic Record* 31, no. 60, May 1955; Beverley Kingston, *My Wife, My Daughter and Poor Mary Ann*, Nelson, Melbourne, 1975; Peter Spearritt, 'Women in Sydney Factories, c. 1920–1950', in Ann Curthoys et al. (eds), *Women at Work*, ASSLH, Sydney, 1975, pp 31–46.

63 Manly Municipal Council, *Manly Diamond Jubilee*, 1927.

64 GS Browne, *Australia: A General Account*, Thomas Nelson, London, 1929, pp 189–91.

65 Eric Reade, *Australian Silent Films*, Lansdowne, Melbourne, 1970, pp 176–80; *NSWYB*, 1921.

66 Browne, *Australia: A General Account*, p 174.

67 Francis Jackson, *Byways of Romance*, EA Vidler, Melbourne, 1927, pp 106–7.

Chapter 4
Shadows behind the bridge

1 *SMH*, 1 January 1932.

2 'Caddie', *The Autobiography of a Sydney Barmaid*, Sun Books, Melbourne, 1966, pp 128, 136.

3 See *ADB*, vol. 11.

4 *SMH*, 18 February 1932, 24 January 1938.

5 See H Radi and P Spearritt (eds), *Jack Lang*, H & I, Sydney, 1977; and Bede Nairn's entry on Lang in *ADB*, vol. 9.

6 Phyllis Peter, Social Aspects of the Depression in NSW 1930–1934, PhD thesis, ANU, 1964, p 59.

7 Bruce Mitchell, *Teachers, Education & Politics*, Cheshire, Melbourne, 1975.

8 JH Bell, The La Perouse Aborigines: A Study of Their Group Life and Assimilation into Modern Australian Society, PhD thesis, University of Sydney, 1959.

9 Peter, Social Aspects.

10 *Workers Weekly*, 16 March 1934.

11 BG Judd, *He That Doeth*, Marshall, London, 1951, pp 152–74.

12 *Workers Weekly*, 16 March 1934.

13 Ambrose Pratt (ed), *The National Handbook of Australia's Industries*, Specialty Press, Melbourne, 1934.

14 Peter Spearritt, 'Depression Statistics', in J Mackinolty (ed),*The Wasted Years? Australia's Great Depression*, A & U, Sydney, 1981, pp 194–212.

15 James Jervis and LR Flack, *A Jubilee History of the Municipality of Botany 1888–1938*, Botany Municipal Council, Sydney, 1938; *SMH*, 8 August 1930; Bankstown Municipal Council, *The Years of Endeavour*, BMC, Sydney, 1972.

16 *SMH*, 8 October 1930.

17 AM Shepherd, *The Story of Petersham 1793–1948*,

Petersham Municipal Council, Sydney, 1948, p 59.
18 *NSWIG*, 30 November 1936, p 1226.
19 This account based on Peter Spearritt, *The Sydney Harbour Bridge: A Life*, A & U, Sydney, 1982.
20 Interview with JT Lang by the author, 28 August 1972.
21 *SMH*, 12 January 1932; Eric Campbell, *The Rallying Point*, MUP, Melbourne, 1965, pp 149–59.
22 A Boswell, 'A High Adventure', unpub. ms, 1936; *SMH*, 2 March 1932.
23 Spearritt, *Bridge*.
24 JM Ward, 'The Dismissal', in Radi and Spearritt (eds), *Jack Lang*, pp 160–78.
25 EJ Ward papers, NLA series 15, item 276.
26 Judith Wright, 'Forty years and Australian cities', *Community*, no. 7, February 1975.
27 Eric Baume, *I Lived These Years*, Harrap, London, 1941, p 147
28 AB Rabone, History of Richardson & Wrench Ltd, unpub. typescript, ML, nd.
29 *NSWPD*, 8 December 1937.
30 N Ingham, 'Sydney Sewerage—A Factor in Metropolitan Growth', *Developer* 9, no. 2, May 1971, pp 34–9.
31 *Cumberland Argus*, 26 October 1938.
32 *NSWSR* 1939–40, pp 202–4; JG Crawford, 'Residential Construction Costs', *Economic Record*, June 1938, pp 74–8.
33 *Cumberland Argus*, 26 October 1938. See also Rosemary Broomham, *First Light*, H & I, Sydney, 1987.
34 Ruth Thompson, Sydney's flats: a social and political history, PhD thesis, Macquarie University, 1986.
35 *SMH*, 15 May 1935.
36 Cumberland County Council, *County of Cumberland Planning Scheme Report*, CCC, Sydney, 1948, p 46.
37 Lane Cove Municipal Council, *A History of Lane Cove 1895–1938*, LCMC, Sydney, 1938; Jervis and Flack, *A Jubilee History*.
38 *SMH*, 29 March 1938.
39 FA Bland, 'Recent Legislation in NSW', *Economic Record*, 14 June 1938, pp 78–82.
40 Robin Boyd, *Australia's Home*, Penguin, Ringwood, Vic., 1968, p 292; *Building*, November 1934, August 1940.
41 *SMH*, 30 March 1938; *Australian National Journal*, September–October 1939.
42 Paul McGuire, *Australian Journey*, Heinemann, London, 1942, p 260.
43 *SMH*, 27 February 1935; *LD*, 24 June 1935; *SMH*, 5 July 1935.
44 *SMH*, 25, 26 July 1935; NH Dick, 'Housing and Slum Clearance in NSW', *Australian Quarterly*, No. 28, December 1935.
45 *LD*, 23 September 1935.
46 *LD*, 20 November 1935.
47 NH Dick, 'Housing Problems: Better Planning Called For', *United Australia Review*, 19 September 1935, pp 9–10.
48 Peter Spearritt, 'Sydney's "Slums": Middle Class Reformers and the Labor Response', *Labor History*, May 1974, pp 65–81.
49 Lane Cove Municipal Council, *Lane Cove*; Hornsby Shire Council, *Back to Hornsby Week*, HSC, Sydney, 1938; Jervis and Flack, *A Jubilee History*.
50 Gavin Souter, 'The Skeleton at the Feast'; and J Horner and M Langton, 'The day of Mourning', in Bill Gammage and Peter Spearritt (eds), *Australia 1938*, Fairfax, Syme & Weldon, Sydney, 1987.
51 AL Haskell, *Waltzing Matilda: A Background to Australia*, Adam & Charles Black, London, 1940, p 137.
52 Edward A Ross, 'Look at Australia', *Publicist*, February 1940, p 12.
53 Haskell, *Waltzing Matilda*, p 136.
54 *SMH*, 10 May 1935.
55 C Wilson, *The History of Unilever*, vol. 2, Cassell, London, 1954, p 361.
56 *University of Sydney Gazette*, June 1974; P Hasluck, *The Government and the People 1939–1941*, Australian War Memorial, Canberra, 1952, p 382.
57 *CPD*, 30 September 1942; *NSWYB*, 1945–46.
58 *SMH*, 1 October 1940.
59 DP Mellor, *The Role of Science & Industry*, Australian War Memorial, Canberra, 1958, pp 470–1.
60 M Terry, *Bulldozer: The War Role of the Department of Main Roads, NSW*, Johnson, Sydney, 1945; MV Aird, *The Water Supply, Sewerage and Drainage of Sydney*, MWSDB, Sydney, 1961.
61 SJ Butlin, *The War Economy 1939–1942*, Australian War Memorial, Canberra, 1955, pp 454–74.
62 *NSWYB*; *Real Estate Institute Journal*, August 1942.
63 *NSWYB*, 1945–46; Helen Nelson, The Politics of Rent Control, PhD thesis, University of Sydney, 1977.
64 Paul Hasluck, *The Government and the People 1942–1945*, Australian War Memorial, Canberra,

1970, p 592.

65 *Salt* , 26 February 1946.

66 *Salt*, February 1946.

67 Kenneth Slessor, *Portrait of Sydney*, Ure Smith, Sydney, 1950, p 14.

68 *NSWPD*, 1 November 1939.

69 *DT*, 11 July 1941.

70 *Sun*, 27 June 1941.

71 AJ Marshall, *Australia Limited*, A & R, Sydney, 1942, p 69.

72 *Real Estate Institute Journal*, November 1942.

73 William McKell, *Five Critical Years*, ALP, Sydney, 1946, p 100.

74 *Century*, 29 June 1945.

75 *SMH*, 23, 25 March 1946.

76 *NSWPD*, 12 November 1946.

77 McKell, *Five Critical Years*, p 102.

78 *NSWHC Report*, 1947–48.

79 *SMH*, 1 July 1947.

80 *SMH*, 4, 2, 3 July 1947.

81 Cumberland County Council, *Report*, pp 69–70.

82 MA Jones, *Housing and Poverty in Australia*, MUP, Carlton, Vic., 1972, p 72; M Neutze, *People & Property in Redfern*, Urban Research Unit, Canberra, 1973, p 76.

Chapter 5
Homes for the people

1 JM Giles, *Migrant Australia*, Mills & Boon, London, 1960; IH Burnley (ed), *Urbanisation in Australia: Aspects of the Postwar Experience*, CUP, Melbourne, 1974.

2 John Collins, 'The Political Economy of Postwar Immigration', in EL Wheelwright and Ken Buckley (eds), *Essays in the Political Economy of Australian Capitalism*, ANZ Book Co., Sydney, 1975.

3 CW Domville-Fife, *Australian Panorama: Land of Golden Opportunity*, Rankin, Bristol, 1949, pp 14–20.

4 JM Giles, *Migrant Australia*, pp 19–21.

5 JH Bell, The La Perouse Aborigines: A Study of Their Group Life and Assimilation in Modern Australian Society, PhD thesis, University of Sydney, 1959; NSW Bookstall Co., *Guide to Sydney and Pleasure Resorts of NSW*, Sydney 1938.

6 Ken Brindle, 'The urban Aboriginal in NSW', *New Dawn*, August 1970; CD Rowley, *Outcasts in White Australia*, Penguin, Ringwood, Vic., 1971.

7 HC Brewster and V Luther, *King's Cross Calling*, HC Brewster, Sydney, 1945.

8 VL Borin, *The Uprooted Survive: A Tale of Two Continents*, Heinemann, London, 1959, p 248.

9 Sarah Dunne, 'Women's Work in 1949', *The Herald Australian Year Book*, Herald and Weekly Times, Melbourne, 1950.

10 GC Bolton, '1939–1951', in FK Crowley (ed), *A New History of Australia*, Heinemann, Melbourne, 1974, pp 482–3.

11 James Jupp, *Arrivals and Departures*, Cheshire-Lansdowne, Melbourne, 1966.

12 Nino Cullotta (John O'Grady), *They're a Weird Mob*, Ure Smith, Sydney, 1957, pp 16, 19.

13 IH Burnley, 'European Immigration Settlement Patterns in Metropolitan Sydney 1947–66', *Australian Geographical Studies*, no. 10, 1972, pp 61–78; IH Burnley, *The Social Environment: A Population & Social Geography of Australia*, McGraw Hill, Sydney, 1976, p 183.

14 Donald Horne, *The Australian People*, A & R, Sydney, 1973, p 235.

15 *SMH*, 2 May 1947.

16 Cumberland County Council, *County of Cumberland Planning Scheme Report*, CCC, Sydney, 1948, p 67.

17 Cumberland County Council, *Report*, pp 68–72.

18 Cumberland County Council, *Report*, p 77; A Birch and DS Macmillan, *The Sydney Scene: 1788–1960*, MUP, Carlton, Vic., 1962, pp 354–5.

19 T Brennan, *New Community: Problems & Policies*, A & R, Sydney, 1973.

20 Frank Hardy, *The Outcasts of Foolgarah*, Allarah, Melbourne, 1971, pp 116–17.

21 *NSWSR*, 1950–51, p 442.

22 Interview, Peter Harrison, 21 November 1974.

23 MA Jones, *Housing and Poverty in Australia*, MUP, Carlton, Vic., 1972, pp 15–16.

24 *NSWYB*; NSWHC, Annual Reports.

25 *NSWYPD*, 13 November 1951, p 43.

26 Gwen Kelly, 'Portrait of a New Community', *Meanjin* XVI, no. 4 (1957), p 402.

27 *NSWYB*, 1959, p 543.

28 *NSWPD*, 1 November 1950.

29 Kelly, 'Portrait', p 400.

30 JR Davis & Peter Spearritt, *Sydney at the Census 1971*, Urban Research Unit, Canberra, 1974, Map 41.

31 Charles Pickett, 'Suburban Fibro', *The Fibro Frontier*, Powerhouse Museum, Sydney, 1997.

32 Measured by the number of years of average male earnings required to buy a house of average price; see Max Neutze, *Urban Development in Australia: A Descriptive Analysis*, A & U, Sydney, 1977, p 162.

33 Graeme Bethune, Home Ownership Policy and Financial Institutions, Urban Research Unit seminar paper, 1975.

34 Bethune, Home Ownership; Helen Nelson, The Politics of Rent Control, PhD thesis, University of Sydney, 1977.

35 Max Neutze, *People & Property in Redfern*, Urban Research Unit, Canberra, 1973; Davis & Spearritt, *Sydney at the Census*, maps 43, 45–7.

36 *Shelter*, No. 9, 1974.

37 *CPD*, 30 August 1973; *Developer*, September–December 1976.

38 PN Troy, *A Fair Price: The Land Commission Program 1972–1977*, H & I, Sydney, 1978.

39 *SMH*, 30 November, 5 December 1977.

40 *NSWYB* 1988, pp 261–7; 1998, pp 222–3. For an analysis of outright ownership and purchase across five income groups in Sydney from 1982 to 1995 see Judith Yates, *Trends in Home Ownership*, Department of Urban Affairs and Planning, Sydney, 1997.

41 RV Cardew, *Flats: A Study of Occupants and Locations*, Buchan Fell, Sydney, 1970; Elzo Vandermark and Peter Harrison, *Development Activities in Four Sydney Suburban Areas*, Urban Research Unit, Canberra, 1972; Max Neutze, *People and Property in Randwick*, Urban Research Unit, Canberra, 1971.

42 *SMH*, 22 July 1976, 4 August 1977.

43 Neutze, *Urban Development in Australia*, p 73.

44 Ruth Thompson, Sydney's flats, PhD thesis, Macquarie University, 1986.

45 Sandra Hall, *Supertoy: 20 Years of Australian Television*, Sun Books, Melbourne, 1976.

46 M Campbell, *Marriage of Convenience: Number 96*, A & R, Sydney, 1974.

47 Hugh Stretton, *Ideas for Australian Cities*, Orphan Press, Adelaide, 1970; PN Troy, *The Perils of Urban Consolidation*, Federation Press, Sydney, 1996.

48 Robin Boyd, *The Australian Ugliness*, Cheshire, Melbourne, 1960, pp 80–1 (emphasis added).

49 Allan Ashbolt, 'Myth and Reality', *Meanjin*, 4/1966, p 373.

50 David Walker, *Dream & Disillusion: A Search for Australian Cultural Identity*, ANU Press, Canberra, 1976.

51 Stretton, *Ideas for Australian Cities*, p 12; Ian Halkett, *The Quarter Acre Block: Use of Suburban Gardens*, Australian Institute of Urban Studies, Canberra, 1976.

Chapter 6
The suburbanisation of work

1 George Wilkenfeld, The Electrification of the Sydney Energy System, PhD thesis, Macquarie University, 1989; Rosemary Broomham, *First Light*, H & I, Sydney, 1987.

2 A Bordow (ed), *The Worker in Australia: Contributions from Research*, UQP, St Lucia, Qld, 1977. See also M Solling and P Reynolds, *Leichhardt*, A & U, Sydney, 1997, chapters 8–10.

3 Ambrose Pratt (ed), *The National Handbook of Australia's Industries*, Specialty Press, Melbourne, 1934; CM Zierer, 'Land Use Differentiation in Sydney, Australia', *Annals of the Association of American Geographers* XXXII, no. 3, September 1942, pp 255–307; JM Holmes, 'Factory Orientation in Metropolitan Sydney', *Australian Geographer*, no. 5, June 1947, pp 96–113. For the nineteenth-century background, see G Linge, *Industrial Awakening*, ANUP, Canberra, 1979.

4 Department of Main Roads, *Main Road Development Plan for Sydney Metropolis and County of Cumberland*, DMR, Sydney, 1945.

5 Alexandria Council, *Alexandria, 1868–1943: The Birmingham of Australia*, Alexandria Council, Sydney, 1943.

6 *SMH*, 3 August 1928.

7 *Sydney Opinion*, November 1929.

8 Department of Main Roads, *Main Road Development Plan*.

9 BM Dale, 'The Location of Oil Refineries in Australia', *NZ Geographer*, vol. 15, October 1959, pp 160–72.

10 M Jones, *North Sydney 1788–1988*, A & U, Sydney, 1988, pp 230–3.

11 *Tribune*, 18 April 1947.

12 Tooth & Co., *Over a Century of Brewing Tradition*, Tooth & Co., Sydney, 1953.

13 *AFR*, 22 April 1967; *SMH*, 8 December 1977.

14 See maps and tables in *SSTT*, pp 120–5.

15 C Keating, *On the Frontier: A Social History of Liverpool*, H & I, Sydney, 1996, pp 189–90.

16 Australian Institute of Urban Studies, *Industrial Land in Sydney*, AIUS, Canberra, 1975; Carol Liston, *Campbelltown: The Bicentennial History*, A & U, Sydney, 1988, pp 219–20.

17 P Murphy and R Freestone, 'Towards edge city: business recentralisation and post-suburban Sydney', in K Gibson and S Watson (eds), *Metropolis Now*, Pluto Press, Sydney, 1994, pp 114–30. See also DC Rich, *The Industrial Geography of Australia*, Croom Helm, London, 1987, pp 159–69.

18 GM Shaw, *Concord Jubilee 1883–1933*, Concord Municipal Council, Sydney, 1933, p 117.

19 Tooth & Co., *The First Hundred Years: A Brief History of the Kent Brewery 1835–1935*, Tooth & Co., Sydney, 1935, p 69.

20 Pratt (ed), *National Handbook*, p 163.
21 *NSWYB*, 1939–40.
22 *NSWPP*, 1940. See G Reekie, *Temptations: Sex, selling and the department store*, A & U, Sydney, 1993.
23 Planning & Environment Commission, *Work Places and Work Trips 1971*, Planning & Environment Commission, Sydney, 1976. See also B Kingston, *Basket, Bag And Trolley: A History of Shopping*, OUP, Melbourne, 1994.
24 B Kingston, *My Wife, My Daughter and Poor Mary Ann*, Nelson, Melbourne, 1975, p 20.
25 Ada A Holman, *Sport of the Gods*, CJ DeGaris, Melbourne, 1921, pp 58–67.
26 Ione Fett, Women Medical Students in Australia, seminar paper, Department of Sociology, Research School of Social Sciences, ANU, 1974; *University of Sydney Calendar*, University of Sydney, 1947.
27 Peter Hall, *World Cities*, Weidenfeld & Nicolson, London, 1971, pp 26–7.
28 Planning & Environment Commission, *Work Places and Work Trips 1971*.
29 Ian Manning, *The Journey to Work*, A & U, Sydney, 1978.
30 *SSTT*, pp 132–3.
31 The 1991 figures here and in the account that follows are based on P Gipps et al., *Journey to Work: Employment and the Changing Structure of Australian Cities*, Australian Housing and Urban Research Institute, Melbourne, 1997.
32 Manning, *Journey to Work*, p 187.
33 *Tribune*, 18 June 1949.
34 *Sunday Herald*, 3 July 1949.
35 *SMH*, 4, 6, 9 July 1949.
36 *SMH*, 24, 3 July 1949.
37 *Building & Engineering*, 25 July 1949, p 63.
38 *SMH*, 29 July 1949.
39 LF Crisp, *Ben Chifley: A Political Biography*, A & R, Sydney, 1963, p 365; Edna Ryan, interview with the author, 13 May 1975.
40 *AFR*, December 1977; *SMH*, December 1977.
41 See M Daly and M Logan, *The Brittle Rim: Finance, Business and the Pacific Region*, Penguin, Melbourne, 1989; and RH Fagan and M Weber, *Global Restructuring: the Australian Experience*, OUP, Melbourne, 1994.
42 P Murphy and S Watson, *Surface City: Sydney at the Millennium*, Pluto Press, Sydney, 1997, p 99. Chapter five examines economic restructuring in Sydney. See also S Fitzgerald and H Golder, *Pyrmont and Ultimo: Under Siege*, H & I, Sydney, 1994.
43 See Sue Rosen, 'Not Bringing Home the Bacon: the death of the State Abattoir, Homebush', in J Shields (ed), *All our Labours*, UNSWP, Sydney, 1992, pp 227–43.
44 State Rail Authority of NSW, *Annual Report 1996/97*, State Rail Authority, Sydney, p 74.
45 ABS, Time Series Community Profile, Sydney Statistical Division, ABS, 1986–96.
46 ABS, Social Atlases, 1986–96 censuses (see Further Reading), maps on unemployment and youth unemployment.
47 Diane Powell, *Out West: Perceptions of Sydney's Western Suburbs*, A & U, Sydney, 1993.

Chapter 7
Public transport and the rise of the car

1 JW McCarthy, 'Australian Capital Cities in the 19th Century', *AEHR*, vol. 10, no. 2, September 1970, pp 107–37. See also Ian Manning, *The Open Street*, Transit Australia, Sydney, 1991, chapter 1.
2 See the entry on Bradfield in *ADB*, vol. 7.
3 I Paddison, *The Railways of NSW 1855–1955*, Dept of Railways, Sydney, 1955, p 190; NSW Archives Office 7/4135.
4 *Australian Town Planning Conference 1917*, Australian Town Planning Conference, Adelaide, 1917, pp 68–73.
5 *NSWPD*, 7 September 1922. For a more detailed account see P Spearritt, *The Sydney Harbour Bridge: A Life*, A & U, Sydney, 1982.
6 *LD*, 19 March 1932.
7 *NSWPD*, 7 September 1922.
8 *Staff*, 21 January 1927.
9 Paddison, *Railways of NSW*, p 192.
10 *SMH*, 22, 24, 29 December 1931.
11 G Reynolds, The Development of Sydney's City & Suburban Railways in the 1920s, Economic History III essay, University of Sydney, 1969.
12 *NSWPD*, 9 November 1938.
13 Don Aitkin, *The Colonel*, ANUP, Canberra, 1969; *SMH*, 21 January 1956.
14 Eleanor Dark, *Waterway*, Johnson, Sydney, 1946, pp 296, 299.
15 Dark, *Waterway*, pp 311, 319.
16 *DT*, 5 November 1927.
17 Graeme Andrews, *Sydney Ferries*, 3rd edn, OUP, Melbourne, 1994.
18 *Staff*, 22 April 1924.
19 Australian Labor Party, Nationalisation of Road Transport, 1930, paper held in the Mitchell Library.
20 Aitkin, *The Colonel*, pp 180–8; *NSWYB* 1938–39 p 399.

21 *NSWPD*, 16 June 1936.

22 *NSWYB*, 1941–45.

23 R Broomham, *On the Road: The NRMA's First Seventy-five Years*, A & U, Sydney, 1996.

24 Peter Spearritt, 'Tramways', *Australian Encyclopedia*, 6th edn, Australian Geographic, Sydney, 1996, vol. 8, pp 2954–6.

25 *NSWPD*, 24 October 1922.

26 Auburn Municipal Council, *Auburn Jubilee, 1887–1928*, AMC, 1928, p 57.

27 Dymphna Cusack and Florence James, *Come in Spinner*, Heinemann, London, 1951, p 144.

28 Martin Painter, 'NSW Political Chronicle', *AJPH*, XXII, 1976.

29 *Tribune*, 7, 21 January 1947.

30 JJC Bradfield, The City and Suburban Electric Railways and the Sydney Harbour Bridge, DSc thesis in Engineering, University of Sydney, 1924.

31 *Australian Women's Weekly*, 24 January 1942.

32 Jon Cleary, *Just Let Me Be*, Collins, London, 1950.

33 DF Dixson, 'Origins of the Australian Petrol Distribution System', *AEHR*, March 1972, pp 36–51; Drummoyne Municipal Council, *Drummoyne 1890–1940*, DMC, Sydney, 1940.

34 L Hovernden, The Motor Car in NSW to 1937, MA thesis, University of Sydney, 1981.

35 *NSWPD*, 20 August 1924.

36 *NSWPD*, 21 December 1926.

37 Auburn Municipal Council, *Auburn Jubilee*.

38 L Moses and HF Williamson, 'The Location of Economic Activity in Cities', *American Economic Review*, May 1967, pp 211–22.

39 PN Troy, Urban Road Planning in the Australian Continent, seminar paper, Urban Research Unit, ANU, Canberra, 1968.

40 Department of Main Roads, *Fifty Years of Main Roads 1925–1975*, DMR, Sydney, 1975.

41 Department of Main Roads, *The Roadmakers*, DMR, Sydney, 1976; Troy, Urban Road Planning.

42 *SMH*, 4 March 1935.

43 *NSWYB*, 1926–27, 1939–40.

44 William Plowden, *The Motor Car and Politics 1896–1970*, Bodley Head, London, 1971.

45 *Truth*, 1 March 1939.

46 *Sun*, 8 September 1938; *DT*, 10 September 1938.

47 Robert Gibbons, Transportation and the Urban Environment, Sydney 1900–2000, MA essay, Dept of Government, University of Sydney, 1974.

48 M Terry, *Bulldozer: The War Role of the Department of Main Roads, NSW*, Johnson, Sydney, 1945, pp 254–5.

49 Department of Main Roads, *Origin and Destination Study of Road Traffic in Sydney*, DMR, Sydney, 1947.

50 Cumberland County Council, *County of Cumberland Planning Scheme Report*, CCC, Sydney, 1948, p 161.

51 Peter Spearritt, 'Cars for the People', in A Curthoys, T Rowse and A Martin (eds), *Australians Since 1939*, Fairfax Syme Weldon, Sydney, 1987, pp 119–29.

52 Cumberland County Council, *Report*, p 158

53 John Black, *Public Inconvenience: Access and Travel in Seven Sydney Suburbs*, Urban Research Unit, ANU, Canberra, 1977; Ian Manning, *The Journey to Work*, A & U, Sydney, 1978.

54 *SMH*, 21 January 1956.

55 *Australian Worker*, 24 April 1946; *SMH*, 20 June 1947.

56 Leonie Sandercock, *Cities for Sale: Property, Politics and Urban Planning in Australia*, MUP, Carlton, 1975, p 176.

57 Cumberland County Council, *Economics of Urban Expansion*, CCC, Sydney, 1958, p 13.

58 Interview by the author with HM Sherrard, 22 June 1972.

59 See A Rattray and A Sinclair, *A Discussion Paper on Transport Planning in Sydney to 1975*, Bureau of Transport Economics, Melbourne, 1978; *Open Road*, October 1977.

60 These issues are dealt with in detail in Max Neutze, *Funding Urban Services*, A & U, Sydney, 1997.

61 See NSW Department of Transport, *Integrated Transport Strategy for the Greater Metropolitan Region*, NSW Department of Transport, Sydney, 1995; and *Action for Transport 2010: An integrated transport plan for Sydney*, NSW Department of Transport, Sydney, 1998.

Chapter 8
Residents and ratepayers

1 AG Austin (ed), *The Webbs' Australian Diary*, Pitman, Melbourne, 1965; JD Fitzgerald, *Greater Sydney & Greater Newcastle*, NSW Bookstall Co., Sydney, 1966; FA Larcombe, *The Development of Local Government in NSW*, Cheshire, Melbourne, 1961.

2 JD Fitzgerald, *The Metropolitan Problems of Sydney*, NSW Government Printer, Sydney, 1918.

3 JR Laverty, 'Greater Brisbane: A Response to Problems of Metropolitan Government', *AJPH*, vol. 18, no. 1, April 1972, pp 34–51.

4 *SMH*, 3 February 1931.

5 GR Curnow, The Sydney Municipal Council 1919–1924, BA Hons thesis, University of Sydney, 1957; JDB Miller, 'Greater Sydney 1892–1953', *Public Administration*, June 1954, pp 110–22, September 1954, pp 192–200; *New South Wales Government Year Book*, 1929–30.

6 *SMH*, 22 May 1931.

7 *SMH*, 17 May 1934.

8 *NSWPD*, 29–30 May 1934.

9 *Who's Who in Australia*, Herald and Weekly Times Ltd, Melbourne, 1939.

10 *SMH*, 6 June 1934.

11 *NSWPD*, 23 October 1935.

12 1932 address, reprinted in F.A. Bland, *Government in Australia: Selected Readings*, NSW Government Printer, 2nd edn, Sydney, 1944, p 549.

13 Eric Baume, *I Lived These Years*, Harrap, London, 1941, p 138.

14 *SMH*, 12 July 1941.

15 Miller, 'Greater Sydney 1892–1953'.

16 Miller, 'Greater Sydney 1892–1953'.

17 Shirley Fitzgerald, *Sydney 1842–1992*, H & I, Sydney, 1992.

18 AM Shepherd, *The Story of Petersham 1793–1948*, Petersham Municipal Council, Sydney, 1948. See also R Cashman and C Meander, *Marrickville*, H & I, Sydney, 1990.

19 Peter Harrison, 'Planning the Metropolis: A Case Study', in RS Parker and PN Troy (eds), *The Politics of Urban Growth*, ANUP, Canberra, 1972, p 64.

20 This description of the boundary changes is an approximation only; see Ruth Atkins, 'Sydney', in WA Robson and DE Regan (eds), *Great Cities of the World*, Sage, Beverly Hills, 1972, pp 929–30.

21 Shirley Fitzgerald, *Sydney 1842–1992*, pp 134–35. See also Paul Ashton, *Planning Sydney: The Accidental City Since 1788*, H & I, Sydney, 1993.

22 P Geeves, *A Place of Pioneers: The Centenary History of the Municipality of Ryde*, Ryde Municipal Council, Sydney, 1970.

23 Leonie Sandercock, *Cities for Sale: Property, Politics and Planning in Australia*, MUP, Carlton, 1975, p 203.

24 Atkins, 'Sydney', p 929.

25 See MJ Painter, Local Council Decision Making in Sydney, PhD thesis, ANU, Canberra, 1973.

26 Harrison, 'Planning the Metropolis', p 65.

27 Harrison, 'Planning the Metropolis', p 65.

28 Denis Winston, *Sydney's Great Experiment: The Progress of the Cumberland County Plan*, A & R, Sydney, 1957; Hugh Stretton, *Ideas for Australian Cities*, Orphan Press, Adelaide, 1970.

29 Robert Gibbons, 'Finance & Planning: The Sydney Water Board and the 1959 Green Belt Releases', *Public Administration*, June 1976.

30 Harrison, 'Planning the Metropolis', p 70.

31 JG Starke, *The Law of Town and Country Planning in NSW*, Butterworths, Sydney, 1966, pp 46–7.

32 Ruth Atkins, 'Cities and Politics', in Australian Institute of Political Science, *Australian Cities: Chaos or Planned Growth*, A & R, Sydney, 1966, p 122.

33 Department of Urban Affairs and Planning, *A Framework for Growth and Change: A Review of Strategic Planning*, Department of Urban Affairs and Planning, Sydney, 1997. See also the rather more substantial *Cities for the 21st Century*, Department of Urban Affairs and Planning, Sydney, 1995.

34 MJ Lewis, Populate or Perish: Aspects of Infant and Maternal Welfare in Sydney 1870–1939, PhD thesis, ANU, Canberra, 1976.

35 Quoted in Dan Coward, *Out of Sight: Sydney's Environmental History 1851–1981*, Department of Economic History, ANU, Canberra, 1988, chapter 12 and p 252. See also NG Butlin (ed), *Sydney's Environmental Amenity 1970–1975*, Botany Bay Project Report no. 1, ANUP, Canberra, 1976; NG Butlin (ed), *Factory Waste Potential in Sydney*, Botany Bay Project Report no. 2, ANUP, Canberra, 1977; NG Butlin (ed), *The Impact of Port Botany*, Botany Bay Project Report no. 3, ANUP, Canberra, 1976.

36 Coward, *Out of Sight*, chapter 13.

37 See Tim Bonyhady, 'The Battle for Balmain', in P Troy (ed), *Australian Cities*, CUP, Melbourne 1995, pp 112–41, for an account of the role of the state government, the Land and Environment Court, the State Pollution Control Commission, local government and dissident residents over the fate of industrial land on the Balmain peninsula.

38 See PN Troy, *The Perils of Urban Consolidation*, Federation Press, Sydney, 1996; and P Spearritt and C DeMarco, *Planning Sydney's Future*, A & U, Sydney, 1989, chapter 4.

39 Office of State Revenue, *Annual Report 96/97*, NSW Treasury, Parramatta, 1998. For a discussion of the implications of corporatising the MWSDB (replaced by Sydney Water) see Max Neutze, *Funding Urban Services*, A & U, Sydney, 1997, pp 191–6.

40 *SMH*, 21 July 1911.

41 See G Aplin and J Storey, *Waterfront Sydney 1868–1920*, A & U, Sydney, 1984.

42 Chris Cunneen, 'Hands off the parks!', in J Roe (ed), *Twentieth Century Sydney*, H & I, Sydney,

1980, pp 112–15. For an account of the administration, vegetation and changing use of one of Sydney's major parks, see P Ashton and K Blackmore, *Centennial Park: a history*, UNSWP, Sydney, 1988.

43 Auburn Municipal Council, *Liberty Plains: A History of Auburn, NSW*, Auburn Municipal Council, Sydney, 1986, pp 220–1.

Chapter 9
The dress circle and the stalls

1 WK Hancock, *Australia*, Benn, London, 1930, p 270.

2 Max Kelly, *Paddock Full of Houses: Paddington 1840–1890*, Doak Press, Sydney, 1978, on the role of landlord-developers and their tenants.

3 AA Congalton, *Status Ranking of Sydney Suburbs*, School of Sociology, University of NSW, roneo, 1961; *Status & Prestige in Australia*, Cheshire, Melbourne, 1969. For a critique of this approach and an overview of class structure in this country, see RW Connell and TH Irving, *Class Structure in Australian History*, 2nd edn, Longman Cheshire, Melbourne, 1992.

4 Blair Badcock, *Unfairly Structural Cities*, Blackwell, London, 1984. This book is a critique of a simple physical determinist notion of urban social geography.

5 *How to Know Sydney*, Sydney, ML, 1895, pp 40–1.

6 Sydney Chamber of Commerce, *Annual Report*, 1920.

7 Peter Spearritt, 'Women in Sydney Factories 1920–1950', in Ann Curthoys et al. (eds), *Women at Work*, ASSLH, Sydney, 1975, pp 31–46.

8 ABS, *Census of Population and Housing*, 1996, cat. no. 2017.1, table 4.

9 ABS, *Census 1996*, cat. no. 2017.1, table 8.

10 IH Burnley et al. (eds), *Mobility and Community Change in Australia*, UQP, St Lucia, 1980; IH Burnley, 'Immigration, Ancestry and Residence in Sydney', *Australian Geographical Studies*, April 1994, pp 69–88. See social atlases listed in Further Reading

11 *SMH*, 7 July 1928.

12 *Eastern Suburbs District Guide*, 1923, p 43, held in ML.

13 *SMH*, 7 July 1928.

14 Dan Coward, *Out of Sight: Sydney's Environmental History 1851–1981*, Department of Economic History, ANU, Canberra, 1988, p 244; IS Indulkor, An Examination of the Planning Implications of the Waterfront Industry, Port Facilities and Shipping of Sydney Harbour on the Formulation of a Comprehensive Port Plan, Master of Town & Country Planning thesis, University of Sydney, 1965. The only notable exception to this is North Sydney Council, which encouraged industry until residents, including Harry Seidler, prevailed in the mid-1950s. See MA Jones, *North Sydney 1788–1988*, A & U, Sydney, 1988.

15 *SMH*, 7 July 1928.

16 *NSWSR*, 1930; Coward, *Out of Sight*, pp 242–3.

17 Charles Whitham, The Book of the North Shore, typescript, 1927, pp 7–8, held in ML.

18 For a detailed account of the Sydney property market written prior to the introduction of the capital gains tax, see MT Daly, *Sydney Boom, Sydney Bust*, A & U, Sydney, 1982.

19 Fieldwork undertaken in Neutral Bay 1976–88.

20 The property pages of the Saturday *SMH* report such sales and run a commentary on the comparative cost of houses in particular suburbs.

21 Whitham, The Book of the North Shore, p 8.

22 Held in ML.

23 On evictions see N Wheatley, 'The disinherited of the earth', in J Mackinolty (ed), *The Wasted Years?*, A & U, Sydney, 1981, pp 27–41. For a superb portrait of a middle-class suburb see Gavin Souter, *Mosman*, MUP, Carlton, 1996.

24 Lennie Lower, *Here's Luck*, A & R, Sydney, 1961 (1930), pp 185–98. See entry on Lower in *ADB*, vol. 10.

25 Miles Franklin and Dymphna Cusack, *Pioneers on Parade*, A & R, Sydney, 1939, p 22.

26 Frank Clune, *Try Nothing Twice*, A & R, Sydney, 1961. See entry on Clune in *ADB*, vol. 13.

27 Allan Martin, interview with the author, November 1974.

28 EF Kunz, *The Invaders: Refugee Doctors in Australia*, ANUP, Canberra, 1975; WC Radford and RE Wilkes, *School Leavers in Australia 1971–72*, ACER, Melbourne, 1975; Elaine Thompson, *Fair Enough: Egalitarianism in Australia*, UNSWP, Sydney, 1994.

29 This age group is the closest approximation of an eligible population available from the census.

30 WC Radford, *Non-Government Schools in Australia*, ACER, Melbourne, 1953, p 53.

31 D Burrows, *History of Abbotsleigh*, Abbotsleigh School, Sydney, 1968, p 3.

32 David McNicoll, 'Sydney's Eastern Suburbs: Where Else Could Anyone Live?', *Quadrant*, August 1975, pp 61–7.

33 Brian Penton, *Think—Or Be Damned*, A & R, Sydney, 1941, pp 31–2.

34 CEW Bean, *Here My Son*, A & R, Sydney, 1950, pp 204–5.

35 Most private school histories are little more than hagiography; an exception is Geoffrey Sherington, *Shore: A History of Sydney Church of England Grammar School*, A & U, Sydney, 1983.

36 *Labor Daily*, 17 December 1931; Sol Encel, *Equality and Authority*, Cheshire, Melbourne, 1970, p 158.

37 HM Storey, *A History of North Sydney High School 1912–1962*, North Sydney Boys High, Sydney, 1962 p 45.

38 Encel, *Equality and Authority*, p 280.

39 There is a rich literature on growing up Catholic or Protestant in Sydney. See for instance Edmund Campion's *Rockchoppers: Growing up Catholic in Australia*, Penguin, Ringwood, Vic., 1982. The impact of religion on education is traced in Michael Hogan, *The Catholic Campaign for State Aid*, Catholic Theological Faculty, Sydney, 1978.

40 Paul McGuire, *Australian Journey*, Heinemann, London, 1942, p 120.

41 Leslie Rumble, *Radio Replies*, Missionaries of the Sacred Heart, Sydney, 1934, pp 144–5.

42 Whitham, The Book of the North Shore, p 9.

43 Ruth Park, *The Harp in the South*, A & R, Sydney, 1948, p 1.

44 HA Johnston, *A Seed that Grew: A Hundred Years of Catholic Life on the North Shore, 1856–1956*, Cresta, Sydney, 1956, p 104.

45 See social atlases for the 1971–96 censuses, listed in Further Reading.

46 See Burnley on ethnic location in Sydney in Further Reading.

47 *Australasian*, 11 June 1932.

48 *LD*, 13 June 1932.

49 *Australasian*, 19 March 1932; Weston Bate, Lang Labor and the New Guard, seminar paper, Dept of History, RSSS, ANU, 1969: and Andrew Moore, *The Secret Army and the Premier: Conservative Paramilitary Organisations in NSW 1930–32*, UNSWP, Sydney, 1989.

50 Don Aitkin, *Stability & Change in Australian Politics*, ANUP, Canberra, 1977; David Kemp, *Society and Electoral Behaviour in Australia*, UQP, St Lucia, Qld, 1978.

51 P Fitzgerald, *The Second Sydney Airport Disaster*, H & I, Sydney, 1998.

52 Owen Donald, Health Care Delivery in Sydney, PhD thesis, ANU, Canberra, 1977.

53 WD Borrie, 'The Family', in G Caiger (ed), *The Australian Way of Life*, Heinemann, London, 1953, pp 25–6.

54 MJ Lewis, Populate or Perish, PhD thesis, ANU, Canberra, 1976; Andrea Mant, Comparative Need for Community Health Care Facilities, MA thesis, ANU, Canberra, 1975.

55 DE Rose, *A Study of Juvenile Delinquency in New South Wales*, Department of Labour and Industry, Government Printer, Sydney, 1942.

56 PN Grabosky, *Sydney in Ferment: Crime, Dissent and Official Reaction 1788 to 1973*, ANUP, Canberra, 1977

57 Rose, *Juvenile Delinquency*.

58 Peter Spearritt, 'Sydney's Slums: Middle Class Reformers and the Labor Response', *Labour History*, May 1974, pp 65–81; Hal Kendig, *New Life for Old Suburbs*, A & U, Sydney, 1979.

59 Rob Hillier, *Let's Buy a Terrace House*, Ure Smith, Sydney, 1968, p 7.

60 John Wong, *The Houses of Balmain*, Horwitz, Sydney, 1969; Rob Hillier, *A Place Called Paddington*, Ure Smith, Sydney, 1970; Bernard Smith and Kate Smith, *The Architectural Character of Glebe, Sydney*, University Cooperative Bookshop, Sydney, 1973.

61 Peter Corris, *Matrimonial Causes*, Bantam Books, Sydney 1993, p 101.

62 Kendig, *New Life*.

63 Hugh Stretton *Ideas for Australian Cities*, Orphan Press, Adelaide, 1970, pp 256–7.

64 Griffith Taylor, *Urban Geography*, Methuen, London, 1949, p 203.

65 Sophie Watson, *Accommodating Inequality*, A & U, Sydney, 1978; Chris Paris, *Housing Australia*, Macmillan, Melbourne, 1993.

66 *Truth*, 22 June 1941.

67 JMD Pringle, *Australian Accent*, Chatto & Windus, London, 1958, p 197.

68 *Evening News Yearbook*, 1929, pp 78–80.

69 Mona Ravenscroft, 'The Housing Problem', *Social Horizons*, no. 1, July 1943, pp 50–52.

70 See social atlases 1971–96 listed in Further Reading.

71 Arnold Haskell, *Waltzing Matilda: A Background to Australia*, A & C Black, London, 1940, p 137.

72 Pringle, *Australian Accent*, p 187.

73 Pringle, *Australian Accent*, p 198.

Chapter 10
Cities and suburbs

1 *SMH*, 10 September 1928. On the range and meanings of street life see A Brown May, *Melbourne Street Life*, Australian Scholarly Publishing, Melbourne, 1998.

2 Florence Harding, A Sociological Study of Sydney's Cultural Life, MA thesis, University of Sydney, 1947; *NSWSR*, various issues.
3 *Daily*, Mosman, 18 December 1928.
4 *Great Northern*, Bridge Souvenir, 18 March 1932.
5 Woolworths 36th Annual Report, 1961. See also B Kingston, *Basket, Bag and Trolley; A History of Shopping in Australia*, OUP, Melbourne, 1994.
6 WB Lynch and FA Larcombe, *Randwick 1859–1959*, Randwick Council, Sydney, 1959.
7 *SMH*, 15 February 1933. See H Wolfers, 'The Big Stores between the Wars', in J Roe (ed), *Twentieth Century Sydney*, H & I, Sydney, 1980, pp 18–33.
8 MI Logan, 'Metropolitan Sydney', in *Economic Geography* 40, no. 2, April 1966, p 450. On Grace Brothers, see N Brash, *The Model Store 1885–1985*, Weldon, Sydney, 1985.
9 *SMH*, 15 February 1933.
10 TJ Redmond, *The History of Anthony Hordern and Sons*, Anthony Hordern, Sydney, 1938.
11 *Sands Directory*, Wise's Directories, Sydney, 1933; P Scott, 'The Australian CBD', *Economic Geography*, October 1959, pp 290–314.
12 *SMH*, 12 October 1965. See P Spearritt, 'Suburban Cathedrals: the rise of the drive-in shopping centre', in G Davison et al. (eds), *The Cream Brick Frontier*, Monash Publications in History, Clayton, Vic., 1995, pp 88–107; and Brash, *The Model Store*, pp 268–78.
13 Spearritt and DeMarco, *Planning Sydney's Future*, A & U, Sydney, 1988.
14 See M Christie, *The Sydney Markets 1788–1988*, Sydney Market Authority, Sydney, 1988.
15 Vince Kelly, *The Bogeyman: The Exploits of Sergeant C.J. Chuck, Australia's Most Unpopular Cop*, A & R, Sydney, 1956, pp 50–3.
16 Jon Rose, *At the Cross*, Andre Deutsch, London, 1961, pp 24–5.
17 Florence Harding, A Sociological Study of Sydney's Cultural Life.
18 Donald Horne, *The Australian People: Biography of a Nation*, A & R, Sydney, 1973, p 192.
19 *SMH*, 10 January 1935.
20 Dymphna Cusack and Florence James, *Come in Spinner*, Heinemann, London, 1951, p 347.
21 *NSWYB*, 1959, p 778.
22 See D Collins, *Hollywood Down Under: Australians at the movies, 1896 to the present day*, A & R, Sydney, 1987.
23 J Davidson and P Spearritt, *Holiday Business*, MUP, Melbourne, 2000.
24 Manly Municipal Council, *Official Jubilee Souvenir ... 1877–1927*, MMC, Sydney, 1927.
25 NSW Tourist Guide, *Hotel, Guest House and Tourist Guide to NSW*, Government Tourist Bureau, Sydney, 1929.
26 *LD*, 15 October 1929; *Textile Worker*, September 1936.
27 *LD*, 2 January 1933; Manly Municipal Council, *Official Jubilee Souvenir*.
28 *Building*, February 1935.
29 Dexter Dunphy, *Cliques, Crowds and Gangs*, Cheshire, Melbourne, 1969, pp 108–15
30 *Commonwealth Home*, September 1926, p 27
31 Lynch and Larcombe, *Randwick 1859–1959*.
32 *Guide to the City of Sydney*, NSW Bookstall Co., Sydney, 1938; *Walkabout*, February 1935.
33 On participation rates, see JA Radcliffe et al., *Social Survey of North Sydney Municipality 1951–52*, Department of Social Studies, University of Sydney, Sydney, 1953, ML.
34 See G Karstens, *Holroyd: a Social History of Western Sydney*, UNSWP, Sydney, 1991, pp 239–40.
35 AJ Rose, *How People Live in Australia*, Educational Supply Association, London, 1959.
36 *Commonwealth Home*, February 1927, p 9.
37 HC Brewster and V Luther, *King's Cross Calling*, HC Brewster, Sydney, 1945, pp 5–7.
38 Brewster and Luther, *King's Cross Calling*, p 6.
39 John Walforth, 'Residential Concentration of Non-British Minorities in 19th Century Sydney', *Australian Geographical Studies* 12, no. 2, October 1974.
40 *Hebrew Standard*, 27 July 1939.
41 Brewster and Luther, *King's Cross Calling*, p 114.
42 Kenneth Slessor, *Life at the Cross*, Rigby, Adelaide, 1965.
43 R Ellis and W Stacey, *King's Cross, Sydney*, Nelson, Melbourne, 1971.
44 Australian Bureau of Statistics, 1996 census. See also JE Coughlan and DJ McNamara (eds), *Asians in Australia*, Macmillan, Melbourne, 1997.
45 J Collins and A Castillo, *Cosmopolitan Sydney*, Pluto Press, Sydney, 1998. The quotes come from the front and back covers of this 492-page guide book.
46 I H Burnley, 'The geography of ethnic communities', in S Fitzgerald and G Wotherspoon (eds), *Minorities: cultural diversity in Sydney*, State Library of NSW Press, Sydney, 1995, pp 187, 179.
47 Australian Bureau of Statistics, *Sydney: a social atlas*, 1991 and 1996 censuses.
48 Australian Bureau of Statistics, *Population Distribution, Indigenous Australians*, ABS, Canberra, 1996. For an account of census practices before and after the 1967 referendum, see *NSWYB 1988*, pp 31–2. On western Sydney see Diane Powell, *Out West: perceptions of Sydney's*

western suburbs, A & U, Sydney, 1993, pp 38–42.

49 See Diana Plater, 'Aboriginal people and community in the Leichhardt municipality', in Fitzgerald and Wotherspoon (eds), *Minorities*, pp 35–49.

50 Ray Archer, 'Market factors in the redevelopment of the central business area of Sydney', in PN Troy (ed), *Urban Redevelopment in Australia*, Urban Research Unit, ANU, Canberra, 1968, pp 273–303.

51 Isadore Brodsky, *North Sydney 1788–1962*, North Sydney Council, Sydney, 1963.

52 Full-page advertisement in the *National Times*, 21–26 July 1975.

53 *AFR* news cuttings, 1975–77.

54 Debate raged in the *SMH* in 1997–98.

55 Peter Thomas, *Taming the Concrete Jungle: The Builders Labourers' Story*, Builders Labourers Federation, Sydney, 1973; see also Meredith Burgmann and Verity Burgmann, *Green Bans, Red Union: Environmental Activism and the New South Wales Builders Labourers Federation*, UNSWP, Sydney, 1998.

56 This is best seen in local studies. Among the best on Sydney are G Karskens, *Holyroyd: A Social History of Western Sydney*, UNSWP, Sydney, 1991; and G Souter, *Mosman: a history*, MUP, Melbourne, 1994. See also J McCalman's two studies of working-class and middle-class Melbourne: *Struggletown: public and private life in Richmond 1900–1965*, MUP, Melbourne, 1984, and *Journeyings: the biography of a middle-class generation*, MUP, Melbourne, 1993; and G Bolton, *Daphne Street: the biography of an Australian community*, Fremantle Arts Centre Press, Fremantle, WA, 1997.

Chapter 11
Demolition and preservation

1 This account of demolitions is based on Historic Houses Trust of NSW, *Demolished for the Public Good*, Historic Houses Trust of NSW, Sydney, 1988, which includes an excellent catalogue (pp 67–96) of major demolitions in Sydney. See also J Hughes, *Demolished Houses of Sydney*, Historic Houses Trust of NSW, Sydney 1999. The scale of the building boom (and by implication, the extent of demolition) is explained in MT Daly, *Sydney Boom, Sydney Bust*, A & U, Sydney, 1982. See also M Simpson, *Old Sydney Buildings: A Social History*, Kangaroo Press, Sydney, 1985.

2 On gas plants see R Broomham, *First Light: 150 years of gas*, H & I, Sydney, 1987. On power stations see G Wilkenfeld, The Electrification of the Sydney Energy System 1881–1986, PhD thesis, Macquarie University, Sydney, 1989.

3 See E Balint, T Howell and V Smyth, *Warehouses and Woolstores of Victorian Sydney*, OUP, Melbourne, 1982.

4 Hardy Wilson, *The Cow Pasture Road*, Art in Australia, Sydney, 1920.

5 CH Bertie, *Old Colonial Byways*, Ure Smith, Sydney, 1928; and Quinton Tidswell, *Sydney of Yesterday* , self-published, Sydney, 1933.

6 See Max Kelly, *Anchored in a Small Cove: A History and Archaeology of The Rocks, Sydney*, Sydney Cove Authority, Sydney, 1997.

7 Mrs AG Foster, *Odd Bits of Old Sydney*, Tyrell's, Sydney, 1921, pp 1–3, 39.

8 Aidan de Brune, *The Dagger and Cord*, Cornstalk, Sydney, 1927, pp 152–3, 80.

9 *SMH*, 4 February 1937. This account draws on P Spearritt, 'Demolishing Sydney: Property Owners versus Public Rights', *Heritage Australia*, Winter 1985, pp 2–5; and P Barnett-Spies, The Early Years of the Preservation Movement in NSW 1900–1939, MA thesis, University of Sydney, 1989.

10 *SMH*, 17 October 1938.

11 *SMH*, 14 October 1938.

12 *SMH*, 10 November 1939.

13 Morton Herman, *The Early Australian Architects and their Work*, A & R, Sydney, 1954; Morton Herman, *The Architecture of Victorian Sydney*, A & R, Sydney, 1956.

14 *NSWPD*, 15 March 1960.

15 *SMH*, 5 April 1956.

16 *SMH*, 12 May 1962.

17 Gavin Souter and Quinton Davis, *Sydney*, A & R, Sydney, 1965, p 36.

18 *National Trust Bulletin*, August 1964.

19 Cumberland County Council, *Historic Buildings Central Area of Sydney*, CCC, Sydney, 1962, pp 34–5; State Planning Authority, *Hyde Park Barracks*, A & R, Sydney, 1965, pp 3–5.

20 On the attitude of the *Herald* in 1972 see Peter Thomas, *Taming the Concrete Jungle: The Builders Labourers' Story*, Builders Labourers Federation, Sydney, 1973, pp 117–18, 122–4; see also Meredith Burgmann and Verity Burgmann, *Green Bans, Red Union*, UNSWP, Sydney, 1998.

21 *NSWPD*, 23 November 1977.

22 *NSWPD*, 23 November 1977.

23 *Annual Report*, Heritage Council of NSW, Sydney, 1998.

24 See for instance P Cuffley, *Australian Houses of the Twenties and Thirties* and *Australian Houses of*

the Forties and Fifties, both publ. by Five Mile Press, Knoxfield, Vic., 1993. See also R Apperly, R Irving and P Reynolds, *Identifying Australian Architecture*, A & R, Sydney, 1989.

25 For a discussion of some of these issues see Graeme Davison and Chris McConville (eds), *A Heritage Handbook*, A & U, Sydney, 1991; J Rickard and P Spearritt (eds), *Packaging the Past*, MUP, Carlton, Vic., 1991; and MC Boyer, *The City of Collective Memory*, MIT Press, Cambridge, Mass., 1996.

Chapter 12
Sydney, Australia and the world

1 See the entries on 'Suburbs' and each of the capital cities in G Davison, J Hirst and S Macintyre (eds), *The Oxford Companion to Australian History*, OUP, Melbourne, 1998.

2 'Australia', in *Holiday* (published in Philadelphia), vol. 8, no. 5, November 1950, p 99.

3 D Williams, *Industrial Victoria*, State Electricity Commission of Victoria, Melbourne, 1930.

4 Quoted in Stephen Salsbury and Kay Sweeney, *The Bull, the Bear and the Kangaroo: The History of the Sydney Stock Exchange*, A & U, Sydney, 1988, pp 450–2, on which I base this account.

5 This and subsequent observations draw on J Davidson (ed), *The Sydney–Melbourne Book*, A & U, Sydney, 1986. See also DC Rich, *The Industrial Geography of Australia*, Croom Helm, London, 1987, pp 135–7.

6 G Boynton (ed), *Guide to the Business Cities of the World*, Simon & Schuster, London, 1988. And see R Jureidini and E Healy, 'A decade of change in industry employment: Melbourne and Sydney compared', in *People and Place*, vol. 6, no. 3, 1998, pp. 54–68.

7 P Spearritt, 'New South Wales—the non-existent state?', *Meanjin* 2/1980, pp 139–49.

8 J Davidson and P Spearritt, *Holiday Business*, MUP, Melbourne, 2000.

9 *Australian Women's Weekly*, March 1988. See also P Spearritt, 'Celebration of a Nation', *Australian Historical Studies*, October 1988, pp 3–20.

10 *Australia*, p 100.

11 G Souter, *Mosman: a history*, MUP, Melbourne, 1994, pp 321–7.

12 M Steketee and M Cockburn, *Wran: An Unauthorised Biography*, A & U, Sydney, 1986, pp 37–8 and 187–227.

13 Trevor Sykes, *The Bold Riders: Behind Australia's Corporate Collapses*, A & U, Sydney, 2nd edn, 1996. See also H Armstrong and D Gross, *Tricontinental: The Rise and Fall of a Merchant Bank*, MUP, Carlton, Vic., 1995, pp.220–221,259.

14 *AJPH* political chronicle 1986–87.

15 See *Age*, 27 November 1997 for a comparison of the Sydney and Melbourne casinos.

16 See D Hickie, *The Prince and the Premier*, A & R, Sydney, 1985; and G Reading, *High Climbers: Askin and Others*, John Ferguson, Sydney, 1989.

17 *Australian Encyclopedia*, sixth edn, 1996, vol. 5. See also accounts in *AJPH* political chronicle 1988–90; and M Gleeson, T Allan and M Williams, *An Act of Corruption? Nick Greiner's Years in Power and His Unorthodox Demise*, ABC Books, Sydney, 1992.

18 See A Green, *1997/98 NSW Redistribution: Analysis of Final Boundaries*, NSW Parliamentary Library, Sydney, 1998.

19 Gary Wotherspoon, *City of the Plain: History of a Gay Subculture*, H & I, Sydney,1991, pp 209–10.

20 *AFR*, 3 August 1998.

21 John Slee, 'Why the showground should always belong to the people', *SMH*, 9 November 1995; see also *AJPH* political chronicle, 1995.

22 *Age* and *SMH*, 31 July – 1 August 1998.

23 See R McGeoch, *The Bid: How Australia Won the 2000 Games*, Heinemann, Melbourne, 1994. The Sydney and Salt Lake City bid sagas ran in the *SMH* and the *Age* from March to June 1999. On tourism see *The Olympic Effect*, Tourism Forecasting Council, Canberra, 1998.

24 Hugh Stretton, *Ideas for Australian Cities*, Adelaide, 1975, p 274.

25 'The Rise of Western Sydney', in P Spearritt and C DeMarco, *Planning Sydney's Future*, A & U, Sydney, 1988.

26 ABS, 1996 census.

27 J Collins and A Castillo, *Cosmopolitan Sydney*, Pluto Press, Sydney, 1998, pp 5–13.

28 On planning for multicultural cities see Leonie Sandercock, *Towards Cosmopolis*, John Wiley, London, 1998.

Further reading

Further reading lists books and articles that are usually available in major libraries. Many of the sources drawn on and listed in the notes are out of print and only available in the Mitchell Library, which contains a magnificent record of the history of Sydney in text, map and photographic form, as do the State Archives of NSW. Most local councils and/or their libraries have good to excellent records. Among the most outstanding are the City of Sydney archives and the Stanton Library in North Sydney.

Many of the most important works about Sydney, for instance JD Fitzgerald's *Greater Sydney and Greater Newcastle* (1906) and Denis Winston's *Sydney's Great Experiment* (1957) have long been out of print and are now rare books, as is the *County of Cumberland Planning Scheme Report* (1948), the most impressive planning document ever produced on Sydney.

This book draws on a rich literature about cities, how they have evolved and how they are experienced.

Adonis, A and S Pollard, *A Class Act: The Myth of Britain's Classless Society*, Penguin, Harmondsworth, Middlesex, 1998.

Badcock, B, *Unfairly Structured Cities*, Blackwell, Oxford, 1984.

Boyer, MC, *The City of Collective Memory: Its Historical Imagery and Architectural Entertainments*, MIT Press, Cambridge, Mass., 1996.

Castells, M, *The Informational City*, Blackwell, Cambridge, 1989.

Davis, M, *City of Quartz: Excavating the Future in Los Angeles*, Verso, New York, 1990.

Garreau, J, *Edge City: Life on the New Frontier*, Doubleday, New York, 1988.

Hall, Peter, *World Cities*, Weidenfeld & Nicolson, London, 1971.

Jacobs, AB, *Great Streets*, MIT Press, Cambridge, Mass., 1993.

Moorhouse, G, *Imperial City: The Rise and Rise of New York*, Hodder & Stoughton, Sevenoaks, Kent, 1988.

Mumford, Lewis, *The City in History*, Secker & Warburg, London, 1961.

—— *The Highway and the City*, Secker & Warburg, London, 1964.

Sudjic, D, *The 100 Mile City*, Andre Deutsch, London 1992.

Urry, J, *Consuming Places*, Routledge, London, 1995.

General works about Australian cities

For the relationship between Sydney and New South Wales see *Atlas of NSW*, Central Mapping Authority, Bathurst, 1987. For the place of Sydney in Australia see *Australians: a historical atlas*, one of the 10-volume series Australians: a historical library, Fairfax, Syme & Weldon, 1987. Held in most major libraries, the series includes volumes on *Historical Statistics* and *Events and Places*.

Bird, J, *Seaport Gateways of Australia*, OUP, London, 1968.

Blainey, G, *The Tyranny of Distance: How Distance Shaped Australia's History*, Sun Books, Melbourne, 1966.

Burnley, IH, *The Australian Urban System*, Longman Cheshire, Melbourne, 1980.

Burnley, IH and J Forrest (eds), *Living in Cities*, A & U, Sydney, 1985.

Cannon, M, *Life in the Cities, Australia in the Victorian Age*, vol. 3, Nelson, Melbourne, 1975.

Cardew, R, J Langdale and D Rich (eds), *Why Cities Change*, A & U, Sydney, 1982.

Davidson, J (ed), *The Sydney Melbourne Book*, A & U, Sydney, 1986 (includes chapters on education, religion, art, culture, crime and sport).

Davidson, J and P Spearritt, *Holiday Business: Tourism in Australia 1870–2000*, MUP, Melbourne, 2000.

Davison, G, *The Rise and Fall of Marvellous Melbourne*, MUP, Melbourne, 1978.

Docherty, JC, *Newcastle: The Making of an Australian City*, H & I, Sydney, 1983.

Forster, C, *Australian Cities: Continuity and Change*, OUP, Melbourne, 1995.

Freestone, R, *Model Communities: The Garden City Movement in Australia*, Nelson, Melbourne, 1988.

Frost, L, *The New Urban Frontier*, UNSWP, Sydney, 1991.

Gibson, K and S Watson, *Metropolis Now: Planning and the Urban in Contemporary Australia*, Pluto Press, Sydney, 1994.

Halligan, I, and C Paris (eds), *Australian Urban Politics*, Cheshire, Melbourne, 1984.

Hugo, CJ, *Australia's Changing Population*, OUP, Melbourne, 1986.

Kendig, H, *New Life for Old Suburbs: Post War Land Use and Housing in the Australian Inner City*, A & U, Sydney, 1979.

Johnson, LC (ed), *Suburban Dreaming*, Deakin University Press, Geelong, Vic., 1994.

McLoughlin, JB and M Huxley (eds), *Urban Planning in Australia: Critical Readings*, Longman Cheshire, Melbourne, 1986.

Neutze, Max, *Urban Development in Australia*, A & U, Sydney, 1982 (1978).

—— *Australian Urban Policy*, A & U, Sydney, 1978.

Parker, RS & P Troy (eds), *The Politics of Urban Growth*, ANUP, Canberra, 1972.

Powell, J M, *An Historical Geography of Modern Australia*, CUP, Cambridge, 1988.

Rich, DC, RV Cardew and JV Langdale, *Urban Australia: Planning Issues and Policies*, Nelson, Melbourne, 1986.

Sandercock, L, *Cities for Sale: Property, Politics and Urban Planning in Australia*, MUP, Melbourne, 1975.

Stannage, CT, *The People of Perth: A Social History of Western Australia's Capital City*, Carroll's, Perth, 1979.

Stretton, H, *Ideas for Australian Cities*, Georgian House, Melbourne, 1975 (1970).

Stillwell, F, *Australian Urban and Regional Development*, ANZ Book Co., Sydney, 1974

—— *Reshaping Australia: Urban Problems and Policies*, Pluto Press, Sydney, 1993.

Sulman, J, *An Introduction to the Study of Town Planning in Australia*, NSW Government Printer, Sydney, 1921.

Troy, P (ed), *Urban Development in Australia*, Urban Research Unit, ANU, Canberra, 1967.

—— *Australian Cities: Issues, Strategies and Policies for Urban Australia in the 1990s*, CUP, Melbourne, 1995.

—— *Technological Change and the City*, Federation Press, Sydney, 1995.

Walter, J, H Hinsley and P Spearritt (eds), *Changing Cities: Reflections on Britain and Australia*, Sir Robert Menzies Centre for Australian Studies, London, 1995.

General works about pre-1900 Sydney

Aplin, G, and J Storey, *Waterfront Sydney 1860–1920*, A & U, Sydney, 1984.

Aplin, G (ed) *A Difficult Infant: Sydney Before Macquarie*, UNSWP, Sydney, 1988.

Birch, A, and D Macmillan, *The Sydney Scene 1788–1960*, MUP, Melbourne, 1962.

Carter, P, *The Road to Botany Bay: An Essay in Spatial History*, Faber, London, 1987.

Fitzgerald, S, *Rising Damp: Sydney 1870–90*, OUP, Melbourne, 1987.

Jeans, DN, *An Historical Geography of NSW to 1901*, Reed, Sydney, 1972.

Johnson, L, *Gaslight Sydney*, A & U, Sydney, 1984.

Karskens, G, *The Rocks: Life in Early Sydney*, MUP, Melbourne, 1997.

Kelly, M (ed), *Nineteenth Century Sydney: Essays in Urban History*, Sydney University Press, Sydney, 1978.

Mayne, AJC, *Fever, Squalor and Vice: Sanitation and Social Policy in Victorian Sydney*, UQP, St Lucia, Qld, 1982.

General works about twentieth-century Sydney

(See also the section on local history for studies of particular municipalities)

Aird, MV, *The Water Supply, Sewerage and Drainage of Sydney*, MWSDB, Sydney, 1961.

Ashton, P, *The Accidental City: Planning Sydney Since 1788*, H & I, Sydney, 1993.

Coombs, A, *Sex and Anarchy: The Life and Death of the Sydney Push*, Penguin, Ringwood, Vic., 1996.

Curson, P and K McCracken, *Plague in Sydney: The Anatomy of an Epidemic*, UNSWP, Sydney, 1982.

Daly, MT, *Sydney Boom Sydney Bust: The City and Its Property Market, 1850–1981*, A & U, Sydney, 1982.

Fitzgerald, P, *The Great Airport Fiasco*, H & I, Sydney, 1998.

Fitzgerald, S, *Sydney 1842–1992*, H & I, Sydney, 1992 (this is a study of the changing territory under the Sydney Municipal Council, but many of its themes are relevant to the entire metropolis).

Kelly, M (ed), *Sydney: City of Suburbs*, UNSWP, Sydney, 1987.

Kirkpatrick, P, *The Sea Coast of Bohemia: Literary Life in Sydney's Roaring Twenties*, UQP, St Lucia, Qld, 1992.

Martin, L and P Spearritt, *A History of Water Management in NSW 1788–1980*, NSW Water Management Audit, working paper no. 2, Sydney, 1984.

Messent, D, *Opera House Act One*, Messent, Sydney, 1997 (includes bibliography of previous books on the Opera House).

Murphy, P and S Watson, *Surface City: Sydney at the Millennium*, Pluto Press, Sydney, 1997.

Parker, RS, *The Government of NSW*, UQP, St Lucia, Qld, 1978.

Pollon, F, *The Book of Sydney Suburbs*, Cornstalk, Sydney, 1996 (1988). Useful alphabetical listing.

Powell, D, *Out West: Perceptions of Sydney's Western Suburbs*, A & U, Sydney, 1993.

Proudfoot, P, *Seaport Sydney: The Making of the City Landscape*, UNSWP, Sydney, 1996.

Roe, J (ed), *Twentieth Century Sydney: Studies in Urban and Social History*, H & I, Sydney, 1980.

Souter, G and Q Davis, *Sydney*, A & R, Sydney, 1965.

Spearritt, P, *Sydney Since the Twenties*, H & I, Sydney, 1978.

—— *The Sydney Harbour Bridge: A Life*, A & U, Sydney, 1982.

Spearritt, P and C DeMarco, *Planning Sydney's Future*, A & U, Sydney, 1988.

Wotherspoon, G, *City of the Plain: History of a Gay Sub-culture*, H & I, Sydney, 1991.

Aborigines

There is not yet a general history of Aborigines in Sydney in the twentieth century. The most extensive research on Aboriginal occupation of the Sydney region prior to the coming of Europeans and in the nineteenth century is to be found in unpublished environmental and heritage reports on particular sites. Some of these are held by the Heritage Council of NSW and the NSW National Parks Service but others are only to be found in the private archives of consulting firms. Copyright in these reports is held either by those firms or the development companies or government departments that commissioned them. This is regrettable. A public archive of these reports should be created.

Mulvaney, J and P White (eds), *Australians till 1788*, Fairfax, Syme & Weldon, Sydney, 1987.

Plater, D, 'Aboriginal people and community in the Leichhardt Municipality', in S Fitzgerald and G Wotherspoon (eds), *Minorities: Cultural Diversity in Sydney*, State Library of NSW Press, Sydney, 1995.

Turbet, P, *The Aborigines of the Sydney District Before 1788*, Kangaroo Press, Kenthurst, NSW, 1989.

Willey, K, *When the Sky Fell Down: The Destruction of the Tribes of the Sydney Region 1788–1850s*, Collins, Sydney, 1979.

Architecture, housing and built heritage

Extensive records on Sydney's buildings are held by the National Trust of NSW (headquarters at Observatory Hill) and the Australian Heritage Commission's Register of the National Estate. Australia's pre-eminent architectural historians, Robyn Boyd, Morton Herman and JM Freeland have written extensively about Sydney's buildings and their architects. The Heritage Council of NSW holds heritage studies of many suburbs and precincts, as well as reports on individual buildings, along with the published reports of inquiries under the Heritage Act and the Environment and Planning Act.

Boyd, R, *Australia's Home: Its Origins, Builders and Occupiers*, Penguin, Ringwood, Vic., 1968 (1952).

Fraser, D (ed), *Sydney from Settlement to City: An Engineering History of Sydney*, Engineers Australia, Sydney, 1989

Freeland, JM, *The Australian Pub*, MUP, Melbourne, 1966.

—— *Architecture in Australia: A History*, Penguin, Ringwood, Vic., 1972 (1968).

Freestone, Robert, 'From Icons to Institutions: heritage conservation in Sydney', *International Journal of Heritage Studies*, vol. 1, no. 2, 1995, pp 79–90.

Haskell, J, *Sydney Architecture*, UNSWP, Sydney, 1997.

Herman, M, *The Architecture of Victorian Sydney*, A & R, Sydney, 1956.

Hughes, J (ed), *Demolished Houses of Sydney*, Historic Houses Trust of NSW, Sydney, 1999.

Irvin, E, *Sydney As It Might Have Been*, Alpha Books, Sydney, 1974.

Jahn, G, *Sydney Architecture*, Watermark Press, Sydney, 1997 (organised around five chronological themes

from 1790–1996, listing 632 buildings with their architects).
Paris, C, *Housing Australia*, Macmillan, Melbourne, 1993.
Rickard, J and P Spearritt (eds), *Packaging the Past? Public Histories*, MUP, Melbourne, 1991.
Simpson, Margaret, *Old Sydney Buildings: A Social History*, Kangaroo Press, Sydney, 1995 (covers the city, inner suburbs, eastern suburbs and north shore).
Spearritt, P, 'Sydney's slums: middle class reformers and the Labor response', *Labor History*, May 1974, pp 65–81.
Sydney Since the Opera House: An Architectural Walking Guide, Royal Australian Institute of Architects (NSW), Sydney, 1990.
Watson, S, *Accommodating Inequality: Gender and Housing*, A & U, Sydney, 1988.
Webber, P (ed), *The Design of Sydney: Three Decades of Change in the City Centre*, Law Book Co., Sydney, 1988.

AUTOBIOGRAPHY, BIOGRAPHY, ORAL HISTORY AND FAMILY HISTORY

The best single source for the architects, politicians, business people, even some of the underbelly of Sydney society is the multi-volume *Australian Dictionary of Biography* published by Melbourne University Press and also available on CD Rom. For politicians see H Radi, E Hinton and P Spearritt, *Biographical Register of the NSW Parliament 1901–1970*, ANUP, Canberra, 1979. There are hundreds of biographies of people who have lived part or all of their lives in Sydney, from judges and novelists (e.g. David Marr's studies of Garfield Barwick and Patrick White) to poets (G Dutton's book on Kenneth Slessor) and artists, archbishops and crooks. Most of Sydney's major state and federal political leaders, from Lang, Askin and Wran to Whitlam, Keating and Howard have been the subject of one or more biographical studies. Autobiographical works range from the political posturing of Jack Lang (*I Remember, The Turbulent Years*) to the feminist political activism of Jessie Street (*Truth or Repose*) to the reflective volumes of Donald Horne. This list is simply indicative, as a comprehensive bibliography would run to many entries.

Campion, E, *Rockchoppers: Growing up Catholic in Australia*, Penguin, Ringwood, Vic., 1982.
Dalton, R, *Aunts up the Cross*, Heinemann, Kew, Vic., 1997 (1967).
Gill, Lydia, *My Town: Sydney in the 1930s*, State Library of NSW Press, Sydney, 1993.
Harmer, R, *Growing Up at Government House*, A & R, Sydney, 1989.
James, Clive *Unreliable Memoirs*, Jonathan Cape, London, 1980.
Langford, Ruby *Don't Take Your Love to Town*, Penguin, Ringwood, Vic., 1988.
Lindsay, Jack, *The Roaring Twenties: Literary Life in Sydney NSW 1921–26*, Bodley Head, London, 1960.
Radi, H and P Spearritt (eds), *Jack Lang*, H & I, Sydney, 1977.
Shields, J (ed), *All our Labours: Oral Histories of Working Life in Twentieth Century Sydney*, UNSWP, Sydney, 1992.

EMPLOYMENT, MANUFACTURING, RETAILING, SERVICE INDUSTRIES

(See the Local History section for accounts of particular suburbs. Many manufacturing and retailing firms have commissioned histories of their organisations.)

Broomham, R, *First Light: 150 Years of Gas*, H & I, Sydney, 1987.
Kingston, B, *Basket, Bag and Trolley: A*

History of Shopping in Australia, OUP, Melbourne, 1994.

Linge, G, *Industrial Awakening: A Geography of Australian Manufacturing, 1788–1890*, ANUP, Canberra, 1979.

Rich, DC, *The Industrial Geography of Australia*, Croom Helm, London, 1987.

Spearritt, P, 'Suburban Cathedrals: the rise of the drive-in shopping centre', in G Davison et.al. (eds), *The Cream Brick Frontier*, Monash Publications in History, Clayton, Vic., 1995, pp 88–107.

Environment and ecology

Benson, D and J Howell, *Taken for Granted: The Bushland of Sydney and Its Suburbs*, Kangaroo Press, Sydney, 1990.

Butlin, NG (ed), *Sydney's Environmental Amenity 1970–1975*, ANUP, Canberra, 1976.

Coward, DH, *Out of Sight: Sydney's Environmental History 1851–1981*, Department of Economic History, ANU, Canberra, 1988 (the major study, but virtually unobtainable).

Taylor, G, *Sydneyside Scenery and How it Came About*, A & R, Sydney, 1958.

Ethnic groups and immigration

Burnley, IH, 'The geography of ethnic communities', in S Fitzgerald and G Wotherspoon (eds), *Minorities: Cultural Diversity in Sydney*, UNSWP, Sydney, 1995, pp 174–91 (lists major articles on the location of particular ethnic groups to 1995).

Collins, J and A Castillo, *Cosmopolitan Sydney: Explore the World in One City*, Pluto Press, Sydney, 1998.

Fitzgerald, S, *Red Tape, Gold Scissors: The Story of Sydney's Chinese*, State Library of NSW, Sydney, 1998.

Jupp, J, *Arrivals and Departures*, Cheshire-Lansdowne, Melbourne, 1966.

Jupp, J (ed), *The Australian People: An Encylopedia of the Nation, Its People and Their Origins*, A & R, Sydney, 1988 (new edition in preparation).

Finance

Most of the literature on finance and banking is at the national or international level. However, as many banks and insurance companies started in Sydney (the Australian Mutual Provident Society (AMP), the Bank of NSW, now Westpac, the Commercial Banking Company of Sydney Ltd, subsumed within the National Australia Bank), their histories are often worth consulting. The *Australian Financial Review* has been published in Sydney since 1951.

Neutze, Max, *Funding Urban Services: Options for Physical Infrastructure*, A & U, Sydney, 1997.

Salsbury, S and K Sweeney, *The Bull, the Bear and the Kangaroo: The History of the Sydney Stock Exchange*, A & U, Sydney, 1988.

Guides to Sydney

The many guides, street directories and handbooks used for this book are listed in the notes. Guides to Sydney are now published in almost all the major international series, from Frommer (first published 1989) to Lonely Planet and the Rough Guide. Some of the more notable guides to Sydney produced over the past 30 years, which take both the history and topography of the city as their starting point, include:

Dirks, J, *Sydney Downtown*, Kangaroo Press, Sydney, 1993

DeMarco, C, B Riera and P Spearritt, *Aird's Guide to Sydney*, Aird Books, Melbourne, 1991.

Huie, J, *Untourist Sydney*, Untourist Co., Balmain, NSW, 1995.

Park, Ruth, *The Companion Guide to Sydney*, Collins, Sydney, 1973 (a geographically organised 448-page guide).
Stone, R, *Sydney: The Harbour City Handbook*, A & U, Sydney, 1981.

LOCAL AND SUBURBAN HISTORY

See Eslick, J Hughes and RI Jack, *Bibliography of NSW Local History*, UNSWP, Sydney, 1987, for works published before 1982. The history of local government is outlined by FA Larcombe in a three-volume study, including *The Advancement of Local Government in NSW 1906 to the Present*, Sydney University Press, Sydney, 1978.

The local histories directly drawn on in this book, as either anonymous efforts at local boosting or as commissioned histories, are to be found in the notes. Most local histories published since the late 1980s are professional in tone and reliable in their evidence and their analysis. Many of these books have been written by members of the Professional Historians Association of NSW. But that is not to suggest that works written before 1980 are not worth consulting. They are usually less critical, but sometimes more illuminating accounts of suburban 'progress'.

Beasley, M, *Sydney Town Hall: A Social History*, H & I, Sydney, 1998.
Cashman, R and C Meader, *Marrickville: Rural Outpost to Inner City: A Social History of Marrickville and the Former Municipalities of Newtown, Camperdown, Petersham and St Peters*, H & I, Sydney, 1990.
Karskens, G, *Holroyd: A Social History of Western Sydney*, UNSWP, Sydney 1991.
Kass, T, C Liston and J McClymont, *Parramatta: A Past Revealed*, Parramatta City Council, Parramatta, NSW, 1996.
Kelly, M, *Paddock Full of Houses: Paddington 1840–1890*, Doak Press, Sydney, 1978.
Keating, C, *Surry Hills: The City's Backyard*, H & I, Sydney, 1991.
—— *On the Frontier: A Social History of Liverpool*, H & I, Sydney, 1996.
Fitzgerald, S, *Chippendale: Beneath the Factory Wall*, H & I, Sydney, 1990
——*Sydney 1842–1992*, H & I, Sydney, 1992.
Fitzgerald, S and H Golder, *Pyrmont and Ultimo: Under Siege*, H&I, Sydney, 1994.
Fitzgerald, S, and C Keating, *Millers Point: The Urban Village*, H&I, Sydney, 1991.
Liston, C, *Campbelltown: The Bicentennial History*, City of Campbelltown, Campbelltown, NSW, 1988.
Solling, M and P Reynolds, *Leichhardt: On the Margins of the City: A Social History of Leichhardt and the Former Municipalities of Annandale, Balmain and Glebe*, A & U, Sydney, 1997.
Souter, G, *Mosman: A History*, MUP, Melbourne, 1994.

METROPOLITAN AND TOWN PLANNING

For a comprehensive listing of key documents until 1988, see P Spearritt and C DeMarco, *Planning Sydney's Future*, A & U, Sydney, 1988, pp 141–4.

Ashton, N, *From Village to Metropolis: A Brief Review of Planning in the Sydney Region*, Department of Environment and Planning, Sydney, 1984.
Ashton, P, *Planning Sydney: The Accidental City since 1788*, H & I, Sydney, 1993.
Cities for the 21st Century, Department of Urban Affairs and Planning, Sydney, 1995.
Coleman, J, *Postwar Planning in the County of Cumberland*, Planning Research Centre, University of Sydney, Sydney, 1968.
Cumberland County Council, *The*

Planning Scheme for the County of Cumberland, NSW Government Printer, Sydney, 1948.
Department of Environment and Planning, *Sydney Into its Third Century: Metropolitan Strategy for the Sydney Region*, Department of Environment and Planning, Sydney, 1988.
Meyer, B, 'Metropolitan Strategies for Sydney 1909–2009', in R Freestone (ed), *Spirited Cities*, Federation Press, Sydney, 1993, pp 209–24.
State Planning Authority, *Sydney Region Outline Plan 1970–2000*, State Planning Authority, Sydney, 1968.
Winston, D, *Sydney's Great Experiment: The Progress of the Cumberland County Plan*, A & R, Sydney, 1957.

NEWSPAPERS AND PERIODICALS

Sydney houses some of Australia's oldest newspapers and periodicals, including the *Sydney Morning Herald* (founded 1842, 1831 as the *Sydney Herald*) and the *Bulletin* (founded 1880) and is the home of many best-selling magazines including the *Sydney Mail* (1868–1938), the *Australian Women's Weekly* (1933), major financial papers, including the *Australian Financial Review* (1951) and a thriving foreign language press. Sydney's rich newspaper history, accounted for in Walker's two volumes, includes the *Labor Daily* (1924–40) and the satirical *Smith's Weekly* (1919–50). *Sydney's Century* also draws on some short-lived but opinionated journals including the *Lone Hand* (1907–20), *Sydney Opinion* (1929–30) and upper middle-class journals including the *Home* (1920–42). Both the Mitchell Library and the National Library in Canberra hold scores of useful trade magazines from the *Journal of the Retail Traders Association of NSW* to the *Real Estate Journal* and the *Employers Review*. Many trade unions also produced periodicals.

Blaikie, George, *Remember 'Smith's Weekly'*, Rigby, Adelaide, 1966.
Greenop, F, *History of Magazine Publishing in Australia*, KG Murray, Sydney, 1947 (a great source, long out of print, by the former editor of *Man* magazine).
Inglis, KS (ed), *Nation: The Life of an Independent Journal of Opinion 1958–1972*, MUP, Melbourne, 1989.
Rolfe, P, *The Journalistic Javelin: An Illustrated History of the 'Bulletin'*, Wildcat Press, Sydney, 1979.
Souter, G, *Heralds and Angels: The House of Fairfax*, Penguin, Ringwood, Vic., 1992.
Walker, RB, *The Newspaper Press in New South Wales 1803–1920*, Sydney University Press, Sydney, 1996.
——*Yesterday's News: A History of the Newspaper Press in NSW from 1920 to 1945*, Sydney University Press, Sydney 1980.

NOVELS SET IN SYDNEY

The best starting point is Patricia Holt's *A City in the Mind: Sydney Imagined by its Writers*, A & U, Sydney, 1983. Hundreds of novels written in the twentieth century have Sydney as their primary setting. Novels quoted in *Sydney's Century* are cited in the endnotes.

PHOTOGRAPHY, PAINTING, CARTOONS AND PICTORIAL WORKS

Alongside the work of famous photographers (Hurley, Cazneaux, Dupain, Moore) are hundreds of coffee table photographic books produced, usually in colour, since the early 1970s. They usually have minimal and frequently unreliable text but some are useful sources for studying the city. Some of the major photographers and artists who have depicted Sydney are the subject of biographical studies, often heavily illustrated. Most cartoons about Sydney and carricatures of its citizens were first published in newspapers, including the *Bulletin*, the *Sydney Morning Herald* and *Smith's Weekly*. Since the early 1950s some of these cartoons have been collected in book form, including works by Mercier, Petty and Molnar. Sources for their work will be found in captions to illustrations.

Brooks, W and N Sutherland, *Sydney: An Aerial Close-up*, Colour Library, Guildford, England, 1986 (160 pp of large format aerial photographs).

Hall, G and N Brash, *Above Sydney*, Weldon, Sydney, 1984 (especially for the pattern of suburban development).

Hurley, Frank, *Sydney: A Camera Study*, A & R, Sydney, 1958.

McCrath, S and R Walker, *Sydney Harbour Paintings from 1794*, Jacaranda, Brisbane, 1979.

Mourot, S, *This Was Sydney: A Pictorial History from 1788 to the Present Time*, Ure Smith, Sydney, 1969.

Underhill, N, *Making Australian Art 1916–49: Sydney Ure Smith, Patron and Publisher*, OUP, Melbourne, 1991.

Statistics and social atlases

The *NSW Statistical Register* (1880–1976) is a superb source of information about Sydney, as is the *NSW Yearbook*, which first appeared in 1904. It remains a major source until the late 1980s, including the bicentennial volume (1988). In the 1990s the yearbook has been reduced to a compilation of public relations handouts from government departments and is almost useless as a source. A handy starting place for statistics about Sydney and NSW is JC Docherty, *Selected Social Statistics of NSW 1861–1976*, History Project Incorporated, Kensington, NSW, 1982. The social atlases cover, in computer map form, core aspects of the city from the five-yearly census of people and dwellings, from 1971 to the present. They include age, gender, housing, employment and unemployment, birthplace, income (from 1976), occupation, education and religious affiliation.

Davis, JR and P Spearritt, *Sydney at the Census, 1971: A Social Atlas*, Urban Research Unit, ANU, Canberra, 1974.

Horvath, R and D Tait, *Sydney: A Social Atlas* [1981 census] ABS, Canberra, 1984.

Horvath, R, G Harrison and R Dowling, *Sydney: A Social Atlas* [1986 census], Sydney University Press, Sydney, 1989.

Poulsen, M and P Spearritt, *Sydney: A Social and Political Atlas*. [1976 census], A & U, Sydney, 1981.

Sydney: A Social Atlas 1991 census, ABS, Canberra, 1993.

Sydney: A Social Atlas 1996 census, ABS, Canberra, 1998.

Transport

Andrews, G, *Ferries of Sydney*, OUP, Melbourne, 3rd edn, 1994.

Broomham, R, *On the Road: The NRMA's First Seventy Five Years*, A & U, Sydney, 1996.

Manning, I, *The Journey to Work*, A & U, Sydney, 1978.

—— *Beyond Walking Distance: The Gains from Speed in Australian Urban Travel*, Urban Research Unit, ANU, Canberra, 1984

—— *The Open Street: Public Transport, Motor Cars and Politics in Australian Cities*, Transit Australia, Sydney, 1991.

Plowden, W, *The Motor Car and Politics in Britain*, Penguin, Harmondsworth, Middlesex, 1973.

Rae, JB, *The Road and the Car in American Life*, MIT Press, Cambridge, 1971.

Wotherspoon, G (ed), *Sydney's Transport: Studies in Urban History*, H & I, Sydney, 1983.

Circular Quay, the city and Botany Bay. Frank Hurley 1950. National Library of Australia

Index

by Patricia Holt